Gentle Genius

Mendelssohn at the age of thirteen. Drawing by Wilhelm Hensel. (Mendelssohn Archive, Berlin)

Gentle Genius

THE STORY OF FELIX MENDELSSOHN

GEORGE R. MAREK

FUNK & WAGNALLS

NEW YORK

Other books by George R. Marek

Puccini: A Biography
Richard Strauss: The Life of a Non-Hero
Opera as Theater
Beethoven: The Biography of a Genius

Designed by Abigail Moseley

Manufactured in the United States of America

L.C. Card 72–184003

1 2 3 4 5 6 7 8 9 10

To Herbert R. Mayes

Acknowledgments

Every block of marble, said Michelangelo, contains a sculpture, and all one has to know is what to chip away. The biographer's task differs: he has to gather the chips of marble—meaning the facts—and assemble them into a statue the outlines of which are already traced. Letters, records of conversations, newspaper articles, testimonies of friends and enemies—these he must search for when he begins, hoping eventually to achieve what Proust in *Swann's Way* called "that accuracy of detail which is easier, often, to obtain when we are studying the lives of people who have been dead for centuries than when we are trying to chronicle those of our own most intimate friends."

For Mendelssohn this task is both relatively easy and relatively difficult. As I have mentioned in Chapter 4, the biographer does not suffer from a paucity but from an overabundance of material. Not only was Mendelssohn so famous that his contemporaries recorded his doings and triumphs in detail, but he was so likable a man that his friends—and he had lots of them—took pleasure in setting down observations about his personality. Some of these observations are overpainted with the rosy benevolence which Felix's nature inspired; they need to be scraped. Since he came from a proud family, his childhood was lovingly chronicled from the time Felix learned to toddle; his father, his mother, his sisters, and his brother, not to mention his cousins and his aunts, indulged themselves in paeans and plaudits about the genius in their midst.

To separate the pieces of sound stone from the sugar cubes and the painted bits is not an easy business. If I have succeeded, it will appear that Mendelssohn was not nearly the simple, straightforward, happy-go-lucky man that he seemed to be on the surface and as which he took pains to show himself to most of his acquaintances.

The quarries of Mendelssohnian data are to be found principally in four places: the Bodleian Library at Oxford, where there is still substantial unpublished material; the New York Public Library at Lincoln Center, containing a collection of his family letters; the Library of Congress at Washington, which possesses not only its own considerable collection but a copy of the Brotherton Collection of the University of Leeds; and richest of all, the Mendelssohn Archive in Berlin.

In all four institutions, people were helpful and patient, as librarians usually are. But I owe a special debt to Dr. Rudolf Elvers, who sat with me on my several visits to Berlin and showed me where to look (the secret of research), gave me suggestion after suggestion, and finally read my manuscript and again was considerate enough to come forth with criticism and corrections. He himself is at work editing Mendelssohn's letters; and being the head of the Prussian State Library, he is hardly a man with time to spare. All the same, he spared it.

As with my Beethoven book, my research was greatly aided by H. C. Robbins-Landon and his wife, Else Radant, who helped me sketch in the historical background and found several Mendelssohn documents whose existence I had not known. Detached Mendelssohn letters and manuscripts are to be found all over the world; they are favorites of private collectors since they can still be bought at a reasonable price.[1] I owe thanks for help given by Dr. Cécile Lowenthal-Hensel, the Wiener Library of London, the Leo Baeck Institute of New York, Professor Felix Gilbert, Paul Hume, the British Museum, the Hebrew Union College of New York, Mme. Susi Heigl-Wach, Otto Lobbenberg, Francis Robinson, Henry Pleasants, Robert W. Gutman, Christopher W. Samuels. Particular thanks go to Bruce R. Carrick, the editor, for his sensible suggestions.

Obviously, I am grateful to the previous biographers of Mendelssohn, much as I may disagree with some of them; the most valuable source books

---

[1] A good Mendelssohn letter will fetch about $100 to $300; a Beethoven letter was sold in 1968 for $5,280.

were Ernst Wolff's *Mendelssohn Bartholdy* (Berlin, 1906), Philip Radcliffe's *Mendelssohn* (London, 1954), and Eric Werner's *Mendelssohn* (London, 1963). A listing of most of the books I have consulted will be found in the back, as well as a calendar of Mendelssohn's life. Virtually all the letters and quotations from German newspapers, periodicals, and books have been freshly translated by me.

"A well-written life is almost as rare as a well-spent one," Carlyle wrote. Mendelssohn's life was well spent; I hope this is a reasonably well-written one.

George R. Marek

New York, 1971.

Contents

List of Illustrations

Gentle Genius

Introduction

GRANDFATHER, FATHER, SON

". . . how can we understand any apparition unless we can observe it on its journey toward us?"

Goethe

*I*N the last week of May, 1833, a cruel heat spell sank down on the region of the lower Rhine. The men of Aachen, Cologne, and Elberfeld, wearing their "sensible" German suits, were perspiring as if they had been transplanted to the African bush country. The thermometer kept climbing, everybody was complaining. What would such temperatures do to the fifteenth Nether-Rhenish Music Festival scheduled to begin on May twenty-sixth in the town of Düsseldorf, an event for which ambitious preparations had been made and from which ambitious results were hoped? Who would want to be cooped up in a hot hall with a neighbor's shoulder touching yours?

Yet at six o'clock on May twenty-sixth, the Düsseldorf Concert Hall was completely filled. Weather or not, no one stayed away. The 1,200 auditors had come from as far away as Holland, arriving by post-chaise, Rhine steamer, private carriage, "extra-post," on foot, and on horseback. The prudent ones had reserved rooms with private families, the less prudent found that they had to bivouac in the fields around town. Well before concert time the audience paraded up the broad Königsallee, which the Düsseldorf fire department had sprinkled, though that didn't help much to keep the dust down.

When Felix Mendelssohn entered, the orchestra and the huge chorus —together they numbered 419—arose. So did the audience. He hardly noticed. He appeared to be utterly cool and isolated, like a statuette protected by glass. He was lithe and svelte and immaculately groomed, resembling more a young eighteenth-century courtier than a nineteenth-century conductor. His immobility lasted but a second or two. Then the glance of his black eyes seemed to add heat to the hall, and he raised his baton.

The program for the first concert consisted of Handel's resplendent oratorio *Israel in Egypt,* a composition which Mendelssohn loved, as he loved most of Handel's music. Since the tradition of these Festivals called for a lively opening number, a piece to get things started, the program committee had suggested preceding the oratorio by a slight affair, Mendelssohn's own "Trumpet" Overture, which he had composed when he was sixteen years old.

Now he was twenty-four. Twenty-four—at that age only Mozart, the unique miracle, had surpassed him in compositional vigor, as he had rivaled him in feats of memory and virtuosity. Yet unlike Mozart, Mendelssohn had become an executive of music, an interpreter of Bach, Beethoven, and Handel, a new kind of conductor, a prodigious pianist, an organizer, a researcher of half-forgotten music. The Düsseldorf Festival Committee in their official letter of appointment had addressed him as "the excellent artist, the honored composer, the proven conductor." Proven—at twenty-four.

He had prepared the concerts with the intensity which was characteristic of all he undertook, and which contrasted curiously with the reserve of his personal behavior, a reserve which his detractors called haughtiness. Mendelssohn was like those little weather-predicting toys, in which one figure appears when the air is dry and another when it is wet.

This was the first Festival he had been asked to conduct, and he did not make it easy for himself. To give *Israel,* to perform Handel, a composer little known in Germany, and to do so with an orchestra and a chorus consisting partly of amateurs—it was not child's play. In London he had searched for the original score and succeeded in finding in the Library of King George III not only the score but a textbook used in Handel's time. He rehearsed the oratorio the whole week, day in and out, culminating two days before the concert in rehearsals which lasted from eight o'clock in the morning till ten o'clock at night, except for brief interruptions for lunch and refreshment. The Dress Rehearsal was open to the public; the house was full, and at a certain point "such jubilation broke out among the listeners and the executants, such excitement as I have seldom witnessed, that it took a quarter of an hour before the proceedings could continue." Yet Mendelssohn was not satisfied, and he called an extra orchestral session on the day of the concert, from eight to ten in the morning. "Everybody performed his task not only conscientiously but smilingly," his father wrote, "as if it were for their own entertainment—and that in the terrible heat."

Felix's father, Abraham, had come to Düsseldorf from Berlin, and it is to his reports home that we owe most of our knowledge of the Festival; they are trustworthy enough, he being a sober critic of his son's achievements. Abraham had arrived in his private equipage, had by chance been met by the panjandrum of Düsseldorf's artistic life, the "Privy Judge of the Royal Appellate Court," Otto von Woringen, who had insisted that Abraham stay not at the room he had reserved—it was "filthy," said Woringen, which was probably a white lie—but at the fine Woringen mansion. After many protests Abraham gave in. There he was, then, in the thick of things, enjoying the adulation offered to his son. "Here they carry him on their hands," Abraham wrote, and while that was a figure of speech, it was certainly true that after the first concert the audience broke out into mighty cheers and then was reluctant to go home.

Woringen, as the head of the Festival Committee, suggested that the second concert consist of new music and of Beethoven's popular Fourth Symphony. New music was acceptable to Mendelssohn, but he preferred to play the "Pastoral," which, though quite familiar to London or Berlin or Vienna, had never been heard on the banks of the Rhine. Accordingly, the second evening offered an Easter Cantata by the Kapellmeister of Weimar, Ernst Wilhelm Wolff, and a Cantata, "The Might of Music," by Peter von Winter, an opera composer, along with the "Pastoral" and the "Leonore No. 3." Abraham:

On the day when a preliminary rehearsal [for the Pastoral] was scheduled and by chance there was no score at hand, he not only conducted it by heart but sang the missing instrumental parts. . . . [At the concert] the Pastoral went quite well, the Wolff Cantata deathly boring, then Leonore stimulating to everybody, and most effective. . . . One of the Woringen daughters, a charming girl, said all that needs to be said about the Wolff Cantata and the Winter composition: "the Might could get you angry, but the Cantata is guaranteed to put you to sleep."

Yet even this boring music could not diminish the general enthusiasm. The female members of the chorus secretly provided themselves with flowers, and at the end of the concert they pelted the young conductor with them. When the first flower struck him, he looked up frowningly, but seeing what was happening, he smiled. He was then offered a laurel wreath. This he refused four times, squirming to the left and right, until a huge man from the chorus pinioned him and one of the Woringen girls succeeded at the fifth attempt in placing the wreath on his head. During all this, orchestra, chorus, and audience kept applauding.

The demand for tickets was so great that the committee decided on the instant to give a third concert, in which part of *Israel* was repeated, as well as the third Leonore, and Mendelssohn appeared as a soloist in a "Composition by Weber," presumably the *Konzertstück*.

Before it was all over, Mendelssohn had not only been wined and dined but had to preside at a banquet and listen to laudatory speeches and poems written to him. The Festival ended with a Ball, and Mendelssohn had enough energy to spare to play the piano for the guests and then to galop and waltz until two o'clock in the morning. After much whispering and consulting with Abraham as to what gift Felix would like, the committee decided to offer him a special signet ring designed by Düsseldorf's famous sculptor, Wilhelm von Schadow.

Of the several reviews of the Festival which began to appear by and by, one may have pleased Mendelssohn. The musical correspondent of the Düsseldorf *Zeitung* was that sour-faced *"ami de Beethoven,"* Anton Schindler, who was living in Aachen and who now, six years after Beethoven's death, had assumed the role of supreme authority and appellate on all matters pertaining to Beethoven's music. Schindler wrote:

I have words only of deep joy and of admiration, not criticism, for every-thing which the artists . . . have accomplished with this music festival. . . . The goodwill and dedication to the noble art of music expressed themselves in the tenacity with which the many strenuous rehearsals were undertaken, with a zeal such as I have never met in my artistic career. . . . The exactness and indefatigable industry of the General Director, the ex-cellent Felix Mendelssohn-Bartholdy, are responsible for the quality of the performances. It is due to him alone that the fifteenth Nether-Rhenish Festival was incomparably superior to all preceding ones. (June 5, 1833)

There was but one slight disturbance. A few students, members of a students' union called the Blacks (*Die Schwarzen*) paraded before the con-cert hall carrying a placard: "Christian music for Christian musicians." The local police dispersed them and no one paid any attention. Mendelssohn probably never knew about it.

He had come to the Festival fresh from his fourth visit to London, where his "Italian" Symphony, possibly his greatest work, had been given its première under his direction (May 13, 1833). It was characteristic of him that he had asked the Festival Committee *not* to include either that symphony or the "Reformation" or any of his popular Overtures in the program. As to the "Italian" Symphony, he vacillated between pleasure at its success and doubt of its worth, just as he himself vacillated between moods of the gayest gaiety, a disposition sunny, charming, and outgoing, and a melan-choly, murky and befogged, during which this most courteous of men could display rage and was quick to take umbrage for an insignificant slight. He slid from high to low, and then climbed up again. There was little in him of Chopin's sureness, of Berlioz's truculent belief in what he was doing, not to speak of Beethoven's awareness of his own immortality. Less than a year before his triumph in Düsseldorf, Mendelssohn had written to Char-lotte Moscheles, the wife of the famous pianist and one of his dearest friends, "I do not know where it will all end with the deep depression (*Verstimmung*) I feel." A few months before Düsseldorf he wrote to his friend Thomas Attwood in London that he was depressed and working on his symphony, but with "diffidence." (Feb. 10, 1833) A few weeks later he felt on top of the world, for no special reason—and the diffidence had disap-peared, the vivacity had returned.

Here we begin to grope for the key to Mendelssohn's character. How was it possible for this young scion of a wealthy family, filled to his finger-nails with talent, to experience the mutability of self-judgment which he did demonstrate all his life? Can an explanation be furnished for the fact that he ascended so quickly to mastery in those superb youthful compositions by which the world remembers him, and never quite gained to higher summits in later life? Why did he drive himself in frantic and fatiguing work—of which this Düsseldorf Festival is but one example—when he never needed to work in the sense that he never needed to earn a penny? Why was his life so short? He was not clawed by the three gray sisters who shorten a man's life. He never knew the humiliation of being pressed under an archbishop's thumb or the fatigue of penury, as Mozart did. He never lacked for fame or was ravaged by disease, as Schubert was. There was nothing but light surrounding him, but he himself created his own darkness.

It would appear that the unmysterious Mendelssohn contained a mystery. To understand him, who, if he was not one of music's greatest geniuses, was certainly one of its most endearing, it is necessary to delve into his background. He was anchored in that background in temperament as much as in musicianship. He never did get away entirely from a family which, far from being nonentities, were each and every one of them remarkable. The father, who was there at Düsseldorf, had a great influence on him. Was that influence beneficial or deleterious? Would Felix have become a greater composer had he been the son of nobody in particular and had had to make his way unaided?

To repeat, we must examine his heritage if we are curious about the man who wrote the music to *A Midsummer Night's Dream* and the *Octet*. Goethe realized that when he wrote, after a visit by the young Felix: "How can we understand any apparition unless we can observe it on its journey toward us?" (Letter to Zelter, June 3, 1830)

Therefore I offer no apology for preceding the story of Felix's life with a sketch of his grandfather and of his father. I was the more tempted to do so since both Moses and Abraham were fascinating men, their story being worth telling even if there had been no Felix.

All three possessed remarkable talent, though along very different lines. Moses sprang from a ghetto to become one of the important philosophers of the eighteenth century, first a fighter for Jewish freedom, then a mediator between the temple and the church. Abraham, partly following Moses' precepts and partly in protest against them, became one of the financial pioneers of the early nineteenth century, gaining not only wealth but a social status rare in his time.

Francis Galton's book, *Hereditary Genius* (1869), largely a statistical investigation, shows that talent running through several generations is by no means a rare occurrence. We all know about the populous Bach family; we can cite the Scarlattis, father and son; or Dumas *père* and Dumas *fils*; or all those Breughels, Pieter the Elder, his two sons Pieter and Jan, Jan's two sons Jan the Younger and Ambrose, and Abraham son of Jan the Younger. Usually, however, inherited talent applies itself to the same "trade." The son is trained by the father. The Mendelssohns possessed dissimilar and almost antithetical talents. One wrote books, one wrote loans, one wrote notes. As to the reason why they showed these differing strengths and why Felix's death ended the procession—that I cannot give. I am unable to pronounce a formula for heredity.

Only one general observation can be hazarded. No talent develops independent of its time, and it is certain that the talents of the Mendelssohns were to a close degree intertwined with the ages in which they lived. To say that their contributions were time-bound is not to diminish these contributions, for Moses, Abraham, and of course Felix left a residue which is timeless. They belonged to those men who tell their age what it needs to be told and accomplish for it what it needs to have accomplished. Such men do not so much make history as does history make them. Hegel thought that this was true of *all* genius and that what great men give birth to is "mothered by the *Zeitgeist*." It is the gift of these men to have "an insight into the requirements of the time—what was ripe for development." They foresaw "the species next in order . . . which was already formed in the womb of time." (*Encyclopedia of the Philosophical Sciences*)

To put it simply, the Mendelssohns were lucky to have been born at the right time and place. Had Moses been born thirty years earlier—before the Enlightenment dawned—he might not have been able to develop his philosophy as fully as he did. Nor would his appeal have been as effective had he lived in another place than the Prussia of Frederick the Great.

Abraham was there when the reconstruction of Europe began immediately after the Napoleonic wars. Had Felix been born twenty years later
and grown up in the hot summer of romanticism, his classically oriented
genius might not have received the understanding it did receive. Was he
not fortunate to come on the scene before Wagner caused all that controversy?

Though any attempt to portray the composer without his ancestors is
a half-told tale, the chief protagonist of the book is, of course, Felix. He
was an artist who didn't fit at all the storybook version of an artist. He
was a man who wouldn't fit at all into our times. But his music does. We
need him now to remind us that to be amiable is not necessarily to be superficial. We need him now as an antidote.

One

THE JEWS IN ATTIC
AND CELLAR

I

LEGAL love was expensive. A Jewish boy and a Jewish girl living in the Prussia of the early eighteenth century could get married only if they paid a special "Marriage Tax." That tax was fixed by an inimical government at so high an amount of thalers that few families could afford it. The law had to be circumvented. It was: bride and groom were secretly united in a ceremony which took place in the attic, while a member of the family kept watch at the front door against the arrival of one of the Police Inspectors who frequently made their rounds of the Jewish quarter. These marriages came to be known as "Attic Marriages."

When the Jews met for discussion of communal problems they met in the cellar. There they proposed this or that plan to help them loosen the latest restriction and slip through the cordon which, physically and mentally, ringed their community. In the cellar, too, were held the debates, dearly loved by the elders, concerning the fine points of the Talmud: they sought stability in their own tradition, and like most traditionalists they lost themselves in a labyrinth formed by the letters of the law. Hence the sifting of every sentence, the search for the meaning of every word, which resulted in endless and sometimes acrimonious discussions. All such conclaves had to

The Frankfurt ghetto, after an engraving by Burger. (The Bettmann Archive)

be held in secret, because they were disapproved by the police. Free assembly was forbidden, and any amount of noise penetrating into the street was a provocation to be avoided.

Above or below, existence was precarious, tomorrow unpredictable. One could never tell when a sovereign on an ill-tempered rampage would level new demeaning sanctions or command a family forthwith to seek the nearest frontier. Because of this uncertainty a Jew addressing a friend or relative would add some superstitious formula to the name: "Isaac, may his light continue to shine," or "Rebecca, may her life go on," or, when making an appointment, write "Next Thursday, if we live to see it."

Attic and cellar, pressure and evasion, silence and subterfuge, humiliation and stubbornness—such were the circumstances of the life of the Jews. Yet, with all its difficulties, a life was possible. And in the German-speaking countries that life was comparatively less dangerous and cruel than it was in the Russia or the Poland or the Spain of the eighteenth century. In Poland or Russia murderous raids, rape, and pillage were, if not exactly sanctioned by law, placidly accepted by the Kremlin or Warsaw Palace. Massacres took place with fearsome regularity when the harvest proved sparse or when the Cossacks were not occupied in war. In Spain the Inquisition was still busy: of the 868 cases tried between 1721 and 1727, more than eight hundred were for the "crime" of Judaism. Of those found guilty, seventy-five were burned.

In German states there did occur occasional hunts of the Jews while the local Duke or Margrave shrugged his shoulders; but out-and-out pogroms were rare. The Jewish citizen was not pricked until he bled. A heavy tome of governmental laws was dropped on his body and he was legally squeezed into impotence. It was all done by due process of Teutonic "Befehl," and as long as the suppression could be documented by ordinance No. 78C, who cared whether it represented an offense against humanity?

A Jew could not pursue a profession. In the first two decades of the century virtually all he could do was to trade in simple unimportant merchandise, in ribbons or trinkets or old clothes. He sold these things at a stall in the market place, or more often went from house to house as an itinerant peddler. He could not be a manufacturer of goods nor become a supplier to the army or to government employees. He could not sell food except to other Jews. He could not own a patch of land. Nor could he live in a corner house, such a location being desirable. If he had musical ability, he could not find employment in the Court bands or orchestras which were supported by the heads of state, though there were cases where the prohibition was relaxed, when a Habsburg or a Wittelsbach needed another violinist to flesh out his musical service. A Jew could not become a Court portrait painter; since his own religion forbade the creation of holy images, he was more or less limited to painting grandfather's face or the white-bearded image of a beloved rabbi. He was unable to teach in a public school. Jews as teachers? Unthinkable, decreed Frederick William I—the "soldier king" and father of Frederick the Great—they were "evidently despoilers of public morality."

However, in some German-speaking countries, a Jew was allowed to study medicine, partly because there was a desperate need for doctors, partly because the Jews had shown exceptional ability in curing ills, and partly because early in the century the medicine man was still considered something of a mountebank.

If a Jew needed clothes, he could buy those only at stipulated hours. If the cloth proved substandard he had no effective redress. A Jew hardly dared to "crave the law" against a Christian citizen. Yet personal relationships between Jew and Christian were not always hostile. More than a few friendships were formed and children of different faiths played together at the edge of the Jewish quarter. Jewish children were not allowed to attend public schools, but went to informal schools of their own. In Bavaria this prohibition lasted until 1804, when Maximilian I annulled it. In most states the Jews lived in a ghetto. They had to obey a curfew. Even in so relatively enlightened a province as the Cologne Electorate, governed by Archbishops residing in Bonn, the Jews lived in a filthy little street—the *Judengasse*—as late as 1770, when Beethoven was born. In Frankfurt the young Goethe often visited the Jewish quarter, observed its life, and flirted with the pretty Jewish girls. So he tells us in *Poetry and Truth*. But Colonel John Trumbull [1] described Frankfurt in the 1780s in more realistic terms.

[1] 1756–1843. He was an American painter who served in the Continental army as an aide to Washington. He lived in Europe for many years and late in life wrote his autobiography, from which this quotation is taken.

The Jews' quarter is a very narrow street or rather lane, impassable for carriages with the houses very lofty, old-fashioned and filthy, not more than a quarter of a mile long—no cross avenue or alley, and a strong gate at each end, carefully closed and secured at tattoo-beat, after which no one is allowed to go out or enter and whoever is found out of the quarter after this time is secured by the city guard and confined. This quarter is said to contain ten thousand of this miserable people, how such a number can exist in such a narrow space is almost incredible, yet here (at one of the entrance gates) I saw them crowded together in filth and wretchedness, calculated to generate disease. And how were they to escape from a fire after the two only avenues were closed for the night?

One of the penalties of being a German Jew was the so-called "Body Tax" (*Leibzoll*). Since the Jews were forbidden to carry arms, the excuse for exacting this toll was the necessity of affording them protection when they undertook a journey. What journeys they did venture on were peddling trips, and there was no protection. They could stay away from home for a maximum of three days. Longer absences were taxed a ducat (approximately $30) for each twenty-four hours.[2] Another tax, invented by some ingenious official around 1727, specified a yearly fee for using the Hebrew calendar rather than the Gregorian one (*Kalendergeld*). In Austria a "Light Tax" was exacted for the lighting of candles on the Sabbath and holy days; but this tax proved difficult to collect. The "Body Tax" was continued even after some of the other restrictions had been lifted: in Austria it lasted to 1782, in Saxony until 1813, in Hanover till 1847. In Prussia it was stopped in 1787, due to the influence of Frederick the Great, who had died the previous year but had bequeathed his nephew Frederick William II a tradition of limited tolerance.

Across the Channel, the Jews were treated more humanely, and many Jews fleeing from persecution in Poland or Russia found a haven in England. There too most of them lived in poverty and were excluded from civil or military offices. But there they were allowed to maintain their own official schools and hospitals. They could engage in major commerce, including the importation of wares, and a few of them managed to become

---

[2] In 1776 Moses Mendelssohn, already famous, paid such a tax on entering Dresden. He had come from Berlin. The tax, he said, was set at exactly the same amount as "for one Polish ox."

wealthy. In 1745, when the Young Pretender advanced on London with the purpose of deposing George II and restoring the House of Stuart, a financial panic gripped the country. Jewish merchants and moneylenders came to the rescue. Confidence was restored and the Pretender repulsed.[3] As a gesture of gratitude the Ministry introduced into Parliament a bill offering citizenship to all foreign-born Jews who had resided in England or Ireland for three years. (Native-born Jews were automatically considered citizens.) The bill was approved by the Commons, but the British public protested against it. Merchants bombarded Parliament with pleas that Jewish competition would render their own commercial lives impossible. Thousands of pamphlets and lampoons were circulated and many women wore broad ribbons across their not always broad bosoms, bearing the slogan: "No Jews, Christianity forever."[4]

If you were unlucky enough to be born a Polish Jew, then your only safety lay in flight. Every year hundreds braved the dark, wolf-infested forests to reach the border. In that unhappy country, torn by internal strife, a Jew was considered little better than a wolf, a creature to be exterminated. There Jews were accused of killing children to obtain Christian blood which, it was claimed, they needed for their religious ceremonies and for baking the unleavened bread they used at Easter time. At least nine such public trials are recorded between the years 1710 and 1760. The accusation was given credibility by a certain Serafinovich, himself a converted Jew, who published a book purporting to be an exposure of Jewish ceremonial. The accused Jews were tortured, some were flayed alive, and some died by being impaled on a stick. The Jews appealed to Pope Benedict XIV. An investigation was ordered through the papal Nuncio in Warsaw, who reported that in none of the cases had there been any evidence of such guilt on the part of the Jews. The Inquisition supported this finding.

France—which later proved to be the country in which the emancipation of the Jews was strongly supported by the philosophers of the Enlightenment—at the beginning of the century treated its small Jewish population alternately with tolerance and with cruelty. The winds blew hot and cold. Coexistence or banishment, it depended whether at the moment sentiment leaned toward trade or toward church. Even so sensitive

---

[3] Cecil Roth: *The Jewish Contribution to Civilization* (Oxford, 1945).
[4] Sir Walter Besant: *London in the Eighteenth Century* (London, 1903).

a philosopher as Pascal had preached: "The Jews should be miserable, because they crucified Him." Religious fanaticism was virulent in every form,
as Voltaire was to discover when he sprang to the defense of the family of
Jean Calas, the unjustly executed Protestant.[5] Yet France, a country which
appreciated the "reasonable" view of life—that is to say the practical, commercial view—knew that the Jews could be economically useful and that it
might be bad for business to pound them into misery. As Arthur Hertzberg
wrote in *The French Enlightenment and the Jews:* "In 1741 the controller-
general of finances wrote a circular letter to all the intendants [provincial
governors] asking them, in all their various provinces, about the commerce
of the Jews. All twenty-five who responded answered unanimously that the
Jews should not be excluded from the fairs and the markets because they
served a useful function in keeping down prices, which would otherwise be
artificially high because of the monopolistic practices of the guilds." Yet
four years previously a book had been published which retold in lurid language the lie about Jewish ritual murders. (François Gayot de Pitaval:
Causes célèbres et intéressantes)

No wonder, then, that the German countries represented comparative
calm to the Jews. In spite of chicanery and individual vindictiveness, in
spite of the pushing and the squeezing, in spite of being dependent on the
whim of this Grand Duke or that little King, the Jewish community developed. By and by Jewish skill in trading and finance was put to use. The
peddlers enlarged their stock to include tobacco, tea, and coffee (some of
it smuggled so that it could be sold at lower prices). By and by a few
added thaler to thaler and learned how to make them breed in an expanding
economy. Artisans came to the fore: we hear of goldsmiths and diamond
cutters and of one renowned optician who knew how to make excellent eyeglasses. Jewish women excelled at needlework; the skillful among them
embroidered dresses, the less skillful sewed buttonholes for uniforms and
greatcoats.

Since virtually all of the German states, from small enclaves and the
so-called Free cities to the relatively sizable kingdoms of Bavaria and Prussia, insisted on minting their own coinage, payments for interstate trade

---

[5] It is curious that Voltaire, the egregious fighter against intolerance, was himself prejudiced.
He disliked Jews because he had been cheated by one in a transaction in which he himself had not
acted honestly.

were complicated transactions. A Prussian thaler had a value different from that of a Rhenish thaler; the caroline, the louis d'or, the Friedrichs d'or, the florin, the ducat, the livre fluctuated to and fro. Jewish "financiers"— at first moneylenders on a small scale—learned how to make sense out of this confusion and some rendered valuable services to various sovereigns. In return, a few were granted special privileges. They were called "Protected Jews" (*Schutzjuden*) or "Court Jews" (*Hofjuden*). The title could not be inherited, though their children were allowed to choose their own domiciles after marriage. Even a "Protected Jew" could at any time run afoul of a willful decree. The convenient accusation was "usurer"; that term could stand broad interpretation. Of course some Jews were usurers; so were some Christians. Lending money being one of the few enterprises in which Jews could engage, some of them no doubt exacted all the profit the traffic would bear.

A famous early case of a Jew who rose high and fell low was Joseph Oppenheimer (1692?–1738), who served both the Elector of Mannheim and Karl Alexander, Duke of Württemberg. He evolved for the Duke a plan for a state bank after the British model. Accused of malfeasance, he was investigated but was exonerated and became a member of the Duke's Privy Council. He invented new taxes, established royal monopolies, and may have accepted bribes, which he divided with the Duke. When Karl Alexander died, Oppenheimer was arrested, tried, and convicted. He was strangled and his corpse was exhibited to public view in a cage in the town square. Such was the fate of the man known as "Jew Süss." (Lion Feuchtwanger told his story, in fictional form, in the novel *Jud Süss* [1925], English title *Power*.)

Two years after Oppenheimer's death, Frederick the Great became King of Prussia (1740). This free-thinker, free-fighter, free-spender had not much use for the Jews, protest though he would that all religions and all peoples were alike to him. But he was sage enough to temper prejudice with prudence. He needed a great deal of money both for his wars and his constructive enterprises. He enlisted Jewish money experts to produce coin of the realm by alchemistic magic—or near magic. What it was, was counterfeiting on a grand scale, and the King was aided in his equivocal deals by his official banker, Veitel Ephraim. They bought up silver and gold coins from Holland, Poland, Hungary, and Russia, melted them down, mixed them with baser metals, restamped them, and sent them back to their respective countries claiming full value. The Berliners sang a ditty:

> Outside silver, inside tin,
> Outside honesty, inside sham,
> Outside Frederick, inside Ephraim.

The cheated recipients blamed the "Jewish counterfeiters" but the pleased Frederick built Ephraim a beautiful little palace.

It was at the crossroads of trade or at the seats of government that—with a good deal of luck—an astute Jew could find his way to affluence, even if modest, and thus buy his way out of the ghetto. Young Meyer Rothschild understood this early when he left the rabbinical school in the country, where his family had placed him, and returned to his native Frankfurt. From the Frankfurt ghetto he began his financial operations, which led him to Landgrave William of Hesse-Cassel, and his sons and grandsons to a fortune which has been estimated at more than $6,000 million.

In short, it was at the beginning of the eighteenth century that the more courageous Jews, driven both by desperation and by hope, gravitated toward the centers where commerce and customers were to be found. A number of them drifted to the capital of Prussia, to the "big city" which was being developed by the Prussian kings.

2

What was Berlin like, in those early days of the eighteenth century? It wasn't much of a city. In 1710 it had 57,000 inhabitants; in 1740, 90,000. Not until the later reign of Frederick the Great did it begin to expand rapidly; by 1800 it had doubled its population. There was no comparison between Berlin and either Paris or London, the two great cities where the main thought of the Enlightenment was hatched. Even Vienna outranked Berlin in liveliness, attractiveness, and, in the old sense of the word, urbanity. Berlin was enclosed by a protective wall (The Ring of the Palisades), as Vienna was. This was completed by Frederick William I (reigned 1713 to 1740). Frederick the Great (reigned 1740 to 1786) thought that his Berliners,

living behind that wall, were little better than barbarians. They knew how
to make war, eat and drink too much, and propagate children. But they
couldn't care less about the life of the spirit. Most of them were incapable
of appreciating any music higher than ditties or dance bands. Emanuel
Bach, Frederick's court composer, was practically unknown outside the palace. What writers they had were primitive storytellers. Illiteracy was still
fairly prevalent. As to the art of life, wit, dalliance, repartee, the play of
thought, the exchange of philosophic or metaphysical ideas—these were
almost unknown in that clumsy German language and to a clumsy people
who wolfed their food, belched, turned over and took a snooze. He, Frederick, was going to change all that. He was going to educate them whether
they liked it or not, and in the meantime he avoided as much as he could
speaking German and spoke and wrote in French. His admiration for everything that was Gallic, which antedated even what proved to be one of the
most famous friendships in history, his and Voltaire's, caused him to dero-
gate his home unduly. Yet he had a point: at the beginning of his reign
Berlin limped behind the other European centers and retained a primitively
rural aspect behind its wall. When Frederick asked the French ambassador
whether Berlin could compare itself in size with Paris, that diplomat, a
certain Marquis de Vabry, answered, "Assuredly. But with the difference
that in Paris we neither sow nor reap."

The city did enclose cow pastures, gardens, fields, and dairies. Berlin's
gardens, landscaped by French and Dutch horticulturists, were famous.
Vegetables and flowers were available in plenty. There were even vine-
yards, although the wine was not very good and could be used for the most
part only for vinegar. The trouble was that there was no canalization, no
water-supply system; in the summer Berlin was covered with clouds of dust
and the fields burned up. Beyond the fields were the forests, and these not
only supplied the wood for fuel but offered convenient hunting grounds.
Hunting was Frederick William I's favorite pastime, when he was not busy
choosing and training his guard of six-foot-tall soldiers, and the wild boar
was the favorite game of these court hunts. The Jews were forced to purchase the superfluity of the slaughtered animals. What could they have done
with them, since their religion forbade the eating of pork? Presumably they
used the skins for leather and sold the meat illegally.

Public conveyances were virtually unknown, nor were vehicles available for hire. If one needed to go to Charlottenburg, the royal center, one could get a place in one of the chaises (*Kremser*, a sort of omnibus) which were queued up near the Brandenburg Gate; then one had to wait, sometimes for hours, until the chaise was completely filled. Otherwise it didn't pay the driver to start on the journey.

Buildings were simple and for the most part ugly. There was little for the visitor to admire. An object of admiration was Berlin's only full-length mirror, which stood in an alcove in the Royal Palace. It was a gift from the Czar and the Berliners pointed it out "with unique astonishment."

The construction of Sans Souci was not begun till 1745 and finished two years after. It was a highly rococo pleasure palace, as French as its name, and did not fit in the least into Berlin's style. Besides, being in Potsdam, it was removed from the city and quite inaccessible to most Berliners.

In the royal gardens Frederick the Great favored the cultivation of potatoes. At first potato plants were used merely as decorations. The King tried time and time again to persuade the Berliners to eat potatoes, but they disliked those brown lumps and it was not until quite late in his reign that he succeeded. He had better success in the development of Prussia's industry. He caused textile factories to be built and competed with progressive and prosperous Hamburg by constructing canals. Hamburg had enjoyed a virtual monopoly on sugar and tobacco. As soon as a commodity could be grown or manufactured within Prussia, restrictive import laws were written. However, there was much smuggling, since the quality of the home-grown goods was not good enough to suit the Berliners. Frederick established a government monopoly on salt. There was plenty of it and the King forced everybody to buy it, sacks of it. Housewives—Christian or Jewish—had to keep "salt books" proving that they had bought the prescribed amount. What to do with all that salt? They hit on the idea of salting the small cucumbers which grew near the Spree forest; they developed the salt-pickle which has remained a staple of German cooking. Sauerkraut, too, owes its existence to the availability of vinegar and salt.

Large stretches of Berlin were little better than wasteland. The most depressing area was the eastern part, where the Rosenthal Portal was located. That was the only portal open to the Jews who came to Berlin on foot. But come they did in ever increasing numbers, to seek opportunities for a livelihood and comparative safety from persecution. Frederick the Great offered them such safety within a corral fenced in by his edicts. By the end of the century half of all the Jews living in German lands—roughly about 200,000—were concentrated in Prussia.

3

Forced to live segregated lives and driven into themselves to feed on their own spiritual resources, they demonstrated a firmness of purpose and steadfastness of family feeling which only gained in strength by opposition. No storms could exfoliate that tree. A German Jew in the eighteenth century could abjure his religion, have himself baptized, and be integrated into the community. Yet few did so. Most of them sought solace not in abdication but in confirmation. They did not mind in the least circumventing the laws imposed by the Christians; their own laws they held in almost superstitious awe.

It was the strength of that bond around the diaspora which accounted for the survival of the Jewish tradition. What this tradition represented was a resistance movement of a force and duration unparalleled in history. Rousseau was to comment on it: the laws of Greece and Rome, he wrote, no longer existed, but "Zion destroyed has not lost her children."

Yet these children of Zion suffered penalties of their own making. If restriction from the outside was the badge of all their tribe, they suffered as well from restriction from within, erected by the very tradition and the very faith to which they clung. Not only were they shut out from the life of the nation, they themselves shut their doors against the draughts of change. Their mental arteries hardened. On the shelf next to the lawbook written by their inimical neighbors stood another tome, heavy with laws written by themselves centuries ago. True, that book could be used as a firm board on which to lean. Yet the unwillingness to raise their eyes from the book and look around set up atrophic boundaries. Surrounded as they were, was it not natural that they feared to strain the boundaries? What Solomon had set down in the tenth century B.C. the eighteenth century A.D.

still obeyed. Wisdom was there; but it was wisdom which lacked flexibility and some of which was no longer understood. The praise of tradition often became a hymn out of tune. The Jews clung to a dozen formulas, a hundred proscriptions, a thousand interdictions, hallowed by history, the meaning and purpose of which had long ceased to be lucid. The old men still insisted on wearing their long white beards. Why? They could not tell you. Was unshorn hair the symbol of a free man? Or did the tradition commemorate the destruction of the Temple? The kosher laws were strictly observed, though the prohibition against pork no longer made sense in Berlin. Under German laws they were forbidden to read a German book or even speak the German language; yet when later—under Frederick the Great—this restriction was annulled, it was the Jews themselves who reinstated it. Only Hebrew and that mixture of Hebrew, Russian, and German called Yiddish were proper languages. Moses Mendelssohn recollected the case of one young Jew who was banished by the Jewish community of Berlin because he was caught carrying a German book. Women were considered inferior creatures, as in antique Athens. They sat in a segregated section in the synagogue. They were forbidden to display outer garments of silk or other fine material; they were forced to dress plainly. A girl could try to make herself attractive, but once the poor creature got married she had to have her hair cut off to make herself undesirable to other men. (Women got around this by wearing wigs, and later women less orthodox hid their hair under caps. Moses Mendelssohn's wife wore one.) Weddings and circumcisions were regulated by sumptuary edicts: in Metz, at weddings where the dowry amounted to less than 6,000 livres (roughly $6,000 in today's equivalent), only three musicians could be employed. At engagement receptions only four plain cakes and four honey cakes could be proffered. Lazarus Bendavid, one of Moses Mendelssohn's disciples, was to write later (that is, after the influence of the Enlightenment): "Thousands and thousands of tiny ceremonial-laws, the transgression of which was considered by other Jews as a mortal sin, were unknown and unnamed in my home. . . . I was educated merely to lead a moral and ordered life . . . my sole religious exercise being a morning and an evening prayer." [6] This was heresy, before the Enlightenment.

[6] Autobiography, Berlin, 1806.

Jews were forbidden to buy or read German books, so their only literature was the Bible in Hebrew, the Torah, and the Talmud.[7] But the man in the street was not supposed to read, let alone interpret, the holy books. The interpretation was delivered either by the rabbis or a host of "Torah Students" or "Talmud Scholars." Many of these were Polish refugees; they had the reputation of being more learned than German students. Some of them were earnest and sincere scholars and teachers. Others took advantage of their status to cadge free meals. It was a strictly observed custom to invite a "Talmud Scholar" to partake of the family meal when he knocked on the door. Isaac Hirsch, himself one of the truly learned Talmudists, wrote: "The teachers were for the most part unsuccessful Torah students who couldn't make the grade either as merchants." [8] It was these teachers and scholars, real or would-be, who proclaimed the good old ways. Reform was apostasy.

To give these Talmud Scholars their due, they were often excellent linguists, having acquired knowledge of German and French (openly or by stealth), in addition to Hebrew and Polish. They made themselves useful by translating business communications, composing appeals to the local authorities, and explaining to their wary listeners the meaning of government decrees. They led the discussions in which the threads of the Talmud were raveled into dark knots. They rocked to and fro on a sea of mystic words, a motion by which propositions "proved" yesterday could be disproved today. The key word of these dissertations was "If." Salomon ben Josua, a late eighteenth-century philosopher better known by the name of Maimon (a name he assumed because of his intensive occupation with the writings of the twelfth-century philosopher Maimonides), once characterized the typical Talmudist: If God were to ask him, "What can you do?", he would answer, "Put any assertion to me and I'll prove the opposite." Lazarus Bendavid tells us that as a young man he indulged in a heated dispute with a shoemaker, the question being, "Precisely how long does Eternity last?" The shoemaker said that a pair of Manchester trousers (trousers made from extremely durable material) would last an eternity. In the resulting argument the shoemaker threw Bendavid out of his shop.

[7] The Torah is the body of instructions and judicial decisions, given by the ancient priests as a revelation of divine command. The Talmud is a compilation of civil and ceremonial traditions; in other words, a commentary on the fundamental laws.

[8] *My Apprentice Years*, translated into German by Moritz Zobel, Berlin, 1936.

Such hair-splitting dialogues were of course not unknown among the clerics of other religions. Did not medieval monks debate the question of how many angels could dance on the head of a pin? But Talmudic interpretation became so involved that "Talmudic" has come to be known as a synonym for "sophisticated" in the sense that Dryden used the word: "I love not sophisticated truth, with an allay of lye in't." Talmudists could demonstrate that a cloud had a shape like a camel or was backed like a weasel.

In Eisenstadt (where Haydn worked), there was a famous "Talmud school"; the local rabbi debated the question, "Was it allowable for Jews to play cards?" The "Talmudic" answer: no, it was not—except to express the joy of life on certain special feast days, such as Chanukah or Purim. When Joseph II opened the Austrian schools to the children of all faiths (1782), the elders had to decide whether the children ought to be exposed to Christian thought. The Jews of Bohemia were all for it, the rabbis of Hungary were all against it. Of what use was knowledge? No study was profitable except that of the holy books.

The German-Jewish community, then, was a priest-ridden group. Like priest-ridden Egypt in its decline, it might have hardened into immobility. The dust of heredity might have covered the Jews with so thick a layer that the shoots of progress could not push through. Their strength could have been crushed by the double burden of Christian prejudice and their own sectarianism. The fires of life which must be stirred by the bellows of new ideas, those fires which must crackle with dissent, could have sunk into ash. This could have happened, as it did happen with other cultures and other nations, had not a few men arisen strong enough to fight on the twin fronts of Christian and of Jewish intolerance. Foremost among these men was a young philosopher, at once a believer and a questioner, by the name of Moses Mendelssohn.

Moses Mendelssohn, after an oil painting by J. G. Frisch.
(Mendelssohn Archive, Berlin)

Two

THE FIGHTING
PHILOSOPHER

Three seekers of the pure truth, Moses of Egypt, Moses
Maimonides, author of *More Neubkim* (Guide of the Per-
plexed) and Moses Mendelssohn . . .

James Joyce: *Ulysses*

I

*H*ALFWAY between Leipzig and Berlin lies the little city of Dessau.
Today it is an unprepossessing conglomeration of industrial buildings, owing
whatever small touristic reputation it may have to annual festival performances of Richard Wagner's operas, but in the Middle Ages it was a resi-
dential city gathered around an impressive castle and the Church of St.
Mary. (Both of these buildings were destroyed in World War II.)[1] In
Dessau lived a peddler known locally as "Mendel" or "little Mendel."
He was an ambitious man, taught himself to read and write Hebrew, and
was soon employed by the Jewish community as teacher and scribe. He
thus experienced the practical advantages of education, and when a son was
born to him, in 1729, Mendel, poor though he was, determined what a
father usually does determine for his child: through education the boy
was to be given whatever opportunities there were possible. German Jews
had then no right to formal names (that right was legally granted as late as

---

[1] In the nineteen twenties Dessau was the seat of the Bauhaus school, under Walter Gropius.

1812); Mendel called his son Moses—half the male Jewish children were called Moses—but the neighbors identified him as "son of Mendel," Mendelssohn.

The first Jewish school Moses attended was probably primitive and was certainly harsh. "Maimon" (Salomon ben Josua, 1754–1800) described his own school:

> Schoolmaster Jossel treated [the children] with exceeding cruelty, whipped them . . . and not infrequently tore them by the ear or administered a blow to the eye. When parents came to complain he chased them away with his cane. The schoolroom was in a little hut, heated by an open, smoky fire; some of the children sat on benches, some on the dirt floor. The teacher, clad in a filthy shirt and sitting on a table, kept taking snuff. . . . [The teachers] appropriated for themselves most of the bread which the children brought for their breakfast . . ." [2]

Yet little Moses had the good fortune to be taught, not by a Schoolmaster Jossel, but by a kindly and learned man, a Rabbi Fränkel. Under him the child studied and absorbed Jewish lore and history and began critically to examine the traditions. David Fränkel was a remarkably broadminded teacher, and the habit of judicative thinking, the habit of taking little for granted, which Mendelssohn was to develop, was instilled in him by this exceptional scholar. Fränkel soon proved too good to be retained in Dessau and was called to Berlin as chief rabbi.

When the boy lost his mentor, he decided that as soon as he could he would follow him. When Moses was fourteen he did so, walking from Dessau to Berlin, a distance of some seventy miles. Fränkel welcomed him, helped him find some attic chamber, and had him at his table on the Sabbath and holy days. The motto of Moses' life, as he himself wrote a bit grandiloquently, was "Eat bread and salt, drink water, and study." (This was modeled after the Talmudic command: "Eat bread with salt, drink water by measure, sleep on the hard earth, live a life of privations, and busy thyself with the Law.") But what he studied was not only the Law, but rebellious material: not content to confine himself to Jewish knowledge, he embarked on conquering the German language. He had to hide this knowledge both from the authorities and from the Jewish community. How

[2] *Maimons Lebensgeschichte*, Dr. J. Fromer, ed. (Georg Müller, Munich, 1911).

was he able to practice and perfect himself? We do not know. We only know that he became a master of style, handling the language with the precision of an architect in the building of his philosophic edifice, and with the stroke of a tennis player in his epigrams.

He learned Greek, Latin, and English. In one of his letters to his future wife, he asks her to procure for him a copy of Johnson's Dictionary, and later, with his friend Lessing, he discusses Sterne's *Tristram Shandy*. At first, says Mendelssohn, he was puzzled by the book, hopping from one divagation to another; as soon as he got acquainted with Uncle Toby, however, he found the whole thing delightful. Presently he found it advisable to study French. If ever he was to appear at the Prussian Court—which seemed a remote possibility then, but nothing was altogether remote from Moses' ambition—if ever he was to speak to the new king, who was in the third year of his reign when Moses came to Berlin, he would need French. More immediate, Moses had heard of the new literature which the French *philosophes* were sending like shafts of sunlight into a murky world. This had to be examined.

Any man who had pretensions to being civilized could at least read French. It was the international language and it was Frederick's language. Voltaire spent six weeks with Frederick in the same year that Moses came to Berlin. Pierre Louis Maupertius, the mathematician and astronomer who in 1736 had headed an expedition to Lapland to confirm Newton's theory of the flattening of the globe at the poles, was now in Berlin at Frederick's invitation and headed the Berlin Academy. Rousseau was as yet unknown to fame; *La nouvelle Héloïse* was not published until 1761. The very year after its publication, however, we find that Mendelssohn had already read it and recommended it to his bride, at the same time advising her to keep the book away from her sister, the little girl being too young for such literature. Jean d'Alembert, developer of the theory of dynamics, and Julien La Mettrie—a materialist who doubted the tenets of Christian doctrine and a hedonist and a glutton who eventually perished in Berlin after eating a spoiled game pie—were friends of and advisers to the great Francophile, King "Fritz." Other philosophers—such as the Scottish skeptic David Hume, whose *Treatise of Human Nature* had just appeared, or Charles de Montesquieu, whose book, *The Spirit of Laws*, was to influence the shaping of the American Constitution, shed their lights from afar. The sum of these lights enabled men to look with new curiosity at old beliefs, though some shaded their eyes against such unaccustomed brightness. Moses was particularly influenced by the philosophy of his contemporary, Christian von Wolff, a follower of Leibnitz, who taught that the salvation of the world lay in "goodness" of man to man, regardless of his creed. For this "atheistic" belief—that a man can be good without being a Christian—Wolff was banished from Germany, but was recalled when the Enlightenment gained strength.

It was an age in which philosophy was necessary equipment for a cultured man and constituted as much a part of conversation as space travel does in ours. "Everything was being discussed under the heading of philosophy," Jean d'Alembert observed in *Eléments de Philosophie*. D'Alembert not only noted the inclusiveness of philosophy, he practiced it: he was interested in the refraction of light, in integral calculus, in the phenomena of matter in motion, in astronomy, in education, in musicology, in the encyclopedia, in the motion of winds.[3]

This philosophic age prepared the way, this new illumination lit the path, for a Mendelssohn, a man belonging to a despised race, to rise to honor and fame. As yet he could hardly have dreamed of honor and fame, except perhaps within the Jewish community; he wanted to become "a wise man," possibly a rabbi like his teacher. Yet his mind impelled him to acquire unclean, "unkosher" knowledge.

Day after day, hour after hour, Mendelssohn sat in his room lit at night by a little tallow light (cheaper than a wax candle) and studied. He must have hidden his books and been beset by fears of discovery; it was dangerous for a Jew to keep company with heretics, be they French or German minds. But Mendelssohn was obsessed by the encyclopedic hunger. He fed that hunger through his eyes, until they became swollen and weakened. For the rest of his life his eyesight was impaired.

Soon enough he acquired a reputation as a serious and learned young man. When he was twenty-one this reputation—and no doubt a kind word

---

[3] His *Réflections sur la cause générale des vents* was dedicated to Frederick the Great. Frederick promptly invited him to come to Berlin; d'Alembert promptly refused. He wanted no part of Berlin.

from Rabbi Fränkel—earned him the post of "house-teacher" in the home of Isaak Bernhard, a Berlin silk manufacturer.

I have mentioned that Frederick the Great, spurred on by the ideas of the Enlightenment, showed a certain tolerance toward the Jews living in Prussia, though he personally had little use for them and certainly no understanding. More important than racial tolerance was the need to support local manufacture. Silk was an indispensable commodity and Bernhard knew how to spin it. Therefore, he was permitted to run a factory which proved successful. He could afford to hire a private tutor for his children.

In time Mendelssohn became what was then called the "bookkeeper" of the enterprise, a position tantamount to manager. He moved out of his little hovel and into Bernhard's house. He no longer looked threadbare. He began to eat more than bread and salt. He showed vigorous business ability, though complaining in his cantankerous moods: "Business, business, all those business deals! Heaped on my back, they are pushing me to the ground. I am a pack mule and yet in my conceit I imagine myself a noble race-horse." He got up at 5 A.M., studied "the sciences," was in the factory at nine, remained till three, studied some more, and spent the evening in discussion. Between the calls of customers he would surreptitiously pull out a book and read. "It is difficult to be a bookkeeper and experience the emotions of beauty." It was difficult, but he managed. Finally, after Bernhard's death in 1768, Mendelssohn became owner of the business. It is a remarkable case of a philosopher who was as well a good businessman. But so was Voltaire.

To the men of the Enlightenment, a question had to be examined like an insect imbedded in amber, put under the lens, turned this way and that, bored into, shattered, and reassembled, before the answer could satisfy. The habit came naturally to Mendelssohn, trained as he was in Talmudic speculation. Yet other thinkers, men who might never have read the Talmud, speculated similarly.

"Generally speaking," writes Frederick Copleston in *A History of Philosophy*, "the philosophy of the Enlightenment included a separation of ethics from metaphysical and theological considerations." All three subjects, ethics, metaphysics, and theology, furnished the food for thought to the German philosophers. Many of these were not original thinkers; they were rather interpreters of French and English ideas to a small educated German public. Occasionally they lost themselves in curious quibbles. Important among these contemporaries of Moses Mendelssohn was Christoph Martin Wieland, more of a poet than a philosopher, much appreciated by Goethe, and the translator of twenty-two of Shakespeare's plays into German. Another was Hermann Samuel Reimarus, professor of Hebrew and Oriental languages in Hamburg, who wrote *Apology for or Defense of the Rational Worshippers of God,* a work he did not dare to publish.

Most important, there was Gotthold Ephraim Lessing, an extraordinary man and an extraordinary mind. He was exactly the same age as Mendelssohn and the two young men met, tradition has it, at a chess game which both of them played expertly. From this meeting developed a friendship which was to have far-reaching consequences for both of them and for their worlds.

However, it was probably not chess which brought them together. Lessing had written a comedy, *The Jews,* a rather primitive piece of work. In it he presented a Jew who was noble and unselfish. The critics fell on the little play and tore it to pieces. Was it not quite improbable and untrue to life that a Jew could be honorable? Mendelssohn answered:

> What temerity for a person who himself has a spark of decency to deny an entire nation the probability of being able to produce a single honest man! . . . Is it not enough that we have had to feel the bitter hatred of Christians in so many different cruel ways? Are these injustices also to be justified by slanders? Continue to oppress us, continue to force us to live in fetters among free and happy citizens, even continue to expose us to the mockery and contempt of the world—but do not attempt to deny us virtue, the sole comfort of oppressed souls, the sole refuge of the helpless.[4]

2

Lessing, like Mendelssohn, was born to poverty. His father was a pastor who wrote pathetic poems on the misery of going hungry. Yet

[4] Quoted in *Diaspora* by Werner Keller, New York, 1969.

somehow the father scraped together enough to send the son to the University of Leipzig, where he was to study theology. He soon turned away from such studies, however, to pursue his literary and critical interests. He expressed his ideas on drama (see his *Hamburg Dramaturgy*) and aesthetics (his famous essay on Laocoön) in so stimulating a style, with such remarkable absence of pedantry and fussiness, with such un-German clarity, that he became an inspiration to the men who followed him, from Ruskin to Berenson to T. S. Eliot.

At a time when the German stage was virtually nonexistent, he wrote plays of such strength—and one comedy (*Minna von Barnhelm*) of such charm—that they still hold a place in the repertoire. Without Lessing there would have been no Schiller and perhaps no Goethe.

Though the stage became his natural pulpit, he never relinquished his interest in philosophical, ethical, and religious disquisition. Along those paths, as much as along artistic paths, he could search for truth. And that is what he wanted, to search for truth. He said that if God were to offer him with the right hand the absolute truth and with the left the unending search for truth, he would choose the left. Absolute truth belonged to God alone.

Lessing would have been considered a heretic a few years previously. He believed that the moral principle of Christianity existed before the Gospels were penned. Like other theologians of the Enlightenment, he rejected the idea that the Bible must be accepted unquestioningly. The lessons it taught were important and Christ was a great teacher, but they were not to be regarded as the end-all in the development of mankind. The Old Testament was mankind's primer; the New Testament represented the youth of man. But the mature stage, the third Gospel, would come to show human beings how to act reasonably and do good for the sake of doing good and not for reward, be it given on earth or in heaven. Only then would true tolerance exist.

Such sacrilege would have been duly punished, had not Frederick the Great declared himself. When he was asked whether a Catholic might become a citizen of Frankfurt an der Oder, a Protestant city, he wrote: "All religions are equal and good, provided those who believe are honest folk. If Turks and heathens were to come and wished to populate our lands, we would build them mosques and temples." [5] Idealistic words, indeed, although Frederick did not quite live up to them. And the distance between what he said and his government's treatment of Jews and Catholics was as wide as the distance between the theory of desegregation and its practical application.

It was in 1754, when both Mendelssohn and Lessing were twenty-five years old, that their friendship began. Mendelssohn had already become a partner in the business and was able to offer Lessing the hospitality of his home. The two men must have made a strange-looking pair: Lessing could have been painted by Rigaud, being more French than German in appearance, proudly erect, his brilliant eyes looking at the world "with the gaze of a falcon"; while Mendelssohn, small, ugly, hunchbacked, and with his enormous nose, looked almost like the caricature of a Jew, but for his luminous, introspective eyes and a forehead high enough to house his knowledge.

Both men's lives were destined to be short—Lessing died in his fifty-second year; Mendelssohn outlived him by only five years—and both men were to attain international fame. But Lessing remained impecunious.

Lessing and Mendelssohn immediately began to collaborate. In 1755 they published an essay over their joint names. The Berlin Academy, one of Frederick's favorite institutions, had announced a prize competition on the subject of Alexander Pope's philosophic creed. Pope's poetic summary of current philosophical beliefs, *An Essay on Man*, had appeared some twenty years previously and had now become popular throughout Europe. The Lessing-Mendelssohn entry was entitled *Pope a Metaphysician!* They pointed out that Pope was in no sense an original philosopher and that as a matter of fact philosophy, dealing with the conceptual, and poetry, dealing with feelings and sensations, were two different matters. The essay won first prize and scored a triumph. Mendelssohn expatiated on these ideas in *Letters on Sensations*, published the same year, in which he wrote that beauty could not be defined, nor was the sensation of beauty related to knowledge. It could be felt only through a faculty which Mendelssohn called "the capacity for approval (*Billigungsvermögen*)." If you possessed this capacity, you would not need to possess the objects of beauty; indeed,

[5] He wrote this famous pronouncement in a faulty German. As I have mentioned, he preferred to speak and write French.

beauty transcended and defied desire or capture. He urged that we think of beauty in the multitude of its forms with "calm pleasure."

These ideas were partly influenced by English writers and more perhaps by Lessing. From the contemplation of beauty Mendelssohn turned to an examination of religious ethics and religious customs, publishing his first book, *Philosophic Conversations*, when he was twenty-six, to be followed by *Philosophic Writings*, issued when he was thirty-one. Both were attempts to arrive at the formulation of his creed. The creed was to bring him in conflict with tradition, the "inert force of history."

3

By the time he was thirty-one years old, the philosopher not only enjoyed considerable local reputation but had become fairly well-to-do.[6]

He fell in love.

Her name was Fromet Gugenheim. He met her on a voyage to Hamburg. Legend has it that she knew him by reputation. She was shocked when she saw him, a little weakling with a hunchback. He told her that God had ordained that it was she who was to be born deformed, but that he had prayed God to "give him the hunchback and let her grow up straight." This, like the tale of Othello's hardships, won her. It is a fine story—but it seems too good to be true.

She was the daughter of Abraham Gugenheim, a fairly prosperous Hamburg merchant, who however had met some business reverses and was now in Vienna to try to rehabilitate his affairs; he did not meet his future son-in-law till long after the couple became engaged. For six weeks Moses spent evening after evening in Fromet's company, discussing philosophy, life, and literature, without telling her his love. Later he wrote to her, half-humorously, berating his own timidity: "How many beautiful hours did I waste, how many left unsatisfied! Only when I seemed to hear the sound of the postilion calling me back did I seize the occasion to declare myself to my beloved."

---

[6] However, the brilliant and beautiful Henriette Herz (1764–1847), wife of the physician Dr. Markus Herz, wrote that even at the time when Mendelssohn's house had become a center of intellectual Berlin and guests came and went constantly, his income from the silk business and from his "scientific writings" was "inconsiderable." I believe she was exaggerating for dramatic effect.

He returned to Berlin and wrote to Lessing:

Berlin, May 1761

Dearest Friend! Our correspondence has long been interrupted; let me renew it. I would never have kept silent for so long, had I not undertaken a voyage to Hamburg which involved me in a thousand diversions. I went to the theater, made the acquaintance of scholars, and—something which you'll find very strange—I was foolish enough to fall in love. And that when I was in my thirtieth year. You are laughing? Never mind. Who knows if a similar fate isn't going to befall you? Perhaps one's thirtieth year is the most dangerous and you are not there yet.[7] The girl I want to marry has no fortune, is neither beautiful nor learned, and yet I, enamored clown, am so much taken by her that I believe I will live happily with her. . . .

You have a full year before you need to compose the wedding poem. Then your lazy Muse must once more reach for her dusty lyre. How could we celebrate our wedding, unsung by you? . . .

It did take a full year, and then a month. Mendelssohn had to apply to the Court for two permissions: being a "foreigner" (from Dessau, the province of Anhalt), he needed a "Permanent Residence Permit" as well as the usual "Wedding Permit" required for Jews. In spite of his reputation, a full year, much running around, and some pulling of strings became necessary. In the intervening year Moses and Fromet corresponded. Her letters have been lost; his have been preserved and they furnish us a picture of the philosopher as a man. They are written in a carelessly conversational style, very different from the carefully shaped writing of his published works, and are sprinkled with Hebrew phrases. He is both steeped in the Jewish tradition and impatient of it. He keeps the Sabbath holy, but not once does he mention having attended service at a temple. He does not seem to have confined himself to a kosher kitchen. He never fails to send proper greetings to her mother and later to her father, adding to the name the usual Hebrew formula of "may her days be long" or "may his Protector guard him." Yet he does not observe the tradition of obedience "to the father and mother of your bride." Father Gugenheim wishes him to

[7] Both men were thirty-two. Why he gave the wrong age for himself and Lessing I do not know.

sign a document acknowledging that he received a certain sum as a dowry. But he is not to receive this sum, as there is no money to pay it, the document being merely an empty attestation to the respectability of the Jewish family. He absolutely refuses to hold still for such a trick. When they become engaged, Fromet's father desires a written contract in which "all details be spelled out punctiliously as was customary at Jewish engagements," and in which the future husband of his daughter furnish guarantees for her maintenance. Moses once again refuses: "The word of a virtuous man is the best security in the world."

He treats his bride now as "my dear child," now as a full equal. He urges her to take French lessons, to read Rousseau [8] and a satire by Friedrich Melchior Grimm, Baron of the Holy Roman Empire, as well as a sentimental novel written for ladies, Riccoboni's *Lettres de Mylady Catesby*. He is delighted that she has read the essay by Shaftesbury, *An Inquiry Concerning Virtue*. At the same time he writes to her that a friend reported to him that she reads too much. "Of this I cannot approve. What is your purpose? To be a scholar? God forbid! Moderate reading becomes a woman, but not scholarliness. A girl who has red eyes from reading deserves to be made fun of."

He adores her but occasionally scolds her and demands the privilege of being "honest with her." He makes fun of the ritual of fashionable courtship: he sends her a ring and writes:

> . . . I accompany this, my most precious friend, with an unworthy trifle as a memento of my devoted love, hoping that you will deign to put it on your incomparable finger.

He adds:

> Was this compliment modishly expressed? I doubt it, since it is too easily understood. Well, let me write in my own way and let's leave the compliments to cleverer writers . . . who express themselves in words which not even a magician can decipher.

He is inclined to be a bit stingy, and when he sends her flowers he tells her how much they cost. Yet he calls himself a spendthrift and hopes she

---

[8] Moses had written the introduction to the German edition of Rousseau's famous *Discours sur l'origine de l'inégalité parmi les hommes.*

will prove more careful of money. He is scrupulously honest. In the course
of the Seven Years' War the Prussian thaler had become devalued, and as
I have mentioned, Veitel Ephraim, "Entrepreneur of the Mint," undertook
doubtful maneuvers to manipulate the debased currency. He tried re-
peatedly to interest Mendelssohn in the enterprise, but Mendelssohn had
no great opinion of Ephraim's character, and refused. He writes Fromet:

February 23, 1762

. . . I thank God daily that I stayed away from the mint; how easy it
would have been to swim with the stream. . . . Everybody blames me:
I should have seized the opportunity to become rich. But I know my limitations and I know that I acted right. . . .

Such were the letters of the philosopher in love who signed himself
in most of the letters, "The unimportant Moses from Dessau." He loved
not only Fromet but her little freckle-faced sister Brendel, who seems to
have been something of a flirt and whom he never wearied of teasing. His
steadfastness never wavered: "It is as impossible for me to cease being
your lover and constant admirer as to cease philosophizing."

And finally he received the two coveted permits.[9] Now the waiting
days—before she could arrive in Berlin—seemed years to him. He prepared
to receive her, but he would leave the details of furnishing their establishment to her judgment and taste. "I want to be like the poet who while sitting in his study heard somebody yell Fire! Fire! The poet replied: 'Tell
it to my wife. I don't want to have anything to do with household chores.'"
Now she must prepare herself to become a Prussian citizen:

March 26, 1762

In true Prussian fashion you will now have to believe everything which
is advantageous to us. The Russians, the Turks, the Americans, they are
all at our service and are only awaiting our wishes. Our money will become
steadier than gold . . . and the whole world will look to Berlin for
security. Our Exchange will become famous from the *Schlossplatz* to our

---

[9] The "Residence Permit" was supported by the French philosopher, the Marquis d'Argens,
who wrote the King: "A poor Catholic philosopher entreats a poor Protestant philosopher to grant
this privilege to a poor Jewish philosopher. There is too much philosophy here for Reason not to
be in accord with the petition."

house. All that you will simply *have* to believe, because you now have the Permit for Berlin. . . .

They were married on June 22, 1762. It proved to be a happy marriage indeed. Eleven years later, when Moses happened to be away from home, Fromet writes to him in one of the very few letters of hers which have been preserved:

July 1773

. . . If it is half as difficult for you to be away from me as it is difficult for me to be away from you, we are never going to leave each other, not even for an hour. I wish my days away. When I awake I want it to be night and when it is night I wish for the next day. The only pleasurable time I spend during your absence is when I get a letter from you. . . .

No doubt that the peace and love Fromet brought Moses helped him to accomplish his task.

4

Frederick the Great was ambitious to develop Prussian industry not only for commodities which were necessities of life but for life's decoration. Jacques Turgot, then the intendant of the province of Limoges and later Louis XVI's brilliant finance minister, had introduced in Limoges new methods of producing porcelain, reviving skills which had lain dormant for many decades. Frederick admired Limoges porcelain; in 1761 he established a Royal porcelain factory in Berlin which was to become famous, though Berlin porcelain never attained the subtlety of Meissen or Derby. Frederick—or rather, a government bureau called *Generallotteriepachtso-cietät* (Society for the Contracts of General Lotteries)—decreed that Jews must buy the product of this factory: when a Jew got married, he had to buy a stipulated amount, more when he bought a house or if a Decree of Protection was awarded him. A third of the porcelain a Jew had to purchase had to be chosen from the best quality, a third from middle quality, and a third from lowest. The Jewish buyer could not choose: obviously the least desirable merchandise was dumped on him. When Mendelssohn got married, he bought twenty china monkeys.

Those twenty china monkeys became a symbol of the house of Mendelssohn. They were passed from father to son and were still in possession of the descendants at the beginning of the Hitler period. Now they have disappeared.

5

Through Lessing's introduction, Mendelssohn joined the "Coffee House of the Scholars" (*Das gelehrte Kaffeehaus*). This was a "club" on the English model, similar to the "Circle of Wits" to which Johnson, Goldsmith, Garrick, and others belonged. Emboldened by the Coffee House scholars, Mendelssohn dared to contribute to a periodical, *Letters Concerning New Literature*, a review of some verses composed by Frederick the Great:

> Almost every verse mirrors the character of this Prince. The whole poem is his portrait, revealing convincingly his great soul and his greater heart, as well as a certain weakness. What a loss for our mother-tongue that this sovereign feels more comfortable in French!

Because of this review, hardly a damning one, Mendelssohn was denounced as an "impudent Jew" and was commanded to appear before the King—and that on a Sabbath. Mendelssohn appeared and defended himself: "He who writes verses, be he King or peasant, plays ninepins. He must allow the pin-boy to tell him how he bowled." The King forgave him. (The scene of the Jew before the King undoubtedly influenced Lessing to write the Jew-before-Saladin scene in *Nathan the Wise*.)

In 1763 the Berlin Academy commissioned several philosophers to write an essay on the theme, "Are philosophic (metaphysical) truths capable of the same exact proofs as mathematical propositions?" Mendelssohn's entry earned him a prize of 50 ducats (about $1,500 in today's equivalent) as well as much praise from the pundits. Probably as a result he was, in the same year, declared a "Protected Jew," to his great joy. (After his death this distinction was, by special decree, conferred upon his widow and children "because of the well-known merits of your husband and father.")

Though to the learned men around him the hunchbacked little man with the great charm became a personality to be admired, to the man in the streets of Berlin Mendelssohn remained that unappetizing creature, "a Jew." In a letter to a friend he describes his taking a walk with his children:

> "Papa," asked my innocent boy, "what is that fellow shouting at us? Why are they throwing stones? What have we done to them?" "Yes, dear papa," another child said, "they pursue us on the street and scream: Jews! Jews! Is it such a disgrace to be a Jew?" . . . I lower my eyes, sigh, and think to myself: "Men, men—whither have you led yourselves?"

So Mendelssohn rented a large garden in which he and his family could take their walks unmolested.

It is a curiously German trait: the burgher derogates the great man of his country while the savants stuff him with honors. As Bismarck was to say, "No nation shows a wider gulf between its men of talent and its ordinary men than does Germany."

Then the Berlin Academy elected Mendelssohn a member, which was the highest honor that could be bestowed on a native scholar, but this was more than King Frederick could stomach. A German *and* a Jew a member of his Academy? He crossed out Mendelssohn's name. Frederick's action may have been as much prompted by prejudice against the Germans as against the Jews. Lessing, a pure Christian, tried hard to obtain the post as head of the Royal Library in Berlin. Several scholars supported his petition. The King chose a French nonentity instead. After his own rejection, Mendelssohn said: "I prefer having been chosen by the scientific society and crossed out by the King's pleasure to being chosen by the King and crossed out by science." It sounds like sour grapes.

Without benefit of the academic title, Mendelssohn continued his work. He became involved in a dispute with Johann Lavater, the Swiss theologian and physician who is remembered as the proponent of the theory of judging character by facial characteristics. Lavater announced that the bump on Mendelssohn's head clearly showed that he had the mind of a Socrates. Could such a man remain a Jew? Lavater wanted to convert him to Christianity. Mendelssohn answered in a suave and affable essay which formed a study for what is stylistically his finest work: *Jerusalem or of the*

Religious Force of Judaism (1783). This work so impressed Kant that he almost became a convert. Mendelssohn had previously journeyed to Königsberg to meet the august professor. According to a contemporary report, Kant's students were astonished to see walking into the lecture room a bent little Jew, unprepossessing and timid. They mocked him and asked him what he was doing there. Mendelssohn replied that he had come to make the acquaintance of the great philosopher. The students were about to throw him out as an officious nuisance when Kant entered, recognized him, embraced him, and presented him to the student body. Perhaps the story is true, though the behavior of the students was one hardly likely from a group studying philosophy.

As to the dispute with Lavater, the Swiss doctor was fair enough to apologize for his "presumptuous" attempt to convert Mendelssohn, and he was handsomely praised for this apology. It was Mendelssohn who was attacked, because in his defense of Judaism he had admitted that it, like other religions, was not perfect, that there were defects in the creed. How could such a distinguished seeker-after-truth defend an imperfect doctrine? Mendelssohn wrote:

> I do not understand what could possibly bind me to this seemingly over-strict and generally despised religion, if I were not convinced in my heart of its truth. . . . I shall not deny that I have detected in my religion human increments and abuses that, unfortunately, much obscure its radiance. What friend of truth can boast of having found his religion free of harmful human additives? We all know this poisonous breath of hypocrisy and superstition, and those of us who are seekers after the truth wish that we might purge the poison without harming the true and the good.
>
> ("Epistle to Deacon Lavater in Zurich")

Pens were crossed, universities debated the issue, clergymen found serviceable topics for their sermons, the philosophic fight raged.

Two years after the *Jerusalem* essay, Mendelssohn took part in another famous controversy, the so-called "Battle of Pantheism." The German philosopher Friedrich Jacobi attacked the pantheism of Spinoza, a creed he felt was nothing short of atheism, and he railed against Lessing—now dead—who, Jacobi believed, was a follower of Spinoza. Mendelssohn

A discussion among Moses Mendelssohn, Lessing, and Lavater. Lessing is standing behind the chess set, while Lavater is pointing out a passage in the Bible to Mendelssohn. Woodcut after a painting by Moritz Oppenheim.

sprang to the defense of Lessing and once again expressed his views in his final work, *Morning Hours* (1785). Eventually Goethe and Herder were drawn into the dispute.

Like most of his philosopher-companions, Moses was a prolific writer. He had something to say on a multitude of subjects, though he hardly rivaled the Voltaires and the d'Alemberts in their passion for pen and ink. Among his minor writings, one finds such essays as "Letter from a Jealous Husband and a Reply" and "Suggestions to Young People on How They Should Read New and Old Poets." He expressed himself strongly against birth control, which was then beginning to be practiced; in the midst of war he wrote, "What times! To choke men to death is the road which leads to honor. To beget children is considered shameful." In a lighter vein, he recommended to the Jews that they attend the theater; he himself was a passionate theatergoer. Orthodox Jews frowned on anything as frivolous as the theater. Mendelssohn wrote:

> At the end of a play when the illusion has ceased, reason comes to the fore, but in the heat of the moment we follow the dictates of our imagination. We forget who, what, and where we are and what our personal concerns are. . . . We do seem to remember, though dimly, that a similar misfortune once happened to us. We fear that a like tragedy might befall us. Such a feeling only heightens illusion, giving additional weight to our emotions. Relating the subject of the play to ourselves is a sympathetic, not a selfish, emotion.

While delivering a manuscript to the publisher, Mendelssohn caught cold. His frail constitution was soon undermined; he died in January, 1786, hardly fifty-seven years old.

The finest tribute to Mendelssohn had been tendered by Lessing: Moses served as the model for Lessing's masterpiece, the play of tolerance, *Nathan the Wise* (1775). Nathan's answer to Saladin's barbed question, "Which of the three religions do you consider the best?" may well reflect Mendelssohn's dialectic. At any rate, the play is a noble monument to the Jewish philosopher, to the spirit of the Enlightenment, and to the idealism of Gotthold Ephraim Lessing.

Mendelssohn's tribute to Lessing—in a friendship so selfless and mutually beneficent that one hesitates to expatiate on it lest the impression remain that such goodness is improbable—that tribute can be found in a letter he wrote after Lessing's death to Lessing's brother:

> Not a word about the loss, the great defeat we have experienced. The memory of the man who left us is too sacred to me to diminish it by plaint. He now appears to me bathed in a light of peace and humor; that light illumines everything I touch. No, I no longer count my loss. Rather I thank Providence for the benison to have known in my youth a man who educated my soul, who acted both as friend and judge in all my actions and for every line I penned. Whenever in the future I will undertake anything important, I imagine he'll be beside me, as friend and judge. . . .

6
Phaedo and the Philosophy of Moses Mendelssohn

The story goes that at the town gate the customs officer asked Moses Mendelssohn, "In what merchandise do you trade, Jew?" He replied, "In Reason, sir, a commodity with which you have no acquaintance."

He attempted to apply reason to thoughts and feelings beyond reason. He wished to prove nondemonstrable concepts, the soul and God, with demonstrable logic. It was reason, he wrote, which led him to postulate both the existence of the soul and the existence of a God.

His mentor was not, as one might expect, his great Jewish antecedent, Spinoza, but that most essential of Greek philosophers, Plato. Lessing had counseled Mendelssohn to study the world of antiquity, writing to him, "Let us go back to the school of the ancients. Could we choose betters, except Nature herself?"

Mendelssohn wrote about Plato:

> His style flows with a soft, easy majesty when he waxes poetic. If you didn't understand the craft of writing, you could believe that his style came effortlessly to him. I have never read Plato without being ashamed that I have taken pen in hand. And by this time I have written enough to understand the art behind that seeming effortlessness. I feel how hard this man must have worked to give his noble and fiery thoughts their fine polish and exquisite smoothness.

The work on which Mendelssohn's contemporary fame rested was a book based on Plato and using Plato's technique of teaching through the give-and-take of dialogue. The book was entitled *Phaedo or On the Immortality of the Soul*. One of Plato's most famous Dialogues is entitled *Phaedo*; in it the philosopher Phaedo discusses the immortality of the soul. The Dialogue contains the description of the death of Socrates; it is one of the most beautiful passages of the world's literature.

Mendelssohn's *Phaedo* became a bestseller and was published in thirty-seven languages; it rivaled the popularity of Voltaire's *Candide*. It was required reading for all who either possessed or pretended to have an interest in philosophy. It was discussed in the ghetto as well as in the palace of Frederick the Great, in the coffee houses of London as well as in the Sorbonne in Paris. The young Goethe read it with delight. Its fame even traveled across the Atlantic. Benjamin Franklin may have had a copy of it in his library.[10]

What is the philosophical argument of *Phaedo*? And why did it make so great an impression in its time?

Mendelssohn postulates, first, that we have a soul because we are able to feel, dream, desire, and be aware of our existence. It is this awareness of ourself which creates our capacity to feel. True, we cannot see or touch the soul. But we see and touch everything *through* the soul. The soul, being the medium of consciousness, exists as certainly as does matter.

> I hear people complain that they don't know what the soul is. I wish they would tell me first what matter is. We do see and feel matter, but not what it is—rather the effect it causes. My question was "What *is* matter?", not what is its effect. Perhaps it is an improper question, because it may only be possible to define things through the effects they cause. Let us now turn to the soul! We know what the soul can cause: it can feel, think, desire, condemn. Our inner consciousness, the awareness of ourselves, teaches us that the soul is part of ourselves because it is we ourselves who feel, think, desire, condemn. We need not, as we do with matter, derive the soul's definition from its effect. We ourselves feel the soul with absolute cer-

---

[10] A copy of *Phaedo* came to *The Library Company of Philadelphia*, which owns many of the books from Franklin's library, through a collection bought by William MacKenzie. He "bought a good many books when the Franklin library was dispersed in 1801–03. Unfortunately this copy of the French translation of 1772 was rebound in the last century, and any shelf mark which would prove it to have been Franklin's is gone." (Edwin Wolf, 2nd Librarian, in a letter to the author.)

tainty because we feel ourselves. Yet people still want to know what the soul is.

Or again:

D'Alembert defined matter as something dimensional and impenetrable. Both of these concepts, the dimensionality as well as the impenetrability, have their origin in the soul. We ascribe these properties to an object outside of us, and that object we call matter. The element in which these concepts are formed within us we call the soul.

   The truth is that as far as we know, matter is only something which can arouse in the soul the ideas of dimensionality, impenetrability, shape, etc. It is the soul itself which gives birth to such images.

Mendelssohn cites another "proof" for the existence of the soul: the process of dreaming. Do we not all dream? Would it be possible for us to dream if we were made of matter? Could we dream these wild "fragments taken from diverse systems" if reason alone—or in other words the brain—operated in us? To be sure, dreams do have a connection with reason, showing that the soul is not some loosely floating substance but something that is linked to the other parts of our being—to reason itself:

When we dream we build our personal worlds. Then when we awake, we move into a communal world. Our dreams are fragments taken from diverse systems; together they do not form themselves into an integrated whole. The only objective truth dreams contain is the existence of the dreamer himself. That existence always remains beyond doubt.

   Dreams are full of the liveliest and most vivid imaginings. When you awake, you realize that you have experienced such excursions of the imagination, but you are unable to remember them, if you cannot remember the subject with which they are connected and which caused them to spring up. The soul can only conjure up a concept if, so to speak, it has a string in its hand with which to pull it forth from the subconscious. If the string cannot be found, the effort is in vain.

Plato too delved into the phenomenon of dreams and brought to the surface a remarkable anticipation of Freud. Here is Plato on dreams (from *The Republic*):

I mean particularly those desires which are awake when the reasoning and taming and ruling power of the personality is asleep; the wild beast in our nature, gorged with meat and drink, starts up and walks about naked, and surfeits at his will; and there is no conceivable folly or crime, however shameless or unnatural—not excepting incest or parricide—of which such a nature may not be guilty.

In all of us, even in good men, there is such a latent wild beast nature, which peers out in sleep.

Plato was certain that we had a soul and that the soul did not die, but possessed "personal immortality." It was this security that our souls would carry on existence which made it possible for us to face our bodily death courageously and to endure the death of the people we loved. Yet Plato admitted that the existence of the soul could not be demonstrated any more than God could be demonstrated. Our gods may be only personifications of our ideals, ideals of love and hope. Whatever the truth of the matter, says Plato in his *Phaedo*, it does no harm for us to believe in the gods and may do us and our children enormous good, by giving us the strength to battle on.

Mendelssohn adopted Plato's reasoning, but instead of admitting defeat in the attempt to demonstrate God, he deduced the existence of God from the existence of the soul. Since man has a soul and since that soul does not age or wither away, the soul tends naturally toward perfection, toward goodness. That is the religious impulse. If the soul is, as Hamlet says, "a thing immortal," then an immortal force exists. That force is God. Philosophically speaking, the existence of God can be proved by the fact that the soul exists. In saying this, he, the philosopher, does no more than give an orderly expression to what human beings feel instinctively and have felt from time immemorial. That feeling, so strong in us, so historic, so long lasting, so ubiquitous, existing as it does in separated tribes and nations, is the foundation of natural religion. Natural religion is as ineluctable an ingredient of the structure of man as the soul itself. Could that structure be possibly based on a false premise? No.

Therefore religion was a true concept and God existed.

There was no conflict between Reason and Religion. On the contrary, Reason led to Religion.

But—and it was a big "but" in its time and place—the religious instinct may not serve as a reason or excuse to enforce acceptance of any one specific religious doctrine. He himself was a Jew and believed in the principles of Judaism. He believed in Judaism because no other religion contained as many admonitions to lead the initiated toward "justice, piety, obedience to law and state, human warmth (*Menschlichkeit*—humanity)." However, it really made no difference what religion one chose.

> All religions are partly theoretical and partly practical. Their theoretical side has no influence on morality. Men often have constructed false moralities from true theories and true morality from false theory. The practical side of any religion classifies virtues and vices. That does not necessarily mean that Reason will agree with this classification. Religion makes it easier to do good because it cites motives for doing so. *Any* religion does that if it holds out the promise to man that doing good will please God and that evil will displease Him. Yet the definition of what is "good" is impeded by the prejudices of various religions. You ask me which religion is least impeded? I answer, the religion which permits the greatest freedom to Reason.

Here again we find Mendelssohn attempting to combine reason and religion, harmonizing what he felt was true though unseen and impalpable with what was evident and observable. Such a combination led to tolerance. That religion was best

> which is most tolerant and which permits us to embrace all of humanity with equal love. A religion which excludes any one [of a different creed] merely constricts our soul. Such a religion creates a loveless pride in our own exclusive worth.

It is clear that he could not accept the doctrine that the Jews were the "chosen people."

All very fine! Yet he was not quite broad-minded enough to embrace all religions with equal calm. He particularly disliked the stricter form of Catholicism. That prejudice came naturally to a man who lived in a Protestant country, whose best friend was a Protestant, and who had imbibed copious draughts of Voltaire:

Despotism has the advantage that it is definite. However much its tenets may offend a sane intellect, at least they are consistent and systematic. Every question has its certain answer. You are not to bother or search or examine. . . . Such is the principle of the Roman Catholic religion. It treats every contingency fully and consistently. If you can accept its precepts, you know at least where you stand. A building has been constructed and there is silence in every room. To be sure, it is only, as Montesquieu says, that terrible silence which reigns in a fortress expecting an assault that night. If you believe that silence and peace make up life's happiness, then you cannot be more securely sheltered than under a Roman Catholic despot.

We have seen that he found fanaticism, a "zeal to condemn," even in the Jewish religion. He found too often "narrow-minded application of teaching that was great of heart." Yes, the ancient traditions were life-enhancing, but some of them had now hardened and were choking the free flow of the soul. Religious thinking, like philosophic thinking, must be kept flexible to be able to stay vital. Slavish observance turns some into bigots, others into freaks, whatever the dogma. He was afraid that bigotry and dogmatism would always exist. We would always have with us the tenacious clinging to outmoded custom; we would not free ourselves from suspicion against the neighbor who looks different and acts differently.

He harbored no optimistic notions of mankind's progress, though individuals were able to perfect themselves:

> . . . considered as a whole, mankind retains, at all periods of time, about the same degree of morality, the same quality of religion and irreligion, of virtue and vice, of happiness and misery. . . .

While mankind was a viscous mass, men could rise and become fluid; the only way they could become so, the only guide on a road upwards, was the soul. One needed to aid the soul, the natural impulse of which was toward progress, by paying attention to it. One needed to "listen" to its impulses, to the voice of God. He spoke through the soul.

7

Why did *Phaedo* create as much discussion as it did? Why did it prove so popular? Why did Mendelssohn become more famous than Kant, an incomparably more original thinker? The reasons must be understood in their historical context. The first of these was solace.

In its effort to break the power of the church, to dispel the fog of religious obscurantism and light the lights in what was to be a brave new world, the Enlightenment had gone very far. Perhaps too far, too far for comfort. What could one now believe in? Where were the devout dogmas of yore, the accommodating superstitions, the comforting mumbo-jumbo? Where was the soothing half-light of mystery and miracle? The light was crass now, the world too bright. The fairy tale was gone out of fashion. Everything was being questioned, in an assault of skepticism whose leader was the Scottish philosopher, David Hume. His *Treatise on Human Nature* had been published in 1740, twenty-seven years before *Phaedo*. Hume denied that the world was built on cause and effect. We are creatures of haphazard sensations and random ideas. We cannot believe in a sequence of whys and wherefores. Everything—including religion and philosophy— is a series of apprehensions on which we try to force a design which does not exist and proves fictitious. At best we deal with probabilities. We cannot know the truth. "God, too, has no real existence."

Once, at a dinner in a friend's house, Hume protested that he could not swallow his food because there was an enemy present. What enemy? Hume pointed to a Bible lying on a table.

Voltaire, who was not nearly the skeptic Hume was, but who was equally devoted to the task of breaking the back of organized religion, rephrased Hume's thoughts when he wrote, "It is given to us to calculate, to weigh, to measure, to observe; this is natural philosophy; almost all the rest is chimera." Voltaire, as he himself said, developed the art of doubt. Only charlatans were certain. "Doubt is not a very agreeable state, but certainty is a ridiculous one."

Hume, Voltaire, and the other *philosophes* had knocked the props from under many a sincere soul. They had closed the door of the church or the temple into which a troubled man could go and ask for aid. The eyes of men were directed to see only what was to be seen, not what was unperceivable. A need was left unfulfilled.

On the other hand, the new skepticism offered a measure of compensation. If the word of God was no longer unassailable, if your particular God could be questioned, if indeed a doubt ascended toward the existence of any God, then it no longer made sense to separate yourself from or fight against those who believed in a deity different from your own.

While Mendelssohn was working on *Phaedo*, in 1765, a sixteen-year-old boy by the name of La Barre was arrested on the charge of having mutilated crucifixes. He was tortured and under torture confessed his guilt. His head was cut off and his body flung onto a pyre. A copy of Voltaire's *Philosophic Dictionary*, which La Barre owned, was burned with him.

This tragedy brought out the finest side of Voltaire's nature. Having expressed skepticism with unparalleled wit and brilliance in a dozen satires, including *Candide* (1759), he now felt that the time for mockery had passed. He no longer felt, he said, like smiling. He rallied "brave Diderot, intrepid d'Alembert," and others around him and poured forth a seemingly endless stream of pamphlets, letters, commentaries, diatribes, essays, culminating in his *Treatise on Tolerance*. Because he wrote in a style so sharp and lucid as hardly a philosopher before or after him, he was read as eagerly as a sensational novelist; his pamphlets, aided by the additional fillip of being "improper" literature, were passed from house to house. The idea of tolerance was borne on a wind of words, carried by thousands of sheets of paper and by thousands of dinner discussions.

Voltaire's eloquence was seconded by the book written by the philosopher of Berlin, its language simple enough to be widely understood, its thoughts expressing clearly what some had as yet felt only dimly. "How true!" must have been penciled on many a margin by many a reader. *Phaedo*, then, proved useful on two grounds. First, it offered a pole to be grasped on a slippery ground, a staff of stability in a newly unstable world. To put it simply, *Phaedo* showed that religion was not foolishness. It had a place even in an "enlightened" world. Men who had been shaken by skepticism, by doubts, by materialistic philosophy, by philosophies which specialized in denial, found here what at that moment they needed, a reaffirmation of the religious instinct. Surely, even at the time when Reason was king, people longed for the comfort and the consolation offered by a God or promised in a Paradise. Second, *Phaedo* buttressed the belief in tolerance, which was gaining acceptance among thinking people.

In short, Mendelssohn brought Reason into consonance with Religion. He offered assuagement without apology. And he not only joined the philosophic chorus, but became one of its leading singers, chanting the hymn to tolerance in a gentle but certain voice.

8

After *Phaedo*, Mendelssohn came forth with a more daring proposition: if belief as a function of the soul was a personal and inward affair, then the forming of a sect and the gathering together of co-worshippers into closed groups was contrary to the very spirit of religion. This was what the Jews had done. They had been separated and had bound themselves together—whether voluntarily or forced by circumstances made no difference—and they now formed a globule within the body politic. A sign of this separatism was the fact that whether a Jew lived in Berlin or in Paris, his religious service was conducted in Hebrew. Mendelssohn believed that the Jews must adopt the language and usage of the country in which they lived. Religious rites, if they were to be observed at all, should be held in the German language in Germany, in French in France. Jewish heritage must be adapted to native heritage, the two amalgamated; then and only then will it become meaningful to future generations. He was against an international Judaism and he opposed the idea of a Jewish homeland which would reunite the scattered people. Even in the eighteenth century many dreamed of and longed for a Zion. No, said Mendelssohn, a Jew is first of all a citizen of the country in which he was born. The true homeland lies where your home is. He recommended assimilation. By all means let the German Jews hold on to the ethical virtues of their religion, in whose virtues he himself strongly believed. But in all other respects—in language, custom, obedience to government—let them become Germans. The wall which surrounded the ghetto must be torn down by men working from within as well as from without. There are to be no more conclaves, forced or voluntary. The governments of the German states must cancel the discriminatory laws against the Jews. Take Frederick the Great at his word: If the Jews wish to populate Prussia, let them build their synagogues there. But let the services of these synagogues be conducted in the German language and let the worshippers become, in truth, German citizens, undistinguishable from other Germans.

He himself began to translate the Scriptures into German. Trained by and encouraged by Lessing, he wrote German adaptations of the Pentateuch, the Song of Songs, and a number of the Psalms. These translations are magnificent examples of linguistic skill; they are prose poems written from a full heart and a noble soul.[11] He said that he regarded the Psalms as great oriental lyric poetry: "Long enough has their clear meaning been adumbrated by mystic equivocation." Gradually these German versions were published, at first with the Hebrew on the left page and the translation on the right, later solely in German.

9

Opposition to Mendelssohn's assimilation program came as strongly from the camp of the Jews as from the tents of the Christians. As new inventions are often opposed most actively by those who stand to benefit most by them, so did the orthodox faction resist reformation. The rabbis, seeing their status as dispensers of mysteries threatened, forbade the congregation under pain of ostracism to read the Pentateuch in German and made very free with the threat of Jehovah's wrath. The translation was declared an heretical act in 1779. A Rabbi Raphael Kohen proposed a set of punishments for Jews who were to be found reading it. It was only the intervention of King Christian VII of Denmark, who had become a subscriber to a special edition of Mendelssohn's works, and who threw the weight of his authority in Mendelssohn's favor, which made it impossible, or at least impolitic, to carry out the Rabbi's plan. "Maimon," whom we have already quoted, tells the story of being found studying a book of Hebrew logic by Maimonides, with comments by Mendelssohn. Maimonides, the patriarch of Jewish scholars, appearing in the same pages as this modern unbeliever?

[11] Schubert's beautiful chorus for female voices, "The Lord is my Shepherd," is a setting of Mendelssohn's words.

"Maimon's" friend was beside himself with fury. He screamed, "A fine book you are reading! . . . I advise you to leave Berlin voluntarily as soon as possible if you do not want to be thrown out."

Gradually, however, there came to the fore leaders of Jewish thought who agreed with Mendelssohn's proposals. His Bible translations became more and more widely employed. Daniel Itzig established and financed the "Free School" (1778), which taught, among other liberal subjects, the correct use of the German language. Markus Herz the physician, Lazarus Bendavid, and "Maimon"—all friends of Mendelssohn—played important roles in Germany's intellectual development. Herz became Kant's assistant. Bendavid recalls in his autobiography that his studies included mathematics, history, theory of the arts and languages; in the evenings, with his parents safely asleep, he sneaked off to the house of a Protestant clergyman to discuss philosophy. The younger generation studied German, using Mendelssohn's texts. The assimilation had begun.

It worked two ways: tolerance and understanding developed as well in Christian circles. Lavater or no Lavater, people—some of them, anyway—began to understand that a crooked nose was no sign of a crooked character.

In 1788, two years after Moses' death, *The Merchant of Venice* was performed in Berlin. The actor Fleck, who played Shylock, felt it necessary to precede the play with a prologue:

> Now that intelligent Berlin begins to esteem the
> co-religionists of the wise Mendelssohn,
> Now that we see among these people whose
> prophets and serious laws we honor,
> Men arise who excel in the sciences and the arts—
> now do we want to sadden them by mocking them?
> Do we want to cause the blush of shame to rise
> to the cheeks of those who as friends of humanity show
> themselves kindly toward Christians and Jews alike?
> No, that we assuredly do not want.

In Prussia the "Jew porcelain" edict was repealed in 1787, the "Body Tax" in the same year, in 1808 "deserving" Jews in Berlin were awarded citizens' privileges, including the right to be elected to honorary posts. The following year Salomon Veit (brother-in-law of Dorothea, one of Moses' children) was elected to the Berlin Magistrate. Finally in 1812 the "Emancipation Edict" was issued,[12] declaring Jews full-scale citizens—or almost so. There were to be no more "Protected Jews," all were permitted to settle in Prussia, and they could choose whatever profession they wished—except the army, the law, or the royal court. Similar measures were taken in other German states, though not in all. In 1798 the elders of the city of Mainz solemnly burned the portal of the ghetto. A Christian family in Breslau took Mendelssohn's name. Christian Wilhelm Dohm, Counsellor in the Prussian War Ministry, wanted to aid the Jews of Alsace and wrote a famous treatise dedicated to Mendelssohn, *On the Improvement of the Civil Condition of the Jews*.

10

As their civil condition improved, so did their economic and intellectual condition. As they became wealthier, they opened homes some of which became the salons and intellectual centers of Germany. Soon French was spoken almost as widely as German. The house of Markus Herz, presided over by Henriette, became a meeting place for such men as the French revolutionary leader Mirabeau (who wrote a treatise *Sur Moses Mendelssohn*); Friedrich Schlegel, one of the founders of the German romantic school; Friedrich Schleiermacher, philosopher and Protestant theologian (who influenced Felix Mendelssohn); Friedrich Gentz, who became Metternich's powerful associate; and the brothers Humboldt—Wilhelm, who became Prussian minister of education, and Alexander, the explorer. Fanny Itzig, daughter of the financier, married Baron Nathan Arnstein and opened a salon in Vienna which Beethoven visited. Schiller wrote: "The circles of the educated Jews of Berlin are the only places where literature is discussed."

While he lived, Mendelssohn's house and later that of his daughter Dorothea served to gather such a circle. Henriette Herz recalled the evenings when new books and plays were read aloud in company:

[12] This followed by some years *The Declaration of the Rights of Man*, issued by the French National Assembly at the time of the Revolution. In 1791 the Jews of France were voted full civil rights.

Mendelssohn listened punctiliously and attentively. How we used to edge up to him and try to hear what he thought! He was kind and mild in his wisdom. Yet he loved a joke. But his humor was never biting. Even when he condemned, he knew how to give his criticism a pleasant and charming turn. . . .

Only rarely did a foreign scholar come to Berlin without calling on him. His friends and the friends of his friends could drop in uninvited. . . . Even some of the old orthodox Jews made their appearance, though only the more intelligent ones among them. Toward them Mendelssohn showed himself friendly and understanding.

Mendelssohn's hospitality was unlimited, though the family had to practice moderation. The refreshments he offered to his guests were hardly lavish. As an intimate friend of his daughters, I knew that the mistress of the house carefully counted the number of raisins and almonds which it was then *de rigueur* to arrange on a platter before she carried it into the salon.

The Mendelssohns had nine children; [13] six of them grew to adulthood. Six out of nine, an excellent record of survival in the eighteenth century, indicating that the children were well cared for, or that the parents were lucky. The six were, in order of birth, Dorothea (Brendel), Recha, Henriette, Joseph, Abraham, and Nathan.

Dorothea married when she was only seventeen. Her husband was a prosperous merchant, Simon Veit. It was not a love match, but one arranged by the parents. Moses Mendelssohn's enlightenment had not reached the state where the wishes of a daughter seemed particularly important. After bearing Veit four children, [14] Dorothea met Friedrich Schlegel. She fell in love with him and he with her, though she was anything but beautiful. She left her husband and lived with Schlegel. The affair created a great scandal, particularly so because Schlegel published a novel, *Lucinde*, which was considered highly immoral and which reflected aspects of his life with Dorothea. Dorothea herself became a writer; she wrote *Florentin*, an obvious imitation of Goethe's *Wilhelm Meister*. Dorothea and Schlegel married in 1802. How Fromet accepted the fate of her eldest daughter is not known.

[13] Some sources say there were ten.
[14] Two of the sons, Abraham and Philipp, became painters. Philipp achieved prominence; he designed the decorations for the Cathedral in Mainz.

Henriette had a long love affair with Friedrich Ernst Schleiermacher, but never married. She became the companion of the daughter of a Count Sebastiani. The daughter married the Duke of Praslin; it was an unhappy union and the Duke killed his wife in 1847. The sensational murder case was the talk of Paris for many weeks. Henriette—the "Tante Jette" of whom Felix was very fond—continued to live in Paris.

The three sons of Moses founded the banking empire. Nathan and Joseph established themselves first in Hamburg, Abraham in Paris, later in Berlin.

I I

Moses Mendelssohn's residual value lies less in what he thought than in what he taught. His legacy is less an original philosophic system than a set of instructions governing the conduct of his people. A second Moses, he led the Jews into the Western world, so to speak, out of Jerusalem into the *Schlossplatz* and the *Place de la Concorde* and the Strand.

Some of the rabbis mocked him as a "circumcised Christian." Yet the men and women who longed to march out of the ghetto and take part in the life of their country were eager to follow him and echoed his demand that they be given a chance at public education and access to arts and sciences. Let us see what they contribute, said Mendelssohn, taking into account that up to now they had "been kept at such a distance from culture that one might almost doubt the possibility of improvement."

If assimilation did not succeed at all times, it succeeded at certain periods, and when it did, it succeeded brilliantly. German Jews tried assimilation so wholeheartedly that some of them became German chauvinists. Then, just when they thought that they had wiped out the damning difference, they were forced to fail. When a demagogue needed a whipping boy, the crash at the Börse or the trouncing of the Seventh Regiment was due to the Jews. At such times, long before Hitler, they were cursed into renewed segregation.

For one or two generations at least, following Moses' death in 1786, the Jews of Germany, a country which is peculiarly subject to violent swings between sentimentality and brutality, lived in a generally clement climate.

Before the winter of discontent once more began to darken, Christians and Jews worked together in comparative harmony. Intermarriage became a commonplace. Was it mere coincidence that this period was Germany's finest season? It was then that Germany produced Goethe and Schiller and its great romantic writers; it was in that era that Germany offered the world its concentration of musical genius.

Not that all was sweetness and light. In 1808, the year that Goethe published the first part of *Faust*, Johann Gottlieb Fichte published his *Addresses to the German Nation*, in which he wrote that equal rights for the Jews represented "an offense against the human rights of the German nation" and that "the Germans alone are carrying aloft the torch of civilization." Friedrich Ludwig Jahn organized German youth into gymnastic associates and called for a "crusade" against everything foreign—that is, Poles, French, Junkers, priests, and Jews. Ernst Moritz Arndt, another German nationalist, wrote, "Humanity be damned! Cosmopolitanism is the way the Jew thinks."

Still, there was no lack of voices to proclaim the morality of and the necessity for tolerance. Among the most impressive was that of Prince Charles Joseph de Ligne, a Belgian nobleman who served in the Austrian army and wrote a *Treatise on the Jews*. Goethe, the foremost European of his time, confessed that as a child he had had prejudice drummed into him. Only later "did respect join the admiration I cherish for the people who created the Bible and for the poet who sang the Song of Songs." Napoleon in his early days assumed the role of liberator of the Jews, as he postured as the savior of Europe. In 1806 he convoked the *Assemblée des Notables* in Paris; the assembly consisted of 112 Jewish representatives. Prompted by Mendelssohn's teaching, the assembly sanctioned intermarriage and voted against self-administration, being content to live within the French law of *égalité*. Later, however, Napoleon proved to be not quite so broadminded.

Similarly, at the Congress of Vienna, the smaller German states juggled Prussia into revoking some emancipatory decisions governing Jews. So it went, back and forth. Fortune remained skittish. The sails of the ketch had to be tacked frequently "the scanty wind to catch." Yet a refreshing wind did blow.

12

Mendelssohn was not an isolated thinker, immured in a tower, as Montaigne was. He was not an angry man of philosophy, as unruly as Hume. He was not one of the detached and daring explorers in the space of thought like a Kant or an Einstein. His achievement was more that of a peace-maker: he wanted to arbitrate the conflicts between Reason and Religion and between Christian and Jew. As an arbitrator he stood in the vanguard of the Enlightenment. Voltaire, Diderot, Franklin, Pope, Thomas Paine, Lessing, Cesare Beccaria—you could have invited all of them for dinner and you would have found that they agreed more or less with Mendelssohn. Their ideas did much to spawn the two great events of the eighteenth century, the American Revolution and the French Revolution, both of which postulated religious tolerance and demanded the separation of church and state.

He was both a thinker and a doer. Greater geniuses than Moses sometimes are inhibited by the very profundity of their thinking; they do not accomplish all they set out to do. Kant died believing that he had been unable to transfer his view of the world from his head to paper. Less profound, Moses knew how to combine cogitative powers with operative powers.

His operative power he bequeathed to his sons, particularly to Abraham, father of Felix. Abraham, firm of purpose, knew what he wanted: wealth and position. What he wanted he got. He inherited as well Moses' intellectual curiosity and his eagerness for knowledge. "Education" was the password of these households. Abraham in turn passed the standard on to his children, perhaps making too much of it.

As to Moses' theory of assimilation, it was interpreted by the next generation in curious combinations. Abraham believed in going all the way, denying Judaism and adopting the religion of his country. Dorothea, mystically inclined, became a devout Catholic.

As a final estimate of the eighteenth-century philosopher, let us say—whether we agree with all his tenets or not—that he was one of the attractive apparitions of the Age of Reason and that the tolerance he preached promoted an understanding of his people and aided their continuance. More than a half century after Moses' death, Disraeli was able to declare to the House of Commons:

> They are an ancient people, a famous people, an enduring people, and a people who in the end have generally attained their objects. I hope Parliament may endure for ever, and sometimes I think it will; but I cannot help remembering that the Jews have outlived Assyrian kings, Egyptian Pharaohs, Roman Caesars, and Arabian Caliphs. (May 25, 1854)

Abraham Mendelssohn playing cards. Unpublished drawing by Wilhelm Hensel. (Mendelssohn Archive, Berlin)

Three

THE BANKER

I

$\mathcal{B}$ECAUSE he was the son of a famous father and the father of a famous son, Abraham's own fame is pint-sized. A short measure of it has been granted to him; most of the chronicles are content to mention that he was a banker and that he became very wealthy, enabling him to give Felix "the best of everything."

His grandson Sebastian Hensel—son of Fanny, Abraham's daughter, and of the painter Wilhelm Hensel—gave a sketch of his grandfather in his book, *The Family Mendelssohn*. Hensel's book, good-naturedly chatty, is as cautious as official family recollections usually are. What emerges there is the picture of Abraham as the devoted family man.

He was more than that. He was more than the "hyphen between a father and a son," as he once described himself in a rare attack of modesty. He represented a new type of businessman of the world, a type which emerged in the industrially advancing countries. Shrewd and determined though he was, he did not live his life locked in the counting house. He read more than the market reports and the bills of exchange. He became a representative of the new educated middle class, a man who believed that the privilege of having money carried with it the duty of enriching the mind. Many of his friends felt that way. Whatever their prejudices and limitations—and Abraham too had his set of prejudices and limitations

—they were not mere money-grubbers. They were not what the Germans call *Spiessbürger* and what we used to call Babbitts. It was these men, almost as much as the poets and painters and politicians, who helped Europe to the vigor it possessed in the early nineteenth century.

Abraham, with his exceptionally keen mind, might have become, as his father's son, a successful philosopher. In his youth his mind was philosophically occupied. His capacity for responding to and understanding the arts, particularly music—a capacity which astonished Felix—could have turned him into a good critic. He chose neither career. His choice was a sign of his times, which offered new opportunities to industrialists and gave new strength to money, because there existed a new need for money.

Abraham saw the possibilities. He perceived the emerging pattern. Most of us can see what is happening right now at the street corner: few of us can weave immediate events into a pattern. We are occupied with the moment. Goethe said that on the day the Holy Roman Empire came to an end his coachman and his servant had a fight: that domestic altercation concerned him more than the dissolution of the Empire.

Abraham Mendelssohn was born six years after Beethoven and outlived Beethoven by eight years (Abraham: 1776–1835; Beethoven: 1770–1827). Both men lived a significant part of their lives under the whip of Napoleon who, heedless of "civil wounds plough'd up with neighbor's sword," plunged on and on and was with nothing pleased "till he be eased with being nothing."

Both Beethoven and Abraham experienced Napoleon's wars. Vienna was invaded twice, Berlin once. Both men had to seek refuge. But while the successful composer became poorer, the successful banker became richer. Abraham's wealth can be traced to four causes: first, the change in the status of the Jews brought about by the Enlightenment and Moses Mendelssohn; second, Prussia's strategic position in the Napoleonic wars; third, the industrial development of Prussia; fourth and most important, his own vision of the changing world to which I have referred. Amidst all the turbulence, his vision never became beclouded. Not even when the smoke of the cannons limited visibility.

During his youth the tricolor was waving over Europe. The storm clouds chased across the skies; whether he looked East or West he saw these clouds and heard the hail of Napoleon's fusiliers. Virtually all of the German-speaking territories had to duck beneath these assaults. Cologne, Bonn, Mainz, Coblenz, Munich, Dresden, Vienna for a time—they all became "French" cities. Yet in the central portion of the German land the Napoleonic fire burned with less heat. "Everywhere the world was aflame," Goethe noted in his diary, "Europe changed shape. Cities and navies were being destroyed on the land and on the sea, but central and northern Germany profited from a kind of febrile peace which enabled us to enjoy a doubtful safety."

That was because Napoleon used northern Germany—and Prussia particularly—for his own purposes. Napoleon's chief enemies, as yet unconquered, were England and Russia. As to Russia, Napoleon wanted Prussia as a steppingstone toward that country and he wanted to make sure he wouldn't slip on that stone. As to England, Napoleon, having failed to invade its island, did the next best thing: he sealed the Continent's sea coasts, including Prussia's, against the importation of British goods. Prussian industry, whatever there was of it, was thereby given a lift. The Berliners became suppliers to the Parisians, and Prussia became Napoleon's ally in spite of itself; it had to do business with the dictator. While doing so its ministers sent secret messages to Moscow and London, preparing for Bonaparte's downfall, just in case it should ever come to pass.

Prussia's double-dealing ended not by a cleansing of its political morality but by its stupidity. The decision-makers in Sans Souci were as myopic as those in the Hofburg or the Kremlin. Having first betrayed the European coalition against Napoleon, Prussia joined it at a moment which could not have been worse chosen: in the autumn of 1806. Napoleon, who had treated Prussia with the arrogance which a rich uncle displays toward a poor relative, now moved against Prussia's war machine, built up by Frederick the Great, and with a tiger's pounce tore it apart in the Battle of Jena (October 14, 1806). Frederick William III (reigned 1797–1840) was king by then; his queen, the vivacious, pretty, and intelligent Louise, said, "We have slept too long on the laurels of Frederick the Great." Napoleon occupied Berlin and from there issued his orders. He was ready for the move against Russia. He was near the zenith of his power, a self-annointed godhead.

After Napoleon's defeat—that great defeat which had begun in the

Russian snowdrifts—Frederick William III faced the task of rebuilding Prussia. Its army, its industry, and its reputation were decrepit. The government's coffers were bare, the thalers had been shoveled into Napoleon's war chest and had vanished from there. The land itself was wounded: 150,000 soldiers had trampled over its fields and meadows.

Fortunately there arose in Berlin a group of able men who began, at first haltingly and later with ever increasing assurance, to design a rebuilding plan. In the vanguard of these statesmen were Karl vom Stein, impetuous and impatient, and his antithesis, Prince Karl August von Hardenberg, calm and cautious. (It was Hardenberg who convinced Frederick William III to join with Russia in the final campaign against Napoleon, despite Napoleon's attempts to drive a wedge between the two countries.)

The task before these men was enormous. Could the wheat once more be made to flourish? Yes, if the peasant were freed of serfdom and allowed to till a piece of land he himself owned. Could silk and porcelain and shoes once more become freely available in the stores? Yes, if the merchant were allowed to buy and sell without ridiculous tax chicanery. Could the roads, many of them built by Napoleon to move armies, now be used to transport goods over the far-flung Prussian territory? Yes, if horses were bred and inns were available along the roads. How could export and import be favored? By opening the toll gates at the frontiers of the German states. In 1790 no fewer than eighteen hundred customs frontiers interrupted the flow of merchandise from one German-speaking principality to the next and proved nuisances to the traveler as well, as he had to alight from his carriage, salute the customs officer, and declare what he was about and why. It took more than forty years before an effective customs-union (*Zollverein*) could be agreed to, under Prussia's leadership. What about navigation, the use of the vital rivers, the Rhine, the Elbe, the Spree, and the others? Hardenberg negotiated new shipping agreements at the Congress of Vienna. Finally, how could Prussia build a better defense machine against future disasters? The new army was to get rid of the indifferent mercenaries and be headed by strong leaders, such as Blücher, Scharnhorst, and Gneisenau. The spirit of Frederick the Great—or "a piece of him"—stalked the Berlin Royal Palace.

None of the Prussian reforms was wholly successful; the Junkers clung to the land they owned and the privilege of doing what they liked with it. Bureaucracy grew on the body politic like a dropsical man's belly. For a reasonable bribe you could buy your way out of army service. The King disliked Stein and was not overly fond of Hardenberg. Still, imperfect though they were, there *were* reforms, and within a few years Prussia could once more hold its head up among the European nations.

This capsulated summary of Prussia's fortunes, which covers the span of Abraham Mendelssohn's life from his early twenties until he was nearly forty years old, is meant to make one point: that Abraham was lucky to have been born in Berlin. If he had to experience war—and who in Europe did not?—he was better off as a Berliner than he would have been in Cologne or Vienna or in burning Moscow. Geography came to Abraham's aid.

Yet his success was built on a broader base than the accident of location.

2

Not only the tricolor but another, imaginary, flag waved through Abraham's life. That flag, too, was tricolored: white for steam, black for coal, and gold for gold.

Moses lived in a period where thinking was directed toward incorporeal verities. God, his existence or nonexistence, the loom of language, the inquiry into the springs of human behavior, the relearning of ancient lessons taught by the Greeks, the definition of beauty—such were the questions to which the philosophers of the Enlightenment addressed themselves. Within one generation, the philosopher more or less abdicated and the engineer took over. Emphasis was placed on the corporeal life, on being better housed and better fed. From metaphysics, thought swung to physics.

Representative of this new thinking was Karl Freiherr vom und zum Stein, who admired the "practical sense" of British institutions, said that he had no use for the "useless cobwebs of metaphysics," and worked toward the ideal of a sane existence within a sane state—free of ambitions of conquest and victory—in which men would help one another to solve the problems of the community. To him these problems were largely economic.

The change was not, of course, immediate or total. Philosophers continued to ponder problems, artists continued to seek and find fresh interpretations of emotions. Still, with some oversimplification, it can be said that the hero of Abraham's era, from having been previously the inventor of abstract ideas, now became the inventor of practical machines.

Machines were required to feed, clothe, and house an expanding population. It was no longer possible to rely on the small farmer, who swung a homemade sickle with his tired arms. The carpenter, who threw together a hovel which the next rainstorm would wash away, no longer sufficed. The mason and the architect who built the castle were too slow and proved too costly. Hand-operated looms could no longer weave enough winter coats.

As the machine took over, people wanted more of the products it could produce. They could afford the cheaper things made by the machines. The eighteenth-century Limoges porcelain was replaced by the less expensive Staffordshire pottery of the nineteenth. There were more teacups in middle-class homes and more homes had tea to serve. If necessity is the mother of invention, invention stimulates the consciousness of necessity. If supply grew with demand, demand grew with supply.

The early industrial expansion has been characterized by W. O. Henderson (in *The Industrialization of Europe 1780–1914*):

> It is something of a paradox therefore that twenty-three years of Revolutionary and Napoleonic Wars should subsequently have marked the beginning of industrial expansion on the European mainland. Naturally Europe suffered. The movement of great armies living off the land, heavy casualties and the massive diversion of manpower from more peaceful pursuits had their inescapable consequences, while Napoleon's "Continental System" and the British blockade ruined one great port after another. Certain industries, however, expanded enormously under wartime pressures. The need to clothe, provision and arm many thousands of soldiers created an insatiable demand for certain commodities—a demand greatly accentuated by the exclusion of British competition. Striking growth was evident in the cotton industries of Ghent, Paris, Mulhouse and Saxony, and in the metal and armament industries of Belgium, Germany and Switzerland.

"Invent and produce" was the theme song of the early nineteenth century, a tune played by an orchestra of a hundred scientists and entrepreneurs and conducted by a man with a slide rule as baton. In 1790 the first rolling mill, powered by steam to flatten iron, was opened in England. Three years later Eli Whitney came forth with the cotton gin. Two years after that Joseph Bramah invented a hydraulic press; in 1798 Philippe Lebon patented a system for using coal gas for heating and lighting; at the turn of the century Alessandro Volta produced electricity from a cell; the Earl of Stanhope perfected an iron printing press; and French engineers began to hew out a carriage road over the Simplon Pass which, because of new road-building equipment at their disposal, they were able to complete within six years. One of the pioneers of "mass production" was the formidable Josiah Wedgwood, Staffordshire potter, who was one of the first to develop an entire industrial community, one of the first to take advantage of the opportunity of a cheap local labor market, and one of the first to treat labor with that mixture of paternalism and ruthlessness—depending on whether things were going his way or not—that eventually led to labor's revolt. In 1803 Robert Fulton propelled a boat by steam. It was the beginning of the end of the poetic sailing vessel. Five years later the *Clermont* began its regular run from New York to Albany. And fifteen years later a monstrous-looking conveyance made of iron, long as a brontosaurus, with a smokestack as tall as a factory chimney, sailed from a dock in London and puffed its way across the English Channel and up the Seine to Paris.

It took longer for railways to transport passengers. Locomotives were built as early as 1804. But they were used mostly for the transporting of goods and particularly of coal. Abraham never rode on a German train; they started operating only in the year of his death. Even to the young Felix, a train ride was something of a frightening experience.

Everywhere inventions sprang from the drawing boards, and factories proliferated. In Berlin, the "Association for the Promotion of Technical Knowledge" received royal patronage. In 1802 Philippe Girard invented a machine for spinning flax. In 1804 a Frenchman, François Appert, opened a canning factory. In 1810 the Krupp works began operating at Essen. In 1819 the *Savannah* became the first steamship to cross the Atlantic; the trip took twenty-nine days and eleven hours. In 1823, Charles Macintosh invented a new kind of fabric which he claimed was waterproof. In 1832 Samuel F. B. Morse introduced the telegraph, and two years later Cyrus McCormick perfected his threshing machine. In this new iron age, wood no longer served as fuel; coke smelting was perfected. Soon the ovens in Upper Silesia belched clouds of smoke and turned the grass brown.

The old Goethe, writing to Zelter in 1825, saw it all clearly: "Wealth and speed are now the gods for which all men strive. Railways, express mails, steamboats, and all conceivable means of communication are what the educated world seeks. . . . This is the century of smart minds, of practical men who possess a quick grasp, who are endowed with facility, but who lack talent for the most exalted tasks." Goethe added wistfully: "We and possibly a few others are the last representatives of an era which will not soon return."

The essential ingredient of industrialization was money. Capital stoked the ovens which furnished the steam which turned the wheels. As soon as the inventor had drawn his latest design, he submitted the sketch to the man who had the money or knew how to raise it. The private banker became the general of the industrial army. The King needed him as well, because in spite of all the taxes and all the monopolies, not enough money could be pressed out of the people to pay the army or officials' fees. The Finance Minister went around hat in hand, though the hat was an elegant one, and the banker still bowed to the minister, not the minister to the banker.

Christian von Rother, who had been for some years the head of the Overseas Trading Corporation (*Seehandlung*), an enterprise founded by Frederick the Great, now negotiated a five-million-pound loan with Nathan Rothschild in London; and later, in 1822, he managed a second loan of three million pounds from the same source. The Pereire Brothers, Emile and Isaac, Jews born in Bordeaux, furnished much of the financing for the first French railroad built solely for passenger travel, the Paris–Saint Germaine line. They were as well co-founders of the Crédit Mobilier, the bank through which they "mobilized" the use of private capital for the development of the French economy. Finance was supported by philosophy: the French philosopher, Claude Henri Saint-Simon, wrote that secular life should be managed, not by the government, but by industrialists and bankers. He recommended a huge supranational program of public works; he even put forward (in 1814) a plan for a United States of Europe. His followers, among whom he counted many young Jewish intellectuals, including Abraham Mendelssohn, became advocates of free trade and world peace.

Still another French banking house of Jewish origin was Fould and Company. A grandson of the original Foulds, Achille, was to become French Finance Minister under Louis Napoleon.

The gold in the flag of industrialization glittered.

3

Abraham was Moses' second son. He was but ten years old when Moses died; yet even at so early an age he had thoroughly accepted Moses' belief in the emancipation of the Jews. When he was sixteen, he joined a "Society of Friends," along with his brother Joseph. The purpose of this society was to combat orthodoxy; in the first year of its existence it attracted more than a hundred members in Berlin. Many of the Berlin Jews had themselves baptized. Daniel Itzig, "Court-Jew," banker, adviser to the King and friend of Moses Mendelssohn, was the president of the society.

Like his father, Abraham was a student. His mother no doubt saw to that, but he himself early developed that appetite for learning which was characteristic of the Mendelssohns. He learned French, Latin, Greek, and Hebrew. (He never learned English.) However, unlike his father, he had no wish to lock himself in a study. Reacting appropriately to the changing world, he wanted to plunge into commercial life and become a banker. His best chance lay in France, the country which had accorded full rights to the Jews and where the young Napoleon was developing his progressive programs. When he was twenty-one (1797) he left Berlin and emigrated to Paris, no doubt accompanied by Fromet's tears. He had obtained a post with the banking house of Fould and Company.

In Paris he developed his admiration for French culture and French manners. He loved breathing its soft air, so different from that of the city on the Spree; he felt the insouciance and the sense of importance which filled the city.

He quickly understood the chance offered to the banker and the rewards which would await him if he guessed right. Fould and Company were lending money to the French Directory with which to purchase armaments. Abraham saw to it that they were not only to obtain a high rate of interest, but were to be granted first options on real estate and investments in mines and factories and shipping. His abilities were soon recognized. He never wanted to return to boring Berlin.

Then he met Lea Salomon. She was the granddaughter of Daniel Itzig, one of his sixteen grandchildren. She was not precisely a beauty, though as a girl she was pleasant and sweet-looking. She was inclined to plumpness which in later life became shapelessness. Her eyes were her best feature, as dark and large as the eyes of Persian women, ringed above by eyebrows as definite as parentheses and below by a soft shadow which gave her a more mysterious expression than her nature warranted. She was an educated woman—she spoke French fluently, English well enough, and she could read Homer in the original—and she was equipped for the task which was eventually to be hers, hostess of an important house and representative of an important family. There were no great depths in her; she could become as enthusiastic over a new ostrich-feather hat as over a new composition by her son. She was a bit of a snob and stood in awe of Baron So-and-So and the Marquis de Something. She loved to dance, she loved to entertain. She didn't give two straws about politics.

Was it really a love match? Yes and no. Abraham no doubt was attracted to her. Yet he had to be gently pushed into the marriage; he hesitated because Lea insisted that she would not live in Paris. She was born a German and she was going to remain a German. Not for her the role of an expatriate, speaking French with a German accent. "I would much prefer," the young girl wrote to a friend, "to receive from you straightforward German information about the book you intend to write rather than those gallant remarks so typically French."

Abraham's sister Henriette was an intimate friend of Lea's. She decided to play the role of matchmaker. She wrote to Abraham:

> My dearest! This marriage would be in every respect so rare and excellent a stroke of fortune for you that I cannot beg you enough not to decide too rashly and not to sacrifice everything to your present situation, which admittedly is a pleasant one but which is subject to change.
> I feel as if I were twenty years older than you [she was eight years older than Abraham] and that I can tell you from experience that at your

Lea Mendelssohn. Drawing by Wilhelm Hensel. (Mendelssohn Archive, Berlin)

age one usually fails to recognize luck, even if one finds it lying loose on one's path. . . .

I hope to read in your next letter that you have spoken to Lilla [Lea]. The oftener you approach her the more will you understand that you will seldom, if ever, find a wife like her. I disapprove of the fact that your dislike of an existence in Berlin should exercise so great an influence on your most important decision. I cannot avoid accusing you of youthful rashness when I read that passage in your letter which says, *"Je préférerais manger du pain sec à Paris* [I would prefer to eat dry bread in Paris]." *Du pain sec* is not to be despised . . . but I fear . . . it could become *pain amer* [bitter bread].

He was soon to eat bread thickly spread with honey. He did approach Lea and he did consent to return to Germany, though a compromise was reached: they were to live not in Berlin but in Hamburg. They were married in 1804. He was twenty-eight, she was twenty-seven.

In the first weeks of her marriage Lea wrote to her sister:

You want to know, dear sister, how things stand at my house and with my domestic arrangements? Indescribably sloppy *à dire le vrai*, just like a looney student's. There is no question of a private room or of an orderly household or of Berlin comfort. When I look at my *remue ménage* I find difficulty in believing that I am really married. Such a change in life is usually accompanied with the possession of pots and pans, candelabras, mirrors and mahogany furniture. For the moment I must forgo the contemplation of such pleasant sights *chez moi*. However, provided Mama's and your own sense of neatness can forgive me, I am not letting myself get grey hairs over the situation; I comfort myself with the prospect that the efficient Martha [the maid] will presently let us hear the melodious rattle of her keys. Tomorrow we are going to try to give the first dinner within our four little walls; it will be sent in from a French restaurant. For the moment I cannot order either furniture or household goods because we haven't got a speck of room here. The chaos will be put in order when we move to the country. We have the prospect of getting a country house, supposedly very pretty, quite near the Elbe and near Neumühlen, and it has a balcony!!! We are going to inspect it soon.

The evening of my arrival I indulged myself and opened my Paris trunk, not only opened it but put on both of the sumptuous gowns. Heavenly! But only suitable for a reception at Emperor Napoleon's. The most wonderful, the richest, the shiniest silken-soft robe of artfully-worked Peking velvet and one in *façonne* pink interlaced with delicate white, trimmed divinely and beautifully tailored! Mendelssohn was all enthusiasm, but I said that such subtle and magic colors were only suitable for Fräulein Hebe.

They did get the house they wanted; it was an old mill (Marten's Mill) and they lived there for six years. Three of their four children were born there: Fanny in 1805, Felix in 1809 (February 3), and Rebecka in 1811.

4

Why did they choose Hamburg in preference to Berlin? First because it was one of the German "Free Cities," a city-state not unlike ancient Athens, with its own government and set of laws. As such its official attitude toward the Jews was a more tolerant one than that of the Prussian capital.[1] Perhaps it wasn't altogether a question of being tolerant: the mercantile city needed the financial skill the Jews could provide. There was the second reason: Hamburg was Germany's most important port, and one of the two largest ports of Europe. Through its vast harbor flowed the goods and raw material which came from England and its colonies and the Orient. The Hamburg Exchange—almost as old as those of Lyon and Toulouse— acted as a hub from which money streamed forth for industrial employment.

The ancient city was beautiful and always in movement, with the polyglot sailors strolling about and the sea gulls crying in the moist air. The frequent fogs held fast the town's odors, compounded of brackish water, raw rope, smoked herring, tea, tar, fishmeal, sandalwood oil, and the cheap perfume of the prostitutes. One could escape the smell by moving to the country: Abraham and Lea breathed happily at the Mill on the bank of the river.

In this city Abraham founded the banking house of "Mendelssohn

---

[1] Unlike the Berliners, the Hamburgers always disliked the "authorities." They called the policemen, who were dressed in red coats, "Lobsters" (*"Hummer,"* pronounced *"Hummel"* in the Hamburg dialect). The street urchins derided the *Hummels;* the grownups did not disapprove.

Brothers and Company" (established January 1, 1805). The Berlin bank had been established ten years previously by Abraham's elder brother, Joseph. It began as "a small and insignificant discounting office." [2] But soon Abraham set out to construct a network of banking associates, one of the first being Fould and Company in Paris. Danzig, Vienna, Amsterdam, Aachen, Coblenz, Trier followed; eventually a Mendelssohn affiliate was to be found in every major city of Europe and in New York.

Two years after Abraham and Lea married, Napoleon decreed his "Continental System." Since England could not be starved to death, its business life was to be choked to death by preventing the shipments of its coal, iron, precious metals, and manufactured goods to the Continent. What England produced was to lie useless within its boundaries, to moulder and rot into a gigantic heap. All harbors were to be closed to British ships. The Continental System was formalized by Napoleon's "Berlin Decree" of 1806, issued after his victory over Prussia. But the measure did not work, the blockade did not block, the Bank of England did not topple. The Continental System was answered by a smuggling system on so vast a scale as to make previous smuggling expeditions appear amateurish. The new United States, for example, took a joyous and profitable delight in shipping wares to the Continent. Nor could the British fleet be stopped. One could not dispense with British merchandise, which kept coming in at night under false flags, false bills of lading, and covered by false wrappings. It is one of the ironies of history that Napoleon's soldiers marched to their death in Russia in shoes "Made in Great Britain."

Hamburg became a center of the smuggling operations. Big ships and little barks, crates and rucksacks, small money and big money, experts and adventurers, honest men and thieves, all served the cause. Across the Elbe lay the city of Altona, then a Danish possession. From time immemorial the Hamburgers had disliked Altona and mocked its provincialism. Hamburg folklore contains the story of God visiting the earth one day and noticing an old man sitting on the side of the road and weeping bitterly. "Why do you weep, old man? Tell me and I am certain I can help you." "I weep," said the old man, "because all my life I have lived in Altona."

<hr />

[2] Paul Emden: *Money Powers of Europe in the Nineteenth and Twentieth Centuries* (New York, 1938).

So God sat down beside him and wept with him. . . . Now Altona became a favorite goal for excursions. The French customs officers were puzzled because so many skinny citizens left for Altona in the morning and returned at night considerably fatter. Yards of British cloth were tightly wound around their bodies. Nor could the customs officials explain why so many natives were dying in Altona and had to be buried in Hamburg, until they opened a coffin and found it filled with coffee beans.[3]

The big smuggling transactions needed capital and the banks were there to furnish it. They bought ships, manned them, and registered them under neutral flags. None of this could have been accomplished had the French officials been incorruptible. They were far from that.

Napoleon bottled up one harbor after another. No sooner did he do so than the British uncorked other ports, using two weapons, bribery of French customs officials and the threat that all ships, of whatever nationality, trading in ports where Britain was excluded were liable to capture. That policy nearly led to another war with the United States in 1807 when the U.S. frigate *Chesapeake* was stopped by the British vessel *Leopard*, ostensibly to demand the surrender of "British deserters."

"Far from being a mere risky adventure, this smuggling became a highly articulated system—a different organization from the usual one, but still a regular organization for a regular trade." (H. Butterfield: *Napoleon*) There is little doubt that Abraham Mendelssohn was a leader of this articulated system. Working with his brother in Berlin, he helped supply Prussia with the necessities of life, ranging from raw iron to coffee beans.

Lea's dowry—a considerable one—gave Abraham the capital with which to operate and which, in four years, he multiplied. But it was Napoleon who helped to make him wealthy. The foundation of the Mendelssohn fortune rested on the trickery of smuggling. The Continental System gave him the cue. Though, as he himself said, even a Napoleon could not be present everywhere at all times, he could command a further tightening of the net. On October 18 and 25, 1810, he issued the Decrees of Fontainebleu which ordered the confiscation and burning of any and all British goods found within Napoleonic states. Further, in December of that year he

---

[3] W. Vogel: *Die Hansestädte und die Kontinentalsperre* (Munich, 1913).

simply annexed Hamburg along with other North German cities such as Bremen and Lübeck, again to strengthen the blockade. He appointed Marshall Louis Nicholas Davout as Governor of Hamburg. Davout was a man of such "firmness of character" (Napoleon's words) as to be beyond the possibility of bribery.[4] His soldiers scanned the sea and peered under the tarpaulins of ships. He became known as "The Terror of the North," his occupation being conducted with dictatorial severity. Homes were searched, men were arrested. Finally, Abraham was suspect, and he knew it.

Lea was pregnant. Soon after Rebecka was born on April 11, 1811, the Mendelssohns decided that Marten's Mill could no longer be regarded as a safe refuge. Abraham had previously transferred most of his money to Berlin. On a spring night Abraham, Lea, and their three children fled from Hamburg. Fanny was six years old, Felix two; the baby was carried in her mother's arms. No servants accompanied them; they were disguised as poor refugees, wearing tattered clothes. They carried false passports. At Hamburg's frontier a carriage was waiting for them. All went well: after a journey of a few days, during which Lea must often have mistaken a tree for a French sentinel, while the fog on the road may have assumed the shape of a Napoleonic cannon, they got to Berlin unharmed.

Berlin, too, was ruled by Napoleon. However, the French ambassador to Prussia happened to be a friend of Lea's aunt, and Abraham seems to have been allowed to pursue his banking activities unmolested. Abraham considered himself now a German through and through: no doubt what he had witnessed of Napoleon's methods had influenced his point of view. Now he was even reconciled to living in Berlin. When, after the retreat from Moscow, the Allies began to close in on Napoleon, Frederick William grandiloquently proclaimed a "War of Liberation" and appealed to his people for support. When the King undertook the formation of a new army, the *Landwehr* and the *Landsturm*, it was the banking houses like the Rothschilds and the Mendelssohns (and British bankers as well) who furnished the wherewithal with which to buy ammunition and feed the troops. Abraham gambled on a Prussia which he did not like much and

---

[4] Or was he? One historian, De Bloqueville, in *Le Maréchal Davout, Prince d'Eckmühl* (Paris, 1883), believed that Davout simply wanted to arrogate all the business of smuggling to himself.

against a France in which he had once been happy. The turn of the political wheel proved right for him: his stake came back with rich interest.

After the Allies' victory over Napoleon at Leipzig in 1813 Abraham was honored as a public benefactor. He was appointed to the Municipal Council of Berlin. "Councillor Mendelssohn"—it was rare indeed for a Jew to be chosen for public office.

5

What sort of man was Abraham? From his looks one could never have told that he was a son of Moses. He inherited none of the gnarled features, the bent back, the Jewish nose, the obstreperous hair of his father. Abraham was straight and angular, clear-eyed and clear-skinned, nose, mouth, lips, and chin drawn in pure Nordic lines. Yet he was not quite that, not quite Nordic: his hands were French, so to speak, gesticulating vividly and animatedly, while his legs were German, walking a pompous gait. In his youth he had been slim as a poet; in his middle age he acquired a rich man's paunch. His belief in himself enabled him to deal as confidently with his business associates as with the statesmen, artists, poets, and writers who by and by began to frequent his home. He could be a chairman of the board at one moment and a respectful disciple the next. His posture changed depending on whether one was discussing steel or sonnets. He made sense in either discussion, for he was not pretending. He was, fundamentally, an honest man. Zelter described him to Goethe as one who "in troubled times was able to become wealthy without suffering damage to his soul."

The diversity of physical characteristics was paralleled by the diversity of his mental characteristics. He admired French wit, the *bon mot* which rounded a heavy topic lightly; but his own style, as we read it in his letters, was German, handling light topics as if they were potato dumplings. His humor was primitive. He was full of wise saws and modern instances, moralizing in his role of father, the words "duty" and "obedience" on his lips. He preached at his children and they must often have been as bored with his Polonian instructions as Laertes and Ophelia seem to have been. Yet, like Polonius' children, his children loved him: they knew that underneath the platitudes lay the affection and concern and pride in and for the family. That was Abraham's chief characteristic: absorption in the family. His was a clannishness which he pronounced in plangent tones: nobody, but nobody, was as important as a Mendelssohn. He would certainly have disagreed with Thomas Fuller's famous epigram: "He that has no fools, knaves, nor beggars in his family was begot by a flash of lightning." According to Abraham, there were no fools, knaves, nor beggars among the Mendelssohns.

A few passages from the letters to his children will serve to illustrate Abraham's family feeling:

Hamburg, October 20, 1817

Your letters, my dear children, gave me much pleasure. I would write each of you an individual letter were it not for the fact that I hope soon to be back with you. That's better than writing a letter.

You, my dear Beckchen, wrote to me very nicely. I praise you because you took pity on the little squirrel and took it into your room. If the weather is as horrible there as it is here, even a squirrelephant couldn't stand living out in the open. But what did Mother say? Work hard and be obedient. I'll bring you a beautiful present, but you will have to earn it.

You, dear Fanny, wrote the first letter in excellent script. The second one seemed to be written more hastily. It does you honor that you didn't find B's bad jokes funny. I too have no particular taste for this kind of thing and consider it a blameworthy ambition to make fun of things which are good and beautiful. Unfortunately, general conversation and social intercourse is limited to such a practice. . . . It's a golden rule that it is better to keep silent than to say something inappropriate.

Mother has written me that she is very satisfied with you, my dear Felix, at least up to now. I am very glad to hear it and I hope that I will find a truthful and pleasant diary [when I return]. Follow my admonition: "Be truthful and obedient." You can't do better than that, and if you are not that you couldn't do worse. Your letters gave me much pleasure but in the second there were a few slips which I will point out to you on my return. You have to make an effort to speak better, then you'll write better.

To six-year-old Paul, the youngest Mendelssohn:

Paris, July 2, 1819

To your question about marrying Mieke [she was the four-year-old daughter of the gardener] I did not respond at once because I wished to ponder the question. I now believe that we let it go until I return home so that I can get a glimpse of this Mieke. If I find that she is neat and clean, and if you manage to behave yourself for all of fourteen days, we'll discuss the subject some more.

6

The symbol of the banking house—presumably designed by Abraham —was a crane standing on a globe with the motto, "I watch." (The crane, according to German lore, spread good luck.) The brothers watched while the safe filled and the securities were heaped up. In 1812 Mendelssohn and Company was among the first twenty banks of Berlin; eleven years later it was among the first three. In 1816 Abraham went once again to Paris to negotiate the war reparations which Prussia was exacting from France. This time he was no longer the carefree bachelor: he took his family along. It was on that occasion that Felix and Fanny took a few piano lessons from a lady who had been one of Beethoven's good friends, Marie Bigot. It was she who had played the rain-soaked manuscript of the *"Appassionata"* at sight and played it perfectly. She was still young, pretty, charming, and gay, though she was to die only four years later. Abraham had little enough free time for music or gaiety; he spent most of his days on the complicated negotiations which he brought to a conclusion favorable to Prussia. His return to Berlin, the contract in his pouch, proved nothing short of triumphant.

Other governments heard of the Mendelssohn skill, and eventually, though after Abraham's retirement, the house became the official bankers to the Czar.[5]

Abraham bought a mansion in 1825 in a section of Berlin far enough removed from the center to assure peace and quiet. The house was located at Leipziger Strasse 3 but nothing is left of it today. The property included

---

[5] Paul Emden, in his *Money Powers of Europe in the Nineteenth and Twentieth Centuries,* notes that in the career of Joseph and Abraham "it was their unique position as bankers for Russia that made their phenomenal rise possible."

not only the main house of many rooms, but several guest houses and a commodious park complete with the features desirable in a retreat for that nature-loving age: the yew alley, the lime trees, the rose bushes, the over-grown gazebo, and the fountain falling into careful ruins. The main house contained large salons in which Sunday musicales were given to invited audiences, as well as amateur theatricals. There was no end of amateur theatricals, all very decorous, the poetry highflown. Felix, the prodigy, was first exposed to admiration at the Sunday musicales, and one can imagine how extravagant was the astonishment tendered by an audience of friends.

Here then was Felix's childhood castle, a fortress filled with love, a stronghold of affection. He loved the park particularly, for there he could ride his horse; there in good weather dances were given for which the trees were festooned with paper lanterns made by the children; and there too he could sneak off and hide and daydream. It was a self-contained community, the children even publishing their own newspaper. They called the little homemade sheet first *The Garden Paper,* then *The Tea and Snow Times (Thee und Schnee Zeitung.)*

Abraham set out to make Leipziger Strasse 3 the intellectual center of Berlin, to form it into a private Circle of Wits. Because his was a strong personality, because Lea was a good hostess, because the food was first-class and the conversation spicy, he succeeded. There was hardly a famous name of the early nineteenth century which was not inscribed in the Visitors' Book: Leopold Ranke, the historian; Jacob Grimm, collector of the fairy tales; Bettina Brentano; E. T. A. Hoffmann; the poets Tieck, Heine,[6] Varnhagen; the philosopher Hegel; the brothers Humboldt—the list is a Who's Who of German talent. But it was the musical talents which Abraham sought and welcomed most eagerly, not only for the sake of Felix and Fanny, but for his own delectation. Friends of the house were Eduard Rietz, the violinist, and his brother Julius, later a good conductor;

---

[6] Heine, who was forever fleeing from Berlin and its "thick sands and thin teas," was a puckish spirit in the Mendelssohn circle. The girls were afraid of this handsome poet who laced his conversation with mockery. Yet he fondly remembered his visits there and wrote to Droysen (Sept., 1829) from the isle of Helgoland: "Greetings . . . to the Palazzo Bartholdy. A respect-ful salute to Madame Municipal Councillor; a less respectful salute to Fanny's beautiful eyes, among the most beautiful I have ever seen. As to fat Rebecka, yes, greet as well that plump little person, the dear child, so pretty, so good, every pound of her an angel."

Adolph Marx, the musical scholar, one of the early biographers of Beethoven and editor of the *Berliner Allgemeine Musikalische Zeitung,* whom, however, Abraham secretly disliked; the composer Ferdinand Hiller; Carl Maria von Weber, Ludwig Spohr, and the mogul of Berlin's musical activity, director of the Royal Opera, Gasparo Spontini. Of Carl Friedrich Zelter, the friend of Goethe, who was later to become Felix's teacher, I will have more details to give. He was the head of the Berlin Singing Academy, an institution to which Abraham contributed financial support. Zelter told Goethe that the Mendelssohn house was always open to him. It was indeed, though he was considered a bit of a rough customer.

Abraham did know a remarkable lot about music. His tastes were turned toward the old, his favorite composer being Johann Sebastian Bach. He wrote to Fanny, who had played one of Bach's cantatas at one of the Sunday musicales: "Once again I am reminded of Bach's loneliness; he stood quite isolated from his world and his surroundings, developing his own pure, mild, but enormous force and his own clear profundity." (March 3, 1835) In early youth, Felix was influenced by his father's predilection.

On the other hand, Abraham did not understand the later Beethoven at all, and this was to become one of the several causes of disagreement between him and Felix. From Rome Felix wrote to his sisters (November 22, 1830):

> Though the terrible world events [the 1830 French Revolution] may have contributed to it, the depression of our father seems to spring from the same cause as it did at the time I determined to take up my "immoral" profession and go my own way. At that time, Father was continuously in the worst mood and scolded Beethoven and all the romanticists. Often he saddened me and made me impatient. Something new had come into the world and my father could not quite stomach that. It frightened him a little. As long as I insisted on talking about Beethoven and praising him, his temper grew worse and worse, and if I remember rightly, he once ordered me to leave the table.
>
> Then I took stock. I thought I could still be speaking the truth without having to speak precisely of the very matters which my father could not abide. After that everything went better and better and finally it came out all right. Perhaps you too have forgotten that you ought once in a while to humour him and not to provoke him. . . . Try to praise a little what

he admires and do not condemn the things he loves, at least not everything that is traditional. And above all, praise the house frequently.

Yes, he loved music and he loved the house and he loved his children. Yet as Abraham grew older and wealthier he could not accept wealth calmly. He could not know ease. It was now useless for him to work hard. But, as if he believed that there was ethical value in work for the sake of work, or almost as if he felt the need of doing penance, he exacted hard work from his children. While placing them in the midst of a luxurious park, he drove them to so demanding a schedule of study that children of less robust constitution would have broken down under it. An insistent fear of idleness haunted the elegant rooms. Self-possessed though he outwardly appeared, and secure in most facets of his personality, there remained in Abraham's mind a Jewish uncertainty, a sense of guilt for having money, a self-lacerating instinct, for which he compensated by demanding excessive effort from his family and often by being more frugal than there was any necessity to be. Abraham's children were *not* to become rich man's sons or daughters. The children were awakened at five o'clock in the morning and set to work. The day was as precisely apportioned as a soldier's food. Most of the education took place at home, partly because in that way more stuff could be crammed into their heads, and partly because Abraham wanted to offer them the better instruction available from private teachers. A succession of such teachers appear in Felix's early years, men who were eminent in their fields. Music was but a fraction of a curriculum which included Latin, Greek, mathematics, an enormous amount of European history, geography, esthetics (which Felix studied with Hegel), political philosophy (with Eduard Gans the historian), German and foreign litera-ture, and drawing and water coloring. Quite early Felix perfected his French and his English; later he learned a serviceable Italian. Only on Sundays could the children sleep late, that is, until six A.M.

From the first it was drummed into each of them that he and she were representatives of a leading German family. Each of them represented the nation. A polished, polite bearing was indispensable. So were the social graces. They had to know how to converse well and listen well. The women of the house were to learn to combine charm with knowledge; there was no need to hide their education, so long as they did not become blue-stockings. Abraham believed that woman's place was in the home. So did most of the fathers and husbands of his time. Like Felix, Fanny early showed extraordinary musical talent, both as a pianist and as a composer. She was good enough for Felix to publish some of her little compositions as works of his own. Yet Abraham would not hear of Fanny's pursuing a professional career. That might be good enough for a Marie Bigot, but not possible for a daughter of a patrician house. He wrote to Fanny: "For him [Felix] music may become a profession. For you it has to remain a decoration. It can and should never be the be-all and end-all of your life." She must be content to rejoice in the applause which Felix would earn for himself. Such contentment was "feminine and only what is feminine is proper for women."

Perhaps Abraham's discontent and lack of ease in these years lay in the contradiction stuck in his soul between artistic instincts and bourgeois leanings. A letter by Lea to Felix gives the clue; it is written at a time when Felix's fame was burgeoning and Abraham's business was prospering:

October 1830

Your father ruins, for him and for us, our good and pleasant life . . . he goes about like a man depressed by grief, gloomy and despondent. Oh God, how happy this man could be and how much happiness he could radiate! Yet he, the soul of a husband and father, is eternally in doubt about something, deep down in his heart. Nor do I know what it is that causes his constant doubts. . . .

Eric Werner (in *Mendelssohn*) ascribes this unhappiness to Abraham's regret at having renounced Judaism. Placing the letter in context with other expressions of his, one arrives at a different conclusion. The cause of his doubt about something deep down in his heart was not religious scruple but the struggle of the banker versus the artist.[7]

The philosophic and artistic bent he had inherited became warped into frustration; he wished he could be more than a man of money; he longed to be a creative artist. Yet he could not create.

When Felix was but six or seven years old it became obvious that

[7] I owe this point to Rudolf Elvers.

there was the artist Abraham wanted to be. The father set out to give him, as well as his brother and his two sisters, for he could not very well make any sharp distinctions, the opportunity along with the severest sort of challenge. His son was to be a great musician while being as completely educated as a Renaissance prince. He was to be a Medici and a Mozart, rolled into one slight body. That is why Felix was made to study with Hegel and Gans, and why the other three were subjected to a like scholastic inclusiveness.

Although the intellectual demands which Abraham laid on his off-spring were taxing, the physical side of their education was not neglected. After all, that side belonged to being a lady or a gentleman, particularly a gentleman. The counterbalance saved them from becoming intellectual freaks. The children skated and rowed on the Spree, went for long hikes, and all of them became expert swimmers; being young Germans, they of course formed a *Verein*; it was a Swimming Club. Klingemann, who was one of Felix's earliest friends, wrote verses which Felix set to music and which were suitable, they claimed, for singing in the water. Riding was Felix's particular enthusiasm. When he was a grown man and had become the musical director of Düsseldorf, he asked his father for permission to buy a horse. Permission was granted.

7

Abraham's attitude toward religion was partly inherited from Moses and partly ran counter to his father's doctrine.

He went a big step further than Moses: he decided to bring the children up as Protestants. This decision fully met with the approval of Lea. Even before she had met Abraham, she declared herself in favor of conversion. She was buttressed in her thinking by her brother, who, originally named Jacob Lewin Salomon, had changed his name to Bartholdy and had embraced the Christian faith. The name Bartholdy had belonged to the owner of a large garden in Berlin, and Jacob assumed the name after having bought the garden, thus gaining, as W. S. Gilbert would have expressed it, an ancestry by purchase. Jacob was an interesting personality, an historian of Greek and Renaissance art who published a study on Mycenae which in its time was considered important. He became the Prussian Consul General in Rome, and there built a beautiful villa which Felix was to visit on his Italian journey. Bartholdy tried to persuade his brother-in-law to adopt the Bartholdy name. It was, he argued, all well and good to show loyalty to one's name and faith, but "loyalty" became an empty gesture if what you were loyal to had become meaningless. If he, Abraham, felt that the Protestant religion was the best, then not only should he assume it but strip the family of the Jewish-sounding name of Mendelssohn. If on the other hand he wished to remain faithful to an oppressed, persecuted religion, let him do so but realize clearly the prospect of leaving his children a heritage of martyrdom. Once one ceased to believe, the martyrdom became silly barbarism. The least he could do was to add the name Bartholdy to Mendelssohn to distinguish his branch of the family from other branches. There was nothing new in that: the custom of adding the name of a relative of one's wife to one's own name was widespread in France.

Abraham followed his advice. The children were baptized in 1816. Fanny was then eleven years old. When four years later she became confirmed, Abraham wrote a letter in which he stated his ethical beliefs:

> Is there a God? What is God? Is a part of ourselves immortal, will it live on after the other parts perish? If so, how and why? All that I do not know, and therefore I have never attempted to instruct you about these questions. I do know that there resides in me and in you and in all human beings an eternal desire toward the good, the true and the just. I do know that there is such a thing as conscience, which warns and guides us if we lose our way. I know this, I believe in it. I live in this belief, that is my religion. . . . That is all that I can tell you about religion because that is all I know. It will remain true as long as man exists, as it has been true since the first human being was created. The historic form of religion which your religion teacher speaks of as being the only true one is, like all human laws, mutable. A few thousand years ago the Jewish form was the dominant one. Then it was the heathen. Now it is the Christian. . . . We have educated all of you as Christians because that is the form of religion to which most of civilized human beings subscribe, a form which contains no precept which could lead you away from virtue. . . .

When Felix's career began to assume international proportions, Abraham felt that the time had come to suppress the name Mendelssohn altogether. Here he ran into serious conflict with his twenty-year-old son. Abraham wrote a long letter to Felix in London (July 8, 1829). Parts of his argument were:

> The suspicion has come to me that you have suppressed or neglected or allowed others to suppress or neglect the name which I have taken as the name of our family, the name Bartholdy. In the concert programs you have sent me, likewise in newspaper articles, your name is given as Mendelssohn. I can account for this only on the supposition that you have been the cause.
>
> Now, I am greatly dissatisfied about this. If you are to blame, you have committed a huge wrong. . . . it is your ineffaceable, as well as reasonable, duty to take for granted that, whatever your father does, he does on valid grounds and with due deliberation.

Now Felix was a Christian, and a Christian Mendelssohn was an impossibility. The name would always stand for Judaism "in transition."

> . . . in transition, when Judaism, just because it is seeking to transmute itself spiritually, clings to its ancient form all the more stubbornly and tenaciously, by way of protest against the novel form that so arrogantly and tyrannically declared itself to be the one and only path to the good.

Since his children showed no particular religious conviction, he, the father, was obligated to do the choosing.

> Naturally, when you consider what scant value I placed on any form in particular, I felt no urge to choose the form known as Judaism, that most antiquated, distorted, and self-defeating form of all. Therefore I reared you as Christians, Christianity being the more purified form and the one most accepted by the majority of civilized people. Eventually, I myself adopted Christianity, because I felt it my duty to do for myself that which I recognized as best for you. . . . Here I must reproach myself for a weakness, even if a pardonable one. I should have done decisively and thoroughly that which I deemed right. I should have discarded the name Mendelssohn completely.

He reminded Felix that he deliberately ordered his visiting cards engraved "Felix M. Bartholdy." In sum,

You can not, you must not carry the name Mendelssohn. Felix Mendelssohn Bartholdy is too long; it is unsuited for daily use. You must go by the name of Felix Bartholdy. A name is like a garment; it has to be appropriate for the time, the use, and the rank, if it is not to become a hindrance and a laughing-stock. Englishmen, otherwise a most formal lot, change their names frequently. Seldom is anyone renowned under the name conferred at baptism. And that is as it should be. I repeat: There can no more be a Christian Mendelssohn than there can be a Jewish Confucius. If Mendelssohn is your name, you are ipso facto a Jew. And this, if for no other reason than because it is contrary to fact, can be of no benefit to you.

Dear Felix, take this to heart and act accordingly.

Your Father and Friend.

For once, however, Felix would not obey his father's command. His answer, written almost immediately though he was as busy as possible with his first London engagement, is a dignified and manly rejoinder. Felix denies that he neglected or could ever possibly neglect his father's "commands and precepts." If that is the impression Abraham received, it could have arisen only through Felix's carelessness: he never realized that it was Abraham's intention to eliminate the name Mendelssohn altogether.

To support his position, Felix cited his recent experience in London. Approximately a week after his arrival, the magazine *Harmonicon* published an article—it went without saying that he was not the instigator of it nor did he know a syllable of it beforehand—and this article said, "Mr. Mendelssohn, the grandson of the famous philosopher of the same name, has arrived; he loves and makes music and is a professional musician." [8] From that moment on, all the musicians called him Mendelssohn, and people whose acquaintance he made wanted information about Moses and said flattering things about his grandfather's work. Then came his appearance with the Philharmonic Society. During the rehearsal somebody showed him the program. He was called Mendelssohn Esq. He said he wanted his whole name and never mind the Esquire. Dixi (?) asked what was the use of the Bartholdy and everybody said the name was too long

---

[8] Felix was telling the truth, as usual. The *Harmonicon* reported his arrival as "son of the rich banker of Berlin and, I believe, a grandson of the Jewish philosopher and elegant writer. He is one of the finest pianoforte players in Europe, and though a very young man, is supposed to be better acquainted with music than most professors of the art."

and both names too difficult to pronounce. He then proposed to omit the Felix and to change the name to Mendelson, anglicizing it. They all got very excited and warned him for God's sake not to change the name. "The British knew my name and knew my grandfather and would take any change ill. I beg you, my dear father, not to be angry with me. The thing is done and no longer to be changed."

What were Felix's real motives? Was it his desire to declare his independence against his father, much as he loved him? Was it a revolt of which he himself was but half conscious? It was surely not any inclination toward Judaism. He felt no such inclination, considering himself a Protestant. Was it out of respect for the grandfather whom he never knew? Felix no doubt valued the reputation of the famous philosopher, but from the evidence of his library it is not at all certain that he managed to plow through all of *Phaedo*. Perhaps we should take Felix at his word and leave it at that: his early successes were scored under the Mendelssohn name and he wanted to leave well enough alone.

For Abraham it was a defeat. He tried again later to change his son's mind. In vain.

It is significant that while the children were baptized in 1816, Abraham himself did not assume the Protestant religion until 1822. He had retired from active business life the year before. It was not, then, business or social advantages he sought in the change of religion. He did it out of conviction. Or shall we say out of lack of conviction? At that, one practical consideration may have influenced him to wait: his mother-in-law was a devout Jewess and he may have feared disinheritance of his children. He did not become a Protestant until the old lady was dead.

8

To summarize Abraham, we meet a man here of talent and force, who, however, never achieved clarification. He achieved both wealth and education, but the philosophy of the son of the philosopher was no better than a primer of stubborn rules. He had set ideas, bourgeois ideas. He was the very model of the German paterfamilias, his home an absolute monarchy. He gave his children love, provided they were willing to accept it on his terms. That love benefited Felix by offering a rich ambience in the home, by opening to the boy advantages of education, social contact, opportunities for sports and travel, freedom from money-grubbing, support in his fledgling music attempts, in short, all the gains which can be adduced for goodwill eased by wealth. No other composer had so easy a childhood.

Abraham concerns us chiefly because he played the pivotal role in forming Felix's personality. Perhaps the father offered the son too much ease. Perhaps Felix's talent would have grown greater had he met deprivation early in life, had he had to struggle, had suffering led him deeper into the human maze. Opposed to ease, but compatible with it, were Abraham's principles of propriety: he designed a matrix of Biedermeier orderliness and pressed Felix into it. Eventually Felix emerged from it, but never quite. I say this because the conventionality of some of his music stands in strange contrast to the originality of his prime pages.

Like his father, therefore, Felix was a divided man. He was a paradox.

Felix Mendelssohn, by Aubrey Beardsley, one of a series of caricatures of musicians that Beardsley never completed.

Four

THE POLITE PARADOX

I

*F*ELIX Mendelssohn—a polite man writing polite music. That is how most of us think of him, at whose cradle kind spirits stood to endow him both with talent and with gentlemanliness. There was no big bad witch around to lay on him the customary curse of genius and twist a sinew of his soul. Not for him the acrid and arrogant unscrupulousness familiar to us from Wagner's character. Not for him the jealousy of Brahms, hidden under an almost coquettish self-derogation. Not for him the snobbishness of Chopin, with his deep bows before the titled. Not for him the tragic secret which pressed on Tchaikowsky's life. And not for him the unreasonable passion which undermined Berlioz's career. Successful from his early youth on, he was widely appreciated and joyfully greeted. Schumann hailed him as "the Mozart of the nineteenth century," Liszt called him "Bach reborn," Chopin deemed his talent "admirable."

As to the man himself—then and even now—a whole thesaurus of complimentary adjectives has been heaped on him: gentle, happy, helpful, kindly, even-tempered, elegant. In the books, we frequently come across the statement that he was well named by being named Felix. Or that his music "very consistently revealed his *real* self—the cheerful, successful, contented, happy man that he was." He was noted for his "generous and impulsive affection for his fellow creatures." Another contemporary wrote:

"The charm of his personality enhanced the effect of his music." In the days when music was considered to possess moral powers, the Reverend H. R. Haweis published a highly regarded book entitled, *Music and Morals*. He wrote:

> In this age of mercenary musical manufacture and art degradation, Mendelssohn towers above his contemporaries like a great moral lighthouse in the midst of a dark and troubled sea. His light always shone, strong and pure. The winds of heaven were about his head, and the STILL SMALL VOICE was in his heart. In a lying generation he was pure, and not popularity nor gain could tempt him to sully the pages of his spotless inspiration with one meretricious effect or one impure association.

(Quoted by Philip Radcliffe, *Mendelssohn*)

As we look upon his picture, the painting done in London by James Warren Childe when Mendelssohn was twenty years old, we see a young man as handsome as Byron, as dandified as the Prince of Wales, as confident as the young Disraeli, as slim as Shelley, with nothing much to distinguish him from any baronet strolling down Piccadilly on his way to the Club. Thackeray's impression was: "His face is the most beautiful face I ever saw, like what I imagine our Savior's to have been." (That at least is how Sir George Grove reported it in *Grove's Dictionary*. Grove wrote a most sympathetic account of Mendelssohn, one of the three he contributed to the *Dictionary*, the others being on Beethoven and Schubert. Still, it doesn't sound much like Thackeray.) His mouth was delicate, his hair was soft and coal black, his eyes, inherited from his grandfather, were dark-brown, "as expressive a pair of eyes as were ever set in a human being's head." (Sir Frederick Pollock) When he was excited, his eyes dilated and gave his face the intensity of an actor's. His hands were strong, with tapered fingers, his feet quite small and always elegantly shod. Though he was a big eater —sweets, particularly; he loved rice pudding—he was lean, and only in his last years did he become a little corpulent. Then, too, he lost some of his hair, which made his high forehead appear higher.

As we look at Mendelssohn's drawings and water colors, we get the impression that the man who sketched these technically excellent pictures enjoyed Nature as long as Nature remained decently behaved. He had a fine sense of the picturesque, but no sense for wildness. Even the ravine becomes tame. The Alps are friendly. Rome has no slums. The Swiss village is spotless.

If we read his letters—in his short life Mendelssohn wrote nearly seven thousand letters [1]—we feel that most of them are written with creamy ink and a honeyed pen. He can be witty and pungent. He can write very well indeed; the travel letters abound in sharp observations, droll tales of his mishaps and vignettes of curious characters he meets; his joy in life and appetite for decorous adventure spring from the pages. He makes amusing comments: Italian clarinet players, he writes, seem to have been born with a wooden leg: when they play you feel as if you ought to throw a coin to them down to the courtyard. Describing a musical evening in Berlin held in memory of Mozart, he says that the music went so-so but the supper went all the better. "That is what my countrymen do best, gorging themselves. . . . By midnight everybody except Spontini was drunk, all in Mozart's honor."

His intellectual curiosity is comprehensive, as is to be expected from a man given so wide a humanistic grounding. His analyses of musical conditions are apt, his descriptions of music in Rome or London being valuable to the historian. Yet facile is the word for Felix the letter-writer: in hundreds of these communications we find a cautious politeness, a wish to please the recipient of the letter, a neutral smoothness and—not always, but often enough—little emotional involvement. Many of his "business" letters, dealing with his own compositions or works he wishes to perform, are almost as matter-of-fact as letters from General Electric.

Dry or enlightening, playful or severely factual, the letters are written in a punctilious hand, the calligraphy as if designed by a draftsman, quite beautiful with spacious circular strokes for the h's and the g's, with hardly a word crossed out or a line smeared, often titivated with small drawings, and finally neatly folded and addressed. "Neat"—a damning word. He hardly ever lets himself go, as if he were aware that these would become autographs to be collected. His hand does not shake; no rage is hurled on the paper. There is little self-revelation.

We do not possess one single love letter by Mendelssohn, either to

[1] One day he wrote twenty-four long letters.

his wife or to a mistress, if there was one. To be sure, that statement is not quite just to Felix: his family and his wife's family deliberately set out to destroy whatever love letters he or she might have written. Still, it is to be doubted that they had to destroy many.

The letters he received he filed carefully, along with programs, diaries, and account books. He stored them in large green boxes, virtually all of which are extant.[2]

His punctiliousness in money matters was that of a Swiss bank teller. Certainly he knew he would never be in want. Yet as a young man he was made to get along on a not overly generous allowance stipulated by Abraham. He *did* get along on it. Then when he began to earn money he refused to accept anything further either from father or from Lea. He insisted on being well paid. He did not throw his money around, though he often helped out friends who were in a financial bind.

He was unselfishly helpful to other composers, even to those for whose personality he had little use. He battled the publisher Simrock and practically forced him to publish Ferdinand Hiller's music. Yet Mendelssohn never said a word about it; the story came to light sixteen years after Mendelssohn's death. His judgment on new music was often good, though his enthusiasm could run away with his critical faculty. (That is true of most creative minds.) His relationship to Schumann was ambivalent: he recognized Schumann's greatness as a composer, but he disliked his hyperbolic prose writings. That romantic business of the *Davidsbündler* (League of David), the device by which Schumann discussed differing points of view and in which such characters as Eusebius, Raro, Florestan, Chiarina (Schumann's wife Clara), and Felix Meritis (Mendelssohn) appeared, was too extravagant for Mendelssohn. Schumann, on the other hand, worshipped Mendelssohn[3] and wrote copiously about his compositions. After Mendelssohn's death, Schumann set down in his diary a few reminiscences (entries are unfortunately brief; Schumann mentions people and topics of discussion, but gives few details):

> His judgments in musical matters—especially on composition—the most trenchant imaginable, go straight to the innermost core.—He instantly and everywhere recognized flaws and their cause.

[2] These "green books" are in the Bodleian Library.

[3] Clara Schumann named her seventh child Felix. Like all the male children of the Schumanns, Felix died young, at the age of twenty-five.

I always considered his praise the highest—he was the highest authority, the court of last appeal.

If he had unjustly offended anyone—spoken of someone adversely to
a third party—he could not rest until he had made amends. . . . When
he had nothing to praise, he said nothing; but where he unmistakably
found talent, he was the first to say so (thus in the cases of Bennett, Gade
and Rietz).

In 1836 when we were talking about ageing composers, he said, "how
sad is the thought of creativity drying up" and added that he could not be
reconciled to this thought. [Mendelssohn was then twenty-seven years old.]

He was free of all the weaknesses of vanity.

The exaltation of associating with him. Highest moral and artistic
principles; for that reason intransigent, sometimes seemingly rude and
unkind.

He never remained in debt. If you said something good or significant
to him, you could be certain of receiving it back twice and thrice over.

Self-criticism, the strictest and most conscientious I have ever encoun-
tered in an artist. He changed some passages five and six times. (Especially
the *Elijah;* his fine remark on that: "I think there are a few things I might
do better.")

. . . The trace of melancholia which is so frequently found in all his
compositions after the *Lobgesang.*[3a]

He loved children and enjoyed himself when his own children filled
the house with their playmates. He invented games for them and drew
funny doodles.

In short, at first glance Mendelssohn seems too good to be true.

This first impression is not a false one. Mendelssohn *was* attractive
and lovable. Very much so. The encomiums fit. But they do not describe
the entire man. There was more to him than the bland and polite picture
he turned so carefully to the world. There must have been—or else how
could he have composed the music for which we still value him in this, our
impolite era, and which conveys to us, along with its insouciance and spright-
liness, the melancholy of a November dusk? Where did he, carefully
nurtured, obtain the sense of pain which he shows in some of the slow
movements of his chamber music? In what corner of his soul lay the poetry

---

[3a] From G. Eismann and G. Rudloff-Hille: *Schumanns Mendelssohn-Tagebuch.* Zwickau,
1949. (Quoted by Jacob)

which enabled him to equal Shakespeare's summer revels in music? He was not just a superb craftsman; he was a genius. However various may be the form that genius can assume, it cannot remain aloof, uninvolved, or just polite.

The biographer attempting to reconstruct the whole Mendelssohn is handicapped not by a paucity but by a plethora of "artifacts." The ground is strewn with paper: not only all those letters—a complete edition in ten volumes is now being prepared by the Mendelssohn Archive in Berlin— but also a long list of personal recollections, books, pamphlets, monographs of friends, partisans, journalists, fellow-musicians.[4] They were honest men and women—but what you get from them is for the most part what Mendelssohn himself allowed them to glimpse. They see him in a mirror placed by himself in a favorable position. Only occasionally do we discern a harsh light or a glint of strife. The witnesses were influenced not only by the man they valued, but by the tone of the times in which they lived. It was a period in which unrelenting introspection was out of fashion. One did not examine psychological motives too closely. After the upheaval of the Napoleonic wars it was natural that one should desire to live life calmly and near the surface. Except in love—and perhaps even there—excessive self-questioning was to be avoided, as was excessive show of sentiment, though in Germany especially there was no dearth of sentimentality; there was much to-do about the German forest and the mumbling brook, which of course mumbled in German. The young people were more attracted to the mellifluous verses of Heine—particularly the sentimental poems such as "On Wings of Song" (*Auf Flügeln des Gesanges*) or "New Love" (*Neue Liebe*) or "Morning Greeting" (*Morgengruss*), all of which Mendelssohn set to music—than to the philosophic probing of Goethe's *Faust* with its dangerous dissatisfaction. Moderation in thinking, behavior, and relationships was a precept of a bourgeois society. Lea admonished her son to be "*ausgeglichen*," to cultivate an "equable" disposition. Mendelssohn disliked frenetic persons and did not choose his friends among the wild-eyed. He couldn't abide Rahel Varnhagen and had not much use for Bettina

---

[4] Among those who wrote personal recollections are: Julius Benedict, Hector Berlioz, Henry Chorley, James Davison, Eduard Devrient, Johann Droysen, Sebastian Hensel, Ferdinand Hiller, Charles Horsley, Joseph Joachim, Karl Klingemann, Wilhelm Lampadius, Jenny Lind, Ignaz Moscheles, Elise Polko, Julius Schubring, Robert Schumann.

Brentano; those female poets were too bubbly for his stomach. He disliked Berlioz with his unruly hair and unruly manner and quite failed to understand Berlioz's work.

Mendelssohn lived his youth in the *Biedermeier* period, so called after a bumbling character featured in Germany's leading humorous periodical, the *Fliegende Blätter*. The period found its expression in homely furniture, simply in design and inexpensive in material. It suited the German people in the years after Napoleon's pomp, and brought with it, along with simplicity in furniture, simplicity in manners. Social gatherings were unpretentious; as Karoline Bauer, the actress, wrote, "A lady could wear the same evening dress several times without being criticized." The "intellectual" salons were often commonplace gatherings of people of like convictions, exchanging views with which everybody had agreed in advance; they lacked the brilliant bitchiness of the salons of eighteenth-century Paris. As one historian of Biedermeier puts it, many a hostess thought she was running a salon when she was merely running a restaurant.[5] Cup after cup of tea was served, imitating the English.

As Mendelssohn grew up, he began to feel very much at home in England. British manners and Anglo-Saxon self-restraint appealed to him. He liked the stiff upper lip. No doubt part of his Anglophile attitude sprang from his great personal success in England. (Father Abraham was far less smitten.) He went to England ten times and became completely bilingual, speaking English idiomatically, though with a slight accent, and only occasionally mixing up those tricky English prepositions, or writing "lead" for "led."

When he was not working, there was nothing solemn about him, and he loved to hear or tell jokes, though it is to be feared that they were all clean ones. (He differed there from Mozart and Beethoven.) But in no sense was he prissy; it was simply that he was uninterested in eroticism, overt or hidden, frank or smutty. He lacked the driving sexual impulse. There is no sign that "carnal stings" overwhelmed him. He did like women and loved to be in the company of girls, though no woman ever moved him to turbulence or misery or foolishness. One woman he did love profoundly; but of that relationship we must speak in a later chapter. Suffice

[5] Georg Hermann: *Das Biedermeier*, Hamburg, 1965.

it to say that his sexual impulse was restrained but "normal." "There was a great deal of manliness packed into his little body," a British friend said (quoted by Grove), but it was a manliness of the drawing room, not the bedroom. He loved convivial evenings of conversation in mixed company, and when he wanted to he could converse brilliantly, speaking with a slight lisp; but suddenly, and for no apparent reason, he would fall silent and cede the talk to others.

It is this reserve, along with a temperament prevailingly considerate and courteous, which delivered to his contemporaries and then to posterity the picture of a man at ease, going about his work. Was he really at ease? Was he always at ease?

2

I do not think so. There were two facets to his make-up, one free, the other encapsulated. He was an extroverted introvert, and his introversion, meditative and troubled, was carefully tucked away behind his smile.

Let us shift our grounds. Let us observe actions and traits of his which run counter to the accepted labeling of Felix as Felix.

"A genius never can be quite still," Dr. Johnson wrote to Mrs. Thrale. Mendelssohn not only could not be quite still but was driven by a pervasive restlessness. The truism that the need to earn a living drives one to work did not apply to him. His need, although traceable to his childhood training, came from an inner disturbance which made him unable to remain tranquil; this disturbance stayed with him all his life, persisting after his father was no longer around. He subscribed to the hortatory German proverb, "If I rest I rust." He feared repose. We could understand his drive had it been solely due to his desire to compose music; the creative urge does push and spur regardless of practical requirements or economic circumstances, simply because grass must grow. Yet it wasn't that, it was not all creativity, it was not wholly a conviction that he had something valuable to give and give it he must, as copiously as possible, which pressed him. It was activity as such which he craved. His day abhorred a vacuum. He filled the interstices of his existence with busyness in various forms. His work as a conductor, music director, pianist, organist, music teacher, and organizer of concerts and music festivals would have been enough to complete a normal measure. He was an enthusiastic traveler, though protesting that he liked to stay home: he ran off to England four months after his wedding day. He liked to travel fast, sometimes through the night. He climbed Swiss mountains and walked up and down the Rhine Valley. His sketchbook was in his pocket and he filled it with pictures of the landscapes he saw. He collected autographs and musical manuscripts and was indefatigable in search for the authentic texts of the works he conducted or played. When he was not standing on the podium or playing the piano or improvising on the organ or writing at his desk, he galloped off on his horse or was bent over the billiard table (he played the game well) or engaged in a chess game (which he played badly) or sat down to a game of cards (at which he hated to lose). It is incomprehensible how he did all that he did. To cite Grove once more: "We may almost be pardoned for wondering how he can have found time to write any music at all." Goethe summarized him: "He has the smallest possible amount of the phlegmatic and the maximum of the opposite quality." He never knew Milton's "lazy, leaden-stepping Hours."

As a compensation, he used suddenly to fall into short sleeps, so profound that when he awoke he had no idea where he was. He could sleep anywhere, any time; when he saw a couch he lay down and off he was. Conversation swirled around him; he heard it no more than one accustomed to the sea hears it at ebb tide.

That wonderful courtesy of his: it was used to hide the irritations under which he chafed, the disappointments that he felt because his co-workers were not able or not willing to be as selflessly devoted to the dissemination of music as he; and deepest of all a realization, which I believe he grasped, of the limitation of his own talent. That talent was fine-grained and radiant, and he knew it. Is any creative artist void of the pride of having talent? Does not every artist possess a sense of importance? Even Schubert, behind those glasses through which he peered up at his contemporaries, felt an inkling of his worth. But Mendelssohn, erudite as he was, forced himself into an historic view of his art and measured himself against his idols, Bach, Beethoven, and Handel. His critical intelligence whispered to him that good as he might be, he could not stand up there on the mountain-top. That is not to say that he brooded about it; his disposition was too hedonistic for sighing, and the praise given him was too densely woven not to cover him with a handsome and protective cloak. Yet a frustration remained. Doubt remained. Of one of his compositions, a little concerto for two pianos, he wrote that every idea in it knocked twenty times before it entered; sometimes there were knocks but no ideas came in. (Letter to Klingemann, April 10, 1833) Such disapproval of his music was not exceptional: he had something derogatory to say of compositions better than that Concerto for Two Pianos. Yet he cared for them as tenderly as artists do.

His most signal failure was his inability to compose a viable opera. He wanted very much to do so. He practically began his musical career with the composition of little operas, which were given in the family circle. His first "professional" opera, as we shall see, was performed when he was eighteen years old. It was a failure. From then on he tried over and over again to find an opera libretto which would suit him—"something between *Fidelio* and *Les deux Journées*," he said—but he never could find it because he was not naturally cut out to be a dramatic composer. He blamed it all on those poor librettos submitted to him, but the true cause was his lack of the theatrical gift, a lack which he did not want to admit. In the year of his death he again began the composition of an opera (to a libretto by the poet Geibel) on a subject which seemed congenial to him as a German who had spent part of his life on the Rhine, the legend of *Lorelei*. He left it uncompleted. Five of his operas remain in manuscript form; they have never been published. Writing to J. R. Planché, an English dramatist specializing in fairy plays (he wrote the libretto for Weber's *Oberon*), who was working on a libretto for him, he is at first delighted with Planché's sketch. As they proceed, he becomes disappointed, he makes objection after objection, and he finally decides to turn down the libretto because "Planché won't change it and I am beginning to fear that we both may be right." When he turns it down, he does so with the utmost consideration of Planché's feelings, continuing to praise the text and writing Planché three very long letters which say nothing more than "No."

Because he held himself in check, he was subject to sudden fainting spells; they seemed to occur when he was bested or crossed. He was extremely sensitive to criticism, never really forgave a harsh review, but usually swallowed his hurt and kept his poise. Yet his moods were unpredictable. As two of his London admirers, the charming Horsley girls—who could have come straight out of Jane Austen—remarked, he would turn in a trice from a clown into a melancholy Dane. Once in Düsseldorf he did lose his temper at Immermann, the Intendant of the theater. It is the harshest letter of his we have:

> In my opinion only one answer to my letter would have been a proper one. Your answer I cannot accept. Therefore our relationship is terminated. We shall not meet again. F. M. B. February 9th, 1835.

Since he was one of the most remarkable musical child prodigies who ever lived, it stands to the credit of his parents that they put a damper on his growing sense of importance. How does one handle a child who, by the time he is fourteen, has composed thirteen little symphonies, several cantatas, a brace of piano concertos, and many organ pieces, and has acquired skill in playing the piano, violin, viola, and organ? Perhaps, however, the damper dampened too efficiently. Not only did Felix remain modest—extraordinarily modest, considering all the temptations he had to become immodest—but his self-doubt resulted in an unwillingness to have his compositions published. It was so with the "Italian" Symphony; he worked at it for fourteen years and in the year of his death he was still considering changing the last movement; it was so with the *Fingal's Cave* Overture; it was so with the "Scottish" Symphony, which he began in 1830 and did not let go until twelve years afterward.

When he was all of nineteen, that is, in September, 1828, he was planning his first trip to England. He wanted to conquer new territory and felt that "people [in Berlin] are tired of me." He had composed the Overture to *A Midsummer Night's Dream* two years previously and had scored a great success. Yet he wrote to the conductor, Ganz (October 19, 1828):

> It is a very long time since the public has had anything of importance from me (a couple of hastily written cantatas cannot be taken into account), nor have I played the piano, or showed myself as a composer, and so I have gently slipped into forgetfulness, in which I wish to remain till after my great journey. The people are tired of me, and to a certain degree I cannot

reproach them for it; therefore I would rather wait till I return fresh from foreign parts before I come into contact with the public again. At present they would only pass over my successes and blame my failures: friends would praise and enemies attack me, each undeservedly—and I dislike both.

(Hardly the language of a nineteen-year-old! Perhaps he was purposely exaggerating a little: he wished to persuade Ganz not to perform the Overture "Calm Sea" with an inimical orchestra.)

Four years later he wrote to his friend Moscheles in London, right after the publication of the first set of the "Songs without Words":

At least twenty editions of this work will be published and with my earning from it I'll buy the house at Chester Place No. 2 as well as a seat in the House of Commons. Then I'll become a professional Radical. Before that happens I hope we'll meet again; it's possible it will be difficult to sell just the first edition. (August 10, 1832)

Three years later, to Moscheles' wife:

You know there are times when I think very little of myself and I hesitate to talk or cogitate much about myself. Such moods creep over me here [in Düsseldorf], worse than anywhere else, because there isn't anybody here in whom I can confide. (January 10, 1835)

One or two biographers have ascribed this "thinking very little of myself" to his abdication of his Jewish heritage. Because he changed his religion he felt unanchored; such is the theory. Only once did he refer to himself as a Jew and that was after his performance of the *St. Matthew Passion*, which was brought about by his courage and the enthusiasm of his friend, the actor Eduard Devrient. "To think," said Mendelssohn, "that it was an actor and a Jew who gave back to the German people their greatest Christian work." Did he really say it? The anecdote, a famous one, comes to us second-hand from Devrient's reminiscences. True or not, Mendelssohn exhibited none of the peculiar anti-Semitism which so many Jews show, and which was rampant even in his own family, Rebecka making fun of a distant relative of her grandfather's because he was an orthodox Jew. To Felix, Jew or Gentile made no difference. But he certainly thought and felt as a Protestant, steeped as he was in the music of Bach and the teachings of

Schleiermacher who, in the year that Mendelssohn was born, became the Pastor of Berlin's Trinity Church.[6]

Did Felix have a guilty conscience about the change of religion? Not at all, as I have indicated. The orthodoxy of religion meant little to him. He was not a churchgoer. He went to churches of whatever denomination —if they had a good organ on which he could play. In his manuscripts he often penned an exclamation—"Let it succeed, God" (*Lass es gelingen, Gott*) or "Help along" (*Hilf Du mit*)[7]—but these were mere formulas. He was not pious. His interest in Christian doctrine was musical, the use of it for motets, oratorios, psalms, hymns, anthems. He knew, of course, of the spitballs which were thrown by the anti-Semites behind his back and sometimes, though seldom, straight at him. He laughed it off. It seems to me significant that his least convincing music is his religious music, except *Elijah*.

His relationship to religion he expressed in a curious connection. Rumors had been floating about that he was losing his hearing and that he was now becoming a devout believer. He wrote to Johann Schirmer, a painter and teacher at the Academy in Düsseldorf, indignantly telling him that his ears were as good as ever, and that was very good indeed. Then:

> I am supposed to have become devout.
>
> If by that is meant the usual definition of the word "devout," and I take it that is what you have in mind, then I must reply that unfortunately I have not become so. Yet I try every day to approach some such goal, knowing, of course, that I shall never wholly succeed. Good enough if I approximate it. If by "devout" one thinks of a pietist, somebody who folds his hands and expects God to work for him, or somebody who instead of trying to perfect himself in his chosen calling prattles of a call to heaven incompatible with earthly endeavor, or somebody who is unable to love either man or thing on this earth with his whole heart—well, I haven't become anybody like that, thank God, and I hope I never will. . . . (November 21, 1838)

---

[6] When a German critic argued that Mendelssohn's music could never become universally valid because it contained "Hebraic elements and psalmodies of the synagogue," Berlioz asked whether the critic would have made such a foolish statement had he not known that the composer of *St. Paul* and *Elijah* was a descendant of the famous Moses Mendelssohn. "It is hard to see how these psalmodies can have influenced the musical style of Felix Mendelssohn, since he never professed the Jewish religion. Everyone knows he was a Lutheran and an earnest Lutheran at that."

[7] He formularized these by using initials only: "*L.e.g.G.*," and "*H.D.m.*"

His ethical striving was as honest as were his intellectual interests. "He could be very irritable when people thought they were bound to converse with him exclusively about music; . . . 'as if I were incapable of talking on any other subject than my profession,' he sometimes said with amusing indignation." (Polko) With equal curiosity he plowed through the muddy philosophy of Herder, for whom Germany was the hub of the universe, as through the serene classicism of Goethe, who found heaven in Helen's eyes. He was a prodigious reader—and again one asks, where did he find the time? Many of his books have been preserved in the Mendelssohn Archive in Berlin: Homer in German; Milton in English; Plato in Greek; Scott's *Waverly* novels, which were then favorite reading in Germany as much as in England; the plays and writings and theatrical essays of Eduard Devrient; a set of Schiller, of course one of Goethe, and a set of Shakespeare in the new German translations by Schlegel and Tieck, the volumes well thumbed. The complete works of Jean Paul are represented. Jean Paul was an early romantic, "buffoon and angel," whose combination of wit and sentimentality made a particular appeal to the young people. Both Fanny and Felix were ardent admirers. So was Carlyle.

Mendelssohn's own carefully compiled inventory of "Books Owned" lists as well a complete Shakespeare in the original, Byron, Burns, the *Decameron* (a present from his mother-in-law), the Greek plays (in German); *Gil Blas, Nicholas Nickleby, The Pickwick Papers*, plays of Molière and Beaumarchais; several poets such as Eichendorff, Uhland, Hebbel; the *Thousand and One Nights* in a fifteenth-century translation; the writings of Moses Mendelssohn, and the Bible with illustrations by Raphael.

His reading was not confined to great works of literature. He was interested in what was going on around him and he was an avid newspaper reader, preferring, however, the English papers to the German ones, deeming them "more honest." They were.

As he was suspicious of the poet's eye in fine frenzy rolling, so was he skeptical of composers who, he said, waited "for the divine spark." Of course he believed in inspiration, but not in trance. He was equally suspicious of high-flown theoretical palaver about music. "What's the use of talking so much about music? It is better to compose well." It is consistent with his personality that his manuscripts are clean and free of corrections.

We know he corrected and amended again and again, but he permits us no glimpse into the workshop. Either he destroyed his sketches or, more probably, he worked it all out in his head. Yet what he produced is sometimes copper coin. Some of the little piano pieces with which he dazzled his audiences or some of his coy songs lie so far below the level of his best work that they detract from his total achievement. We think of him as a composer of gay music; that is because his most popular works, such as the "Italian" Symphony, the *Midsummer Night's Dream* Overture, the *Octet*, or the Violin Concerto, are prevailingly happy in mood. To value him as a whole, we should include the elegiac music, plaintive and subdued, to be found in his chamber works.

His co-workers spoke of his modesty—but, genuine though it was, that modesty contained a contrary component. Schumann's statement that he was "free of all the weaknesses of vanity" is absurd. Devrient, a close friend, said that Mendelssohn could be quite vain, more of his person than of his work, and with all his amiability and graciousness he liked to be the center of attention. That is, for a time; then he would suddenly draw isolation around himself.

As we retrace his life, there emerges a man who did not wear his heart on his sleeve for daws, friendly or unfriendly, to peck at; but who carried in that heart, along with gaiety, more than a pinch of sorrow. Perhaps his almost frantic restlessness was due to a feeling that he was not going to live long. After a rehearsal of his oratorio *St. Paul*, he sat in a Weimar hotel room with Christian Lobe, flutist of the Weimar orchestra. Lobe, who was a hypochondriac, said that "he was not destined to enjoy many of Mendelssohn's later works. Mendelssohn answered, 'Oh, you'll long outlive me. I will not grow old.' But then, as if he regretted what he had just said, his mien at once assumed a smiling expression." [8]

The smile was there when he stepped from the penumbra of self-examination. He was not smiling all the time.

[8] *Goethes Schauspieler und Musiker*, Eberwein and Lobe, Berlin, 1912.

3

It is obvious that his mastery of himself in speech, letters, and be-havior, the restraint which he practiced so successfully most of the time, he inherited from his father. The *bürgerlich* virtues were inculcated in him every day by that exemplary citizen, Muncipal Councillor Abraham. Polite-ness, consideration for others, advantage of connections, husbandry, good manners, the belief that it was not shameful to have money, the creed that a certain amount of conformity—when in Berlin do as the Berliners do—facilitated life, and the pleasures of sociability: all these made up Felix's tradition. Something of Abraham's conservatism, his suspicion of the wide sweep and the grandiose gesture, remained in Felix's musical make-up. It is, I think, significant that he formed his closest friendships not with the musical revolutionaries of his age, not with Liszt or Chopin, but with men of conservative hue. He liked Spohr, Felix said, because the man was "re-served and elegant."

From his grandfather he inherited elegance of style, the tenacity to think through a problem, and personal charm: both of them, one ugly, one handsome, knew how to captivate people.

Through the three generations runs one streak: a mighty will to suc-ceed. The result of that power took three different forms, but a similarity exists: in each of them a brain operated under tension and with tyrannical earnestness.

Tension—there lies the paradox. He laughed and he flirted and he played the piano and he bantered and he danced and he conducted and he composed and he sketched—and everything he did he seemed to do so easily. Yet, as we study him, we feel that tension underneath the ease. Per-haps it was that tension, a clock overwound, which suddenly and at a very early age made it all come to a stop.

Five

YOUTH, ZELTER, GOETHE, BACH

I

THE scene in the Mendelssohn home must occasionally have resembled the scene in *The Would-Be Gentleman* in which the Music Master, the Dancing Master, the Fencing Master, the Tailor, and the Philosopher all swarm around Monsieur Jourdain. The teachers swarmed around the Mendelssohn children: Ludwig Heyse, philologist and father of the poet Paul, was the *"Hauslehrer,"* fulfilling the same function that Moses had in the silk manufacturer's home; Ludwig Berger, himself a pupil of Clementi, taught them piano; Carl Henning and Eduard Rietz, two eminent violinists, taught them the violin and viola and, though Mendelssohn remained a pianist, his expertness in quartet writing owed much to the understanding of these instruments instilled by these two teachers; a droll, gnomish professor of the Berlin Academy, "the little Rösel," instructed Felix in landscape drawing. When Felix was fifteen Ignaz Moscheles came from London to spend some time in Berlin. He was invited to the home; he heard Felix play; he marveled; he at once started to give him lessons until Moscheles declared, "I can teach him nothing more."

All the children made music; Rebecka sang, Paul played the violoncello, and Fanny showed pianistic talent fully equal to that of Felix: when she was thirteen she surprised her father by playing from memory the twenty-four Bach *Preludes* and playing them well.

The child Felix was as winning as he was handsome. Early he made friends, some much older than he, many of whom he retained all his life. There was no resisting this serious boy, serious but exuberant, with his long hair falling over his shoulders, his inquisitive eyes, his hesitant soft voice. When he sat at the piano, the wisdom of the mature musician was in him; when he jumped down from the piano stool, he was as ready for a prank as any child, climbing on the roof at night and meowing like a tomcat, or thrusting a banana into the window of an indignant Polish lady.

Some of his best friends were greatly to distinguish themselves: Eduard Devrient, eight years older than Felix, who came from a family of famous actors,[1] was a successful actor, singer, playwright, and later Director of the Dresden Theater. Julius Schubring, about the same age as Felix, became a renowned theologian. Gustav Droysen achieved fame as a historian, his books on Alexander the Great and his *History of Hellenism* influencing the later works of Theodor Mommsen and Jacob Burckhardt. Felix probably felt closest to Karl Klingemann, who was eleven years older, but a youthful and luminous spirit, idealistic and a bit of a poet. He was the son of a poet and theater director from Braunschweig, and therefore was from childhood on accustomed to the ambience of the arts. Later (in 1828) he became Secretary of the Hanoverian Legation in London, where his house often served as a home for Felix. He was highly regarded in British Court circles. The year before Felix died, he called Klingemann, in an excess of sentimentality rare for him, "his one and only friend." None of these friends, except Moscheles, was Jewish.

2

Two teachers were most influential in shaping Felix's musical thinking. One was Adolf Bernhard Marx, the other Carl Friedrich Zelter, of the two Zelter being not only the stronger personality but the longer-lasting mentor. Marx was a dialectician of music, a brilliant conversationalist, but a

---

[1] Several of Eduard's descendants became well-known actors, one of them a superb Shakespeare interpreter at the *Burgtheater* in Vienna.

jejune composer. The children liked him and called him the "Abbé" (after the initials of his Christian names), but Abraham did not trust his influence on Felix and told Devrient: "People who talk so aptly but produce nothing apt exercise a bad influence on productive talents." [2]

However, he was an honest teacher and forthrightly voiced his regret that his pupil wasted time on sentimental trifles; he warned of his being led astray by the adulation offered him. Felix listened to him. It was Marx who introduced Felix to the wonder of Beethoven; by the time Felix was in his late teens he knew the nine symphonies, the piano concertos, and many of the sonatas by heart.[3] It was Marx too who helped Felix improve his Overture to *A Midsummer Night's Dream,* suggesting changes of conventional turns of phrase. Later he and Marx agreed to write oratorio librettos for each other. Marx wanted to compose a "Moses," Felix was thinking of "St. Paul." So Mendelssohn wrote the words to a "Moses" and Marx to a "St. Paul." Neither was satisfied, and the relationship became cool though outwardly remaining pleasant. When Marx had finished his oratorio, he took a train to Leipzig, where Mendelssohn was music director, and played the score for him, hoping that Felix would see fit to perform it. He had finished only the first part when Mendelssohn said, "Don't be angry with me—but I can do nothing for this work." Marx closed the book, got up, and left without a word. Back in Berlin, he took all the letters he had received from Mendelssohn and threw them in the lake in the Tiergarten. They never saw each other again.

Carl Friedrich Zelter was the son of a mason and, after having been thrown out of the *Gymnasium* for some transgression or other, he had begun to follow his father's trade. But music had attracted the mason. He was especially drawn to vocal music, perhaps because, having injured one of his fingers, he could not play an instrument. His taste ran to the past, to old music, and he avidly collected manuscripts of Bach, Handel, Graun, etc. (Of course only the Germans could compose music. Zelter ignored Palestrina and knew next to nothing of Rameau or Lully.) He had genuine talent which was soon recognized; first as a member and later as the director,

[2] Quoted from Eduard Devrient: *Meine Erinnerungen an Felix Mendelssohn-Bartholdy* (Leipzig, 1869). The book is a valuable source book, if like all recollections written by friends it is read with caution. Wagner criticized the book unmercifully.

[3] Beethoven, who died when Mendelssohn was eighteen years old, never met him. But there is an entry in one of the Conversation Books: "Mendelsohn (*sic*) 12 years old promises much."

he developed the artistic standards of the Berlin *Singakademie* and its allied male chorus, the *Liedertafel,* an approximate equivalent of a glee club. In the year Mendelssohn was born, he was appointed professor at the University of Berlin.

Zelter, through self-education, had become a learned and sensitive man; but he was one of those who hide their learning and sensitivity behind a mask of ignorance. His ruffian manner was laid on with a trowel. He was so afraid of being considered "arty" or *précieux* that he purposely used the language of the day laborer or the drill sergeant, sprinkling his conversation with the kind of expletives which were to be heard in the barracks of Berlin. In company it was only a question of minutes before Zelter would say something coarse and contrary. He was visibly delighted when he could slaughter a sacred cow; his huge face with the long nose and the furrowed cheeks lit up. The men who knew him saw through the pose and found it refreshing. They liked this tall, burly, blunt man, who knew much and pretended to know nothing. He was on friendly terms with such different personalities as the philosophic Hegel, the aristocratic Schiller, and the fussy Varnhagen.

Zelter's best friend, the white plume of his later years, was Goethe. This was indeed a curious friendship. Goethe, the great cosmopolitan, that subtle and diamantine genius, the rays of his mind illuminating the most diverse subjects, the man who could turn from his incomparable lyric poetry to an inquiry into the theory of color or the descent of man, the diplomat who inhaled and exhaled the air of the courts as if it were mountain air, the master of supple language—what could he have possibly found in common with this gruff German with his beer-soaked talk and his interest concentrated on the one subject of which Goethe knew comparatively little? Yet there it was, a friendship which lasted for many years. It began when Zelter had set some of Goethe's poems to music and Goethe had liked the settings. That was characteristic of the poet; he liked those musical treatments which gave precedence to the words, the music being "accompaniment." As a consequence he preferred the songs composed by mediocrities.

After the death of Schiller, Goethe needed another friend to serve him as a partner in the play of ideas. With Schiller he had an equivalent partner. With Zelter he did not, but he knew how to adapt the play to the

Carl Friedrich Zelter, Mendelssohn's teacher. Pencil drawing by Wilhelm Hensel, 1829. (National Gallery, Berlin)

player. One of Goethe's modern biographers [4] has this to say about the relationship:

> Goethe's friendship with Zelter was the only real male friendship of his later life; it was a friendship strengthened in times of crisis, when Zelter would hurry over to Weimar to console his friend, and pleasantly cultivated in quieter days, when parcels of Teltow turnips, a great favorite of Goethe's, would arrive in Weimar, and drinking songs with the refrain *Ergo bibamus!* were sent in return. Nor was this all. After Schiller's death Zelter became Goethe's chief correspondent, and in these letters Goethe "deposits" many of his ideas, in the same way as he did with Schiller. In the same way, too, the correspondence was done up in volumes and sent to the binder, in preparation for its publication as a supplement to the posthumous works; it gave the old man pleasure to see the collection grow—finally Riemer was able to publish it in six volumes. Zelter, of course, was a very different foil to Schiller; he had no original philosophic ideas and no claims in that direction, but he was a character, a personality, a *Natur* as Goethe used to call people with strongly defined individualities, a man with a keen eye for men and situations. Goethe, who in his protean way adapted himself to each of his correspondents, took care to pull himself together so as to appear as resolute as Zelter, and to discard his "moaning and groaning," as he termed it in one of the *Tafellieder* he wrote for his friend. In spite of the gulf between them, Zelter exerted an educative influence over Goethe, not by advice and admonition like Schiller, but simply by his example.

Whatever the reason for the friendship, there it was, and Zelter was the only man who addressed the aging Privy Councillor of Weimar by the familiar *du*. Zelter once had a stepson whom he loved very much and who committed suicide. Goethe knew about it and without acknowledging the tragedy by a single word he addressed Zelter with the *"du"* in the next letter. (Over five hundred letters were exchanged.)

It is revealing of Zelter's character that he made careful drafts of his letters to Goethe, then edited them to insert those kernels of uncouth expression of which he was fond. Goethe, of course, never knew about this purposeful vulgarization. It is equally characteristic that Zelter was jealous of Marx. To Goethe he berated him as "a certain Marx or Marcus from

[4] Richard Friedenthal: *Goethe, His Life and Times*, New York, 1963. Quoted by permission of World Publishing Company.

Halle, who must have been baptized with soda, for his defecations are greenish-gray. They, like flies, stain even the food they enjoy."

I have mentioned that Zelter's musical taste looked back in time. He thought Weber's *Der Freischütz* a ridiculous opera and he felt, at least for some years—he later changed his mind—that Beethoven was an undisciplined composer, that he used an unduly heavy apparatus to express small ideas, "like Hercules using his club to kill flies." Bettina Brentano, furious, called Zelter "a Philistine with large bones and a long waistcoat." As to Schubert, Zelter ignored him entirely. Yet he was a wise enough teacher not to impose his own tastes on Mendelssohn, who was greatly moved when as a twelve-year-old he heard *Der Freischütz* at its first performance in Berlin. That was in the same year that Mendelssohn met Goethe.

Such was the man, then, to whom Abraham entrusted the vital part of the musical education of his extraordinary son. The lessons began when Felix was eight years old; Zelter was fifty-nine. Again we must record it to Abraham's credit that he would not only repose confidence in a man who came to his home and behaved like a bear, but that later he gave due acknowledgment to Zelter. In 1835, when Mendelssohn had become famous, Abraham, reminiscing about Zelter, wrote to Felix: "Beyond the shadow of a doubt your musical education would have taken quite another path without Zelter." Felix too did not cease being grateful to him, writing from Paris that due to Zelter's training he would under all circumstances remain a member of the *école allemande,* and signing the letter, "Your faithful pupil, F. M. B." The old Zelter, who hated to praise, wrote with love about Felix, adding immediately, "Admittedly I speak like a grandfather who spoils his grandchildren."

The grandchild showed every promise of becoming an artist. At the age of eleven he began to pour out one composition after another; these included fugues, songs, operettas, and little operas (*The Two Pedagogues, Soldiers' Loves, The Uncle from Boston*), a little Violin Concerto in D minor (which has come to light only recently), two Piano Concertos, and a Piano Quartet in C minor which he published as his Opus I. Much of this is apprentice work, done between the ages of eleven and fourteen, and displays his delight in experimenting in various styles. The famous English critic Henry Chorley, who was, to be sure, an ardent partisan of Mendelssohn and whose dicta therefore need to be discounted, thought them "rebel" works:

> But they are knotted up, as it were, with close care and pains, not dashed off with insolence. They were the works of a boy anxious to prove himself a man among the double-refined intelligences of those by whom he was surrounded; and parading his science, his knowledge of the ancients, his mastery over all the learning of his Art.
>
> (From *Modern German Music*, London, 1855)

Felix used to perform these works at the Sunday concerts in his home. Occasionally Abraham hired a small orchestra for him and the boy stood on a chair and conducted with great gravity. The scene would strike one as tasteless, were it not for an absence of the sorry mannerisms of the prodigy; the gifted child showed off as little as the gifted man.

3

Zelter was proud of Felix's progress. He decided to take him to Goethe, to show his prize pupil to his prize friend. Joyfully Abraham and Lea gave permission. Zelter wrote to Goethe:

> Berlin, October 21, 1821
>
> Tomorrow morning I depart with my Doris [his daughter] and a young, lively boy twelve years old, my pupil, son of Herr Mendelssohn. We are going to Wittenberg, to the festival. . . . I would love to show Doris and my best pupil your visage before I have to depart from this world, though I have every intention of remaining in it as long as possible. He is a good, handsome boy, spirited and obedient. Admittedly he is the son of a Jew but he is no Jew. His father has made the children learn something real; and with considerable effort on his part he educated them in the right way. For once it really would be *eppes rores* if a Jewish boy were to become an artist.

(We need not take Zelter's anti-Semitic remarks too seriously—they were his idea of humor, but many years later when the Goethe-Zelter correspondence was published, the Mendelssohn family understandably took offense at them.)

On a fine autumnal morning, a private carriage stood in front of the Mendelssohn home, Zelter inside. The boy jumped in and off they went on the journey to Weimar, but not before Felix had had to endure much parental instruction, such as to sit straight at the dinner table, not to be forward, to be respectful to all he was to meet in Goethe's house, and to answer questions in a few words and to the point. It was enough to frighten an adult visitor. Fanny told him that if he were not to remember every word that Goethe said and report on every detail of how he looked, she was never going to speak to him again.

Why did Goethe invite the boy? In his long life he must have had his fill of child prodigies. He was not overfond of children, including his own grandchildren, whom he kept at a safe distance. It had become difficult to meet the aged poet; he had to shield himself. Tranquility was a necessity to him, a law of self-preservation. He was not a selfish man and would take any amount of trouble to help people. For years he worked for the benefit of the little state of Weimar. He gave generously to his friends in need—and he was not wealthy—as long as the pain and the sorrow of these friends would be kept removed from personal contact with himself. He could not bear to go to a funeral. Once when his daughter-in-law fell from a horse and cut her face, he could not bring himself to visit her until the wound was healed. Schiller wrote: "He binds men to him by small as well as by great attentions. But he always knows how to hold himself free—like a god, without giving himself."

Here then was an opportunity to please and honor his friend Zelter. No personal involvement was required: he merely had to act his role "like a god, without giving himself." Another reason lay in Goethe's insatiable curiosity, a curiosity which embraced things and ideas and people. He wanted to see this "something rare." He was now seventy-two years old, in love with an eighteen-year-old girl—his cycle of poems, *Trilogy of Passion*, was the result of this infatuation—and he liked to ask the young for a loan of their youth. He filled his house with young people—if they were handsome.

Perhaps a more cogent reason prompted him: now that he was enjoying greater leisure, he turned to music with greater attention. His relationship to music was equivocal. He liked "strong fresh sounds," and in his

Goethe, painted by Joseph Stiller in 1828. A copy of this portrait was given to Mendelssohn.

youth he had enjoyed playing the violoncello and the harpsichord. Yet he appreciated music not for itself but largely as a stimulant to his moods, a magic carpet on which his thoughts could ride. He never penetrated into the true nature of the art, as he did into Greek sculpture or Raphael's drawings. He was puzzled by Beethoven and so little interested in Schubert that he did not even open a package of songs which Schubert had mailed to him; in that package were some of the great Goethe poems, destined to be freed of the limitations of language and to become international heritage through Schubert's music: songs such as *"Gretchen am Spinnrad," "Heiden-röslein," "Erlkönig," "Rastlose Liebe,"* and *"Wanderers Nachtlied."* He did hear the *"Erlkönig"* sung long after Schubert's death, by Schröder-Devrient. He seems to have been struck more by the magnificence of her singing than by the song itself and he preferred the setting of the poem by Corona Schröter, an actress and composer of sorts in Weimar who happened to be a very beautiful woman.

The other part—perhaps the deeper part—of Goethe's musical interest was prompted by scientific curiosity. He wanted to apply to music the same method of reasoning and research which had led him to the discovery of the vestigial intermaxillary bone in man. What was it that caused music's agreeable sensations? What were the laws of sound? How was scale structure to be defined? He had written to Johann Friedrich Reichardt, composer and music critic,[5] inviting him to "attack acoustics together." Nothing came of the plan. But Goethe had never given up. Zelter could still teach him and Zelter himself held a somewhat scientific view of music.

Zelter, Ottilie (Goethe's daughter-in-law), and Ludwig Rellstab, the famous critic who later rebuffed Wagner, were waiting in the house. Goethe had not appeared, and the atmosphere was constrained and expectant. Zelter, who usually affected a careless, workman's way of dressing, now was dressed in a formal, old-fashioned mode—knee-breeches, silk stockings, black patent leather pumps with silver spangles; men had not dressed like that since Mozart's time, but Zelter dressed like that when he was in Goethe's presence. It was his policy not to pay any attention to Felix and so nobody else did, since the others, including some ladies who assembled

[5] Author of *Confidential Letters Written on a Journey to Vienna,* a book which contained much information about Beethoven.

by and by, were unacquainted with his gifts. Felix must have felt forlorn and uncomfortable. However, the company began to make little jokes with him and pet him, and his shyness vanished. Yet Goethe did not appear that afternoon. Only in the evening did he emerge, and for that evening he had invited a sizable company to a musical *soirée*. As he entered, everybody rose.

In his old age he appeared taller than in his youth and held himself more stiffly erect. The brow was smooth and broad, his nose hawklike, his hair not yet quite white. His mouth was young, soft, small, and extremely mobile, but when he smiled one saw that his teeth were crooked and had become yellow. His brown eyes were serious but friendly and his manner free of any trace of self-importance. When he addressed a person he lowered his glance. He usually kept his hands folded behind his back.[6]

Goethe greeted Zelter with great warmth, glanced at Felix, and opened the piano. While the candles were placed, Felix was asked to play. The boy asked Zelter, "What shall I play?" "Well, whatever you can," Zelter replied in a condescending tone. "Something that is not too difficult for you." Rellstab thought this remark in poor taste because Zelter knew perfectly well that there was virtually nothing in the piano literature which Felix had not mastered. After some discussion, it was decided that Felix ought to improvise, and he promply asked his teacher for a theme. Now Zelter purposely mentioned a humdrum, old-fashioned ditty. "I don't know this song," Felix said. "Then I will play it for you." Zelter sat down at the piano and with his stiff fingers played the song, which contained a triplet figure.

Rellstab writes:

Felix first repeated the song, and without reflection—taking the triplet figure *unisono* in both hands, brought his fingers into the track of the main figure, so to speak. . . . But then he plunged without more ado into the wildest *allegro*. The gentle melody was transformed into a surging figure which he took first in the bass, then in the soprano voice, developing it with lovely contrasts—in short, created a torrential fantasia that poured out like liquid fire—Hummel's manner of dealing with such tasks must have been most in his mind. The whole company was thunderstruck; the boy's small

[6]This description is based on a little-known letter which David Veit wrote to Rahel Varnhagen.

hands worked into the masses of tone, mastered the most difficult combinations; the passages rumbled and dropped like so many pearls, flew by in ethereal whispers; a stream of harmonies flowed forth; surprising contrapuntal phrases were built up among them—only the banal melody was rather neglected and scarcely had a voice in this brilliant parliament of musical tones.

Rellstab noticed Felix's remarkable instinct for form: he did not improvise one second longer than he should have. He knew when to stop. A silence fell on the company. Zelter cleared his throat and boomed out, "What gnomes and dragons were you imagining to embark on so wild a ride?" Goethe stood up, quite enraptured, and hugged the boy

in whose childlike features happiness, pride, and embarrassment were limned. Goethe took his head between his hands and gave him rough kindly caresses, saying: "But you will not get away with that alone. You must play more for us before we acknowledge you fully."

Goethe asked for a minuet. Felix said, "There is only one," and played the Minuet from *Don Giovanni*. Now Goethe was curious to hear the Overture to the opera. This Felix firmly refused to play, saying that the music could make no effect on the piano. The Overture to *Figaro*, that was a different matter. Yes, he could play it if Goethe wanted it. Rellstab continues:

He began to play it with a lightness, sureness, roundness and clarity such as I have never heard since. At the same time he reproduced the orchestral effects so excellently, so transparently, and by little touches in the instrumentation produced so cunningly the illusion of accompanying voices, that the effect was utterly enchanting and I might almost say that it gave me more pleasure than any orchestral performance ever did.

Goethe became more and more fascinated. Teasing the boy, he said, "So far you have only played pieces you know. Let us hear whether you can play something you do not know. Wait a minute." He left the room and presently returned carrying some manuscripts. He placed those on the piano. Felix at once recognized the beautiful handwriting as being Mozart's. In great excitement his eyes perused the manuscript. It was a little

Adagio, not very difficult, which he then played with perfect assurance. "Very good," Goethe said. "Now let's see what you can make of this." He placed another sheet of music on the rack. What was this? The manuscript looked as if ink had been sprayed all over it and the notes, when you could make them out, seemed to have been thrown helter-skelter onto the page. Zelter had got up and gone to the piano to look over Felix's shoulder. "Why certainly," he said, "this is written by Beethoven. You can see that a mile away. Beethoven always writes as if he were using a broomstick and as if afterwards he had rubbed his sleeve over the page." With intense concentration Felix tried to make sense out of the chaos. It was one of the Goethe songs set to music by Beethoven. Rellstab, too, stood at the piano, trying to make it out; it was difficult, but finally Felix was able to take in the whole page at one glance. He first played it through tentatively and with mistakes; whereupon he attacked the song for the second time and played it well, at one time interrupting himself to exclaim, "This is pure Beethoven."

The news of the boy's prowess spread through Weimar and all Weimar was eager to hear the young virtuoso. Yet he was still a child; a few days later, attending a function given by the Grand Duchess, he was asked to play after Johann Nepomuk Hummel performed, the famous virtuoso and friend of Haydn and Beethoven. Felix said he could not—and burst into tears.

Such is Rellstab's account of the first meeting between Felix and Goethe. Two musicians, Karl Eberwein and Christian Lobe, respectively concertmaster and flutist of the Weimar orchestra, reported: [7]

> At the beginning of November 1821, four members of the Weimar Court Orchestra were summoned to the house of Privy Councillor von Goethe. We were shown by the servant into the familiar room. Three music desks stood there at the side of an open piano. On the piano lay a bunch of musical manuscripts. Curious as I always was about new music, and still am, I perused the manuscripts and saw one, "Studies in double counterpoint," another marked "Fugues" and a third "Canons." Then a Quartet for piano, violin, viola, and cello. The sheets carried a name: Felix Mendelssohn-Bartholdy, the notes were written in a firm smooth hand, and as

[7] *Goethes Schauspieler und Musiker, Erinnerungen von Eberwein und Lobe.* Dr. Wilhelm Bode, ed. Berlin, 1912.

far as I could tell at first glance, the compositions hinted at an accomplished artist. The name Mendelssohn as a musician was unknown to us.

As we unwrapped our instruments and began to tune, a tall man entered. With his stiff military bearing one could imagine him to have been a former corporal. But I knew him, having visited him the year before in Berlin. It was Professor Zelter, the renowned Director of the Berlin *Singakademie*, the friend of Goethe and his "*du*"-brother . . . "Gentlemen, I preceded the others," he began, "to ask you for a favor. You will make the acquaintance of a twelve-year-old boy, my pupil. It is probable that his ability as a pianist and more, his talent as a composer, will awaken your enthusiasm. The youth has a peculiar nature. The oh's and ah's of the dilettantes do not touch him. But to the judgment of professional musicians he listens avidly and takes it all for coin of the realm. The young rapscallion is as yet unable to distinguish between benevolent encouragement and strict measurement of merit. Therefore, gentlemen, if you are going to sing a song of praise, something which I both wish and fear, do it in moderate tempo. Do not orchestrate your praise too loudly and do it in C Major, the least colorful of the scales. Up to now I have been able to protect him against vanity and conceit, those two God-damned enemies of artistic progress" . . .

A handsome boy of a distinctly Jewish cast bounced into the room. He was slender. His rich black locks cascaded down to his shoulders, his eyes sparkled with spirit and life. For an instant he looked at us curiously and then he shook hands with every one of us in a friendly way. . . . Goethe had entered with Felix. . . . He said, "Let's hear, my child, what your young head has created," and patted the boy's locks.

Goethe listened to what followed with complete attention, without saying much except a "Good!" after one movement and a "Bravo!" after another, and to incline his head as a sign of approval. We remembered Zelter's admonition and we showed our approval to the boy, whose face had become redder and redder, only by our facial expressions. When the last movement had ended, Felix jumped up and gave every one of us a questioning glance. . . . Goethe, no doubt prompted by Zelter, became the spokesman and said, "Very good, my son! The expression of these gentlemen tells you clearly that your music has pleased them. But now go down to the garden and cool off . . . for you are burning like fire." Without a word Felix ran outdoors.

A long conversation now developed. Goethe regretted that we only had had the opportunity to make the boy's acquaintance through one Quartet. He said, "It is true that these days musical prodigies are not such a great rarity, particularly in their technical facility. Yet what this little man is capable of in improvisation and in sight reading borders on the miraculous. I would not have thought it possible in one so young."

Zelter said, "And yet you heard Mozart in Frankfurt when he was seven years old." "Yes," responded Goethe, "but remember I was only twelve years old at the time. Like all the world, I marveled at Mozart's ability. But your pupil—he seems to bear the same relation to the Mozart of that time as adult speech to baby talk" . . . "Ah," remarked Zelter, "many began like Mozart but no one ever reached him." [Zelter obviously disapproved of Goethe's ridiculously exaggerated statement.]

Felix wrote home that Goethe was kindness itself, that he showed him his collections of minerals, engravings, fossils, statues, and the other things that a boy might want to see. "Just think, every morning I receive a kiss from the author of *Faust* and *Werther* and every afternoon two kisses from my fatherly friend, Goethe." He had to play for him almost every afternoon. Goethe would say, "I haven't heard you yet today. Make a little noise for me." In the evening, whist was occasionally played and Zelter told Felix, "Whist means keep your mouth shut." That must have been hard for the excited boy to do.

Goethe was clearly enraptured by Felix, who brought youth, impetuosity, talent, and, with all his hero-worship, a certain insouciant independence to the poet's house. He stirred the air in a room where the atmosphere was now often all too hushed. When Zelter wanted to leave for Jena, as was his original plan, Goethe became very angry. He shouted, wrote Felix, "like ten thousand warriors." He absolutely refused to let them go, the upshot of which was that they stayed for sixteen days. It is characteristic of Mendelssohn that he had brought along a few songs which Fanny had composed. He showed them to Goethe and Goethe thanked Fanny by sending her a poem which, though hardly one of his masterpieces, must have delighted the girl beyond measure.

Felix saw Goethe again. He visited him next the year after, with Fanny and his parents, in the course of a journey the whole family took to Switzerland. Goethe talked privately to Abraham about Felix. He said that after Felix had left he lost interest in music and the piano remained closed. Would Felix come again soon and play David to his Saul?

The meetings with Goethe made an indelible impression on Felix, not only because the boy had the opportunity to gaze at the enshrined idol of his people, but because he came in contact with characteristics of the poet which were echoed in Mendelssohn's own artistic constitution as it developed in the years following: these were the classicism of Goethe's view, his sense of form, the aristocracy of his expression, and the largeness of his intellectual interests. Mendelssohn's first successful composition, the *Octet*, was inspired by some lines from *Faust*, and the Overture "Calm Sea and Prosperous Voyage" by Goethe's poem. He read Goethe all his life and he corresponded with him until the poet's death in 1832.

And Goethe's feeling for Felix? These days it would be fashionable, not to say mandatory, to place a psychoanalytical interpretation on the affection shown by the disciplined and distant genius for the handsome twelve-year-old boy, and to speak of submerged tendencies. Was a stirring involved, akin to Aschenbach's emotion in Thomas Mann's *Death in Venice?* Extremely improbable in a man so strongly masculine as Goethe was! He had just proposed marriage to the young Ulrike von Levetzow, and he was now gazing into the dark eyes of the beautiful Maria Szymanowska, a Weimar pianist of whom Felix realistically reported that "they confuse her unpretty playing with her pretty face." It is more probable that Felix revived in him the feelings Goethe once sensed for his own son August as a little child. Later Goethe withdrew from his son in deep disappointment, and August, drifting like the typical son of a great man, died a drunkard's death. However self-sufficient Goethe may have been, his son's fate must have left a gap. Felix filled it, at least temporarily. When Felix wrote home that Goethe acted like a father to him, we may believe him. At any rate, we need no help from psychoanalysis to conjecture that Goethe was drawn to this talent-in-the-bud because he recognized and responded to talent in whatever form, and that he loved the boy because Felix went out to him in trust and openness and communication unfogged by the fear of fame.

4

As one reads the Zelter-Goethe correspondence in chronological order, one can review a miniature panorama of the young Mendelssohn's progress. The letters reveal Zelter's joy and Goethe's satisfaction. Here are a few brief samples from the letters:

Zelter to Goethe

Berlin, November 5, 1825

. . . Felix is good and industrious. His third opera is completed and written down and will soon be given among friends. After his return from Weimar, he finished a Gloria, half a piano concerto for his sister, and he began a Magnificat. Even if I myself am unable to create anything decent, I have the satisfaction of my disciples. There are a dozen who give me pleasure.

Zelter to Goethe

February 3, 1823

. . . My Felix has begun his fifteenth year. He is growing under my very eyes. I take his marvelous piano playing for granted. It is possible that he will master the violin as well. . . . Everything [he composes] comes from the inside. What is superficial in our times touches him only superficially. Just imagine my joy if we both live to see the boy growing up and fulfilling what in his innocence he promises. . . .

Zelter to Goethe

Berlin, December 10, 1824

Felix is still on top of the world. His industry is the result of good training. His sister Fanny has composed her thirty-second fugue. . . . When they accomplish something, they are as proud as if they had conquered Mexico. They love me, just as I am. They hover around me like bees around flowers.

Zelter to Goethe

Berlin, November 5, 1825

My Felix continues to work. He has just finished an Octet which really makes sense. In addition, he gave his teacher Heyse a few weeks ago a most charming gift: without saying anything to anybody, he translated Terence's comedy, *The Girl of Andros*, into metric [German] verse. I am told the translation is very good, though I have not seen it yet. He plays the piano like the very devil and he is not so bad either when he plays a string instrument. In addition, he is healthy, strong, and a good swimmer, even upstream. In the newspaper his quartets and symphonies have been somewhat coldly criticized. That is not going to hurt him. That kind of critic is a nit-wit who cannot find his hat when it is on his head. Only if one were unable to remember how Gluck's and Mozart's pieces were judged forty years ago would one be inconsolable.

Zelter to Goethe

February 20, 1827

. . . His last opera . . . is lying at the *Königliches Theater* for more than a year and has not managed to come to light, while French slop and swill are put on the stage and the stuff hardly lasts till a second performance. Since we are young and enjoy advantages for which another has to slave half his life, the damage is not so terrible. . . .

Zelter to Goethe

March 9, 1829

. . . You will have read in the newspaper that we are going to perform the Passion of J. S. Bach. Felix has practiced the music under my tutelage [8] and he will conduct, while I cede my podium to him. I'll send you the text soon, for which I have written a foreword. Moscheles has invited Felix to London and from there he may go to Italy. The boy is my consolation. It is good that he is getting away from the parental home. . . .

[8] A slight exaggeration!

Zelter to Goethe

March 12, 1829

Yesterday [March 11] Bach's music was given a fortunate performance. Felix turned out to be an exigent but calm conductor. The King and the whole court witnessed a sold-out house. I hid myself with the score in a corner, from where I could observe both the public and my young charges. . . .

Goethe to Zelter

Weimar, November 9, 1829

. . . Now I wish to learn whether you have received favorable news from Felix. I take the greatest interest in him. It is frightening that so valuable a person should be hindered in his activity by a pernicious incident [an accident which happened in London]. . . .

Zelter to Goethe

Berlin, May 10, 1830

Felix was going to start his journey any day and bring a letter to you. Friday at my house he played a concerto of old Bach and he played like a master; the concerto is as difficult as it is beautiful. I wish old Bach himself could have heard it. I can't wait for the time for him to get out of the miserable shallow swamp of Berlin and get to Italy, where he should have gone long ago, in my opinion. There the very stones have ears—here the people eat pigs' ears served with lentils. . . .

Goethe to Zelter

Weimar, June 3, 1830

Just now, half-past nine on a morning of beautiful sunshine and clearest sky, Felix departed with Ottilie, Ulrike and the children. He spent fourteen delightful days with us and charmed everybody with his endearing art. He is going to Jena, to the benefit of his good friends there. He left with us a memory which will be forever treasurable. His presence was especially beneficent to me. My relationship to music is still the same: I listen to it with pleasure, with participation and with thoughtfulness [but] chiefly I am fond of the historical viewpoint. For how can we understand any apparition unless we can observe it on its journey toward us? Felix too understands this desire to walk step by step; fortunately his excellent memory allows him to draw forth examples at will. Beginning with Bach and his epoch, he brought to me living accounts of Haydn, Mozart and Gluck. He gave me a sufficient idea of the modern technicians [9] and finally he made me feel and think about his own creations. Therefore he departed with my best blessings. . . .

Zelter to Goethe

Berlin, November 2, 1830

By this time Felix is probably in Rome. I am very glad he is, because his mother was always against Italy. I feared he would be reduced to a jelly here in this country and in the midst of all the flatulent family gossip. . . .

Goethe to Zelter

Weimar, June 28, 1831

. . . A word about our Felix. The Herr Papa is absolutely wrong not to let him go to Sicily. Why should he long for something unnecessarily? . . .

[Felix longed to go to Sicily. Abraham thought Sicily, infested by bandits, not a proper place for a young man to visit. Goethe and Zelter tried to change Abraham's decision. He wouldn't.]

5

There was no gradual development. He went in one door as a gifted child and came out the other door as a master. The transformation seems to have been accomplished by legerdemain, like changing the two of clubs into a living rose. His Piano Quartet Op. 1, composed when he was twelve, "is still undistinguished, and the finale is built on a single, rather dull theme." Of the Sextet in D, composed when he was fifteen, Radcliffe says: "The first movement contains some pleasant ideas, but they are usually drowned in a flood of conventionally brilliant bravura work, and the finale, with its polka-like rhythms, is still more vapid." In the same year he com-

---

[9] No doubt he counted Beethoven among the "modern technicians." Mendelssohn played him the first movement of the Fifth Symphony on the piano. Even on the piano it was too much for Goethe. He said, "It is tremendous but quite mad. The whole house might collapse—imagine a whole orchestra playing it."

posed what he designated as his First Symphony, Op. 11. Actually it was preceded by no fewer than twelve little symphonies which he never published. Symphony No. 1 is nimble and fluent, and in its slow movement he does give us a taste of those mild songs which are characteristic of Mendelssohn. Yet on the whole the symphony is the work of somebody who has recently learned his lesson from Weber and Mozart. A few months later—no more than that—and along comes the Octet Op. 20, fresh, individual, charming in form and content, as easy to like as a painting by Vermeer, one of his finest compositions and one of the indispensable works of all chamber music. It is treated as an heirloom whenever a few string players get together. It is completely assured Mendelssohn. Of the famous Scherzo of the *Octet* Fanny wrote:

> The entire movement is to be performed *staccato* and *pianissimo:* the isolated, spasmodic tremolandos, the lightning flash of trills, all is new, strange, and yet so ingratiating and pleasing—one feels so close to the world of spirits, so lightly carried up into the air, indeed, one might even seize a broomstick so as to follow the airy procession with more alacrity. At the end, the first violin soars feather-like aloft—"Then all must quickly fly."

That last phrase is a reference to Goethe's *Walpurgisnacht,* the source of Mendelssohn's inspiration:

> *Wolkenflug und Nebelflor*
> Train of clouds and flow'ring mist
> *Erhellen sich von oben,*
> Illuminate the sky;
> *Luft im Laub und Wind im Rohr*
> Reeds and leaves by wind are kist,
> *Und Alles ist zerstoben.*
> Then all must quickly fly.

Now he is seventeen. In July he writes to Fanny, who is away from home, that he has become accustomed to composing in the garden and there "today or tomorrow he'll start to dream *midsummer nights dream* [sic, in English]. I have a lot of nerve!"

The Overture to which he owes much of his fame was supposed to have been written in a single flow of nocturnal inspiration, and it is true that the score does not show any extensive corrections or alterations. Yet one must doubt the story of its creation with one stroke of the pen: there is no reason to disbelieve Marx when he says that he suggested extensive rewriting and Felix, after first being provoked and hurt and running away from him, came back to tell him that he was right and that he would follow his advice.

Taking the composer himself at his word, if he did begin the day after he said he would, then that date would have been July 8 or 9. The manuscript bears August 6 as the date of completion. The Overture then was composed in a month—and by a seventeen-year-old boy; familiar though it has become, it remains an utterly astonishing achievement.

What new is there to say about this music set in a forest of Athens as unreal as the Forest of Arden? We know that Felix began to read Shakespeare early and read him both in English and German, in the new translations which were then making their appearance. After all, Schlegel was a relative, having come into the family by way of his aunt Dorothea. We can guess that Goethe talked with Felix about Shakespeare. The poet not only knew Shakespeare intimately, but he had absorbed the plays so thoroughly in his artistic consciousness that occasionally scenes or speeches emerge in Goethe's plays which are almost exact Shakespearean quotations. Ophelia's song is sung in *Faust; Götz von Berlichingen,* an early work, starts with a brawl of secondary characters modeled on *Romeo and Juliet;* in the crowd scenes of *Egmont* there are similarities to speeches in *Julius Caesar,* sometimes almost word for word.

What is extraordinary about the Overture is that it so adroitly presages and expresses the play: it does "awake the pert and nimble spirit of mirth"; it seems to sound "in grove or green, By fountain clear, or spangled starlight sheen." . . . But we shall postpone further comments to the story of the *Incidental Music.*

The year following the completion of the Overture to *A Midsummer Night's Dream,* Mendelssohn was ready with the first opera he destined for professional performance. He had been working on it since he was sixteen. It was called *The Wedding of Camacho* and was based on an episode in *Don Quixote*. It is a lively and pleasant little work, though not very different from a dozen others of the Auber-Lortzing variety. He had to submit it to Gasparo Spontini, King Frederick William III's Kapellmeister and general director of music in Berlin. Supported by the King—who liked any music as long as it was French or Italian Grand Opera—Spontini's sway in the Prussian capital was absolute, and he himself was a jealous man, having no use for Weber or any of the other young German composers. In Mendelssohn's biography he plays the role of an incidental villain because he lectured Felix on his little opera as not being "important" and managed to postpone production for more than a year. It is just possible, of course, that the composer of *La Vestale*, an "important" opera, honestly did not like the slight work or its libretto by Klingemann. The Mendelssohn family had enough influence to order the production of the opera, no mean feat of string-pulling. Spontini waved his lorgnette and gave in. Understandably, he never after felt kindly toward the Mendelssohns. Years later he wrote to Richard Wagner: "Believe me, there was hope for German music as long as I was the Sovereign of Berlin's musical life. Now that the Prussian King [Frederick William IV] has delivered his music to the confusion created by the two Wandering Jews [the other was Meyerbeer, Spontini's successor] whom he summoned, all hope is lost."

Spontini's doubts about *The Wedding of Camacho* were justified by the première. The house was filled with friends of the family and the applause after the first act was encouraging. But during the second act the audience got bored and became restless. Even the friends began questioning whether this opera was good enough for a Berlin theater. Would it not have been more prudent to confine it to the family circle? Felix, sensing a failure, fled from the opera house before the final curtain fell; Devrient had to appear in his place. After the performance, the interpreter of the role of Don Quixote fell ill, and before he could recover the work was shelved. Felix did not press for a second performance. He was enraged by an unfavorable review which appeared in a Berlin paper. Before he could get over the smart, he himself began to feel detached from the opera; he had outgrown it. The work was never again performed anywhere.[10] Yet there lingered in him a resentment against Berlin.

[10] Except, surprisingly, in one performance in Boston in 1885.

It was the arena of his first failure, experienced when he was eighteen. He could not, then or later, take a failure lightly. In his mind one failure sounded louder than a dozen fanfares of success.

6

The year after Felix's first meeting with Goethe, the whole family decided to make an excursion to Switzerland, to show the thirteen-year-old boy the beauty of the mountains. They started off in a number of carriages, a caravan of a group of servants, the house teacher—for of course Felix had to take lessons even while on vacation—three other teachers, all the children. In the excitement of beginning the journey, Felix was left behind in Potsdam, which was the first stop. Everybody thought he was in some-body else's carriage. A few miles after, they realized with a great shock that there was no Felix. Heyse borrowed a horse and galloped back to Potsdam. After an hour Heyse saw him with a stick in his hand, calmly walking along on the main road, dusty but quite self-possessed. The boy had struck up an acquaintance with a peasant girl and had decided to walk toward the next stop in company with her.

The family's pilgrimage took them to Cassel, where they met the composer Ludwig Spohr, and to Frankfurt, where they became acquainted with another prodigy, Ferdinand Hiller, two years younger than Felix. Hiller was a pupil of Johann Nepomuk Hummel, and with his teacher visited Beethoven in 1827, to write the heartbreaking story of Beethoven's last days. Hiller became a famous conductor and one of the most vital figures of the romantic movement; he was friend and confidant of Schumann, Rossini, Chopin, Meyerbeer, Berlioz, Liszt—in fact, all the musical stars. In his Memoirs he remembers the first meeting with Mendelssohn: he was even more impressed with Fanny's piano virtuosity than with Felix's. From Frankfurt the Mendelssohns traveled south through Switzerland as far as Chamounix—Felix's lifelong love for Switzerland dates from this first experience—and on the return journey stopped off at Weimar.

More important than this and other small journeys was an expedition to Paris. For Abraham it was a business trip; for Felix, just turned sixteen, it was to prove decisive. Abraham was still not sure that his son should become a professional musician. He had seen too much of the struggle of the Berlin aspirants who came to his house, sometimes glad to get a meal, and he had observed too many of the chicaneries with which one tried to nudge the other away from the starting post, not to know that only the exceedingly talented—or the egregious charlatans—could succeed. Did his son possess enough talent? He wanted to be quite sure. He decided to consult one of the supreme authorities, a man equally admired for his genius and his vast musical knowledge, Maria Luigi Carlo Zenobio Salvatore Cherubini, author of sixteen Masses, Professor of Composition at the *Conservatoire,* composer of *Les deux journées* and *Medée.* With this in mind, Abraham took Felix to Paris.

Even before he was examined by Cherubini, he had the opportunity of meeting a number of French and foreign celebrities gathered in the French capital.

His Parisian impressions, as detailed to Fanny in several letters, show Felix's less attractive side. He must have gone to Paris carrying in his young head the typical German conviction that French culture was not serious, that frivolity and superficiality reigned, that these sparkling people lacked the *Innigkeit* on which the Germans pride themselves. As most travelers take from a foreign country what they have brought into it, so Felix misunderstood a way of thinking different from what he was used to. His remarks on the famous musicians he met smack of a young boy's know-it-allness. Of Rossini he writes: "I was introduced to the famous Rossini. He pulled a sly face, a mixture of roguishness, boredom, and weariness. He went to the piano and played Mozart's '*Ave Verum,*' which happens to be in fashion. As a scholarly composer, he wished to modulate all dissonances . . . for the benefit and profit of all listeners, or rather, *non*-listeners. . . . There you have the great Maestro Windbag." (April 6, 1825)

A decade later, when Felix was less green in judgment, he understood that behind Rossini's façade of "boredom and weariness" lay a genius. To his mother and sister Rebecka he wrote from Frankfurt on July 14, 1836:

> Early yesterday I went to see him [Ferdinand Hiller], and whom should I find sitting there? Rossini, big, fat, and in the sunniest frame of mind. I really know few men who can be so amusing and witty as he, when he chooses; he kept us laughing the whole time. . . . Intellect,

animation and wit sparkle in all his features and in every word, and whoever does not consider him a genius ought to hear him expatiating in this
way, in order to change his opinion.

Of Franz Liszt, then only fourteen years old, whom Felix heard in
Paris, he said, "He has many fingers but few brains, and his improvisations
are miserable." Again he was to change his mind later.

He writes to Fanny, "You tell me that I should play the role of
proselytizer and teach Onslow [French composer and later Cherubini's
successor at the *Conservatoire*] and Reicha how to learn to love Beethoven
and Sebastian Bach. Well, I will do my best. But, my darling, remember
that the people here don't know a single note of *Fidelio!* That they think
of Bach as a wig stuffed with scholarliness."

That is the presumption of a talented and pampered youngster. Anton
Reicha was a pupil of Haydn and Albrechtsberger, a friend of Beethoven
(the one who gave Baron de Trémont a letter of introduction to Beethoven)
and it is of course impossible that he did not know Beethoven's compositions
well or that he was ignorant of *Fidelio*. Mendelssohn continues in the same
letter: "Recently I played at the request of Kalkbrenner Bach's Organ
Preludes [in E-minor and A-minor]. The people thought they were very
'charming' and somebody remarked that the beginning of the A-minor
Prelude bore a remarkable resemblance to a popular duet from an opera by
Monsigny. I saw red." Kalkbrenner, though a snob who pretended to be
of noble birth—Heine said of him that he looked as if "he had been . . .
turned out by a confectioner, his speech almost but not quite concealing
Berlinisms of the lowest order" [11]—was nevertheless a serious and knowl-
edgeable musician, and it is inconceivable that he did not appreciate the Bach
Preludes. Even Fanny did not accept her brother's general condemnation
of French conditions, whereupon Felix rather testily replied, "Are you the
one who is in Paris, or am I?"

Now, at sixty-five, Cherubini was as imposing a figure in real life as
his friend Ingres had painted him in imagination, the Muse of Music hover-
ing over his head, ready with the laurel wreath. He was Sir Oracle, and

---

[11] Chopin, Liszt, Hiller, and Mendelssohn once played a trick on him: they dressed themselves as ragged beggars and accosted Kalkbrenner in a fashionable café, greeting him affectionately and mortifying the poor fellow beyond speech.

when he oped his lips, let no dog bark. Certainly no dog in Paris. He made Berlioz's life miserable. In his memoirs Berlioz never wearies of scoffing at Cherubini's pedantry and his French spoken with a spaghetti accent; Berlioz assures his readers that "if he chastised me with whips I gave him a few scorpions in return whose sting he had cause to remember." The ogre, however, was a superb musician; even Beethoven respected him.

Felix must have looked forward to the meeting with a mixture of trepidation and eagerness. He was writing to his sisters several anecdotes designed to show how difficult the man was: how Cherubini was auditioning a young composer and at the end of the session Cherubini asked, "Is it possible that you have a talent for painting?" and how the best one could hope to get out of Cherubini was silence. Felix chose his Piano Quartet in B-minor, Opus 3, as a sample of his ability. Cherubini listened carefully—in spite, wrote Felix, of a very bad performance—smiled, got up, went over to Felix, and nodded his head. Then he said to the others present, "This boy is wealthy. He will do well; he has already done well. But he is spending too much money and he uses too much material for his clothes." The remark was obviously meant metaphorically. Whatever it meant, everybody was astonished. Cherubini approved: nothing like it had ever happened before.

All the same, Felix described Cherubini as "an extinct volcano still throwing out occasional sparks and flashes but now almost entirely covered by ashes and slag." However, in later years he frequently performed Cherubini's music, partly perhaps out of gratitude and partly because Cherubini's classic style appealed to him.

At any rate, now Abraham was sure.

7

The St. Matthew Passion

One of the commonplaces of musical history is the statement that Johann Sebastian Bach had sunk into the ocean of oblivion a half-century after his death, that few people knew who he was, that some of those who did know considered him a powdered wig stuffed with learning, that others thought him to have been a great teacher but a dull composer, and that in short his spirit no longer walked the world of music—until Mendelssohn called him from the vasty deep. All this makes for good storytelling, but truth compels some modification of it.

Bach was never entirely forgotten. His smaller church works, though too difficult for use in the ordinary Protestant service, were much admired by theologians. Serious pianists, such as Moscheles or Czerny, were playing this or that composition of his in their better concerts. We know of a chamber group in Vienna which presented several if not all of the Brandenburg Concertos in public performances. Every organist worthy of his calling knew and played Bach's organ works. Zelter's *Singakademie* intoned some of his Motets at the Friday morning meetings. The young Beethoven played Bach fugues for Baron van Swieten in the quiet hours of the night. "Old Sebastian," as many musicians called Bach affectionately, though perhaps a little condescendingly, had never ceased to be a force. The works which could be performed by soloists or small groups, the "practical" works, were known to many and appreciated by many.

It was his larger works which were unknown, and by this lack Bach's stature could not be justly measured nor the extent of his contribution surveyed. The unknown Bach was the Bach of the *St. Matthew Passion*, the *St. John Passion*, the *B-Minor Mass*, the *Christmas Oratorio*. These works were unknown not because they were beyond the public's ability to understand and appreciate but because the music was not accessible to concert organizations, the manuscripts or copies of them lying in libraries, abbeys, museums, or other receptacles of dead storage. Only a few bespectacled scholars knew of their existence. Not one of Bach's works, except the *Musikalische Opfer*, was printed between 1750, the year of his death, and 1800.[12]

In 1802, however, the first biography of the Leipzig cantor appeared, written by Johann Forkel. E. T. A. Hoffmann, that romantic spinner of strange tales and a composer as well, who early recognized Beethoven's genius, now issued a panegyric on the older "genius of all mankind." Because Hoffmann was one of Germany's most popular authors and a spokesman for the early romantic movement, people took notice. Other musicians, including Weber, chimed in. The climate was propitious for a "Bach

---

[12] Under Carl Philipp Emanuel Bach's sponsorship, an edition of his father's *Art of the Fugue* was published on 1756. Johann Sebastian himself had prepared the edition. Only thirty copies were sold, discouraging further attempts to publish Bach's work. To publish the large works was, of course, a very expensive undertaking.

revival." Yet between climate and actuality a gap remained. Who could grapple with these enormous works, with their double choruses and double fugues, their depth of expression, the large casts required, the rehearsals necessary to turn a lost tradition into living sound? The tradition had been lost for a long time. Discussing Bach, Leopold Mozart wrote, "With the old music one arrives at the most diverse meanings: everything is in a great muddle."

Zelter was one of the most active of the scholars who searched for Bach manuscripts in likely and unlikely places and, having found them, shut himself off in his library and gloated with delight. Abraham Mendelssohn gave Zelter quite a few original manuscripts of Bach Cantatas as a gift. Zelter would lock up his collection in a large commode; standing before it he would exclaim mysteriously, "What treasures are hidden here!" but would refuse to specify. Even Felix had difficulty gaining access to these valuables. Other collectors gave Zelter competition, chief among them one Georg Poelchau (1773–1836), the most successful of the Bach collectors of the early nineteenth century.

Even before the "rediscovery" of the *St. Matthew Passion*, its publication was being contemplated. Adolf Bernhard Marx, that strong scholar and weak composer, told the story:

> As a matter of course I spoke to one and all who would listen to me about the new spiritual experience which I had undergone. I had no definite purpose in mind—I simply couldn't help myself. That is how old Schlesinger heard about the work. He asked who was the publisher. It was never published. He asked is this music really so extraordinary, and do I have a score. I was able to answer yes to both questions. "Then I will publish it," he exclaimed, and at once the printing of the full score and of the piano score was decided. But his associates were of a different opinion and they tried to throttle the project. A lunch at the firm was arranged for the purpose of putting a formal question to me: "Did I think that one could 'do something' with this work." All the guests were renowned musicians and they eagerly waited for my answer. There was a general silence while I declared, quite calmly, that I had no idea whether or not one could derive a profit from this publication. I only knew that the work was the greatest example of church music. "And I will publish it," exclaimed the old gentleman, with his lion voice, and he banged the table. "Even if it were to

cost me 3,000 thaler I would do it for the prestige of our firm." The *Passion* was published—and it even brought the firm material advantages.[13]

In short, Bach was by no means the forgotten man which sentimental history pictures him to be. Yet his fame smelled of the lamp. His works were considered by many as bizarre and "bristly" (an appellation often applied to him), and even Zelter felt it incumbent on him to simplify some of the Motets or Chorales when he performed them at the *Singakademie*.

Zelter owned what he thought was the manuscript of the *St. Matthew Passion*, but what was actually only a fairly faithful copy. He guarded this like Fafner. How did it come into Felix's possession?

Here I must destroy two favorite musical anecdotes. The first of these is that Zelter had bought the manuscript from a merchant who had used the pages to wrap cheese in. Devrient is the author of the story, repeated innumerable times after him. It is wholly untrue. The Bach manuscript (as well as one or two copies) had been carefully preserved and catalogued, and we know its provenance. No cheese dealer had made free with it. In 1828 the existence of the work was well enough known for two publishers to consider publication, one of them being Johann Anton André in Offenbach, who questioned Georg Poelchau about it. There was no mystery about it; it was merely unpublished and not easily available.

The second beloved anecdote concerns Felix's possession of Zelter's copy of the manuscript. According to the story as it is usually told, Felix's grandmother, Babette Salomon, wanted to give him as an appropriate Christmas present a manuscript of music unknown to Felix. The old lady was musically highly educated, she and her sister Sarah having been favorite pupils of Friedemann Bach. She knew about the *St. Matthew* and asked Zelter for a copy of it. Zelter refused. Nothing daunted, Babette applied pressure, pointed out that the Mendelssohns were contributors to the *Singakademie* and he had better cooperate; she finally wheedled the copy from the unwilling Harpagon. Well, Grandmother did give Felix the work for Christmas 1823, when Felix was fourteen years old. But the score from which he conducted—it has recently come to light in England (now in the Bodleian) and contains Felix's notations—indicates that it was not Zelter's copy he possessed but Poelchau's. As Martin Geck says in his fine

[13] In *Erinnerungen*, Berlin, 1865.

monograph,[14] this is all the more probable because Poelchau was a friend of the Salomons and was often invited to their house. "Hardly a doubt exists" that the score from which he conducted was the one "which Mendelssohn received as a present from his grandmother"—that is, Poelchau's copy. Zelter did not refuse; he wasn't asked.

Whatever the origin of the text, Felix delved into it and so immersed himself in this music that it became part of his musical self. He "lived" with it for four years. During the winter of 1827 or 1828—Felix was eighteen or nineteen then—a small group of amateur singers met in his home; burning with enthusiasm, Felix led them through some of the numbers. Devrient took part in these home-grown performances. His wife, Therese, wrote:[15]

> His mother [Lea] sent invitations to about twelve musical persons, the sisters copied the voice parts and so we could begin in a modest way but with serious intent. Felix sat down at the piano. He was pale and excited. We, the singers, stood around him, so that he could at all times look at us and help us out. That was very necessary, for things went miserably. Not only did we experience difficulty in singing this music by reading it from the notes, but both the notes and the text were written so illegibly that it was almost impossible to make sense out of them. And yet, we were terribly moved and felt that we had been transported into a new world of music.

This happened, according to Therese, in October of 1828. Devrient was not only overwhelmed by the beauty of the music, but he perceived how fine a part the role of Jesus was for a singing actor. In January, 1829, he took part, again in Mendelssohn's house, in a complete performance of the first section. He went home that night in great agitation. Was it possible to give a public performance of this work? Was it feasible to bring this mammoth creation, now exactly a hundred years old, before a Berlin audience, to resuscitate it after a century-long slumber? Was it mad to present "a whole evening of Bach [16] and nothing but Bach, who had a reputation for being unmelodic, calculating, dry and incomprehensible"? "Even Felix's parents could not hide their doubts; Marx was extremely dubious and the academicians shook their heads. Felix thought the undertaking impossible . . . and answered all suggestions with irony and jokes."

[14] *Die Wiederentdeckung der Matthäuspassion im 19. Jahrhundert*, Regensburg, 1967.
[15] Therese Devrient, *Erinnerungen*, Stuttgart, 1905.
[16] The *St. Matthew Passion* is approximately 3 hours 17 minutes long.

That night in January Devrient slept little. Impatiently he waited for the break of day and hurried over to the Mendelssohn house.

Felix was still asleep, but his brother Paul thought it was time to wake him and began that complicated operation. He grabbed him under the arms, shook him violently, shouted, until finally Felix blinked his eyes and, astonished to see Devrient, said, "What are you doing here so early?" Devrient told him that he had something important to discuss with him but not until after breakfast. Felix breakfasted with his usual voracious appetite, and presently Devrient, in ill-suppressed excitement, blurted out that he had come to the decision during the night that the *St. Matthew Passion* must be performed in the *Singakademie*. Felix laughed. "Who will conduct?" "You." "The devil you say!" "Now don't fob me off again with your bad jokes. I have reasoned the whole thing out." "Well, you are very solemn. Let's hear." [17]

Devrient then argued that the *St. Matthew Passion* was the greatest and most important "monument of German music." It was their artistic duty to bring it to life. There was nobody around who understood the score as well as Felix. Only he could do it; he had to do it.

Devrient further argued that the *Singakademie* owed him, Devrient, a favor; since he had worked for it for some years, they could not now refuse him something on which his heart was set. Felix replied, "You are right. And of course I love your plan for both of us to undertake this great venture. But it will come to naught because of Zelter's objections. He thinks that a performance of the *Passion* is impossible—because he has not dared to tackle the music up to now. Much as he admires Bach, he believes this work as a whole indigestible."

Devrient himself thought better of Zelter's artistic sense. However, if need be, he was prepared to go over Zelter's head and appeal to the Trustees. Felix would not hear of that, and the two friends argued back and forth. They determined to call on Zelter in his office. Before they entered Felix said, "Listen. If he starts to get nasty, I'll go away. I can't stand bickering with him." Devrient answered, "He certainly will get nasty. But leave the bickering to me."

The old giant was sitting there wrapped in a cloud of dark smoke, with a long pipe in his mouth. The swan quill which he still used for writing

[17] This account is based on Devrient's memoirs, though given in an abbreviated form.

was in his right hand and a sheet of note paper was in front of him. He looked at the two over his spectacles and said, "Well, well! Two such handsome young people so. early in the morning! To what do I owe the honor?"

Now the two exposed their plan. Zelter was more than dubious. The work needed greater executant skill than could be mustered nowadays. It needed the kind of flexible choruses which Bach had trained at the Thomas School. It needed a double orchestra, with expert string players who would know how to phrase the music. It needed a willingness of all forces to devote themselves to arduous rehearsals. If any of these elements had been available, then all four *Passions* of Bach would have been performed long ago.

While Zelter talked, he became excited and marched up and down the room.

The two friends trotted out counter-arguments, flattering the old man by saying that the *Singakademie* was so excellently trained by him that the chorus would be able to master their parts. And as for the role of Jesus, he, Devrient, was burning to enact the part. Surely both of them could transmit their enthusiasm to all who were to help with this glorous undertaking. They had tried out the parts of the *St. Matthew* privately and knew what an effect it could create; nor was the work as difficult as all that. Because Zelter was accustomed to having his word accepted as final, and now it was not, he became more and more angry—"Experienced people have given up the task and now two snotnoses behave as if the whole thing were child's play"—and the two friends edged toward the door, Felix pale, with his hand on the doorknob. Yet suddenly there was a break in the clouds. In a softer voice Zelter said, "How are you going to do it? The Trustees have to consent and you will never get agreement. Don't forget there are those women Trustees. They'll think it is much too much work. Those women! Ten come to a rehearsal today and tomorrow twenty stay away." It was an old standard joke of his; it showed them that they had softened him up.

Felix now went into the practical details of procedure, scheduling, and casts. Finally Zelter said, "In God's name, all right! I can't fight you. Let's see what you can do."

They had called on Zelter dressed formally, Felix in a blue jacket and wearing gloves. Felix had been temporarily short of money and had borrowed from Devrient the trifling sum necessary to buy a fresh pair of yellow gloves. When they returned to Mendelssohn's home to report the news, Abraham was overjoyed but Lea was annoyed that Felix had borrowed money. He could perfectly well have called on Zelter without gloves.[18]

Such, in substance, is Devrient's account. He does not explain adequately why Zelter, the champion of Bach, at first opposed the project. Surely it was not mere contrariness. He may have thought that a twenty-year-old, however gifted, could hardly stand on the podium and command the multiple forces to be employed. Would he falter, disgrace his teacher? And would Zelter then be blamed for letting the *Singakademie* in for an embarrassing failure? Even if Felix did well, would an audience used to a bald and bearded *Hofkapellmeister* accept a stripling? Zelter knew that most of the *Herren Professoren* of the Royal Berlin Orchestra were against Mendelssohn as being a rich man's son and an "amateur" who did not have to earn his living by music. There, in the animosity of the professionals, lay Zelter's severest doubt. Devrient does not mention it, but the facts are clear. Nevertheless, Zelter decided to chance the project. He had courage.

Now Felix and Devrient sprang into action. It was decided to give the concert as a benefit for the "Sewing School for Indigent Girls." (A typical charity of the Industrial Age!) Felix was, of course, to receive no remuneration. As it turned out, the Mendelssohns had in the end to pay for the hire of the hall—fifty thalers (about $450 in today's equivalent). The two friends decided on the soloists and called on each personally. The soprano was Anna Milder-Hauptmann, of whom Haydn had said that she "had a voice like a house," and who had been Beethoven's first Leonore. Mendelssohn had known her since she appeared in a concert in which he performed a concerto. That was seven years previously: then he was a *"Wunderkind,"* now he faced her as conductor and organizer. His feat as an organizer was at least as remarkable as his artistic accomplishment. He imbued one and all with his enthusiasm, enlisted one and all in hours of work, watched over every interpretive detail, and did it all with the air of a man who had done that sort of thing for years. The women of the

---

[18] Devrient relates the glove incident as occurring when the two called on the soloists. It should probably be ascribed to the call on Zelter. Felix was always carefully dressed when he visited his teacher.

Singakademie did not come one day and stay away the next: they came every day and more came than the rehearsal room could hold and for whom parts had been copied. The rehearsals were soon transferred to the large hall. The chorus finally numbered 158 (not three or four hundred, as is usually stated in the musical histories).

The orchestra was constituted of members of the *Philharmonische Verein*, an amateur organization, but the section leaders were drawn from the Royal Orchestra. Eduard Rietz and Ferdinand David—then a young man of nineteen and later a famous violin virtuoso and teacher of Joachim [19] —functioned as concertmasters of the double orchestra. If any animosity remained in the minds of these musicians, it disappeared after the first rehearsals. Though in the beginning Zelter kept an anxious eye on the proceedings, he relaxed and decided by and by to withdraw and let the pupil have his way; he took a seat in the hall and smiled contentedly. Mendelssohn now for the first time used a baton, a practice by no means usual.[20] Since there was a tradition at the *Singakademie* that the leader was not to turn his back to the public, Mendelssohn stood at a right angle in front of a diagonally placed piano, turning his head as necessary, his eyes flashing the cues. He conducted without a score, knowing the music by heart.[21] There were nine full-scale rehearsals.

The rumor of what was going on spread through musical Berlin. Musicians and music lovers asked to be admitted to the rehearsals. People sat and marveled. The newspapers began to discuss the work. Before and after the performance, the *Berliner Allgemeine Musikalische Zeitung,* Marx's publication, published five analytical essays, pages and pages long, which in addition to enthusiastic elucidation contained philosophical implications of such a nature as would have astonished Bach himself. The Germans must have philosophy dished up with their music, and Marx knew how to dish it. At any rate, it was a "promotion campaign" of great strength, and it achieved its purpose. The Mendelssohn family and Felix himself saw to it that the "right" people were invited to the performance; we have

---

[19] Mendelssohn later dedicated his Violin Concerto, Op. 64, to David.

[20] Spohr had used a baton conducting the London Philharmonic (1820). He alarmed some of the directors, but after they had seen the result they allowed that the baton might be a useful weapon. Later Weber used it.

[21] It was considered impolite to conduct without a score. At the concert a score was placed before Mendelssohn; it turned out to be the music for another work, but Mendelssohn punctiliously turned the pages, in order to preserve appearances. The truth of this anecdote—widely told—seems extremely doubtful.

a letter from Felix to the important *Hofkapellmeister* of Dessau, Friedrich Schneider, asking him to "brave the trouble of the journey" and to "spend his precious time" and come to Berlin.

All the same, Mendelssohn was not quite confident that he could hold the audience's attention through an uncut *St. Matthew*. He made excisions, and he did a bit of retouching here and there, such as orchestrating the recitative, "And behold, the veil in the temple was rent in twain," an unnecessarily theatrical effect.[22] It was not, however, an exaggeratedly romantic interpretation, insofar as one is able to judge from Mendelssohn's tempo and dynamic marks in his score. While he used the fast tempos he favored and here and there may have indulged in overstressing the drama, conveying the kind of impression that the age in which he lived found to its liking, he was true to the spirit of the work. No other judgment seems just.

When the tickets went on sale, the house was sold out within ten minutes. (There were only six complimentary tickets, of which Spontini had two.) More than a thousand people clamored in vain for admittance. Social and intellectual Berlin was represented among the eight hundred to nine hundred who did have tickets: the King was in the royal loge with members of the court. We know that Schleiermacher, Hegel, Heine, Droysen, and Rahel Varnhagen were present. The date of the performance was March 11, 1829. A spirit of almost religious excitement pervaded the listeners. "Like a church," wrote Fanny, "deepest silence." Felix conducted with absolute authority, his gestures sparing, his glance touching the artists like a devoted custodian who surveys each constituent of a treasure. He was able to make all participants perform as if it were the last time they were ever to make music. To be sure, there were slips, false entrances, a few bad intonations. They did not matter to an audience prepared in advance to admire and enter into the beauty and drama of the towering tale. Emotion filled the hall; a few men and women wept.

The news of the performance leaped through the city. Twice as many people claimed to have heard the *Passion* than could have been there. Immediately a repetition was demanded, and this was duly scheduled ten days later, on Bach's birthday. Again sold out; even the lobby and the rehearsal rooms were filled with people and all the doors were opened. Zelter, who now believed that the whole thing had been his idea right along, gave a

---

[22] There is no evidence of a "mutilation" of which Alfred Einstein wrote.

festive supper after the concert. Devrient's wife, Therese, was sitting between Mendelssohn and a man who kept urging her to drink, and showered her with inane and flirtatious compliments, until Therese, bored with his prattle, whispered to Mendelssohn, "Who is this idiot beside me?" Mendelssohn whispered back, "That idiot is the famous philosopher Hegel."

A flood of reviews, essays and reports spread through Germany. Marx wrote: "History will recompense his [Mendelssohn's] deed with fame, as his contemporaries who were privileged to witness the work will offer him warm thanks and honor. All this is external; the true reward lies in the deed itself." Rellstab,[23] by this time Berlin's most fearsome critic, who had been twice arrested—once for insulting Spontini and once for being mean to the singer Henriette Sontag—wrote of the "eternally great, infinitely miraculous power and nobility of the work," and said, "Almost never have we heard so perfect a performance. If a few details were spoiled by a few, that was never the fault of the conductor: he accomplished the extraordinary through his devotion and unique talent." Martin Geck writes:

> Never before was Society as involved in and appreciative of a musical event. No other work of music called forth at its premiere or rediscovery a comparable chorus of famous contemporaries, respected critics and anonymous contributors. The celebrated premieres or early performances of Handel's *Messiah*, Haydn's *Creation*, or Beethoven's IX Symphony hardly equaled it, though these were necessary antecedents to prepare the ground for the enthusiastic reception of the *St. Matthew Passion*.

Zelter sent two reports to Goethe, in which (as I have noted) he overplayed his own part in the affair. Goethe was much moved and noted in his diary (March 26): "Professor Zelter's letter about the performance of Bach's music." He wrote Zelter that he was made to feel as if he could "hear the roar of the ocean from afar" and he compared the experience of hearing the work to his own emotion when he looked again at Mantegna's drawings.

A third performance was given on Good Friday, April 17. Mendelssohn had left Berlin and the performance was conducted by Zelter. According to a detailed report by Fanny to Felix, Zelter conducted miserably, now forgetting to take up his baton, to which he was unused, now failing to give the choruses their proper cues; then Milder-Hauptmann got mixed up in her important solo, and so on and so on. Nevertheless, Fanny con-

---

[23] It was Rellstab who called Beethoven's Sonata in C sharp minor "The Moonlight Sonata."

cludes, "all in all the public thought it a good performance." The sisterly letter (April 18, now in the Bodleian) should be taken for what it is: propaganda of love. If Felix wasn't there, it couldn't be any good.

Around this time Fanny became engaged. For five years or longer she had been wooed by Wilhelm Hensel, a handsome but indigent painter. Lea had objected to the match on the usual bourgeois grounds: a painter's prospects were less certain even than a musician's. The parents had exacted a waiting period during which the two young people were neither to see each other nor correspond. Hensel had gone to Italy and Fanny accepted the parental interdict. In Italy Hensel had achieved some reputation and had now returned, still in love. They were married in October of that year. But Fanny before her wedding seems to have been more excited about the *St. Matthew Passion* than her own life.

The performance exercised a profound influence on the appreciation not only of the *St. Matthew*, but other major Bach works. The *St. Matthew* score was published the following year by Schlesinger. Other performances followed—Breslau, Frankfurt, Stettin, Cassel, Dresden, etc. Not all of them were successes. In Königsberg the critic wrote in 1832: "One part of the audience already fled during the first part, another called the work outdated rubbish."

Obviously the *St. Matthew* would have been heard sooner or later had there been no Mendelssohn. His achievement nevertheless was a pivotal one. He turned the light on, shining it on a monument which stood half in the shadow. He destroyed the fear there was in approaching these super-life-size creations. He stimulated the willingness to understand. He was instrumental in urging publication of the works. He showed, then and in later Bach performances, that this music, which makes no concession to prettiness, does reach the sentient. All this he did without becoming a "Bach specialist." Years later he wrote to Rebecka:

July 22, 1844

If you truly feel what is beautiful, if the beautiful truly gladdens you, then your mind becomes enlarged and not specialized. Everything which is genuine and good gives you pleasure. I always get angry when some praise only Beethoven, others only Palestrina, and still others only Mozart or Bach. Either all four, or none of them. . . .

Florence with a view of the Duomo, from a sketch by Felix Mendelssohn made on his journey to Italy.

Six

THE TRAVELER

I

*A*s I have suggested, to Mendelssohn, traveling represented a necessity of existence. Even had there been no need to show himself as virtuoso, conductor, or composer in the cities of Europe—and at times when there was no such need—he packed his bag. When he accepted posts at Düsseldorf, Leipzig, or Berlin, he was always careful to stipulate "free" periods during which he could fulfill guest engagements in distant cities. He voyaged both as a musician and as a man, an impressionable and intelligent tourist. Did he travel to enrich his mind, to gladden his heart with the view of a waterfall, to gaze in self-forgetfulness at a painting, to work through a new musical thought while seated on an antique pedestal? Surely. But more than that, motion itself was to him what rest is to most people, the jouncing of a post chaise as soothing as the swinging of a hammock.

He was in Stettin in 1827 for the first performance of *A Midsummer Night's Dream* Overture. Then to Heidelberg and Cologne. A little later he set out on an extensive walking tour of southern Germany, in the course of which he landed in a casino in Baden. There he was induced to perform, to the fury of the manager, who told him that his piano playing had been so fascinating that it had stopped people from playing roulette. He, the manager, was going to make sure that there would be no piano in the gambling room from then on.

After the performance of the *St. Matthew Passion* he could not wait to get away from Berlin. With all his love for his family, he must by this time have been anxious to assert his independence and to annul the pejorative designation of "rich amateur." Granted, Berlin was a city of musical and theatrical activity. Granted that it was flattering to stroll down the Unter den Linden on a sunny Sunday, to watch the girls, and be greeted by acquaintances. Granted that it was pleasant to sit at the Café Kranzler at the intersection of Unter den Linden and the Friedrichstrasse and dip into whipped-cream pastry. But Felix was not much of a café-sitter, and there were coarse aspects to his home city, coarse and retrogressive, which were becoming repellent to its youth. Rights of seniority restricted a twenty-year-old ambitious musician who needed to prove himself. How could he, in a city where everything went by title and officialdom? After the *St. Matthew Passion* the King did *not* offer Felix a post.

In the opinion of quite a few visitors, Berlin was a "sandy nest," a somnolent city. Sophie Müller, one of the famous actresses of the period, went there just at that time. This was her impression:

> . . . Finally we came to charming Potsdam. It has beautiful streets, sumptuous houses, and is occupied by the Prussian military. We left this friendly place and after two stops we entered Berlin through the Leipziger Tor. A cold shudder overcame me. It was ten o'clock at night. The streets were deathly silent. Only an occasional light here and there showed me that the city was not, like Herculanaeum, uninhabited. After being rudely jolted on the uneven pavement, we finally reached our lodging. They showed us to our rooms. I went to the window; suddenly two sharp whistles, which sounded like Hell's mocking laughter, assaulted my ears. Hardly pleasant auspices, I thought. Now I know what it was. It was the night watchman who announced the passing of the quarter of the hour.

> (Letter to Margarethe Carl, August 2, 1827)

Heinrich Laube, one of the leading playwrights of German romanticism and a guiding spirit of the "Young Germany" movement, describes Prussia around 1834 as an out-and-out police state. King Frederick William III, who had begun by inaugurating reforms under the influence of his intelligent queen, Louise, had now become increasingly reactionary. Louise was long dead and the King had become withdrawn, suspicious, un-

certain, and inimical to anything youth wanted. He called all reform proposals "effusions by unripe poets, certain to lead to perdition." He refused
to give his people the constitution he had promised. "Berlin," writes Laube,
"is a 'dead' city; in a considerable part of the Friedrichsstadt district, grass
is growing between the cobblestones." When the King went to the theater
—chiefly to light comedies and the ballet, aside from grand opera performances—a red carpet covered his loge and hid him from public gaze. His
morganatic wife, the Duchess of Liegnitz, would peek out and relate what
was happening on the stage. Only when some turn in the play particularly
interested him did he himself draw the curtain aside and brave being seen
by the audience. The main street which led to Charlottenburg was the only
one on which smoking was permitted. Anyone caught smoking in other
streets was liable to a fine of two thalers; a friend of Laube's always carried two thalers with him in his vest pocket, "to abrogate the proceedings."
As they were talking, another friend whispered, "Throw away your cigar.
The King is behind us!" "There he was, in an open carriage, and hardly
responded to our greeting." . . . "Woe to you if he noticed you were
smoking. You will be put in prison." (Laube *was* arrested, though not for
smoking, being accused of writing seditious articles in the Leipzig revue,
Die Elegante Welt. He spent several months in jail.) He summarized his
impressions of Prussia: "The majority of educated men were no doubt
liberally inclined, but they thought that their liberalism could be made
compatible with an absolute and bureaucratic government."

Even assuming that Laube exaggerated, he does give us the feeling
of a city in which everything and everybody was watched, in which life was
a series of regulations, and the policeman was walking behind you.

The good men withdrew: Stein had long ago retired, disappointed in
his hopes for reform. (He died in 1831, two years after Mendelssohn's first
London journey.) Hardenberg had died in 1822; in the last years of his
life the liberal chancellor had turned conservative under Metternich's influence. Wilhelm von Humboldt, the reformer of the Prussian educational
system, friend of Goethe and Schiller, renounced public life in 1819, protesting against the spirit of reaction. Now even the sermons of the beloved
Friedrich Schleiermacher were being scanned by the police for subversive
content.

Mendelssohn was not a man of politics. He may not have read attentively the fall of the political barometer of his country. He may not have been aware of the conflict which was developing in Prussia—and not in Prussia alone—between the monarchical wish for the *status quo* and the demands created by industrial labor. Still, to some extent he must have been conscious of what was going on in governmental Berlin; at least he must have heard the friends of the house discuss it. It may be that what he heard and saw spurred his wish to get away.

2

London

Why did Felix choose London, the formidable city, then perhaps twenty times the size of Berlin, as his first ground for conquest? Why not Vienna, the home of Beethoven, who had died but two years previously? Why not Paris, which he had already visited?

There were several reasons. First, the Mendelssohns liked everything British, including tea: it was a family tradition. Second, Felix's good friend Klingemann was there and had posted home enthusiastic descriptions of life by the Thames. Third, Ignaz Moscheles was there, and that counted for a lot. A wonderful friendship had sprung up between the two, the older man full of affection, kindness, and enthusiasm. Harold Schonberg, in his book *The Great Pianists*, calls Moscheles "a sensitive musician, a gentleman, as noble and respected a figure as music has shown." Fourth, Moscheles must have told Felix how warmly foreign talent was welcomed by the British. At that period London attracted nearly all the leading European pianists: Muzio Clementi, Johann Baptist Cramer, Hummel, Franz Dussek, John Field, Kalkbrenner, and others. Pianistic virtuosity was appreciated; Mendelssohn's virtuosity would find appreciation.

Altogether, London's musical life was vigorous and had remained so since the days of Handel and since Haydn had come, bringing along the superb symphonies he had especially composed for the British.

Perhaps London audiences did not take their music as seriously and surely not as ponderously as the Berlin intellectuals. To succeed in London with the ladies and gentlemen who paid for their tickets, one needed to stand in well with a member listed in the Almanach de Gotha: audiences applauded whom the Duchess of Devonshire approved. "Concerts" were often farragos of long duration mixing instrumentalists with singers with small orchestral groups. Almost all artists had to relieve serious music with titillating but insignificant tidbits, sentimental titles such as "The Shepherd's Dream" or "The Love Letter," or show-off pieces such as the "Grand Chromatic Gallop," or fantasies on popular operatic melodies. Solo recitals were rare, except that Moscheles did play them occasionally and present a sonata by his beloved Beethoven. Liszt gave a one-man concert in London; after playing a piece or two on the program, he

> would leave the platform and, descending into the body of the room, where the benches were so arranged as to allow free locomotion, would move about among his auditors and converse with his friends, with the gracious condescension of a prince, until he felt disposed to return to the piano.
>
> (Quoted by Harold Schonberg, *The Great Pianists*)

The largest audiences were attracted by visiting vocal stars. At the Drury Lane or Covent Garden, Maria Malibran and Giuditta Pasta exchanged high notes for good guineas. Italian operas predominated, the sadder the better, the more arias the more applause. That was a tradition which went back to the eighteenth century, when Addison had scolded his readers in *The Spectator:* "For there is no question but our great-grandchildren will be very curious to know the reason why their forefathers used to sit together like an audience of foreigners in their own country, and to hear whole plays acted before them in a tongue which they did not understand."

Even if there were deficiencies in London's musical life, even if some listeners would gossip and nibble oranges during the performance, and come and go as they pleased, there still existed a substantial group who sincerely wanted and loved music.[1] Indicative of such a demand was the establishment in 1813 of the London Philharmonic Society, a brave cooperative venture undertaken by prominent musicians, Johann Peter Salomon (Haydn's Salomon) and Muzio Clementi among them. Its purpose was to promote symphonic music as a change of diet from operatic offerings. Only members could play and only excellent musicians could become members.

---

[1] Where did the English get the reputation for being unmusical? Was it because England has produced few great composers? What the nation lacked in creativity it made up in appreciation. Today I believe London to be the musical capital of the world.

The Society had prospered from the beginning, and while at first the musicians played for the love of it, earning no fees, now they were not only being paid but there was enough money at the disposal of the Society to enable them to invite visiting celebrities to come and conduct (Cherubini and Spontini, for example), and to commission new works. It was from this Society that Beethoven had received help on his deathbed. In addition to this Society—soon called The Royal Philharmonic Society—there were other institutions devoted to orchestral music: "The Concerts of Antient Music," which specialized in old music, and "The City Concerts," founded in 1818 by George Smart and consisting partly of amateurs.

London then was a place where orchestras performed regularly, in contrast to Paris, where a friend had told Felix, and Felix had repeated it, *"Ce n'est pas ici le pays des orchestras."* [2]

One of the founders of the London Philharmonic Society was the conductor George Smart, recently knighted. In 1825 he conducted the astonishing new symphony of Beethoven, the Ninth. At the end of the season, Smart decided to visit the continent to find out what new music he could corral and what new performers. He called on Beethoven in September and tried in vain to persuade him to come to England. To whatever concert Smart went, he took along his pocket tuning fork to check whether the music was being played in tune. By October he and the tuning fork had reached Berlin. He was invited to the Mendelssohns and found himself very much in tune with them and their music-making. From Sir George's diary:

> October 12: . . . On our return from the Charlottenburg palace at seven o'clock, I went by invitation to Mr. Mendelssohn's. There were present his lady, his two sons and two daughters, Mr. Rietz, who is they say a good violin player, and the only pupil here of Rode. . . . Young Mendelssohn played a clever fugue, pastorale and fantasia of Sebastian Bach, all on the organ with a very difficult part for the pedals. . . . Next he played a clever kyrie of his own composition, the voice parts well put together but difficult. . . . He and his sister played on two pianofortes an

[2] This was before 1828, when Habeneck established the Conservatoire Orchestra, which developed into one of Europe's best organizations, rivaling the Leipzig *Gewandhaus*. When Mendelssohn heard the Conservatoire in 1832, he was fair enough to declare it "the best orchestra I have ever heard."

overture of his own composition, which was learned and good. The piano-forte young Mendelssohn played on was one of Broadwood's, the compass only up to C, which Mr. Mendelssohn bought in Paris. We had . . . excellent tea and a fishy supper.

October 16th: . . . At three o'clock I dined, by invitation, at Mr. Mendelssohn's and spent a pleasant day. There were about eighteen persons present. Mrs. Mendelssohn spoke English well, as did a very agreeable medical man. . . . We had music after dinner, I played Mozart's duet in F with Miss Mendelssohn, and Mozart's fantasia with Mr. Mendelssohn, junior, who also played three extremely difficult and clever exercises of his own composition. . . .

October 25th: . . . I then called to take leave of the Mendelssohn family. Mr. Mendelssohn was out but I had a pleasant conversation with Mrs., Miss and Mr. Felix Mendelssohn. Mrs. Mendelssohn gave me the printed rules of Zelter's Singing Academy and I gave Miss Mendelssohn a set of Maundy pence for 1825, which seemed to please her. . . . I took a Droschke [a carriage] and arrived at the Liedertafel—which means literally Singing-table—at the "Englisches Haus," Mohrenstrasse, at about twenty minutes to nine. . . . There seemed about sixty gentlemen present. Those I knew were . . . Count Brühl, the two Mendelssohns, Zelter, Maurer, a Mr. Russell. . . . Supper began about a quarter past nine. Between each dish, as they were brought round, they sang a short piece something in the style of a glee but not so good or long. The pitch was rather flatter than my fork. About eight or ten pieces were sung, some in Latin, and most of them composed by Zelter, one, "St. Paul," was good. . . . The whole was over soon after twelve. . . . Zelter is a pleasant, unassuming man. One of his fingers is crooked. He was formerly a mason. He said he had built ten or twelve houses in Berlin, and did not begin music before he was twenty. I went upstairs into his library, which is large. . . .

[Later] . . . I strongly recommended young Mendelssohn to visit England when I was in Berlin in 1825, which he then seemed inclined to do.

These, then, were the most cogent reasons why Mendelssohn chose London: the availability of orchestras which might perform his orchestral music—which now numbered, in addition to the *Midsummer Night's Dream* Overture and the First Symphony, the Overture "Calm Sea and Prosperous

Voyage"—and his acquaintance with London's eminent conductor, Sir George.

3

Business was good in England that year. The administration was Tory, under the Duke of Wellington. The Duke set the fashion. George IV was still King; he was to die the following year. The division between the fox-hunting set and those "in trade" was as unbridgeable as ever, in spite of a few new industrialists who schemed to be admitted to closed clubs. One still had to know who your father and great-grandfather were before you could be trusted. In the year we are discussing—1829—the first race was rowed between Oxford and Cambridge, but no commoner touched the oars.

England was playing the arbiter in the stresses of the Continental nations, and playing the role skillfully. In March, Parliament approved the "Greek Protocol," assuring that country its hard-won independence. The wealth of England was increasing through iron, coal, and overseas trade. So was its poverty. So was its crime. London had recently been plagued by a wave of thievery, and just as Felix got there Sir Robert Peel managed to have his plan approved for what was to become London's famous Metropolitan Police Force. The Force was not entirely successful in stamping out the crimes born in the back alleys and midwived by the filthy air. There was a law on the books which prohibited anyone under sixteen years to work in cotton mills and factories "more than a twelve-hour day, excluding time for meals," but the law was circumvented and it took until 1833 to pass the "British Factory Act," which made it a criminal offense to employ children under nine to work in factories. Dickens was to write of these conditions in later years and Mendelssohn was to read Dickens, but now the young Mendelssohn saw the sores of London only from afar, if at all, and was overwhelmed by its vitality and dazzled by the lights that glittered in the stately homes.

Abraham and Rebecka accompanied Felix as far as Hamburg. A letter from Fanny, a loving farewell, reached him there. He embarked on April 10—and disembarked, much the worse for seasickness, cold, boredom, and homesickness, on April 21. Eleven days the stormy crossing took. But as

Felix crawled down the gangplank, he saw Moscheles and Klingemann waiting for him and he felt better at once.

Moscheles had arranged lodgings for him at 103 Great Portland Street. The landlord was a German who was immediately captivated by Felix's personality. So was virtually everybody else. His letters of introduction and the fame of his grandfather, along with Moscheles' sponsorship, opened both the musical and the aristocratic circles to him. With enormous gusto he plunged into London's life. He and friend Klingemann were two young men about town, observing, laughing, dancing, reveling in their second language, freed both of Berlin's provincialism and parental pressure. Both Klingemann's and Felix's reports about their new environment and the curious natives make charming reading. I give a few excerpts from the letters which reached Berlin—first, one from Klingemann: [3]

Most Honored Herr City Councillor and Frau City Councillor, Incomparable Young Ladies, Most Excellent Squires Felix and Paul:

. . . *How do you like England?* This is the question which every Miss or Mistress to whom I am *introduced* holds like a dagger against my breast, whereupon I invariably puff out my cheeks and parry with a fearless *"exceedingly well."* I am not lying, because everything here seems so strange to me that it gives me enough food for thought to last ten years. It is true that my front teeth have suffered quite a bit while trying to pronounce the TH. It is true that my back is only with difficulty restrained from performing the usual courteous German bow, a gesture unheard of here, where you merely nod your head. It is also true that like a person learning to swim and dangling by a rope, I am still trying to master the one-two-three of English, without attempting wit or pun, happy that I can manage the home-cooked diet of ordinary language. . . .

But the comfort here! The British comfort is the most marvelous Philistine invention I have ever known. It begins about ten o'clock in the morning, and makes its appearance in my "small," homey room, only half as high as the reception room in the Embassy in Berlin, and very pleasantly furnished. A merry fire is burning in the fireplace, the water is cooking, the breakfast table is laid, and everything needed for breakfast is right there. My eye scans with great satisfaction that mile-long newspaper with

[3] The italicized words are in English in the original.

leading articles, news, lawsuits, police investigations, and all kinds of scandals. Everything is made public and described in a personal way, dramatically, as if it were happening just then. Frequently I have the impression that I am reading a comedy by Aristophanes. The coal is crackling, the coffee is steaming, and between each sip I learn about an interesting *elopement* of a romantic young miss, or a daring burglary (by the way, thievery here is unbelievable), or a *dreadful accident* caused by bolting horses or an overturned carriage. . . . The Turks menace, the Spaniards hang, the French oppose, the shares in the Stock Exchange sink, the waistlines of the women rise—what grave portents of our times!

I only wish I were less myopic: that's because of the English girls. They don't know how to bake an egg-cake, and they spend their time doing silly things, but how marvelous they do look! It is a peripatetic girls' *Pension* which one can observe every day in Regents Park, and they look to me like so many Peris, one more beautiful than the other. They parade in pairs, the taller ones together, and they are quite conscious of their charms; they are protected by a stern aya [an Indian nursemaid] who stares at every man like a natural enemy. . . . Even the chambermaid at Goltermann looks like a princess or a Hebe, and by the way, they are incredibly educated, these girls. At Moscheles' one of them asked me if I had read Kant, to which I could hardly answer in the affirmative. She assured me that she had read him. All I was able to bring forth was that old story about Kant and his student's coat button; on the other hand, she was astonished that I had read all of Walter Scott.

. . . Regents Park and Regent Street is truly the most impressive sight I have seen, almost more beautiful than the Linden. Best of all is *The City.* What a pleasure it is to make one's way through the mass of carriages, coal carriers, crooks, and other honest folk . . . There is something demonic in this enormous, intense activity, yet somehow an order reigns without even having to invoke laws. On Sunday when one walks through the same streets in which, on workdays, you literally can't hear yourself talk, one is almost frightened by the silence. However melancholy we on the Continent imagine an English Sunday to be, the reality is more severe. It's the boredom which fills the churches. The incredible, thick yellow fog hangs over the city and penetrates into the rooms, all stores are closed, and there are no newspapers; a plaintive little bell calls the pious community together. . . . They can't understand at all that we have theatre in Germany on Sunday. That seems to them out-and-out sinful. It did not help a bit when I argued with a *Miss* whether she took less pleasure from her dress on a Sunday, or ate with less appetite, or drank her tea with less gusto—it remained a sin once and for all. But in one respect we Germans have an advantage here: everybody thinks that all of us were born smoking a pipe and owning a piano and every German is a priori musical. These good people have a touching sense for music and an extraordinary stomach for listening. Like ostriches, they swallow gravel and candy together. And long—long—everything is long here! I think Beethoven must have been English. . . .

I am absolutely mad about the theater here, particularly the English comedies. I haven't yet been able to decide whether the actors are really so expert and natural as they appear to be, or whether my impression is due to the newness and strangeness of the plays I witness. . . . The public too participates more than at home. It displays a certain critical innocence. Well-declaimed speeches move it to applause, and when there are jokes people really laugh at them. At the entrance of the theater, before the doors are opened, the policemen call out, *"Gentlemen, take care of your pockets when going in—take care of pickpockets, Gentlemen,"* and everybody guards his belongings. A newspaper here, *The Herald*, estimates the number of pickpockets of both sexes to be between 80,000 and 100,000. . . .

Felix's first reports read like companion pieces:

London, April 25, 1829
(After three days in London)

It is fearful! It is mad! I am mixed up and confused. London is the most grandiose and most complicated monster on the face of the earth. How can I compress into one letter what I have experienced in the last three days! I hardly remember the chief events, and yet I dare not keep a diary, for then I should have to see less of life; that I do not want. On the contrary, I wish to experience everything that offers itself. Things toss and whirl about me as if I were in a vortex, and I am whirled along with them. Not in the last six months in Berlin have I seen so many contrasts and such variety as in these last three days. Just turn to the right from my lodging, walk down Regent Street and see the wide, bright thoroughfare with its arcades (alas! it is once again enveloped in a thick fog today) and the shops with signs as big as a man, and the *stage-coaches* piled

up with men and women. . . . Look how a horse rears before a house because his rider has acquaintances there. See men carrying advertising signs
on which the graceful achievements of trained cats are proclaimed. See the
beggars, and the Negroes, and those fat John Bulls with their slender,
beautiful daughters hanging on their arms. Ah, those daughters! However, do not be alarmed, there is no danger from that quarter, neither
in Hyde Park, so densely populated with girls, where I drove about yesterday with Mme. Moscheles (as the fashion demands), nor at the concerts, nor at the Opera (for I have already been to all these places); only
at the corners and crossings is there any danger, and there I sometimes say
softly to myself, in a well-known voice: "Look out lest you get run
over . . ."

If you could but see me beside the heavenly grand piano—which
Clementis have sent me for the whole of my stay here—by the cheerful
fireside within my own four walls, with shoes and grey filigree stockings
and olive-coloured gloves (for I am going out to pay calls), and could you
see the immense four-poster bed in the next room, in which at night I can
walk to sleep, and the gay curtains and old-fashioned furniture, my breakfast tea with dry *toast* still before me, *the servant-girl* in curl-papers who
has just brought me my newly hemmed black kerchief, and asks for further
orders, whereupon I attempt a polite English backward nod; and could you
but see the highly respectable, fog-enveloped street and hear the piteous
voice with which a beggar down there now pours forth his ditty (he is almost drowned out by the street-vendors); and could you suspect that from
here to the *City* is a three-quarters-of-an-hour drive, and that along the
whole way, at every cross street of which one catches a glimpse, the uproar
is the same, if not far greater, and that one has then traversed only about
a quarter of inhabited London, then you might understand how it is that
I am half distracted. . . .

After I had sent off my last invalid letter to you, Klingemann took
me first of all to an English coffeehouse (for here everything is English)
where, of course, I read the *Times*. As, like a true Berliner, I looked first
for the theatrical news, I saw that [Rossini's] "Otello" and the *first appearance* of Mme. Malibran were announced for that very night. In spite of
weariness and sea-sickness, I resolved to go. Klingemann lent me the
necessary grey stockings, as I could not find mine in a hurry, and yet had
to appear in full dress, with a black cravat, like all the rest of the aristo-

cratic world. Then I went to my lodgings, and from there to the Italian Opera at *king's theater*, where I got a seat in the *pits* (cost me half a guinea). A large house, entirely decorated with crimson stuff, six tiers of boxes, out of which peep the ladies bedecked with great white feathers, chains and jewels of all kinds; an odour of pomade and perfume assails one on entering, and gave me a headache; in the *pits* all the gentlemen, with fresh-trimmed whiskers; the house crowded; the orchestra quite good, conducted by a Herr Spagnoletti (in December I will give you an imitation of him; he is enough to make you die of laughter). . . . Mme. Malibran is a young woman, beautiful, with a gorgeous figure, a towering wig, full of fire and power, and at the same time coquettish; setting off her per-formance partly with clever embellishments of her own invention, partly with imitations of Pasta (it seemed very strange to see her take the harp and sing the whole scene exactly like Pasta and finally even in that very rambling passage at the end which I am sure you, dear father, must re-member). She acts beautifully, her movements are convincing, only it is unfortunate that she should so often exaggerate, which borders on the ridiculous and disagreeable. However, I shall go to hear her every time—only not tomorrow when "Otello" is to be repeated. This I only wish to hear again when Sontag appears in it; she is expected daily. . . .

After the second act came a long divertissement with gymnastics and absurdities, just as with us at home, that went on till half-past eleven. I was half dead with weariness, but held out till a quarter to one, when Malibran was dispatched, gasping and screaming disgustingly. That was enough and I went home. . . . In between I constantly had to keep a firm hold on my seat because I still felt as if the whole house were swaying to and fro; nor did this giddy sensation leave me until yesterday, and last night for the first time did not disturb my sleep. On the day after "Otello," when I was still fast asleep, a soft hand touched me very gently, and that could be nobody but Moscheles, who sat at my bed for a good hour, and immediately gave me all kinds of suggestions.

I can find no adequate expression for the way Moscheles and his wife behave toward me. Whatever could possibly be agreeable, useful, or ad-vantageous to me, they have procured for me. . . .

Felix's judgment of Maria Malibran is just: we know from con-temporary testimony how the fiery artist threw herself into her tragic roles, her acting stopping just this side of the ludicrous. Indeed, Delacroix

thought that as she "ripped her handkerchief and even her gloves to tatters" so did she rip a passion to tatters. But such men as Liszt, Rossini,
Donizetti, Bellini, and Moscheles adored her and Felix's admiration went
beyond the artistic. He was attracted to the beautiful Maria, a year older
than himself, and father Abraham was worried lest his son would tangle
himself in a dangerous alliance. Nothing came of it.

To continue with Felix's first impressions of London, here is his light-
hearted account of a "science" whose founder had had a brush with Felix's
grandfather:

London, May 1, 1829

. . . The other day I went to see Dr. Spurzheim's phrenological cabinet,
shown by a young physician. A group of murderers placed in contrast to a
group of musicians interested me greatly, and my belief in physiognomy
received strong confirmation; really, the difference between Gluck's forehead and that of a parricide is striking and indubitable. But when people
want to enter into minute details and show me where Gluck had his bump
of music and where his inventive power, or exactly where the philosophy
is lodged in Socrates' skull, they seem to me to be on precarious, unscien-
tific ground, although it may lead to interesting results, such as the following: a beautiful young English girl who was there desired to know whether
she had a propensity for stealing, or other crimes, and it ended in a phrenological examination of everybody present. One was pronounced good-
natured, another fond of children, this lady courageous, that lady avari-
cious; and as the aforesaid young creature had to undo her long fair hair to
allow the doctor to feel her bumps, and looked very beautiful with her hair
loose and when doing it up again before the mirror, I gave three cheers
for phrenology, and warmly praised everything concerning it. That I
possessed a taste for music and some imagination was an obvious conclusion; the doctor found afterwards that I was rather covetous, loved order
and little children, and liked flirting; music, however, he declared to be
predominant. . . .

He who was used to the plainer customs of Biedermeier Berlin now
had his eyes filled with the white and gold shimmer of Georgian London.
He was the petit bourgeois transported into the midst of Vanity Fair. He
could not observe the English aristocracy from any but a superficial point

of view, unable to see its backbiting, snobbery, or arrogance. Nor could he know the money worries which lay behind the toothy smiles. Felix was be-glamoured. He speaks of a ball at the Duke of Devonshire's: how the sumptuousness of the house seemed to him to spring from an Oriental fairy tale; how the equipages choked the traffic in Piccadilly; how he saw, as he ascended the stairs, that the two men behind him were none other than Wellington and Peel, which set him to gaping open-mouthed at the two celebrities. He reports on the way the rooms were lighted: all the candela-bras were hidden by huge wreaths of red roses; they seemed to grow in an upside-down garden from the ceiling. He marveled at the paintings: here a life-size portrait by Van Dyck, there a Titian, other walls covered by Correggios, Leonardos,[4] and Flemish painters. In all these rooms the young girls danced; the dancing couples flowed into an adjacent hothouse which was opened to spread the aroma of the flowers through the palace. The buffets were heaped with "the fruits of all seasons." The young men flirted and they waltzed "very badly"; the older men lolled on the couches while they engaged in tender conversations with the ladies.

He plunged into the social stream so enthusiastically that Devrient felt it incumbent to ask whether he had forgotten his musical career. The sharpness of Felix's answer suggests that there might have been something to Devrient's reproof:

June 19, 1829

. . . Now I have to be a little angry. That is about one passage in your letter which I wish to refute. You tell me that my letter helped me with your wife because she had disliked the way I live here and you had agreed with her. If you were here I would march up and down your room and I would vent my anger quite clearly, and then I could spare myself the sermon which I am now about to write (luckily you can't see my furious expression). . . . Life and art are not two separate concepts, and if you are not afraid that I could here become a Rossini or a John Bull, then there is no reason for you to be afraid that this life would overwhelm me. . . . I don't want you ever to think that I have changed. Really, Devrient, if I ever become better or worse I will send you a special delivery letter. Until that time, don't worry. . . .

[4] Surely not! England did not possess many Leonardos and at that time several paintings by Leonardesque painters were falsely attributed to him.

Like Klingemann and "like a true Berliner," he went to the theater. He saw *Hamlet* with the famous Charles Kemble, who was a friend of Sir George Smart. It was a rotten performance, and Felix rightly waxed sarcastic about it, but he jumped to the conclusion, so widely held in Germany, that "the English sometimes don't understand Shakespeare." He thought it bad taste that Kemble [5] appeared with one yellow and one black trouser-leg to indicate madness, that the scene in which Hamlet comes upon Claudius at prayer was cut—"for me one of the most beautiful passages" —that Hamlet behaved continuously like a bravo whom the King ought to have executed at once, that he openly threatened Claudius with his fist during the play scene, etc. "At the end, when Hamlet expires with the words, 'The rest is silence,' and I expected the trumpet-flourish and Fortinbras, Horatio let him lie there, proceeded to the footlights, and said, *'Ladies and Gentlemen, tomorrow evening the Devil's Elixir.'* Thus ended *Hamlet* in England." (Letter of June 25, 1829)

4

Among the British musicians he met was Sir Thomas Attwood. He was a church composer who had been a pupil of Mozart, a fact he never forgot and never let his friends forget. He was then sixty-four years old, but still an outstanding organist, and he held the important position of principal organist in St. Paul's Cathedral.

William Horsley was a composer of glees, and he introduced Mendelssohn to the English glee-club style. Mendelssohn's choral music benefited by it, but perhaps more important, he and his two daughters became intimate friends of Felix, who enjoyed the hospitality of the house, was charmed by the daughters though evidently not amorously attracted to either of them—and left so great an impression on the family that his visits resulted in a book of reminiscences written by both of them, Sophy and Fanny. The book, based on letters (*Mendelssohn and His Friends at Kensington*), is full of humor and sly observation, because the girls, with all their adoration, saw Felix's foibles.

Yet with all the welcome mats which were spread out for him, with

---

[5] Kemble was regarded by general consensus as more adept at lighter parts (Orlando, Benedick, Romeo) than at tragedy.

several of London's leading musicians supporting his cause, he nevertheless did not find it quite so easy to make his mark in music. Not at first. The fact that he was a gentleman-musician, an amateur, counted as much in his favor in London as it counted against him in Berlin. He was there to bring them music, not to take away money. What could be more pleasing? Yet he was unknown as a composer and untried as a performer; the season was far advanced, the remaining events had been programmed. He applied to the Philharmonic Society, wishing to show himself first as a composer rather than as a virtuoso, but they took their time about answering, and his first appearance did not take place until May 25, more than a month after he had reached London. Felix blamed Sir George Smart for the delay, and in his letters home he complained that Sir George brushed him off with excuses. Later, he even called Smart an "intriguing, deceitful and untruthful man." Mendelssohn's accusation does not jibe with what we know of Smart's character: he was an honorable and dedicated man, surely anything but an intriguer. What motive could he have had for standing in Mendelssohn's way? Perhaps he thought that Felix's First Symphony was not quite good enough for the Philharmonic Society, or more likely, Felix, already accustomed to success, became impatient and blamed the almost inevitable slowness of getting started on ill will. At any rate, details were finally arranged, and his First Symphony was to be given at the seventh concert of the Philharmonic season, May 25.

The day after, Felix wrote home:

May 26th

When I came to my rehearsal of the Symphony in the *Argyll rooms*, I found the whole orchestra assembled and about two hundred guests, mostly ladies, many of them foreigners. First the Mozart Symphony in E flat was rehearsed, and mine was to come next. I felt not precisely afraid, but very keyed-up and excited. During the Mozart rehearsal I took a little walk in Regent Street and looked at people. When I came back everything was ready and they were waiting for me. I mounted the podium, drew my little white baton from my pocket, one which I had had made for the purpose . . . and the concertmaster, Fr. Cramer, showed me how the orchestra was placed. Those in the back had to stand up so that I could see them. I was introduced to all, greetings were exchanged. A few snickered, seeing a little fellow with a stick instead of the powdered and bewigged *Conductor* to which they were accustomed. We began.

Considering it was a first run-through, it went well and strong, and it pleased them even in the rehearsal. After every movement the people present applauded and so did the orchestra (by tapping their bows against the instruments and stamping their feet). After the last movement they made a great to-do. I had to repeat the finale because it went badly, and again they broke out in approval. The directors [of the Society] came to me. I had to go down to the audience and bow my thanks right and left. . . . I must have shaken two hundred hands—it was one of my happiest moments. All those strangers became acquaintances and friends within a half hour. The success of the concert last night was greater than I could have dreamed. J. Cramer led me to the piano as if I were a young girl and I was received with loud and long applause. They wanted the adagio *da capo*; I preferred to indicate my thanks and to go on, for fear of boring the audience. But after the Scherzo [6] the demand for repetition was so insistent that I had to play it again. At the end they applauded as long as I kept thanking the orchestra, and I *handsshakte* till I left the hall.

A few days later he gave a piano recital in the same hall. He got there early to try the piano but found it locked. While they sent for the key, he tried another piano, one "gray with age," and presently fell to improvising, forgetting his surroundings and unmindful of the passage of the quarter hours, until the first of the audience arrived at the hall, and he realized with a shock that he had now no chance to try the piano on which he was to perform. He disappeared to get dressed; when he then appeared and saw the full hall and an audience consisting mostly of women in gay summer hats, he was seized by panic and felt feverish. The heat of the hall beat against his face. He flushed and the perspiration ran down his nose. But he was cordially received and the instrument proved to be an excellent one. He lost his stage fright and played with abandon, observing that the field of hats swayed in time to the music like a field of tulips. He was happy when he happened to glance in the direction of Sir George Smart and saw him smilingly take a pinch of snuff.

That the English made an attentive audience for his superb playing,

---

[6] For the original Scherzo of the Symphony he substituted a charmingly orchestrated version of the Scherzo from the *Octet*.

playing which with all its conviction and intimacy and power never o'er-stepped the bounds of modesty, is further attested to by Felix himself:

June 19, 1829

By God, I play better here than in Berlin, and that is because the people listen better. Don't take that as a conceited remark, but it *is* exalting when you feel that you succeed and give others pleasure.

(Letter to Devrient)

He played Weber's *Konzertstück*, several of his own piano composi-tions, and earned a special triumph with Beethoven's "Emperor" Concerto which, to the audience's astonishment, he played by heart, this at a time when such a practice was by no means common. Even Liszt usually had the score before him.

His acceptance as an artist "one has to hear," a socially desirable musician, a "gentleman" one could not only go to admire but send an in-vitation to, a marvel of manners as well of music, that special distinction of his which was to remain in all of his subsequent nine visits to England, came about through a generous gesture. Felix's uncle Nathan had written to him asking for help for the poor people of Silesia. The region had been inundated by a flash flood; many were homeless, the misery was widespread. Felix galvanized into action. He enlisted the help of Henriette Sontag, the capricious and pretty soprano who was the darling of London, after having conquered Berlin and having charmed Beethoven himself. (She had sung in the première of the Ninth Symphony in Vienna.) At first she refused, or rather, "her *homme d'affaires* and her companion (she is sur-rounded by a court of her own and one is but seldom admitted to her presence) refused," but Felix simply would not take no for an answer. He persuaded first her, then Malibran—what a coup to have Sontag and Mali-bran appear together!—then Moscheles, then the flutist Drouet, then a number of other stars. He secured, through Sontag, the patronage of several members of the peerage who were moved by the fate of the Silesians, in spite of the fact that "misery is widespread in London and nobody knows how to relieve it," as Felix himself admitted. The whole affair was en-gineered with remarkable organizational skill: when Felix really wanted a thing he would get it. He even obtained the use of the hall gratis. The concert was sold out, hundreds were turned away, and a few important people were finally seated on the stage behind the orchestra, where they peeped out at the proceedings between the double-basses. He finally obtained so many participating artists that none could sing a solo aria; Felix combined them in quartets and other ensemble numbers. He himself played his two-piano concerto with Moscheles and conducted the *Midsummer Night's Dream* Overture. It enchanted the audience, which sat through four hours of music-making and wanted more.

This concert then—July 13, 1829 was the date—established Mendelssohn as the darling of the British public. His relationship with England became a mutual love affair. England he considered his second home. "There is no question," he wrote from Naples, "that that smoky nest [London] is my preferred city and will remain so. I feel quite emotional when I think of it."

Felix's only unpleasant experience in England was a quarrel with the famous music critic François Fétis, who took Mendelssohn to task for some remarks the young man had made about Purcell. It was a tempest in a teapot, but it firmed Mendelssohn's prejudice against the French.

Klingemann summed up the impression which Mendelssohn left behind him: "Contrary to Satan, the odor which he leaves behind is one of *high talents* and *perfect gentleman* [in English]. A foreigner can hardly understand how much an Englishwoman includes in this expression; it contains a whole volume of approbation. I can imagine that Apollo himself could appear and play irresistibly on his lyre, but if as a liberty-loving Greek he were to decide not to drink wine with the mistress of the house, he would be tagged with the definitive curse, 'He is no gentleman.' It is the severest curse of the civilized world."

5

Immediately after the concert, the *Wanderlust* was once more upon Felix. With faithful Klingemann and another friend, Neumann, he set out on an extended tour of Scotland. He visited Glasgow, Edinburgh, Perth, Inverness, and Loch Lomond. And, like Boswell, he made the tour of the Hebrides, enduring, sometimes with a grumble, more often with a laugh, dreadful weather, primitive inns, and post-stages in which one was sure to contract a heavy cold. What he could not stomach was the sound of the bagpipes and other folk music, much of which he thought dreadful and dishonest. He and Klingemann made a special point of visiting Sir Walter Scott at Abbotsford. Scott was then a vital figure of international literature, as important to his time as Hemingway to his. Today, as his recent biographer, Edgar Johnson, has called him, he is "The Great Unknown." Then he was the great known, spokesman for derring-do and love in the glade. Felix and Fanny had read virtually every word of his novels, and Schubert and Beethoven too had enjoyed reading Scott. Now, on the journey, they got to him after endless trouble and delay. And when they did get there, they found him old, harassed, about to change his domicile, and indifferent to the admiring visitors. All they obtained was "a half-hour of inconsequential conversation."

Yet the silence of Scotland, wrapped in fog, the beauty of its wet fields, its cliffs above which the gulls were watching, the heath where the red grass swayed in the continuously blowing wind, the smell of the oat cakes, the waterfalls, near which the sawmills turned—all that gave Mendelssohn his ideas for the "Scottish" Symphony, ideas which he was to work out later. And on the voyage to the Hebrides he jotted down the beginning of the "Hebrides" Overture, one of his finest works.

In August he began his return trip to London. Now he found a few days of sunshine and blue skies; yet most of the time the bad weather pursued him. "Yesterday," he wrote, "was a *good* day. That means that I was soaked through only three times. I wore my coat continuously and got a glimpse of the sun through the clouds once or twice."

He visited a well-to-do family, the Taylors, who had a large property near Chester called Coed-du. What attracted him were the Taylor girls, all three of them. They were all clad in white and they made a fuss over him. He enjoyed the compliments and flirted with the three of them together. At the Taylor estate he found a superb piano of English make, and very willingly he played for the girls both compositions of his own and a few lieder by Fanny. He rode with the Taylor girls, he sketched with them, he made excursions, he visited a mine which belonged to Mr. Taylor —Felix called him the most English of the Englishmen—and he composed three piano pieces which he dedicated to the three girls.

Yet the thought of returning home now became attractive to him. He wanted to be back in Berlin in time for Fanny's wedding in October. The plan was to meet his father in Holland, and together they were to return to celebrate both the wedding and shortly afterward the twenty-fifth anniversary of Abraham and Lea's marriage. The Mendelssohns were always strong for celebrating anniversaries and birthdays.

A nasty accident intervened. The accident occurred on September 17 in London. Felix was riding in a carriage. Presumably the horse shied, the carriage turned over, Felix fell to the sidewalk and fell so unluckily that he suffered a severe injury to his knee. For two months he was bedridden. He suffered considerable pain, but what irked him more than the pain was the forced inactivity and the fact that he could not be with Fanny. A week after the accident, he wrote to Fanny:

September 25, 1829

This then is the last letter which you will receive before your marriage. For the last time I address you as Fräulein Fanny Mendelssohn-Bartholdy. There is much I would like to say to you. But I am not really able to. True, since yesterday I am allowed to sit up a little every day and therefore it is easier for me to write. But still my head is completely confused from all that lying around in bed and from that long period of thinking nothing. . . . I feel as if I had lost the reins with which formerly I was able to guide my life. When I think about everything which is now going to change and take a different shape, everything which I have long taken for granted, then my thoughts become unclear and half wild. I am unable to organize them. . . . Well, live and prosper, marry and be happy, build your life in such a way that I will find it beautiful and comfortable when I come to visit you (and that will happen very soon), and stay the same as you were. Outside let the wind blow. I know both of you and that suffices. Whether I call my sister Fräulein or Madame is unimportant. The name is unimportant. . . .

Reading between the lines, the letter seems sad not only because he is lying in bed and cannot join the festivities, but more because he realizes that Fanny will henceforth divide her love between brother and husband. She will no longer be solely "his" Fanny.

While Felix was slowly recovering, he observed how quickly the large chunks of time passed, though the minutes crept at a snail's pace. There were continuous visits from his British friends, gifts of fruit, books, and delicacies, and Klingemann was with him every moment that he could spare from his work. "I shall never be able to thank him adequately. Soon it is dusk again. The fat servant-girl appears with my dinner. Soon the little sparse night-light will be burning near my bed. I lie here and peer out to see when the day will break once again."

After almost two months he was allowed to take a short ride, the weather being clement. He was so moved by seeing the sun once again that he wrote to his father an emotional letter in which he thanked him for all his love. Such sentimentality was unusual between the two, and Felix immediately changed his tune and reported that when he was not daydreaming he was burying his nose in eighteenth-century literature, and that if only he had a long pipe and a nightcap he could easily be mistaken for a well-preserved old uncle who had the gout.

Later he visited his friend Attwood in the country. Rummaging through a cabinet in his room there, he discovered among other treasures the full score of *Euryanthe*. Attwood had obtained it in Germany years before and it had become quite a rarity. Felix was overjoyed to study the score; he wrote to Fanny, "It gives me a peculiar pleasure to examine Weber's favorite work particularly here in England, where nobody knows this music . . . where they treated Weber quite shamefully and where he died." (November 15, 1829)

Finally he left London to return home. He could not be in time for Fanny's wedding—which had taken place on October 3 and for which Fanny had composed her own wedding music, to be played on the organ— but he was in time for the parental silver wedding, which was to be celebrated on December 26.

For this silver anniversary, Felix had composed a little *Singspiel* entitled "The Return from Foreign Parts" (*"Die Heimkehr aus der Fremde"*). The libretto was written by Klingemann. It was an innocent piece with the usual complications of the lost son who returns incognito to test his bride. The music is delightful, and if the libretto were not quite as innocuous as it is, the work might not be forgotten. The performance was to be a surprise for Abraham and Lea, who of course were not surprised at all. All the young members of the family and some of their friends took part and rehearsed secretly in the garden. For Hensel, Felix had written a role which consisted entirely of one note: Hensel was unable even to hum "*Oh Tannenbaum.*" At that, he messed up his role. An important part was assigned to Devrient. Felix oversaw the rehearsals with his usual punctiliousness, and everything was in perfect order, when at the last moment the Crown Prince ordered a Court Concert and commanded that Devrient appear in it on the very evening on which "The Return" was to be given. The whole enterprise was shipwrecked. When Felix was told what had happened, he fell into a paroxysm of anger. He began to speak in disconnected broken words and suddenly he could no longer express himself in German but mumbled in English. There were fearful signs of a brain disturbance. The doctor came and Abraham put his son to bed. Felix sank into a deep sleep, from which he did not awake for twelve hours. When he awoke, he was perfectly normal. Abraham then made a personal appeal to a friend of his, the Intendant of the Royal Opera House, and matters were so arranged that Devrient could appear first at the Court Concert and be dispensed with for the rest of the program so that he was able to rush over to the Mendelssohns. The little opera could be given. It was, needless to say, a huge success within the circle of family and friends. Felix, however, was dissatisfied with it and refused to publish it. It was published posthumously.

6

Italy

Even as he was returning from London, working on "The Return from Foreign Parts," and beginning the composition of the "Reformation" Symphony, as well as smaller works, he was dreaming of further travels. In the German-romantic tradition, he longed to go to the country "where the lemons bloom." Goethe, who had derived plenary mental and visual profit from Italy, aside from a love affair or two, urged Felix to go. But who living in the nineteenth century and living in a northern climate did not possess the desire for Mediterranean meditation? Who did not want to journey to the fabulous peninsula? Keats or Ibsen, Berlioz or Turner,

Wagner or Corot—they all pilgrimaged thither. At first Felix thought that the whole family ought to make the southern journey, a project which was immediately vetoed by Lea, who disliked travel. Then Felix did get the permission and the means to undertake the kind of Grand Tour which had become the thing to do for young gentlemen, ever since the eighteenth century. He was ready to leave on the morrow, but in March Rebecka came down with the measles and Felix and Paul caught it, so that it was the beginning of May before he could set out on a journey which was to keep him on the move for the better part of three years. It is significant of Felix's temperament that he undertook this tour of learning, seeing, and studying in spite of the fact that his reputation had now become firm enough for the Berlin University to offer him a chair in the department of music. At the age of twenty-one! He refused this extraordinary offer and suggested Marx, who accepted.

His first important stop was Weimar. He wanted once more to see the man who in his youth had been greatly inspired by antiquity and had held fast his impressions in the *Italian Journey*, the *Roman Elegies*, and the *Mignon* poems. It was to be Felix's last visit, and he described the eyes of the aging Goethe as those of "an old lion who wants to go to sleep." Goethe tried to interest Felix in science and in natural history. How could anybody be content with "a one-sided mentality," Goethe asked Felix. But Felix could not or would not go along, and suddenly Goethe angrily turned his back on him. At that moment Felix was sitting before the piano, and frightened and saddened he began to touch the keys and improvise as if to comfort himself. After a while, Goethe re-entered the room, stood again before him, and said in a soft voice, "You have enough. Hold fast to what you have."

He would not let Felix go, and twice he had to postpone his departure. Felix wrote home:

Munich, June 6, 1830

Then the old gentleman himself entered and said, "What is this about your leaving in a hurry?" He still had a lot to recount to me and I had a lot to play for him. As to the goal of my journey, that was quite unimportant; Weimar should have been its true goal. He could not understand that anything was missing here. What could I find at other tables d'hôte? . . .

He tried to keep Felix longer by inviting all the beautiful women who were around, and he who now lived a rather unsocial life gave a number of gala evenings for the young man. But finally Felix simply insisted on leaving, and Goethe gave him as a memento a page of the *Faust* manuscript with a personal dedication: "To my dear young friend, Felix Mendelssohn, that strong and tender master of the piano, in happy memory of great May days, 1830." Later he sent him a copy of the famous painting of himself (see p. 116). In the original version of the painting (by Stiller), Goethe holds a letter from the King of Bavaria in his right hand, while in this version he holds a little poem written for Mendelssohn. (The painting now hangs in the Mendelssohn Archive in Berlin.)

Then to Munich. Here the story repeated itself: he captured high and low by his playing, made fun of the pomposities of the court, befriended fellow-musicians, heard a good deal of music, including a performance of *Fidelio*, about which he wrote:

Munich, June 6, 1830

> Isn't Germany a crazy country? It brings forth great men and does not honor them. It produces a quantity of great singers, many thoughtful artists, but no minor ones who play a part simply and unaffectedly. Marcellina tears her role to pieces, Jacquino is an idiot, the Minister a sheep. If a German like Beethoven writes an opera, a German like a Stuntz or a Poissl (or whoever) cuts the ritornello and similar "unnecessary" passages. Another German adds trombones to [Beethoven's] symphonies. Then a third one states that B. is overorchestrated.

His most significant experience was his friendship, if that is what it was, with a young and beautiful pianist, Delphine von Schauroth. Whether he actually had an affair with her is impossible to say. It is probable that he fell in love with her, though he speaks of Delphine in his letters in his usual light, half-joking manner. "The King of Bavaria wants me to marry her," he writes. His feelings may have cut deeper than he let on. Years later he told Schumann that Delphine "could have become dangerous to him." He played duets with her and said that Delphine was rightly worshipped as an artist but that she was as well a remarkably cultivated woman. "When the day before yesterday we played together for the first time . . . she made an extraordinary impression on me. Yesterday I

heard her play alone and again I admired her very much," he writes to
Fanny. Immediately he adds that in his own backyard there is a female
who knows how to play the piano quite as well as Delphine, perhaps better,
and who has a total admirer in him. Later he writes to Fanny (June 26,
1830): "I run day after day to the museum and twice a week to Schauroth,
where I stay for a long time. We flirt outrageously but it is not dangerous
because I am already in love with somebody else. And that is a Scotch girl
whose name I do not know." The "Scotch girl" is probably a cover-up. As
to the twice a week, he kept a diary of his journey in which he noted the
people he saw, and in this diary Delphine appears a good deal more often
than twice a week (the diary is now in the Bodleian Library). In later
years Delphine's name crops up once or twice in the correspondence, but
they never met again, at least not on terms of intimacy.

She undoubtedly inspired him to compose his famous Piano Concerto
No. 1 in G Minor (Op. 25). He dedicated it to her and played it first in
Munich in 1831. In a letter to Fanny (undated, from Munich), Felix tells
her that Delphine "composed a passage for my G Minor Concerto which
makes a startling effect." Did she, really? What the passage was we do
not know, but it is astonishing that Mendelssohn should have allowed anybody to touch a composition of his. Was it love which permitted it? The
Concerto had an immediate success, which was repeated every time Felix
played it—in London, on his next voyage, "the audience went wild"—
and for generations afterward. Berlioz tells us of a piano which, having
endured the Mendelssohn Concerto played by a host of budding pianists,
suddenly begins to play the piece by itself. The piano is possessed, it has
gone mad, nothing can stop it:

> M. Erard arrives; but try as he will, the piano, which is out of its mind,
> has no intention of minding him either. He sends for holy water and
> sprinkles the keyboard with it—in vain: proof that it wasn't witchcraft, but
> the natural result of thirty performances of one concerto. They take the
> instrument and remove the keyboard, still moving up and down, and
> throw it into the middle of the courtyard next to the Warehouse. There
> M. Erard in a fury has it chopped up with an ax. You think that did it?
> It made matters worse: each piece danced, jumped, frisked about sep-
> arately—on the paving stones, between our legs, against the wall, in all

directions, until the locksmith of the Warehouse picked up this bedeviled mechanism in one armful and flung it into the fire of his forge to put an end to it. Poor M. Erard! Such a fine instrument! We were heartbroken, but what could we do? There was no other way to loose its grip.

(*Evenings with the Orchestra* by Hector Berlioz)

Poor Concerto! It has now been rescued and when it does appear in concert performances, played with a light touch, it still makes the audience happy.

From Munich he went to Salzburg, Linz, and Vienna, always absorbing and observing, and trying to meet expenses within the allowance his father gave him. He wrote to his brother:

Linz, August 11, 1830

Oh Paul! Do you understand this business about money? Gulden notes, gulden W.W., heavy gulden, light gulden, convention gulden, and the gulden of the Devil and his grandmother. I do not understand it at all and I wish you were with me.

On to Budapest, where he witnessed the crowning of the King and admired the magnates in their uniforms of oriental luxury, driving to the ceremony in carriages beaded with emeralds and rubies, all this contrasting strangely with the dirty gypsies and the humble servants with the long mustaches and their singsong speech, of which he did not understand a word.

From Budapest he drove south. He got to Venice the first week of October, when that magic city was in its autumnal glory, the sunshine still strong enough to glisten with a thousand highlights on the Grand Canal and to bring out the gold of the mosaics on St. Mark's Cathedral. Felix was caught by the strangeness of it all, by the hoarse cries of the city, by its dubious odors, by the alternations of menacing darkness in the little canals and the proud brightness of the open waterways. As long as he could escape listening to the band playing in St. Mark's Square, he was enthralled. What thrilled him most was the churches and their contents and above all Titian's Entombment and Ascension.

Venice, October 10, 1830

I knew . . . he [Titian] had enjoyed life and life's wealth. But he must have known as well the profoundest sorrow. Equally, he must have known what it is like to be in heaven. That is proved both by his divine Entombment and his Ascension. Maria floats on a cloud and the air stirs through the whole picture. One feels her breath, her uneasiness and yet her devotion. A thousand emotions all in one painting! And what words can one use which do not sound banal and dry, compared to what the painting conveys? . . .

In Venice he completed the first volume of his "Songs without Words" (Op. 19). These include some of what have now become his most hackneyed melodies, including the "Venetian Boat Song No. 1."

From Venice he journeyed to Bologna and then to Florence. Like all the fugitives from the dank north, he marveled over the blue skies of Tuscany and the clear air, the wealth of the flowers still blooming, the opulence of the villas and palaces. But again it was the paintings and the statues which called forth his most ardent enthusiasm, and he writes particularly of Raphael's Madonna del Cardellino and the Venus of Medici. The only trouble was the innkeepers, coachmen, and porters with whom the traveler had to do business. Felix fretted and called them "disgusting crooks," and they probably were disgusting crooks. "Finally I became quite dizzy with all the cheating. I no longer knew to whom they were lying. So whatever they said, I protested and declared, 'I am not going to pay,' whatever they asked. That made things bearable."

After a week, he left for Rome and reached that city early in the morning, "in bright and shining moonlight, the sky a deep blue." He must have thought of Goethe, who had entered Rome almost half a century before under similar circumstances and on the same day of the year.

He spent the entire winter in Rome, sightseeing, working, and making innumerable friends. In an early letter to his family (written a week after his arrival), he describes his lodgings and his life:

November 8, 1830

Imagine a small, two-window house on the Spanish Steps, No. 5. The sun shines warmly the whole day long. In my room on the first floor there is a good Viennese piano. On the table lie some portraits of Palestrina, Allegri, etc., with their scores and a Latin psalm book, from which one can compose a *non nobis*. Here is where I reside. . . .

When in the morning I come into this room and the sun sparkles brightly on my breakfast (in me a poet was lost), I feel wonderful at once. Is it not late autumn? And who at home would dare to ask for warm, clear skies, grapes, or flowers? After breakfast I set to work, I play and sing and compose until midday. After that, the whole immeasurable Rome lies before me like an exercise in enjoyment. I do it very slowly, choosing every day something different, something of historic interest. One time I go walking among the ruins of the antique city, another time to the Galleria Borghese or the Capitol or St. Peter's or the Vatican. That is how every day becomes unforgettable, and because I take my time every impression remains firm and indelible. When I am working in the morning, I do not want to stop, I want to keep on writing. Then I say to myself, "You must see the Vatican." Then when I am there, I do not want to leave. Each occupation gives me the purest pleasure and one enjoyment follows the other. Venice with its past seemed to me like a gravestone; those crumbling modern palaces and the continuous reminders of a former splendor put me out of sorts and saddened me. Rome's past seems to me like history itself. Its monuments inspire, whether they make one feel serious or gay. It is satisfying to think that human beings can accomplish something which continues to refresh them and strengthen them after a thousand years.

He was fortunate to be in Rome during an eventful period. He took part in the Roman Carnival and its gaiety, though political disturbances ended the festivities precipitously. During his sojourn, Pope Pius VIII died, and he witnessed not only his funeral but the conclave which followed, the choice of the new Pope, and the festive ceremony of the election of Gregory XVI. He wrote Zelter a detailed quotation and analysis of the music of the Catholic ritual used during Holy Week, showing his extraordinary musical memory.

Because he was who he was, furnished with all sorts of introductions, he was received not only in the German society of Rome but in Italian circles. He made a friend of the historian Baron Christian Bunsen, who was Prussian minister to Rome. He made an equal friend of the Duke of Torlonia, whose family was in the banking business and was connected with the Mendelssohns. He visited the Danish sculptor Bertel Thorvaldsen, was welcomed in Bartholdy's villa, and became particularly intimate with Horace Vernet, the painter, who was the director of the French Academy of the Villa Medici. For him Mendelssohn played frequently, while the painter stood at his easel. Vernet was so impressed by Mendelssohn's improvisations of themes from *Don Giovanni* that he painted his portrait and sent it as a gift to Felix's parents.

Eager though he was to meet people, "particularly Italians," and companionable though his temperament led him to be, he nonetheless saw clearly through the pretensions of the would-be musicians and the half-and-half painters gathered in the city:

Letter to Fanny:

Rome, November 16, 1830

. . . Yesterday for lunch at Bunsen's. I met among others a German composer. Dear God, dear God! I wish I were a Frenchman. The man said to me, "One has to come to grips with music every single day." "Why?" I responded; that embarrassed him. Then he immediately pontificated about "serious endeavor" and how Spohr lacked "serious endeavor." However, he perceived quite clearly serious endeavor in me, particularly in my *Tu es Petrus*. If they had served crow at the table, I would have devoured it. As it was, I had to make do with macaroni. . . .

The bohemian painters fared no better:

To his father:

Rome, December 10, 1830

. . . Really horrible people sit around in the Café Greco.[7] I hardly ever go there, because both they and their hangout make me shudder. . . . They wear broad hats, great big mongrel dogs crouch beside them, and their face, neck, cheeks, are entirely covered with hair. They puff up a terrible cloud of smoke (only on one side of the room, where smoking is permitted), they hurl insults at one another, and the dogs see to it that the bugs are spread around. A tie or a decent coat would be a novelty. Whatever the beard does not cover the eyeglasses hide. So they drink coffee and prate of Titian and Pordenone as if those two sat next to them and also wore beards and storm hats. And what they paint are sickly ma-

---

[7] Still in existence, on the Via Condotti.

donnas, weakly saints, milksops of heroes. One feels like kicking them.
. . . If I never accomplish anything in my life, the least I will do is to
show my contempt to those who have no respect for genius.

He was shocked by the paucity of first-class music. With all the
Italians' love for singing, they lacked discipline. He used to say in later
years that the best Italian singers came from any country outside of Italy.
The Vatican chorus was a tired group of voices over-the-hill and couldn't
even sing the traditional pieces correctly. The orchestras were "beneath
contempt." When he voiced his disgust they called him a *barbaro tedesco*.
Few people knew how to read music. In Venice the customs officer had
confiscated his musical manuscripts, suspecting that they represented a
secret code. Here and there he found a kindred soul who cared passionately
about music; that was the exception, not the rule. Yet the country was so
beautiful and Rome so exciting that it stimulated him and he was composing
with a will. He derived inspiration from nonmusic, he wrote Zelter—from
ruins, paintings, the sweetness of Nature. "In the antique columns—there
music was hidden." At any rate, why should he complain about musical
conditions? It was just as bad in other arts:

Rome, December 7, 1830

If one sees that a part of the loggias of Raphael are scratched out with
unspeakable crudeness and unimaginable barbarism in order to make room
for inscriptions scrawled in pencil, when one sees that the beginnings of
the rising arabesques are altogether ruined because the Italians destroy
them with their knives or God knows how, just to incise their miserable
names, when one sees that somebody wrote in large letters and with great
emphasis "Christ!" right underneath the Apollo Belvedere, when one sees
that in the center of Michelangelo's Last Judgment an altar is erected large
enough to cover the middle of the picture and thus to disturb and ruin the
whole effect, when one observes that through the magnificent rooms of the
Villa Madama, where Giulio Romano painted his frescoes, the cattle are
driven and cabbage is stored merely out of indifference toward the beautiful—so is all that much worse than having terrible orchestras, and it ought
to pain painters more than second-rate music pains me. The people are at
the same time involved and scatterbrained. They have religion and do not
believe in it; they have a Pope and clerics and mock them; they have a

brilliant lucid past and quite remove themselves from it. No wonder that art means little to them, they take the sublime so indifferently.

In the spring he went to Naples, Ischia, Capri and its Blue Grotto, Pompeii, Paestum, etc. He traveled light—"three shirts and Goethe's poems"—and sent home vivid descriptions of all he saw. From morning to evening he was the passionate sightseer and had enough energy left over to read Sterne at night: "Sterne has become one of my favorites. I remember that Goethe once talked to me about *A Sentimental Journey*; he said one could not express the heart of man better: it is both stubborn and despairing."

Naples to him was superficially a "merry place"; yet he was not impervious to its "mass of misery":

Naples, April 27, 1831

I am pained by the incredible mass of beggars who pursue one at every step and who surround one's carriage as soon as it stops; above all the white-haired old people whom one sees. Such a mass of misery is difficult to imagine. If I go walking along the strand and direct my gaze toward the ocean and the islands, fine. But when I turn around, I see that I stand in the midst of cripples who make capital of their disability. Or as happened to me recently, I am surrounded by thirty or forty children, who chant, "*Muio di fame*" and knock on their cheekbones to show that they have nothing to chew on. What a disgusting contrast! Even more hateful is it never to have the pleasure to see a satisfied mien; if one has given a plentiful tip to a custodian, a workman, a waiter, anybody, the customary response is, "*Niente di più?*" Then I am sure that I have given too much.

Eventually he retraced his steps and spent more time in Florence. It was not easy to get there in the days before the railroad. Discussing the *vetturino*, the Roman carriage driver, evidently the enemy of traveling mankind, he writes to his sisters:

June 26, 1831

He doesn't permit you to sleep and lets you starve and thirst. In the evenings when he ought to allow time for a *pranzo* he drives in such a way that one arrives toward midnight, when everybody is asleep and one must be glad to find a bed. In the mornings he departs at 3:15. At midday he stops his five hours, choosing for sure the one inn where there is nothing to eat. He drives his six German miles a day and drives *piano* while the sun shines *fortissimo*. I was particularly unlucky, my travel companions being quite unsympathetic, inside three Jesuits and outside, where I preferred to sit, an unpleasant Venetian woman. If I wanted to escape her, I had to listen to the praise of Charles X and how Ariosto really should have been burned as a seducer and despoiler. Outside it was worse still and the carriage made no progress. The first day, after a journey of four hours, the axle broke and we had to halt for nine hours in front of a country house where we happened to be. Finally we were forced to spend the night there. If we passed an open church, we saw the most beautiful and pious pictures of Perugino, Giotto, and Cimabue. One vacillated between rage and ecstasy and back to rage. Misery! If Nature near the lake of Trasimeno had not served up a little moonlight, if the country hadn't been so beautiful, if every sizable town had not boasted a marvelous church, and if every day we had not passed such a town, and if—well, don't let me go on. . . . In Incisa, half a day's journey from Florence, I no longer could stand the carriage driver's rudeness and insults. I just had to unload my things and tell him to drive to the devil, advice which he did not appreciate. It was St. John's Day, and in the evening there was to take place the famous festival in Florence. I was dying to be there. The Italians take advantage of such an opportunity and the woman inn-keeper in Incisa immediately offered me a carriage at four times the price. When I refused, she said, "Go and find your own." I tried that and learned that there were no carriages for hire, only the postal service. So I asked for that, to be told that the post horses were the very ones which the inn-keeper had offered me at the fantastic price.

I went back to her and demanded to be transported by the postal service. She replied that if I didn't want to pay her price for the horses, I couldn't get the postal service. I called for the rule book which they are obliged to have. She said she wasn't going to show it to me and turned her back. Force here plays a major role, so I went up to her, grabbed her and threw her into the room. . . . I then ran down the street to look for the *podesta* [mayor or head of police]. He wasn't there; he lived four miles away. The affair became ever more unpleasant: with every step the crowd of street urchins increased. Fortunately I came across a decent-looking man for whom the mob seemed to have some respect. I approached him and explained my situation. He took pity on me and led me to a vintner who owned a little carriage. The entire population surrounded his house, some penetrating into it and screaming that I was crazy. All the same, the carriage was brought and I gave a few coins to an old beggar. Promptly everybody shouted that I was a *bravo signore* and *buon viaggio*. The modest price which the vintner demanded only proved the outrageous trickery of the innkeeper. The vehicle was light and rapid and off we went across the mountains toward Florence. After half an hour we passed the vetturino. My umbrella protected me from the sun. I have seldom traveled as pleasantly and amusingly as in these few hours, my troubles behind me and the prospect of the fine festival before me. . . .

He reached Florence in time for the festival, enjoyed it to the hilt, mingled with the people, went to a masked ball which lasted till 1 A.M., and finally watched a procession of brightly lighted barges on the Arno.

Incidentally, Mendelssohn's experience with the vetturino was not exceptional. It parallels a description by William Hazlitt:

Vetturini bargain to provide you for a certain sum, and then billet you for as little as they can upon the innkeepers . . . who consider you as common property or prey, receive you with incivility, keep out of the way, will not deign you an answer, stint you in the quantity of your provisions, poison you by the quality, order you into their worst apartments, force other people into the same room or even bed with you, keep you in a state of continual irritation and annoyance all the time you are in the house.

In Florence he once again haunted the museums. "Today I spent the whole morning, from ten to three, in the [Uffizi] Gallery. It was heavenly." Raphael's self-portrait was to him:

Florence, June 25, 1831

. . . almost the most touching picture I have ever seen by him. In the middle of a tall wall, covered to the top with portraits, hangs a smallish and not particularly famous painting. My eyes were riveted on it at once: that was Raphael—young, very ill, pale, longing to go on, mouth and eyes filled with desire and yearning. It is as if I could gaze into his soul. He cannot yet express all he sees and feels. How something forces him to persevere and how he must die an early death—that is expressed in that

A landscape drawing of a Swiss scene. Mendelssohn drew this when he was thirty-three.

SKETCHES BY FELIX MENDELSSOHN

The vegetable market in The Hague. (Bodleian Library, Oxford)

Mürren, in Switzerland, a spot that Mendelssohn particularly loved. Taken from a watercolor painted shortly before his death. (Mendelssohn Archive, Berlin)

Frankfurt, a view from Cécile's house across the Main River. He drew this while courting her. (Bodleian Library, Oxford)

cloudy, suffering, fierce face. As you look into those dark eyes with their gaze springing from the depths or at the lips drawn in pain, you almost shudder. . . .

He sat once again in his favorite armchair in a little room, where he could immerse himself in the sight of Titians, Peruginos, and Raphaels. He spent two hours sitting there.

Mendelssohn's receptivity toward pictorial art was no by-product of well-bred curiosity. It was genuine. He carried in his heart an open range in which to receive a work of line and color as readily as a work of sound. From childhood on he was held by the past in painting as by the past in music. Yet Samuel Butler in later years doubted Mendelssohn's sincerity. We read in *The Way of All Flesh*:

> I wonder how many chalks Mendelssohn gave himself for having sat two hours on that chair. I wonder how often he looked at his watch to see if his two hours were up. I wonder how often he told himself that he was quite as big a gun, if the truth were known, as any of the men whose works he saw before him, how often he wondered whether any of the visitors were recognizing him and admiring him for sitting such a long time in the same chair, and how often he was vexed at seeing them pass him by and take no notice of him. But perhaps if the truth were known his two hours was not quite two hours.

That may be funny—but it isn't true.

7

In spite of new impressions and distractions, he had not forgotten music. He kept working on the "Scottish" Symphony, more seriously on the "Italian" Symphony, completed the *Hebrides* (*Fingal's Cave*) Overture in its first form, and wrote the setting of Goethe's *The First Walpurgis-Night*, which, however, he completely revised at a later date. In addition, he composed considerable church music, of a Protestant cast, motets, setting of psalms (including Psalm 115, *"Non nobis Domine,"* which was intended as a birthday present for Fanny), chorales, and the prayer *Verleih uns Frieden* for chorus and orchestra (it became Abraham's favorite).

Yet while he had begun much he had issued almost no music since he had commenced his journey. His genius was developing haltingly. He was being critical with himself. He squeezed his work hard, before he could let it out of his hands. Ideas came quickly, execution slowly, approval more slowly. He had now become, and was to remain, the hesitant composer.

When Devrient questioned him, he replied:

Milan, July 15, 1831

You reproach me because I am already twenty-two years old and not yet famous. I can only answer that if God had willed me to become famous at the age of twenty-two, it would probably have happened. It is not my fault. I write as unconcerned with fame as I am unconcerned with obtaining the post of a Kapellmeister. It would be pleasant if both were to happen. Yet as long as I do not exactly starve to death, so long is it my duty to write as my heart dictates. The result I leave to Him Who concerns Himself with greater issues. My only thought, ever present, is honestly to compose as I feel things and less and less because of outer considerations. If I have composed a piece and it has flowed from my heart, I have absolved my duty. I care not whether it brings me fame, honors, distinctions, or snuffboxes. . . . You want me to write only operas and think that I am wrong not to have done so long before this. I answer: Give me the right text and the work will be composed in a few months. Every day I long anew to write an opera. And I know it would be something fresh and agreeable, if I could find the subject. Yet I haven't got the words. A text which does not set me aflame I will not compose. If you know anybody who is capable of writing such a text for me, then name him for God's sake! It is he I am looking for. Isn't it preferable that I do nothing (even if that were possible) until such a text comes along? . . .

8

Berlioz

In Rome Mendelssohn met Berlioz. One would have thought that the romantic element in Berlioz—that imagination which produced *Romeo and Juliet* or the second movement of the *Fantastic Symphony* or *Harold in Italy*—would have reached the man who composed the Overture for *A Midsummer Night's Dream.* Yet Mendelssohn wore his romanticism with a difference. Goethe, though he himself was a poet who braved midnight specters, had infused him with too strict a sense of classicism, Zelter with too clean a sense of form, for him to be able to take a walk to the scaffold or descend into an opium den. Mendelssohn represented the light, Berlioz the dark side of romanticism; the light was dispirited by the dark. Mendelssohn did not understand Berlioz artistically, and his feelings about him as a man were, to say the least, equivocal. He may have been prejudiced against him before they met; it is probable that Zelter had shown his pupil one of the two copies of *Huit scènes de Faust* which Berlioz had sent Goethe. When they did meet, Berlioz was twenty-seven and had finally, on his fourth attempt, won the coveted *prix de Rome*. He was now a student at the Villa Medici, excitable, irrepressible, unruly, his hair flying, and of course unhappily in love. In Rome, as everywhere, Berlioz proclaimed his views in a rebellious *fortissimo*. The gentle Felix, whose nature was *moderato* and whose voice *piano*, must have felt estranged by Berlioz's vehemence; as Berlioz's lack of critical faculty, which often allowed a page of mediocre matter to stand after pages of sublime inspiration, must have struck the all too self-critical Felix as indulgent. Even so, it is strange that Mendelssohn could be so impervious to this geyser of feeling, the flow of which could be traced to the same source which at least in part fed Mendelssohn's talent. Could he not sense that this music set up its own and valid laws? [8]

Curious how much they had in common, those two, with their adoration of Shakespeare, their veneration of Goethe, their passion for Beethoven, their contempt for dilettantism, their knowledge of the orchestral apparatus, a knowledge in which Mendelssohn stood only a little behind the older man. Yet Mendelssohn called Berlioz "twisted"; he had "not even a speck of talent," "he was groping in the dark and yet thought himself to be the creator of a new world." He wrote to his mother:

March 29, 1831

. . . You say, dear Mother, Berlioz ought to know what he wants artistically. I am not at all of your opinion. I think he wants to get married. I think he is worse than the others because he is a poseur. I do not like

[8] This is not a unique case: we need only remember Tchaikovsky's dislike for Brahms, Wagner's for Verdi.

his demonstrative enthusiasm nor the despair which he shows in front of women, nor the black-and-white grotesqueries of his genius. If he weren't a Frenchman I could not stomach him at all, but it's always pleasant to have contact with a Frenchman because they always have something interesting to say.

Compare this with Berlioz's impression of Mendelssohn:

To Ferdinand Hiller

May 6, 1831

. . . We got along very well. He is an admirable fellow and his executant talent is as great as his musical genius, which is really saying a great deal. Everything by him that I have heard delighted me. I firmly believe that he is one of the highest musical talents of our epoch. It was he who acted as my guide [in Rome], and every morning when I called on him he played me a sonata by Beethoven, and together we sang *Armide* by Gluck. Then he took me to see the celebrated ruins which, however, impressed me very little. Mendelssohn has one of those candid souls which one finds rarely. He believes firmly in his Lutheran religion, and I used to scandalize him sometimes by making fun of the Bible. He was responsible for the only tolerable moments which I enjoyed during my stay in Rome.

Later Berlioz wrote to Hiller: "He has an enormous, extraordinary, superb, and prodigious talent. I cannot be accused of flattering him in telling you this, because he told me frankly that he did not understand my music at all."

These letters, written at the time of their being together, give a more direct testimony of Berlioz's feelings than the *Memoirs*, written many years later.

Mendelssohn said that he sometimes felt like taking a good bite out of Berlioz, so furious did he become at Hector's posturing. But just at that moment Berlioz would begin to rave about Gluck, and Felix had no choice but to agree with him whole-heartedly and to respect him. What Mendelssohn took for affectation was certainly not that, for whatever Berlioz's faults, he was nothing if not honest. It is of passing interest that Berlioz felt exactly about the sham artists and the Greco coffeehouse as Mendelssohn did. He writes in the *Memoirs:* "The Café Greco is the most odious place imaginable—dark, dirty and ill-lit. . . . They sit there killing time, smoking abominable cigars . . ."

Mendelssohn had questioned Berlioz in a tone of quizzical surprise about his enthusiasm for Gluck, the implication being: "How can your kind of musician possibly have sufficient intellectual understanding and feeling for grandeur of style and truth of expression to like Gluck?" (*Memoirs*) So Berlioz played a trick on Mendelssohn by placing a manuscript copy of one of Gluck's little-known Italian operas on the piano. Mendelssohn came, at once sat down, and began playing. He was making fun of the music until Berlioz told him that this was a composition by Gluck "and not by Bellini as you thought."

As to Mendelssohn's knowledge of Berlioz's music, Berlioz's *Memoirs* have this to say:

At that time I had hardly produced anything. Mendelssohn knew only my *Irish Melodies,* with piano accompaniment. One day he asked to see the score of the *King Lear* Overture, which I had just composed in Nice. He read it through slowly and carefully, and was about to begin playing it on the piano (which he did, with incomparable skill), when he stopped and said, "Give me the right tempo."

"What on earth for? I thought you said that any musician who couldn't guess the tempo was a duffer."

He would not admit it, but these ripostes, or rather unexpected thrusts, annoyed him intensely.

He never mentioned Sebastian Bach without adding ironically, "Your pupil." In short, he was as prickly as a porcupine whenever the talk was of music; you never knew where to take hold of him without getting your fingers hurt. But being fundamentally good-tempered and blessed with a naturally sweet and charming disposition, he never minded being contradicted on any other point, and I on my side used to abuse his forbearance during the heady discussions on philosophical and religious arguments that we sometimes engaged in.

This does not agree with a letter Mendelssohn wrote to his father (March 12, 1831) in which he tells him that he had played through, with Berlioz, the latter's symphony,

. . . which is called "Episode in the Life of an Artist" and for which a printed program is passed out. In the last movement, the poor artist goes to the devil, where the audience would love to have gone long ago. Then all the instruments have a hangover and vomit music, making us very uncomfortable. And yet he is a very pleasant man and speaks well and has fine ideas, and you can't help liking him. . . .

So Felix did know the Fantastic Symphony in the Roman days. Even in later years Mendelssohn's estimate of Berlioz's music failed to unbend. "His instrumentation is terribly dirty," he writes to Moscheles. "One feels like washing one's hands after handling one of his scores."

Nevertheless, and with all of Mendelssohn's lack of sympathy with Berlioz's aims, and with all of Berlioz's mocking of Mendelssohn's quirks, there was mingled in the relationship of these oppositely charged personalities a quantity of wonderment and admiration. They were not indifferent to each other. For indifference they were both too vital. And it is certainly true that Mendelssohn "came to regard Berlioz as something more than a poseur and an eccentric." (David Cairns) When in 1843 Berlioz wanted to have his compositions performed in Leipzig, where Mendelssohn was music director, Mendelssohn spared neither time nor effort to help Berlioz, going so far as to hunt for instruments which the orchestra did not possess but which Berlioz needed, correcting the choral parts with his own hand, and himself playing at the concert the harp part on the piano, since the harpist was missing. Berlioz said that he behaved like a brother. Similarly, Berlioz, however he might personally have felt, conducted Mendelssohn's music with complete devotion. J. W. Davison, the critic of the London *Times*, wrote that in Berlioz's performance of the "Italian" Symphony every tempo was gauged perfectly—for the first time in his listening experience. (May 29, 1852)

Would that there had been a little of Berlioz in Mendelssohn, and a little of Mendelssohn in Berlioz!

9

Northward he made his way, though still in no hurry to come home. He stayed a week in Milan, and there he met the Ertmanns. The report of his visit plays a part in the biographical literature of Beethoven, Dorothea Ertmann having been an intimate friend, and probably more, to Beethoven; he dedicated the Sonata Op. 101 to his "dear and beloved Dorothea Caecilia."

July 14, 1831

. . . I asked by chance on my arrival at Milan the name of the Commandant, and the *Laquais de place* named General Ertmann. I instantly thought of Beethoven's Sonata in A major, and its dedication; and as I had heard all that was good of Madame Ertmann, from those who knew her; that she was so kind, and had bestowed such loving care on Beethoven, and played herself so beautifully, I, next morning, at a suitable hour for a visit, put on a black coat, desired that the Government-house should be pointed out to me, and occupied myself on the way thither by composing some pretty speeches for the General's lady, and went in boldly.

I cannot however deny that I felt rather dismayed when I was told that the General lived in the first story, facing the street; and when I was fairly in the splendid vaulted hall, I was seized with a sudden panic, and would fain have turned back: but I could not help thinking that it was vastly provincial on my part to take fright at a vaulted hall, so I went straight up to a group of soldiers standing near and asked an old man in a short nankeen jacket, if General Ertmann lived there, intending then to send in my name to the lady. Unluckily the man replied, "I am General Ertmann: what is your pleasure?" This was unpleasant, as I was forced to have recourse to the speech I had prepared. The General, however, did not seem particularly edified by my statement, and wished to know whom he had the honour of addressing. This also was far from agreeable, but fortunately he was acquainted with my name, and became very polite: his wife, he said, was not at home, but I should find her at two o'clock, or any hour after that which might suit me.

I was glad that all had gone off so well, and in the meantime went to the Brera, where I passed the time in studying the "Sposalizio" of Raphael, and at two o'clock I presented myself to Freifrau Dorothea von Ertmann. She received me with much courtesy, and was most obliging, playing me Beethoven's Sonata in C sharp minor, and the one in D minor. The old General, who now appeared in his handsome grey uniform, covered with medals, was quite enchanted, and had tears of delight in his eyes, because it was so long since he had heard his wife play; he said there was not a person in Milan who cared to hear what I had heard. She mentioned the trio in B-flat major [the "Archduke"], but said she could not remember it. I played it, and sang the other parts: this enchanted the old couple, and so their acquaintance was soon made. . . .

She plays Beethoven's works admirably, though it is so long since she studied them she sometimes rather exaggerates the expression, dwelling too long on one passage, and then hurrying the next; but there are many parts that she plays splendidly, and I think I have learned something from her. When sometimes she can bring no more tone out of the instrument, and begins to sing in a voice that emanates from the very depths of her soul, she reminds me of you, dear Fanny, though you are infinitely her superior. When I was approaching the end of the adagio in the B-flat major trio, she exclaimed, "The amount of expression here is beyond any one's playing"; and it is quite true of this passage. The following day, when I went there again to play her the symphony in C minor, she insisted on my taking off my coat, as the day was so hot. In the intervals of our music she related the most interesting anecdotes of Beethoven, and that when she was playing to him in the evening, he not infrequently used the snuffers as a toothpick! She told me that when she lost her last child, Beethoven at first shrank from coming to her house; but at length he invited her to visit him, and when she arrived, she found him seated at the piano, and simply saying, "Let us speak to each other by music," he played on for more than an hour, and, as she expressed it, "he said much to me, and at last gave me consolation."

Another acquaintance Felix made in Milan was Karl Mozart, one of Mozart's two sons, who was employed there as an Austrian official. He was a lonely, gentle man, and Mendelssohn, as he did with so many, brought light into his life by playing Mozart's music for him, while the Ertmanns listened; later, when Karl and Felix were alone, Felix played him some of his own *Walpurgisnacht* score. In return, Karl gave him some letters of introduction to friends of his in Como, one of them a doctor. There Felix had an amusing encounter:

From Isola Bella, July 24, 1831

One began as well to discuss Shakespeare's plays, now translated into Italian. The doctor said: "The tragedies are good, but these fairy plays, they are stupid and childish. Above all one called 'Il Sonno d'una notte di mezza state.' [sic] There the worn-out device is used of a play to be rehearsed on stage. The piece is full of anachronisms and childish ideas." Yes, agreed everybody, it was quite naïve and I ought not to read it. I kept mum like a coward.

The next two months he spent in the country which "of all countries I know is the most beautiful and is the one where I want to live if I get to be really old." That was Switzerland. His letters from Switzerland sparkle with the reflection of glaciers and exude breaths of mountain air. Most of the way he traveled on foot, often up and down, marching through the passes and ravines and climbing the celebrated mountains such as the Jungfrau, the Rigi, and the Faulhorn, with snowflakes on his hair. On sunny days he would stretch out on some Alpine meadow and get out his sketchbook. He "learned what green was," and "made friends with glaciers." It did not matter that he ran into horrible weather; in August the central portion of Switzerland was inundated by an unprecedentedly heavy rainstorm which destroyed much property, tore away bridges, and left many poor people poorer. It did not matter that he had to find refuge one night in a private house, the inn having no room for him, and there he found "vermin as in Italy, a rasping clock which struck the hours with an enormous noise and a baby who screamed the whole night long." It did not matter that his traveling companions were occasionally less than desirable people:

August 18, 1831

Sometimes when I observe people who run through Switzerland and find nothing remarkable there, or anywhere else except in their own egos, when I observe how little moved or impressed they are, how cold and matter-of-fact they stand before the mountains, I would like to hit out at them. Two Englishmen are now sitting next to me and an Englishwoman is sitting on top of the stove. They are as wooden as sticks. For a few days I have to journey along with them. . . . All they do is complain that there are no fireplaces here. They never mention that there are mountains here. Their whole travel experience consists of picking on the guide, who laughs at them, quarreling with the innkeeper, and yawning at one another.

A similar observation, as he was crossing Lake Maggiore: "There was a mustached German on the boat with me. He looked at the beautiful landscape as if he had considered buying it and found it too expensive."

Nothing could dampen his enthusiasm as he journeyed over the Simplon Pass, through the Valley of the Rhone, Chamounix, to the Lake of Geneva, to Interlaken and the Vierwaldstättersee. In Lucerne he rested for a while—or what passed for rest for him—and having been silent for some weeks, he addressed copious letters to his friends and family, including one to Goethe which contained a description of his Swiss journey and which so impressed Goethe that he had it published. In this letter he describes the raging storm and a primitive performance of Schiller's *Wilhelm Tell* which amused him particularly.

Switzerland remained the country in which he sought peace when he was troubled. It was not only the natural beauty of the country which appealed to him but the fact that this beauty had to be conquered by strenuous physical exertion. There were few, if any, funiculars then. There was no lazy way to get to the top of a mountain. "I have never felt so completely free, so completely confronted by nature, as in these unforgettable weeks."

He arrived in Munich in September and remained there for two months. It was then that his relations with Delphine became closer and it was then he played his G Minor Concerto, in a special festival performance on October 17. His First Symphony and the now inevitable Overture to *A Midsummer Night's Dream* were on the program as well, and at the end of the concert he had to improvise on Mozart's *"Non più andrai."* The applause was led by the King himself. He went away from Munich with a contract for the composition of an opera in his pocket.

He stopped at Stuttgart, where he praised the orchestra, and traveled by way of Heidelberg to Frankfurt. There he received the joyful news that Rebecka had become engaged to a professor of mathematics, Gustav Peter Lejeune-Dirichlet. She married Dirichlet and it proved to be a very happy marriage. Rebecka was a more "normal" girl than Fanny, less talented, but possessing the light touch.

The opera project was very much in Mendelssohn's mind, and he went to Düsseldorf to call on the famous poet and dramatist Karl Immermann, author (or adaptor) of the *Münchhausen* tales. They agreed that *The Tempest* would make a good operatic subject, and Mendelssohn was so enthusiastic about the idea that he refused to heed his father's warning that Immermann was too cerebral a writer to produce a serviceable libretto. Abraham asked whether Felix ought not to search among the new French playwrights. Felix said no, he could feel no sympathy for French playwrights, at least not for the living ones.

10

Paris

But to Paris he did go, knowing full well that he could hardly dispense with making his name known in the intellectual capital of Europe. He arrived there in December, 1831.

Paris had come through the July revolution of the previous year with renewed strength. In his attempt to control the press, dissolve the Chambers, and change the electoral system, Charles X had lost his throne. Louis-Philippe became King on August 7, 1830. A week later he issued the Constitutional Charter, which guaranteed elective monarchy, the initiation of legislation by the Chambers, the permanent suppression of press censorship, and an end to Catholicism as the official state religion. The climate was propitious and the minds of France could flourish. Victor Hugo published his revolutionary *Hernani* in 1830, Stendhal his *Le Rouge et le Noir*, and Balzac his *Peau de Chagrin* a year later. *Le Roi s'amuse,* the play by Hugo which spelled out *lèse majesté* in clear language, was given in 1832. In the pictorial arts Delacroix, Daumier, and Delaroche gave a social and political tinge to their drawings and paintings. As Felix wrote home, in Paris it was politics, politics, all the way. Paris had once again, as in the eighteenth century, become the alembic of liberal ideas. In addition, France's industry was progressing, Paris was growing, Parisians were becoming prosperous, and Paris society demanded that it be entertained. Rossini was there, his *William Tell* being only two years old; Meyerbeer's opera, *Robert le Diable,* was given its première in 1830. Cherubini, old though he was, was still active, and Auber, master of light-hearted operas, stood at the zenith of his fame.

Yet it was not these but the new romantics who gave Parisian musical life its unique stamp. Chopin and Liszt were both young—twenty-one and nineteen—and both eager to open new paths. Paganini, who was then forty-eight years old, inspired the younger virtuosi; he played what turned out to be an historic concert on March 9, 1831. Although so wasted by syphilis that he looked like a cadaver, an effect purposely heightened by dark blue spectacles which made it appear as if his face had black holes instead of eyes, the Mephistophelian figure materialized on the stage of the Paris Opéra and performed incredible and incomprehensible feats on the violin, thrilling the packed audience. Liszt sat there, and the experience had a profound influence on him. After that concert Liszt closeted himself and practiced for "ten, twelve, sometimes fourteen hours a day . . ." "He wanted to do for the piano what Paganini had done for the violin; he drove himself mercilessly to conquer the keyboard's last remaining secrets." (Alan Walker: *Franz Liszt*) Mendelssohn heard Liszt play and changed his first opinion: henceforth, though he still harbored some reservations, he was "thoroughly impressed both by his playing and his striking personality."

That personality demanded that society adopt a new viewpoint toward the artist. Too long had the artist been the performing horse. He might have been adjudged a noble horse, but he was still a horse and belonged in the stable. The main stairs were still closed to him. He was still the performer who was not supposed to dine with the host who paid him his fee. Moscheles or Pasta, Malibran or Spohr, were still forced to enter aristocratic houses by the back stairs. Chopin, whose genius opened rich houses for him, was nevertheless considered socially inferior to some weakling descended from a Bourbon branch. With all the worship which spilled around him in the candle-lit salons, he was made to feel that inferiority. Liszt, who surely had no cause to complain of the general popularity bestowed on him nor the adoration with which women covered him, realized clearly what he called the "*subalternité*" of the artist in the social structure. He was himself much more than a "performer." He was a man of literary and philosophic culture. It was that kind of artist who was needed in modern society, he said, and such a one was not likely to swallow slights humbly. In a series of articles, "The Situation of Artists and Their Condition in Society," which were published in the *Gazette Musicale de Paris* in 1835, Liszt spoke of a "new aristocracy of intelligence" which had risen since the Charter of 1830; that new aristocracy was composed of writers and lawyers and had been duly recognized. Where, however, was the musician?

> Alas, music and musicians still live merely a factious and mutilated life on the surface of society. Condemned, by I know not what fatality, to vegetate without any common possession, without dignity, without consecration, the artists are at the mercy of the first comer even as regards their material existence; and as for what I have called institutions, society has scarcely more regard for them than for individuals.

Mendelssohn was that new type of artist for whom the young Liszt pleaded, a man of dignity and wide education, not content to live a factious life on the surface of society. On this, his second stay in Paris (he was never to return there), his personality must have been buttressed by the ideas which his fellow-workers exposed. No doubt, it was easier for him to achieve social stature than it was for a Chopin, because Mendelssohn was wealthy and a gentleman. In England he had been accepted. Yet he was quite conscious that he was an exception. Devrient writes that Mendelssohn "was totally indignant at the way in which paid artists were separated from these [the British aristocratic] circles. He could never forget having seen Malibran sit in a remote corner of the drawing-room, shut-out and looking intimidated."[9] In London he must have been told the story of how in the great houses the musicians were divided from the guests by a cord stretched across the room. One night the bass, Luigi Lablache, let this cord down and no one had sufficient nerve or rudeness to put it up again. The practice fell into disuse.

In Paris, then, in the bubbling and quivering of its artistic life, and hearing the new self-assured voices of the new artists, Mendelssohn found an ambience very different from that of bumpy Berlin. It influenced him, if only by osmosis, though he "never felt really at home there," and though he continued to make fun of the politicking and the French respect for titles and distinctions. (Was this respect not even more extensive in German life?) He wrote to Rebecka that everybody was wearing the *légion d'honneur* ribbon or some other ribbon in his buttonhole and only a man who had really achieved something was allowed *not* to wear it. He would perhaps have liked Paris better had his musical success there been greater.

[9] *Meine Erinnerungen an Felix Mendelssohn-Bartholdy*, Leipzig, 1872.

The Conservatoire Orchestra under François Habeneck did play his Overture to *A Midsummer Night's Dream* (February 19, 1832), and a month
later (March 18) Mendelssohn performed Beethoven's G Major Concerto
to great applause. Among musicians he earned admiration for his *Octet*
and his two Quartets in E-flat Major and A Minor. But his "Reformation"
Symphony, which was then ready in its first form, was rejected after a
rehearsal or two by the members of the Conservatoire Orchestra as being
too learned and too dry. For the young man who had been fortune's
favorite, this must have been a severe disappointment; it is significant that
he says nothing about it in his letters home. He was both shocked and
grimly amused when he heard at a memorial service for Beethoven the
Scherzo from his own *Octet* being played. He describes how the priests
functioned solemnly at the altar while the measures of the music tripped
by gaily: nobody found it strange. "What an absurdity!" he exclaims.

His disappointments were counterbalanced by many new relationships he formed in that Paris where every third man you saw on the
Boulevard des Italiens was a non-Parisian arrived there in search of fame.
He had already met Chopin in Munich, and now cemented an admiration
which was to last and was to be mutual, though they were never to become
intimate friends. He showed Liszt his Piano Concerto, whereupon Liszt
played it at sight from the manuscript in such a way that Mendelssohn
cried, "It was a miracle, a real miracle . . . it could not be played more
beautifully." He saw something of the poet Heinrich Heine, with whom,
however, he was not very sympathetic because Heine "maligned everything
that was German, speaking bad French." Meyerbeer, too, he disliked; when
he was told that he resembled Meyerbeer, he had his hair cut and arranged
differently to cancel the resemblance. He made the acquaintance of Pierre
Baillot, the superb violin virtuoso and now conductor at the Paris Opéra.
He renewed his acquaintance with Ferdinand Hiller, who was the first to
play Beethoven's "Emperor" Concerto in Paris, and whose musical *soirées*
—Mendelssohn played there—given in company with Baillot, were evenings to be invited to.

For the first time in his life, the shadow cast by time darkened Felix's
life. Eduard Rietz, whom he had loved and who had helped with the
performance of the *St. Matthew Passion*, died suddenly on January 23,

1832, and Mendelssohn set a memorial to him by dedicating to him the Adagio of the A Major Quintet.[10]

A greater sorrow followed hard upon. Goethe died on March 22, 1832. The man who had been Mendelssohn's friend and inspiration, almost his second father, the greatest figure of Germany's greatest period, was no more. Mendelssohn must have expected the old poet's death, but at the news he burst into tears. He wrote home (March 31), "The loss of Goethe impoverishes us all. How different our country now looks! It is one of the messages which I have received here and which I will always connect with the name of Paris. Not all the friendliness here, not all the coming and going, not all the merry life, can cancel the impression left by these messages."

There was still a further blow in store for him. Just about when he was ready to leave Paris, the cholera which had been striking erratically in various parts of Europe ever since the great epidemic of 1830 reached Paris, and Mendelssohn caught it. Fortunately it was a light case. He recovered and was able to leave for London, which he reached on April 23, 1832.

Drawing the balance, his stay in Paris had not been an unqualified success, perhaps partly because of his own anti-Gallic prejudices. He couldn't wait to get to London. Yet, as Felix wrote his father (February 21, 1832), "People now know that I am alive and that I intend to accomplish something. If what I do turns out to be good, they will accept it."

I I

London, again

"I wish I could describe to you," Mendelssohn wrote home as soon as he had arrived in London, "how glad I am to be here, how everything seems dear to me, how I rejoice over the friendship of the old friends." He stayed again in the rooms in Great Portland Street which he had oc-

---

[10] The Quintet (Op. 18) was composed in 1826, but Mendelssohn now substituted a new movement for the original second movement. Of a recent performance of this work Harold Schonberg wrote: "The A major Quintet represents his well-bred classicism and expert writing. The scherzo is remarkable, almost on the order of the *Midsummer Night's Dream* Scherzo, and this kind of music was unheard-of at the time. It buzzes along in its elfin manner, light as bees' wings, suddenly dissipating. Lovely."

cupied before. Klingemann, Moscheles, Attwood, and another friend, Friedrich Rosen, professor of Sanskrit, were all there to embrace him. He wandered into a rehearsal of the Royal Philharmonic just to hear how they were treating the "Pastoral" Symphony, and he was at once recognized. One of the musicians exclaimed, "There is Mendelssohn!" whereupon the whole orchestra began to yell and clap, and when the noise died down somebody else called out, "Welcome to him!" and the shouts began anew.

With more will than he could ever summon in Paris, he went to work. He finished his B Minor Capriccio for Piano and Orchestra (Op. 22). He conducted his *Hebrides* Overture, now once more revised, which "sounded very quaint between two Rossini selections." Twice he played his Piano Concerto. In a concert which Moscheles had arranged, he conducted his *Midsummer Night's Dream* Overture and again the *Hebrides,* and then performed with Moscheles the Double-Concerto of Mozart, for which he wrote special cadenzas. On Sundays he used to go and play the organ in St. Paul's, and there, on June 10, he gave a public organ concert which crowded the huge cathedral's capacity. Right and left he was praised. The *Harmonicon,* the leading review devoted to musical matters, called him "One of the finest and most original geniuses of the age." It was sweet medicine.

His first collection of the *Songs without Words* was published by Novello under the title, *Original Melodies for the Pianoforte,* and soon became all too popular with freshly perfumed young lady pianists.

One sad piece of news did penetrate the English pleasures: Zelter was dead. Felix had foreseen his death; he thought that Zelter would not long outlive Goethe. And indeed, when Goethe died, Zelter bowed before his statue and said, "Your Excellency has of course the right of precedence. But I shall soon follow." They were both gone now, the worldly genius and his rough-hewn musician. Two columns of Felix's temple had fallen. He felt as if he had lost blood, and to seek strength and comfort he went to the country home of Sir Thomas Attwood in Surrey. Yet he was not so far gone in grief as to forget that Zelter possessed that considerable collection of Bach manuscripts. From Surrey he wrote his father, "If you can possibly do so, see to it that these manuscripts are not disposed of until my return. At all costs, I wish to see them all together before they are dispersed."

Zelter's death left open the directorship of the *Singakademie*. The question arose whether Mendelssohn should or should not make a bid for this post. He was not at all sure that he wished to bind himself to a steady obligation. If the post were to fall into his lap, he might accept it, he told Fanny, but under no condition would he lift a hand to reach for it. Nor would he leave London prematurely to be on the scene in Berlin when the *Singakademie* successor to Zelter would be discussed. He would come home when his London concerts were finished, but simply because his "father wished it."

Coming home, that wish was supported by his own desire. The realization had been growing on him that what he wanted to do most, what was his real goal, was the creation of music. "As a composer I wish to earn my livelihood," he wrote, but of course it was not a matter of thalers or guineas, but of the fulfillment of a talent which, in spite of the symphonies and chamber music and overtures, was as yet largely unfulfilled. No major opera had come from his pen, nor had he composed an oratorio, though for some time now the subject of the Apostle Paul had been in his mind, Paul's conversion, his life and his death as a martyr. In composition, then, lay his future. If so, he could only be a German composer, that tradition being the warp and woof of the talent he knew he possessed. He wanted to live in Germany. He did not want to become an expatriate. That resolve had become firm during his stay in Paris and even in beloved London. The seriousness of that resolve becomes apparent in the letter to his father to which I have already referred (from Paris, February 21, 1832):

> The right moment has arrived to write you, dear Father, a few words touching my traveling plans. I wish to do so in a more serious strain than usual. First, let me review in general what, on the occasion of my departure, you defined as the purpose of my journey, a purpose to which you commanded me to adhere strictly: I was to observe closely various countries and to select the one in which I plan to live and work. Further, I was to make my name and my capabilities known so that the people among whom I finally decided to settle would receive me well and not be wholly igno-

rant of my capacities. . . . I am happy to be able to say that I believe I have done this. . . .

Your direction that I choose the country in which I preferred to live, with that I have complied as well, at least in a general way. That country is Germany. I am now absolutely certain of that.

So in his own good time, at the end of June, 1832, he was back in Berlin. The Grand Tour was over. "The use of traveling is to regulate imagination by reality," wrote Samuel Johnson. For Mendelssohn the use of traveling was to stimulate imagination. The reality he had seen in many cities of Germany, in Italy, Switzerland, Paris, England, Scotland, had helped to firm him in his own realm.

All the same, his love for motion, his desire to be up and away, never left him.

Contemporary caricature of an old-fashioned conductor using a roll of paper.
Mendelssohn used a baton and did not "carry on" while on the podium.

Seven

THE CONDUCTOR

I

BEFORE we discuss Mendelssohn as a conductor and evaluate his contribution to that art, it is necessary to review the events of his life which led to his becoming a full-fledged practitioner of the baton.

After he returned from London, both his father and Devrient pressed him hard to enter the lists of official candidates for Zelter's post. The whole family concurred, even Fanny, who might have known better. He was doubtful at first, in which doubt his reluctance to stay home must have played a part, but he let himself be persuaded, and once persuaded he went after the position earnestly. No one in the Mendelssohn entourage thought that there would be the slightest difficulty about his obtaining it. Was Felix not a musician whose London triumphs had been widely discussed in the Berlin newspapers? Was he not a home-town boy who had made good? Was he not the leader who had brought about the performance of the *St. Matthew Passion?* Had he not been Zelter's favorite pupil? And were not Abraham Mendelssohn, plus various relatives, donors to the *Singakademie*'s collection of musical manuscripts and therefore deserving of a favor? The only one who wasn't sure was Felix himself, who wrote that the Berliners "considered him an arrogant eccentric."

A number of candidates were proposed, but the only rival to be considered seriously was Karl Friedrich Rungenhagen, a reasonably good chorus master who had served as Zelter's assistant for eighteen years. But when would the matter be decided? As time dragged on and the decision was again and again being delayed, Felix became more and more desirous of getting that on which he had at first set little store. He now wanted the fruit beyond immediate reach, and he even proposed sharing the director-ship with Rungenhagen. He had no illusions about musical conditions in Berlin and the difficulties he would encounter; earlier he had written from London to Devrient:

> As a whole, musical conditions in Germany are miserable. They make music there as if it were a business, they speculate, pay [the least possible], and haggle. Defects are apparent everywhere. If one compares German musical life with English, one unfortunately finds a great difference. How-ever calculating and money-mad people might be here, they do remain gentlemen. . . . And that is a quality which our dear *Kammermusiker* assuredly lack. When I think of the musicians in Berlin, Devrient, I be-come fierce and ferocious.

The directors of the *Singakademie* deliberated for an unconscionably long period, from the middle of August, 1832, when they met for their first general meeting, until the end of January, 1833, indicating that there were internal factions at work and that agreement was difficult to reach. The final vote was 148 for Rungenhagen, 88 for Mendelssohn. A decisive defeat.

It was a blow to Felix. He reacted badly. Though Devrient exagger-ated when he said that his friend "would not get over it all his life," Men-delssohn's letters of the period do reflect a dark mood, further depressed by the realization that the opera libretto which Immermann had fashioned was not at all to his liking and that he had to return it to the poet. To one of his friends, who was later to work with him, Pastor F. Bauer, he wrote that the autumn of 1832 was "the bitterest time which I can imagine and which I have ever experienced." That the Mendelssohn family resigned in a huff from the *Singakademie* goes without saying.

The rejection by the directors of the *Akademie* is often ascribed to anti-Semitism among its members. Devrient, who naturally took Mendels-sohn's part, wrote that plenty of hugger-mugger was going on and that during one of the debates the argument was brought forward that the *Singakademie* was "a Christian institution occupying itself almost exclusively with sacred music, and therefore it would be quite unthinkable that one would propose a Jew-boy as director." It may be so; but lacking the minutes of the *Singakademie* meetings, which were destroyed during World War II, no real proof exists. The period was not one in which religious prejudice predominated, nor did Lea—or Felix himself—mention anti-Semitism as a cause. She wrote to Ferdinand David: "Carelessness, pity, and mediocrity have determined the choice, as is customary here. Besides, no young woman and no member of fewer than two years' standing was allowed to cast a vote; the old members want only the traditional and cannot reconcile themselves to the idea of seeing a lively young man at the head."

Other reasons than Felix's youth may have prompted the directors: perhaps they felt that a young man of such growing fame could hardly be retained long in Berlin. In his application Felix had stated that he insisted on free time to travel, and this might have given the directors the impression that he would not devote himself wholeheartedly to their cause. Putting the kindest possible interpretation on the matter, the directors may also have believed that they owed a certain amount of loyalty to that faithful worker, Herr Rungenhagen. After his election, he stayed with the *Akademie* for another eighteen years and condemned it, said Devrient and others, to mediocrity.

Felix was not to remain long in the role of rejected suitor. He heard from London. In November, 1832, the Philharmonic Society offered him a commission, at a very respectable fee. He was to compose "a symphony, an overture, and a vocal composition, the performance rights of which would belong to the Philharmonic Society exclusively for two years." The honorarium was 720 Rheinthalers (approximately $9,000 at today's equivalent). How well timed! Felix rejoiced and felt that "the fog is beginning to lift." He now went to work to finish the "Italian" Symphony.

A second invitation, quite unexpected, came from the Rhineland. He was asked to conduct the Lower Rhenish Music Festival of 1833, which that year was to be held in Düsseldorf, a city ambitious to form itself into one of Germany's cultural centers. Even without a Goethe it hoped to become a second Weimar. It was a town which because of its picturesque surroundings attracted a group of young painters, under the leadership of Friedrich Wilhelm Schadow; the Academy he formed attracted talents from all of Germany, some of whom, to be sure, were more adept at tasting wine than at testing new ideas. In Düsseldorf, too, Immermann was trying to develop a national theater. No doubt it was he who recommended Felix, who accepted at once. Then he got a letter from Moscheles with more joyful news: his wife was expecting a baby in February. Would Felix come and be godfather? Please, he *must* come.

These various musical and personal temptations decided Felix to be once again on the move. He did spend the winter in Berlin, conducted several concerts, and played the piano publicly once or twice, always with success. In the spring he was ready to visit England once more. Moscheles' son had been born in the meantime, had been christened "Felix," and the godfather had sent the parents a charming letter illustrated with drawings of toys and musical instruments which he wished for the child, and better still, enclosing a lovely lullaby which he had composed to words by Klingemann.

He stopped off at Düsseldorf to discuss the details of the forthcoming festival and hurried on to London, where on May 13 the "Italian" Symphony received its world première with the Philharmonic, Mendelssohn conducting. Up to the first rehearsal Mendelssohn had still felt uncertain of its value. Its success now reassured him—though not for long. The *Harmonicon* wrote that it was "a composition that will endure for all ages." Even Paganini, who usually was chary of praise, loved the work and invited Mendelssohn to play Beethoven violin sonatas with him. Nothing came of it, for shortly afterward Paganini had to submit to serious jaw surgery.

2

We have noted (in the introductory chapter) how great was the success which the Festival enjoyed and how that success was witnessed by Felix's proud father. Their being together there and later, Abraham observing his son at work, Felix having Abraham to himself, the two of them conversing till long past midnight and for once exchanging views rather than talking at each other—all this led to a new intimacy between father and son. Felix, who perhaps admired Abraham more than he loved him, now entered into a relationship in which filial respect was tempered with an ease that cancels years. Abraham now perceived the son as artist, with an artist's problems. Felix now perceived Abraham as a friend of his art, willing to be led, no longer wholly a mentor. The father had become more flexible, Abraham had become a softer man. (His eyes troubled him. He began to have more and more difficulty in seeing clearly and he must have been aware of his fate. He was going blind.) Abraham expressed his admiration for Felix in his usual restrained way, writing to Lea: "It is possible that we will derive some joy from this young man; sometimes I bless Martens Mill [where Felix was born]."

But then he waxed more enthusiastic:

Often I think it is miraculous that four hundred people of different nationalities, background, and age, here blown together like the snow, let themselves be led as if they were children and ruled by a youngster . . . without title or official distinction. . . . It used to be the fashion here for the members of the orchestra who were arriving one by one from all parts of the land and were meeting local friends to use the rehearsals as an opportunity for a lively exchange of conversation. The chatter was incredible. The rehearsals went badly, the conductor had to scream his lungs out, and nobody paid attention. New musicians arrived at the last moment and the disturbance became insupportable. All this happened again during the first rehearsals. Then Felix said that he was not going to stand for it. He was neither able nor willing to shout; it was their duty to listen to him and he insisted on absolute silence and quiet while he was talking. After he had repeated this command very firmly and seriously, I can assure you that one cannot imagine a more punctilious obedience. Everybody understood that what he wanted was necessary and reasonable. The moment he taps his baton and wants to say something, there is a general *psst* and then deep silence.

The authority which Mendelssohn showed at the Festival—that conductor's mastery of the orchestra which is constituted of equal parts of tyranny and cajolery—earned him an immediate offer: it was a three-year contract at a salary of 600 Rheinthalers (about $7,500 in today's equivalent, certainly not enough to live in the style in which he did live), for which he was to lead Düsseldorf's church music, give four to eight concerts a season with the orchestra, and direct another yearly festival. He accepted for the following season.

In the interim he went to London in Abraham's company. Father did not share the son's enthusiasm for England. Abraham said that Felix found the yellow meadows green and the gray horizon blue. "Today at 9.14 A.M. the sun had just enough power to color the fog yellow. And the atmosphere looks like the thick smoke during a major fire; 'a very fine morning,' my barber (here called *hairdresser*) said to me. 'Is it?' I replied. '*Yes, a very fine morning.*' . . . By midday the fog was victorious . . . and at four o'clock I had to move my table right to the window in order to see not *what* I was writing but *that* I was writing. Felix is playing the organ in St. Paul. I cannot bring myself to leave my room. When he returns, he will surely tell me that nowhere is the summer as fine as in London."

Though his son's friends made much of Abraham, he did not feel comfortable in London, partly because he was shocked at the high prices and partly because he was unable to speak English. "With Horsley I converse in Italian, because he speaks neither German nor French and neither of us is able to speak Italian. . . . As far as my English is concerned, I am able to articulate *How do you do, Sir?* and *Waiter, a mutton chop* and a few other such profound phrases."

Abraham met Malibran in London, and he who had disapproved three years earlier of Felix's infatuation now fell under the spell of that orchidaceous woman. In a letter home he raves about her for more than a page. Father and son also met Wilhelmine Schröder-Devrient, then twenty-nine years old. Here was the actress famous for her Leonore, a role for which she had been praised by Beethoven himself. With all the force and passion with which she infused her stage life, Wilhelmine had still quite as much left over for her private love life. She had married three times and had many lovers. Her first marriage had been annulled on grounds of adultery, after she had borne her husband, Karl Devrient, four children. She not only admitted adultery but she proclaimed that such bourgeois proscriptions as marriage laws were not applicable to her. As an artist, she needed the stimulant of love if she were to portray the heroines of love. In London she was called "the Queen of Tears," and when she enacted Leonore,

H. Fothergill Chorley wrote of her, "There was something subduing in the look of speechless affection with which she at last undid the chains of the beloved one, saved by her love—the mere remembrance of which makes the heart throb and the eyes fill." It is strange that she, a better dramatic actress than a singer, became one of Mendelssohn's favorite interpreters of his undramatic songs. Rellstab called her singing "the art of declamatory song," an art which degenerated into a style of barking out notes, and not the right ones at that. She knew it, too: at the end of her career she wrote to Clara Schumann, "Whether I accomplished anything, whether I have left anything for those who came after me, that is the question! . . . Unfortunately I can point to no results, and only throat-clearing and spitting succeed from time to time." [1] In spite of her fame she was often discouraged; she wrote to Mendelssohn that her art was limited and signed herself sarcastically, "Your *famous* singer." Yet, whatever her limitations, she inspired Mendelssohn—as she did Wagner.

By what one is tempted to describe as a mystic coincidence, soon after Abraham arrived in London he suffered a leg injury similar to the one Felix had sustained. Felix nursed him with the most tender care and Abraham preserved his good humor as well as his ironic attitude toward the English. The two Mendelssohns had to spend the entire summer in London; Abraham never did learn English.

3

The two years or so during which Felix worked in Düsseldorf were in a sense an apprenticeship for him as a conductor. As a composer he continued to labor on what he then considered his first *magnum opus*, the Oratorio on the Life of St. Paul. He completed as well that romantically clear and fresh overture, *Die Schöne Melusine*—which bears so remarkable a resemblance to the preludial passage of *Das Rheingold*—and the *Rondo Brillant* for piano and orchestra (Op. 29), an inconsequential piece.

As an executant musician he was extremely adventurous, widening the repertoire, experimenting with the orchestra, scouring the nearby libraries

---

[1] Quoted by Henry Pleasants: *The Great Singers*, New York, 1966.

and archives for church music and bringing forth much that was totally unknown by Palestrina, Pergolese, Lassus, etc. All this in addition to his
favorites Handel, Beethoven, Weber, and Mozart.

His head was full of plans. Indeed, he was expected to act and did
accept to act as the Pooh-Bah of Düsseldorf's artistic life, adding to his
other duties the post of Intendant of the opera house and helping Immermann develop his plans for a national theater.

Before his tenure commenced, Mendelssohn thought that he would
be long content to live in the charming green and moist city which seemed
to have grown up in the midst of a vineyard. In London he had told the
Horsley girls about Düsseldorf:

> Mendelssohn showed us, on a panorama of Düsseldorf, which is in a book
> of the Rhine which the Langs lent us, the place where he is to live, the
> Belgrave Square of the town he says, and also the fashion-walk where he
> pretends he shall promenade every day from 1 to 3, dressed in a short coat,
> and with large moustachios and a small riding whip in his hand. Fancy
> him! I advised, Mary begged him, not to come over for at least three
> years to come, at which he looked rather offended and tearful. Mary and
> Sophy give him two years, Mamma one. He says himself that he shall not
> think of leaving Düsseldorf (excepting to go to Switzerland with Klinge-
> mann) next year, and that Moscheles has offered to conduct his overture
> at the Phil. He wants to compose a great deal I believe, and I think he
> had better at the same time compose himself, for his mind wants a little
> settling in my opinion. He is looking much handsomer than he has yet,
> for his hair is long again like it was last year, which is so very becoming.
> (From *Mendelssohn and His Friends at Kensington*)

Mendelssohn, like most reformers who stride too fast, soon got into
trouble. What he wanted to give the Düsseldorfers was more than the city
wanted him to deliver. He and Immermann scheduled at the Opera what
they termed a series of "Model Performances." It was not a happily chosen
designation, implying that previous performances had been something less
than model. They prepared *Don Giovanni*, and Mendelssohn insisted on
twenty ensemble rehearsals. Advance publicity may have raised expectancy
too high and, more important, the price of tickets was increased. "Pre-

sumptuous," quite a few people thought. At any rate, on the night of the première, there suddenly occurred a noisy scrap of the kind that one had come to expect in Parisian theaters but which must have been rather a novelty in the Rhenish town. Cries of "Arrogance!" and "Money back!" bounced through the theater. A group of young people whistled and howled and threw newspapers onto the stage. Three times during the first act the curtain had to be lowered. Immermann's nerves went to pieces; Mendelssohn kept calm. During the second act things quieted down a little, and at the end the audience applauded for the artists to show themselves. No one came before the curtain.

Mendelssohn declared that until the instigators of the row would extend a public apology to the personnel of the opera house, he would not conduct again. At the same time, a deputation of the orchestra declared that if Mendelssohn were not to conduct, they would not play. The instigator gave himself up: he turned out to be a minor town official who hated Mendelssohn. He was duly and ceremoniously punished. The second performance went fine.

Though other "Model Performances" followed, Mendelssohn had had enough of it; he had no stomach for operatic intrigues:

> I shall never become an Intendant again, and shall always remember those few weeks. To hell with it! To quarrel with people about two thalers, to be strict with the good ones and indulgent with the bad ones, to make noble faces so that they won't lose the respect which they don't even have, to act angry without being angry—these are all things which I can't do and don't want to do. . . .
>
> (Letter to Devrient, November 26, 1834)

He peremptorily threw up his position. It was probably the only time in Mendelssohn's life that he walked out on an obligation. He did so without taking into account the fate of the opera house or its employees. It was lucky for Mendelssohn, though he had not planned it that way, that the assistant whom he had engaged turned out to be highly competent. This assistant was Julius Rietz, the younger brother of Eduard Rietz, who was to take over the leadership of both the opera and the orchestra after Mendelssohn's departure.

Mendelssohn, in an angry mood, wrote to Klingemann:

The pleasure of reigning I do not feel, in the development of the German stage through Düsseldorf I do not believe, with Immermann I do not get along, to praise mediocrity I will not consent, *and be damned to it* [in English].

(November 30, 1834)

Both Devrient and Abraham severely criticized Felix, his father telling him that more than once he had been guilty of "grabbing things quickly and dropping them just as quickly."

Beneath the overt reasons for Mendelssohn's desertion lay a personal reason, his dislike of Immermann. The poet was an idealist, provided the ideal could be reached according to *his* plan. Immermann felt that the German national theater needed a head of absolute authority, "a Napoleon"—he himself resembled Napoleon to a startling degree. Mendelssohn disagreed: he thought nothing could be accomplished by dictatorial methods and, at any rate, Düsseldorf was too provincial a city in which to form a center of theatrical activity. Moreover, he could hardly have endeared himself to Immermann, the author, by discoursing on the English novel, proclaiming that Sterne and Swift were superior to German writers, Goethe excepted. The two men became openly inimical, but Felix did not care: "Such a thing usually troubles me very much; this time it runs off me like water off waxed linen." He now said that the best thing about Düsseldorf was its geographical position: it wasn't far from London.

Yet Mendelssohn's stay in Düsseldorf was not entirely unhappy. He continued work on *St. Paul* and was supposed to have enjoyed a liaison with a widow—the matter is not certain—which rather scandalized his mother, who must have heard about it through the Düsseldorf town gossip: what she really was afraid of was that Felix might impulsively propose marriage. There was no such danger.

He was invited to direct another music festival of the lower Rhine, to be held in Cologne in 1835. He spent the late summer of 1834 with his family—he was drawing closer than ever to Abraham—and on his return to Düsseldorf at the end of that year, he received an inquiry from the Leipzig Gewandhaus Orchestra asking if he would be available soon and willing to head the orchestra. Now the finer facet of his nature turned to light. Of course he wanted to head the Gewandhaus Orchestra; very much so, because it was the most prestigious post to be obtained in Germany. Of course he saw at once the opportunity to work with an orchestra which had tradition behind it and a soundly financed future before it. Of course he knew that Leipzig was the city where orchestral music was considered more important than the opera. Yet his first answer was that he would under no circumstances push another man from his position. The directors of the Gewandhaus assured him that this would not be the case. In point of fact, the Gewandhaus was led by the concertmaster, one Heinrich Matthai,[2] who was now mortally ill. He died the following year. Christian Pohlenz, the so-called conductor, was now more or less inactive and was called on only when oratorios or large works such as the Ninth Symphony were to be performed.[3] Felix insisted on a suitable retirement compensation for Pohlenz, and only when this had been settled did he accept the position. He stipulated other sensible and honorable conditions: five or six months free time for composing, as one clause; and as another that there would not be given any benefit concerts for himself (as was the practice at the time). The salary was 1,800 gold marks (about $18,000), actually less than another position which had been offered him at the Munich Opera House.

During the negotiations, which lasted six months, Abraham was the only one who was aware of every step, Felix consulting him at every turn.

Thus to Leipzig he went, the city of the St. Thomas Church and its still excellent choir, the center of Germany's book and music publishing industry, the seat of a great university, and, perhaps most attractive to Mendelssohn, the city of Johann Sebastian Bach.

4

What was the German orchestra like at the time Mendelssohn came to the fore as a conductor? What was its constitution? How well did it play?

---

[2] "To him was largely due the credit of having made the Gewandhaus orchestra a fit instrument for Mendelssohn to exercise his skill upon." (Adam Carse)

[3] Wagner had heard Pohlenz conduct the Ninth Symphony in the 1831–32 season and had criticized him sharply. The playing was so bad that Wagner began to believe that Beethoven had composed nonsense. Things were at sixes and sevens until a double-bass player "in rather coarse and determined language" told Pohlenz to stop conducting. After that the orchestra did better. Wagner may have exaggerated.

How and how well were its members compensated for their work? How much authority did the conductor of the orchestra possess?

The world had grown louder and so had its music. The "Hammer-klavier" had replaced the harpsichord, wind instruments had been constructed which were capable of greater fullness of sound, the number of players in the orchestra had increased. Romanticism was to demand for its expression an ever widening apparatus. For the première of his Ninth Symphony in Vienna (1824), Beethoven requested, and got, 24 violins, 10 violas, 12 violoncellos, and 12 double-basses, a string complex larger than he had had at his disposal for the première of the Seventh at the special gala concert of the Congress of Vienna. Even the Ninth's orchestra was small compared to Berlioz's orchestra. "I am told you compose music for an orchestra of three or four hundred men," the King of Prussia was supposed to have said to Berlioz. "No, Your Majesty," he replied, "sometimes I write for as few as two hundred." In the King's capital, the Berlin Court Opera Orchestra, led by Spontini, numbered 65 in 1830 and had grown to about 80 in 1843. The Leipzig Gewandhaus Orchestra represented a total of 33 instrumentalists in 1802, but by 1839 it had swelled to about 50 good men and true. For the Munich Odeon Concerts which were reorganized in the same year, 90 men could be mustered, if the need arose.

While the orchestras in the major German cities were beginning to approach in size the modern symphony organizations, in the smaller cities, the Düsseldorfs or Darmstadts, they remained modest aggregates. For smaller halls and smaller audiences, a smaller group of players had to make do. In Weimar, "the city of the Muses" (population about 15,000), the Court Orchestra numbered 35 as late as 1843, and there Liszt gave *Lohengrin* with a total of 38 men in the pit (1850).

Orchestras were still largely, but no longer exclusively, the "property" of King, Elector, Margrave, or whatever Transparency resided in the *Schloss*. A certain amount of democratization had taken place. In a city where the seat of government was located, the orchestra was occasionally and partly supported by local subvention, duly legislated, though His Royal Highness had the final "yes" or "no" and the "how much?" The state of harmony still depended on his nod. It was just that the orchestra was no longer regarded as a private royal toy. In a few cities—Düsseldorf and Frankfurt were two of them—a group of public-spirited citizens got together to raise money, to form musical committees, to make musical propaganda, in short, to tend the musical life of their habitat, independent of town grants, or supplementing such grants. While in France only Paris boasted a fully functioning orchestra and London served as the musical hub of England, in Germany musical life was decentralized.

In one way or another there was a good deal of fiddling, thumping, and piping going on. But paying the piper—there was the rub. The Napoleonic wars had left many a princeling pinched for cash. Town coffers were depleted. Money for music and the theater had to be carefully doled out. Star attractions—Italian singers and violin virtuosi—could command decent fees. But the anonymous graying fellow in the viola section, him one could underpay. The salary of the average orchestral musician was about 6,000 thalers a year (equivalent to about $5,400 in today's buying power). It was just enough to keep him from starvation, but certainly not enough to keep him from looking threadbare. A uniform—or, better, a livery— was given to him and he was required to wear it. Perhaps he thought this demeaning—Wagner did when in the forties he had to wear the official court uniform while conducting in Dresden—but surely it saved wear and tear on his one Sunday suit. In spite of the poor pay, orchestral posts were so desirable that "most of the larger court orchestras included a number of probationers who played for little or nothing in the hope of securing permanent appointments when vacancies occurred." (Adam Carse: *The Orchestra from Beethoven to Berlioz*)

Most orchestral musicians aspired to becoming Kapellmeister. How well off were you then? Otto Nicolai became Kapellmeister in Vienna in 1837 at a yearly salary of 1,200 gulden (equivalent to $7,200 in today's purchasing power). As Ernest Newman writes:

Nicolai soon found that he was unable to live on his salary, and he was compelled to take up teaching in addition to his other work. He was already 100 gulden in debt when he went to Vienna, and had to ask for an advance on his salary from the theater. In 1842, when he had become a person of some importance in the German musical world, he was appointed first Kapellmeister at the Vienna Court Opera, for something like three years, at a salary of 2,000 gulden a year, payment to be stopped, however, if he were ill and unable to discharge his duties for more than a fortnight. He congratulated himself on his bread and butter being secure for a while at least: his financial condition may be surmised from a letter of the 6th February, 1842, to his ever-borrowing father, in which he says that the 10 thalers he is sending are the half of his total possessions—the product of the pawning of a brilliant ring given him by the heir to the Russian throne. In 1844, at the age of thirty-four, he had been able to lay by nothing at all for sickness or old age, a prospect that filled him with terror. In December, 1847, he could congratulate himself heartily on being appointed Kapellmeister at the Berlin Royal Opera at a salary of 2,000 thalers a year, less the payments for a small pension for his mother and sister.

(From Ernest Newman, *The Life of Richard Wagner*, Vol. I.)

Poorly paid, but as a civil employee fairly assured of steady employment, with a tiny pension at the end when lips had become dry and fingers no longer could form the notes, emerging slowly from the status of servant and gaining a little respectability, usually overworked and always struggling to feed the family—that is how we may picture the man sitting in the third row of the *Philharmonische Verein*. He was overworked not because he had to play many orchestral concerts: the number of concerts given in a season were less than a quarter of those performed by the New York Philharmonic today or the Philadelphia Orchestra. Sometimes the regular subscription concerts numbered as few as six to ten a season. (However, concerts were much longer than they are today.) But he was expected to play at the opera house, and indeed in many towns his chief duty lay there, opera being a greater favorite than symphonic music. That opera house could be a *Schauspielhaus* or a *Nationaltheater* or a *Stadttheater*, meaning that spoken plays were performed as well as operas. Hardly ever was a spoken play given without incidental music, that music ranging from Beethoven's copious music for *Egmont* to a casual strumming during intermission. In addition, musicians could be called on to play at official receptions or diplomatic functions, at church services, and at choral societies. A musician dragged his instrument from one hall to another, and what with rehearsals on which no time limit was set, he spent much of his life in artificial light and bad air. No wonder that some of them became surly characters and others husbanded their energy when an uninspired and uninspiring conductor was standing before them. Then, as now, the conductor was the lazy player's natural enemy. Then as now he was legitimate prey if he was a pale leader. But then disrespect showed itself more crassly, by loud gossiping, yawning, arguing, playing schoolboy pranks, and altogether defying authority. (Berlioz relates in his memoirs a vindictive trick the oboist played on him in Dresden.)

The standard of performance was variable, with a north to south compass far exceeding the good to bad, the inspired to the humdrum, of a performance in our day. It seems to me, however, that we now have a tendency to exaggerate the incompetence of the early nineteenth-century orchestra. From all I have read of contemporary accounts—and how else can one judge?—I would guess that though many performances were careless and dull, not *all* performances were meretricious. I do not think it is true that most orchestras could not play a diminuendo or crescendo smoothly, or that the sound they produced was "awful" and the "intonations of the violins . . . unbearably false"; this according to Spohr's recollections. If Spohr was generally right, how was it possible for the public to understand and respond to the new music of Beethoven, which demanded so high a skill of execution? It is flattering to think how much better our orchestras are. Indubitably they are better, incomparably better. But we must be careful not to conclude that everybody a hundred and forty years ago was a duffer.

Let us call Mendelssohn as a witness. In Düsseldorf he did lacerate the orchestra:

I assure you that at the downbeat, they all come in separately, not one decisively, and in the *pianos* it is apparent that the flute plays sharp, and not a single Düsseldorfer can play a triplet clearly, but all play a quaver and two semiquavers instead, and every *allegro* leaves off twice as fast as it began, and the oboe plays E natural in C minor, and they carry their fiddles under their coats when it rains, and when it is fine they don't cover them at all—and if you once heard me conduct this orchestra, not even four horses could drag you there a second time. And yet there are one or two musicians among them, who would do credit to any orchestra, even to your Conservatoire; but that is just the misery in Germany—the trombones and the drum and the double-bass excellent, and everything else quite abominable.

(Letter to Ferdinand Hiller, March 14, 1833)

Possibly this letter was written in a bad mood; it overstates the case. In a decade or so Julius Rietz developed the Düsseldorf orchestra into a very respectable ensemble. Possibly Mendelssohn did not take much trouble with what he soon considered a temporary position. It was different in Leipzig, even at the beginning:

The whole orchestra, which includes very able men, strive to guess my wishes at a glance; they have made the most extraordinary progress in finish and refinement, and are so devoted to me that I often feel quite moved by it.

(Letter to Fanny, January 30, 1836)

As to the variability of execution:

[Arrived] in Berlin the very first evening we went to hear Gluck's *Armide*. Rarely, if ever, did I enjoy anything at the opera as much as this. That great complex of thoroughly trained musicians and singers, ably conducted by Spontini, the magnificent house crammed full with people, the good scenery—all united in the cause of this wonderful music—made such an impression on me that I was obliged to admit to myself that there was nothing to be done with small towns, small means, small circles. It was quite another story here. How often since then have I had to retract my thoughts! The very next day they gave a so-called Beethoven Memorial Festival and played the A Major Symphony [the Seventh] so atrociously that I had to beg pardon of my small town and my small means. The coarseness and impudence of the execution were such as I have never heard before. I can only explain it through the nature of the whole Prussian officialdom which fits music as a straightjacket fits a man. . . .

(Letter to Ferdinand Hiller, July 15, 1838)

The point is that good musical material was to be found in the orchestral forces of Germany and that they made conscientious music, often plunging intrepidly into difficult scores. What was lacking was the shaping spirit, the man who could mold the sounds made by thirty or fifty men into a work of art as observed, thought through, and interpreted by one man.

In Mendelssohn's youth the practice of divided leadership of an orchestra had not become extinct. There was the so-called "conductor" and there was the "leader," and both of them functioned at the concert. In the eighteenth century the leader sat at the harpsichord, from there indicating tempo. Later he was often recruited from the violin section; the concertmaster (first violinist) of our orchestras is his successor. The conductor as well indicated tempi, watched out for mistakes, and sometimes played along on his violin. (That practice had largely been abandoned in Mendelssohn's time.) If leader and conductor disagreed, too bad. Perhaps both props were needed to keep things straight. The conductor stood in the midst of the orchestra, often facing the audience, the musicians standing around him. All except the cellists. For operatic performances, when they played in the pit, the musicians sat; for concerts they stood. (At the Gewandhaus the violin and viola players continued to stand until 1905; Nikisch had by then been the conductor for ten years.) It "would be a mistake to look upon these two figures—leader and conductor—as interpretive musicians in the modern sense. Basically their function was to correct rather than to initiate." (Schonberg) The beat was given not only visually but audibly by striking a desk with a roll of paper or by stamping one's foot.

As orchestras grew larger and could no longer huddle closely together, and as the new music became more irregular in rhythm and complex in dynamics, the need for a unifying impulse became apparent. Before Mendelssohn, Weber, Spontini, and subsequently Spohr, appeared, all composer-conductors. The baton had been used as early as 1810 in Halle by one Daniel Türk,[4] who sawed the air so energetically that he sometimes hit the chandelier above his head and brought down a rain of glass. It took time, however, for the baton to be adopted. Schumann, who himself was a poor conductor, never liked it. Neither did Zelter. Mendelssohn and Berlioz used it. When the two met in Leipzig they exchanged batons, as a gesture of amiability. Berlioz tells the anecdote in his *Memoirs:*

> As Mendelssohn stepped down from the rostrum radiant with the sense of achievement, I came forward, thrilled by the experience of hearing the work [Mendelssohn's *Walpurgisnacht*]. The moment could not have been better chosen. Yet, after the first exchange of greetings, the same melancholy thought struck us both.

[4] Haydn used a baton at the first performance of *The Creation* in 1798. (This fact has only recently been discovered.)

"What? Twelve years? Can it really be twelve years since we day-dreamed together in the Campagna?"

"And in the Baths of Caracalla."

"Ah, still the same scoffer, I see, always ready to mock me!"

"No, no, my mocking days are over. I said it to test your memory and to see whether you had forgiven me for my irreverence. In fact I mock so little that I'm going to ask you at once in all seriousness to make me a present of something which is of great value to me."

"What is that?"

"The baton with which you have just been rehearsing your new work."

"With the greatest pleasure, on condition that you let me have yours."

"It will be copper for gold. Still, it's a bargain."

And Mendelssohn's sceptre was brought to me forthwith. Next day I sent him my heavy oak cudgel, together with the following letter (which the Last of the Mohicans would not, I hope, have disowned):

To Chief Mendelssohn—Great chief! We are pledged to exchange tomahawks. Here is mine. It is rough-hewn. Yours too is plain. Only squaws and palefaces love ornate weapons. Be my brother; and when the Great Spirit sends us to hunt in the land of souls, may our warriors hang our tomahawks side by side at the door of the council chamber.

Mendelssohn was the first of the great interpretive conductors; at the very least he was one of the first to envisage the conductor's task as going beyond ferreting out mistakes, beating time, and holding the men together. He and Wagner, each in his own way, were pioneer expositors. They differed in their approach to music, Mendelssohn's concept being cleanly musical while Wagner searched for the dramatic idea behind the music. Wagner set music within the frame of the totality of the artistic imagination. He saw in Beethoven's Seventh a central programmatic theme; Mendelssohn saw a symphonic structure which had no need of programmatic interpretation. Let us say, with some oversimplification, that Mendelssohn was a descendant of Bach, Wagner of Gluck.

Mendelssohn's experience as a conductor dated back to his childhood days when he stood on a chair and led the little orchestra his father had invited to the home. His extraordinary memory helped him to hold fast every note and nuance and accent.

The composer H. Dorn related that he played one of his compositions for Mendelssohn when Felix was only sixteen years old. When they chanced to meet again sixteen years later, Mendelssohn played for Dorn twelve bars of this composition which the composer himself had forgotten. Mendelssohn's phenomenal retention of music was similar to that of Toscanini. While it must be an exaggeration to claim that "he knew every bar of every work of music," as Charles Halle, English pianist and conductor asserted, he undoubtedly encompassed a vast repertoire. What he knew he knew profoundly: there was no faking about him.

He came to conducting by way of the piano and it is reasonable to conjecture that his style of pianism transferred itself to his style of conducting. The characteristics of that style were: clarity; avoidance of excess mannerism (little "Schmalz"); [5] rhythmic certainty, with a predilection for "keeping things moving" which now and then drove the music at too fast a pace; a marvelous sense of color (musicians said that when he played an orchestral work on the piano, they could "see" the orchestration of the full score); power when needed, delicacy when needed (only very occasionally would that delicacy fall into trivialism).

Contemporary tributes to Mendelssohn's piano playing, which may also apply to his conducting, are plentiful. Here are two of them:

Clara Schumann:

> Of mere effects of performance he knew nothing—he was always the great musician, and in hearing him one forgot the player and only reveled in the full enjoyment of the music. He could carry one with him in the most incredible manner, and his playing was always stamped with nobility and beauty.

Ferdinand Hiller:

> He possessed great skill, certainty, power and rapidity of execution—all, in fact, that a virtuoso could desire; but these qualities were forgotten while he was playing, and one almost overlooked even those more spiritual gifts which we call fire, invention, soul, apprehension, etc. When he sat

[5] He hated sentimental *ritardandos* at the close of lyric pieces. His favorite expression was: "That is not written" (*Es steht nicht geschrieben*).

down to the instrument music streamed from him with all the fullness of
his inborn genius.

His behavior on the podium was unostentatious, as was to be expected from his personality. He did not carry on. "His movements were
short and decided, and generally hardly visible, for he turned his right
side to the orchestra. A mere glance at the concertmaster, a slight look
this way or that, sufficed," said Ferdinand Hiller. When he was pleased
with the orchestra, he let them know it: he nodded his head and pushed
out his lower lip "as if there were nobody in the room." Joachim, too,
spoke of his "almost unnoticeable but extremely lively gestures." He "corrected little errors with a flick of his finger." Robert Schumann compared
him favorably to those magnates "who threaten with their scepters to
thrash the score, the orchestra, and even the audience." Yet not even a
Mendelssohn could keep his temper all the time in the battle of rehearsal.
Once in Düsseldorf when the musicians appeared to be particularly indo-
lent, he flew into a rage and tore the score in two. Later, he subdued the
Berlin orchestra, who were tough boys when their martinet, Spontini, was
away. He stood it for one rehearsal and then fined the more recalcitrant
members. "Now they regard me as another Spontini. . . . Instead of being
haughty, they are now obsequious."

W. A. Lampadius, who wrote an early biography of Mendelssohn
(Leipzig, 1849), said that "when once his fine, firm hand grasped the
bâton, the electric fire of Mendelssohn's nature seemed to stream out
through it, and be felt at once by singers, orchestra and audience."

At the outset, when he took his place at the music-stand, his countenance
was wrapped in deep and almost solemn earnestness. You could see at a
glance that the temple of music was a holy place to him. As soon as he had
given the first beat, his face lighted up, every feature was aflame, and
the play of countenance was the best commentary on the piece. Often the
spectator could anticipate from his face what was to come. The *fortes* and
crescendos he accompanied with an energetic play of features and the
most forcible action; while the *decrescendos* and *pianos* he used to modulate with a motion of the hands, till they slowly sank to almost perfect
silence. He glanced at the most distant performers when they should
strike in, and often designated the instant when they should pause, by a

characteristic movement of the hand, which will not be forgotten by those who ever saw it. He had no patience with performers who did not keep good time. His wondrously accurate ear made him detect the least deviation from the correct tone, in the very largest number of singers and players.

He heard a work of music as a whole, knowing from the first bar where it was going, and he interpreted it as a whole, finding the dynamics and phrasing which in his view best expressed the style of the composition. The sense of fitness, the perception of proportion, is one essence of the conductor's art, and that art he carried much beyond his predecessors. Whether today we would find his conducting satisfactory is a moot question. Perhaps his restraint was too restrained. Those fast tempos might bother us.[6] They bothered Schumann. In the chorus of praise a few dissonant voices can be heard. Schindler, who praised Mendelssohn after the Düsseldorf Festival, later turned against him. Listen to him rant in his biography of Beethoven:

> In regard to Beethoven's music, it was largely Mendelssohn who set the standard: this was a great misfortune for the music. No music will ever recover from the wounds inflicted upon it by this artist, highly esteemed both as a pianist and as a conductor. For the bad seeds he has planted north and south, east and west throughout the musical state have already borne fruit that can never be rooted out, despite the efforts that certain art journals may bend in that direction, for the effects have already poisoned the flesh and blood of a whole generation. Not that there were no conductors before Mendelssohn who, being also virtuoso pianists, saw all music from a virtuoso's point of view and would chase whole orchestras in double quick-step through a piece of music—Conradin Kreutzer is an example—yet their influence was confined to a single place beyond which their authority did not extend. Mendelssohn, on the other hand, even while still a youth, carried his authority as a true aristocrat of music from

---

[6] Brahms favored "moderate tempi": only such enabled "modern music" (Beethoven, Schumann, Wagner, and himself) with its frequent harmonic changes to make its full effect. Tempo, to Brahms, was a "relative concept," capable of different interpretations. However, once decided upon, the relationship of tempi within a composition must remain consistent and not be subject to a whim. Brahms liked Handel's tempo indication: "*Tempo giusto.*" And he admired the "Mendelssohn tradition," especially as practiced by Joachim. To Joachim and Bülow, whom he admired equally, he gave "*plein pouvoir*" in the performance of his music. (From the Introduction to *Billroth und Brahms im Briefwechsel*, Berlin, 1935)

country to country, from one music festival to another, until it was inevitable that he should be regarded everywhere as the highest model for the performance of every type of music, especially as his productions were supported by eminent qualities of another sort.

This condemnation is suspect, both because Schindler thought he possessed the exclusive secret to the "Beethoven style" and because he may have been Mendelssohn's disappointed rival: evidence suggests that he tried for the conductor's post in Düsseldorf.

Equally suspect is Wagner's judgment. He thought Mendelssohn a superficial conductor. In his treatise *On Conducting* (1869) Wagner takes Mendelssohn to task for his fast tempi, particularly in the third movement of Beethoven's Eighth, accusing him of covering up inaccuracies by speed, though he did acknowledge that the "modern orchestra" owes something to Mendelssohn. But, as I say, we must take Wagner's judgment with a grain of bitter salt.

6

The Wagner-Mendelssohn relationship was a profitless and dim one, its facts obscured by self-serving remarks of Wagner's, set down chiefly in his autobiography, and by silence on Mendelssohn's part. Certainly the two men were unsympathetic to each other. Wagner's anti-Semitism became sharper when it was directed toward a musician who seemed to be insufficiently in sympathy with him. As Robert W. Gutman wrote in *Richard Wagner: The Man, His Mind, and His Music:*

> He passionately believed in the theater as a temple of Germanic art where mystic rites might redeem the erring and exorcise the Semitic demons Mendelssohn and Meyerbeer. (The latter had joined Felix in the Wagnerian Gehenna.) And need one ask whose works Wagner imagined should form the Proper and Ordinary of this cleansing ritual?

Certainly, Mendelssohn neither understood nor shared Wagner's ideas. As to Wagner's great music, that Mendelssohn could not know: by the time the *Ring* [7] or *Tristan* came along, Mendelssohn was dead. *Tannhäuser* and possibly *Lohengrin* were the latest he could have perused.

[7] Curiously, Mendelssohn considered the Nibelungen Saga as a possible subject for an opera of his own. He asked Fanny about it. The idea vanished, as did so many others.

It began with a courteous enough letter from Wagner to Mendelssohn (April 11, 1836, when Wagner was twenty-three years old) in which he sends him the score of his C Major Symphony as a gift. He composed this symphony—he tells Mendelssohn—when he was eighteen years old and he could imagine no finer destiny for it than the possibility that Mendelssohn would leaf through the work in an idle hour. He would be even more pleased were the score of this symphony, which he had executed with conscientious labor, to lead to a nearer acquaintance with Mendelssohn. The letter was a covert suggestion to have his symphony performed. But it had already been performed by the Gewandhaus Orchestra, and presumably Mendelssohn did not like the piece and had no wish to perform it again. What Mendelssohn did with the score is unknown; it was not among the papers he left behind nor has it been found in the Leipzig archives. Did he destroy it? According to Du Moulin Eckart, Wagner said that he believed Mendelssohn must have done so, "perhaps because he detected in it a talent that was disagreeable to him." But Eckart was a notoriously unreliable biographer.

In *Mein Leben* Wagner tells us that on the occasion of their working together in a concert in Leipzig—the concert was given in honor of Sophie Schröder, the famous actress and Schröder-Devrient's mother—he "became conscious of the peculiar unrest and excitement with which this master of music, who, though still young, had already reached the zenith of his fame and life's work, observed or rather watched me." Mendelssohn appeared to be jealous of Wagner for two reasons: first, Wagner's triumph with his *Rienzi*, while Mendelssohn had failed in his "most ardent desire . . . to write a successful opera." Second, because he "probably found it no less exasperating that Devrient, whose gifts he acknowledged, and who was his own devoted admirer, should now so openly and loudly sound my praises." Mendelssohn, says Wagner, put his *Ruy Blas* Overture on the program because it was "operatic," while Wagner conducted two arias from *Rienzi*. It sounds improbable; Mendelssohn was not as childish as all that.

All the same, Wagner respected Mendelssohn's technical skill, though he found him "cold." In the concerts Wagner conducted in London in 1855, he programmed Mendelssohn's compositions. It was an unhappy experience for him; the memory of Mendelssohn was still green, and the critics did not forgive Wagner for not being Mendelssohn. Davison of *The*

Times was particularly acerbic, whereupon Wagner took a poor revenge by calling the press a bunch of Jews. Wagner's comments to his friend Ernst Kietz:

London, April 27, 1855

For the most part I am being torn apart by the press *à cause de* Mendelssohn and the other Jews who would like to pack me off to eternal life. . . . This evening, while conducting the concert, I kept my gloves on for the first time, out of *malice* over a very bad symphony of Mendelssohn [the "Italian"]; for the *Euryanthe* Overture I took them off.

Eleven years previously, when *Der Fliegende Holländer* was produced in Berlin, Mendelssohn merely murmured, "Well, you ought to be satisfied now," and never referred to the work again, though the two met several times during the next few days. Thus Wagner's recollection in *Mein Leben*. It quite contradicts his letter to Minna, his wife, written at that time:

. . . Mendelssohn, with whom I dined once, gave me great pleasure; after the performance he came on the stage, embraced me, and congratulated me most heartily. . . .

The year before, Wagner had written to Mendelssohn: "I am proud to belong to the nation which produced you and your *St. Paul*" and he sent an enthusiastic report on this oratorio to the Intendant Lüttichau. Yet later Wagner, who had deplored the standards prevailing at the Gewandhaus before Mendelssohn's tenure, now wished for the return of Leipzig's "pre-Judaic age." As Wagner grew older, and as he thought about Mendelssohn when he was dictating *Mein Leben* to Cosima, his antipathy deepened. He could never forgive Mendelssohn's silence about the youthful symphony. Not to recognize Wagner at once as a supreme genius was, in Wagner's view, cause enough for permanent malediction.

A year before his death, Mendelssohn conducted the *Tannhäuser* Overture in Leipzig. Bülow called it an "execution" in more ways than one. Mendelssohn was accused by the Wagnerites of purposely holding the work up to ridicule. There exists a report [8] by Natalie Planer, Minna's daughter, which calls Mendelssohn "a smooth Jew, slippery as an eel," and says that he "purposely mutilated and damaged" the overture. No doubt Mendelssohn gave the piece a bad performance: he could not warm up to this music. Yet it is unthinkable that he conducted badly on purpose. Such behavior was incompatible with his character.

Wagner himself took the opportunity of another side-swipe at Mendelssohn when Eduard Devrient—who had been Wagner's friend as well as Mendelssohn's—published his *Recollections of Felix Mendelssohn-Bartholdy*. Wagner wrote a review of the book, attacking it venomously. Ernest Newman, in *The Life of Richard Wagner*, writes:

> If there was any need at all in Germany for a brochure of this sort there was certainly no reason why Richard Wagner should have wasted his time in writing it—except the desire to find a personal victim for the rancour against the German world in general that filled his soul just then. Knowing well that he was doing something that hardly presented him in the most favourable light imaginable, he issued the Devrient pamphlet under the pseudonym of "William Drach"—one more instance of his preferring to fire at someone he disliked from behind a hedge rather than in the open.

To be fair about the Wagner-Mendelssohn relationship, it must be added that there is not the slightest evidence that Mendelssohn made an effort to understand the music of Wagner or that he perceived in him a growing giant, destined for a different measure than that of a Niels Gade or a Sterndale Bennett. Lack of vision beset both Mendelssohn and Wagner.

It is a calamitous commentary on the smallness of which large minds are capable. Is this illiberality, this bias, which admits only one way and charges ahead on that way, a mark of talent? It would almost seem so, for it occurs so often. A man of talent, drawing the cloak of his occupation tight around himself, is frequently impervious to signs of talent around him, or, if he does recognize other talent, he faults it because it is not like his own. "A vulgar barbarian," said Voltaire of Shakespeare. "He didn't know how to draw," said Michelangelo of Botticelli. "Against stupidity the very gods contend in vain," wrote Schiller. But even the gods have their own stupidity.

[8] In the Burrell Collection (No. 288).

7

Returning to the theme of Mendelssohn as a conductor, H. F. Chorley, the English music critic, in whose eyes and ears Mendelssohn could do no wrong, was yet impartial enough to say that Felix obtained better results with the Leipzig orchestra than with other groups. On the other hand, Miles Birket Foster, in his *The History of the Philharmonic Society of London, 1813–1912* (London, 1912), writes that Mendelssohn "did much to make it rise Phoenix-like from the ashes." In Leipzig he really felt at home. The members of the Gewandhaus were no great virtuosos, but he formed them into a homogeneous group. Practicing together daily, he developed a fine *esprit de corps*. That is attested by observers less friendly than Chorley: by Bülow, by Berlioz, and by Schumann, who spoke of the orchestra's "family feeling."

He was greatly helped by Ferdinand David, whom he called to Leipzig in 1836 as the "leader" and who, once Mendelssohn had settled the business of unilateral authority over the orchestra, became its concertmaster. He was devoted to Mendelssohn with all his heart and remained with the Gewandhaus until his death.

Mendelssohn took a personal interest in the lives and welfare of his musicians. Letter after letter can be read, addressed to him by one grateful member of the orchestra or another. He fought for a statutory pension fund. He got salaries raised:

> . . . If they wish to honour Handel in Halle, Mozart in Salzburg and Beethoven in Bonn by founding good orchestras and performing their works properly, I am their man. But I do not care for their stones and blocks as long as their orchestras are only stumbling-blocks, nor for their conservatories in which there is nothing worth conserving. My present hobby is the improvement of our poor orchestra. After no end of letter-writing, soliciting and importuning, I have succeeded in getting the salaries raised by five hundred thaler; and before I leave them I mean to get them double that amount. If this is granted, I will not mind their setting

up a monument to Sebastian Bach in part of the St. Thomas School; but first, mind you, the grant! . . .

(Letter to Moscheles, November 30, 1839)

He was unable to do away entirely with the "mixed" programs which were the custom. As late as 1848 the young Bülow heard a concert at the Gewandhaus consisting of first an overture by Niels Gade, followed by an aria from *Figaro*, followed by Ferdinand David playing "some bad variations of his own very cleverly," followed by the Sextet from *Don Giovanni*, followed by a Mendelssohn Rondo played by Moscheles, followed by two songs of Rietz and one of Mendelssohn. After all that antipasto came—the Ninth Symphony!

Mendelssohn introduced himself to Leipzig with a little more consistent evening (Oct. 4, 1835):

Mendelssohn: Overture *Calm Sea and Prosperous Voyage*
Weber: Scene and Aria from *Der Freischütz* (Mme. Grabau)
Spohr: Violin Concerto No. 8 (Gehrke)
Cherubini: Overture and Introduction to *Ali Baba* (with the Leipzig
    Singakademie and the St. Thomas Choir)

Intermission

Beethoven: Fourth Symphony

From variety entertainment he proceeded to present all-Beethoven programs—in one of which he gave all four overtures to *Fidelio*, which was probably rather overdoing it—a Bach-Handel concert (exceedingly copious), a series of "Historical Concerts" which ranged from Viotti to Weber, the *St. Matthew Passion* again, *The Messiah*, Handel's *Salomon*, and much contemporary music. Among the contemporaries he preferred the less problematical; polite stuff which has been washed through the sieve of history: Ferdinand Hiller, Sterndale Bennett, Franz Lachner, Heinrich Marschner, Étienne Méhul, etc. But he did bring Schumann's music to the fore and he gave the world première of Schubert's great C Major Symphony. Schumann had discovered it in Vienna among a pile of manuscripts in Schubert's brother's house; he arranged to have it copied and sent it to Mendelssohn. It was most carefully rehearsed and performed on March 21, 1839. Bülow:

I recall the impression—never again so powerful in subsequent performances—which was made on me by Schubert's C Major Symphony under
Mendelssohn's direction. At that time it was not yet fashionable to install
Schubert on the heights of Mt. Olympus; he was loved, admired, and
enjoyed as a *minorum gentium,* but there were complaints about the ex-
pansiveness of his forms and the monotony of his rhythms. But under
Mendelssohn's baton, one was not aware of these faults. Without using
the blue pencil [9]—simply through his elastic sensitivity and the magnetic
eloquence of his gestures, the brilliant leader was able completely to con-
ceal the abovementioned deficiencies. What wonderful nuances of color,
what intelligently thought-out shadings of tempo he used! How easily he
caused us to glide over the varied steps of the "endless" Allegretto, so
that, at the end, the hearer had no conception of the duration of the
acoustical phenomenon! For we had just dwelt in eternity in a timeless
world.

Hans von Bülow: *Ausgewählte Schriften*
(Leipzig, 1896)

One of Mendelssohn's splendid achievements as a conductor was his
presentation of the Ninth Symphony. When Felix was seventeen and the
Ninth two years old, he had played it on the piano and elucidated the as yet
obscure work to an invited audience. London had heard it both with enthusiasm and puzzlement; in Paris Habeneck and the Conservatoire Orchestra had worked at the symphony for three winters before daring to play it;
but it was still more or less of a stranger in Germany. Now, on Feb. 11,
1836, Mendelssohn and the Gewandhaus presented it to an expectant and
absorbed audience. Ten years later Wagner conducted it in a famous performance, one which must have been very different from Mendelssohn's,
of larger outlines, more dramatic design, and perhaps profounder understanding. Yet it is absurd to claim as Ernest Newman did that Wagner
alone, or almost only he, then "really understood the greater Beethoven."
Chorley could not have been altogether wrong when he wrote: "Never,
indeed, did I hear the Symphonies of Beethoven so intensely enjoyed as at
Leipzig and never so admirably performed."

As against these doughty deeds—how is this for a program conducted
by Mendelssohn at the height of his fame?

---

[9] Mendelssohn seems, however, to have made some slight cuts.

Nov. 2, 1840

1. Overture by Beethoven (not specified)
2. Aria from *Fidelio*
       sung by Louise Schlegel
3. *La Melancolia* by Prume
       sung by Uhlrich
4. Duet from Bellini's *Il Pirata*
       sung by Wild and Schlegel

Intermission

5. Overture to Cherubini's *Les deux journées*
6. Duet from Bellini's *Romeo und Julie* [sic]
       sung by Schloss and Schlegel
7. Aria sung by Wild [not specified]
8. Crusell: *Andante pastorale* for clarinet
       played by Heinze, Jr., member of the orchestra
9. "The Farewell": Song by A. Pohlenz
       sung by Schlegel

On the other hand:

FIFTEENTH SUBSCRIPTION CONCERT
Feb. 4, 1841

W. A. Mozart

1. Overture to *La Clemenza di Tito*
2. Recitative and Aria *"Non temer, amato bene"*
       sung by Mme. Schloss and Herr C. M. David with violin obligato
3. Piano Concerto [not specified]
       played and conducted by Mendelssohn
4. Two Songs
       sung by Schloss (*"Das Veilchen"* and *"An Chloe"*)

Intermission

5. "Jupiter" Symphony

We may think of Mendelssohn, then, standing on the podium as a slight figure, immaculately dressed in the fashionable *Frack* of the early nineteenth century, flushed with enthusiasm, not too solemn, perhaps too nervous, kind and courteous but nevertheless brooking no nonsense or slovenliness from the orchestra. He made them work: extra and long rehearsals were the rule, not the exception. He wore white gloves at the concerts—as was the custom—but he certainly took his gloves off when he prepared the program. He took an intense interest in the entire musical life of the city, all phases of it. He became active in planning the Leipzig Conservatory (opened in 1843) and was one of its first teachers. To this institution he attracted so famous a faculty as Robert Schumann (piano and composition), Ferdinand David (violin), Ignaz Moscheles (piano), and Moritz Hauptmann (music theory).

The Gewandhaus concerts became overcrowded events and Leipzig turned into a musical mecca. Mendelssohn had to conduct as many as twenty concerts a season, not counting charity affairs and special concerts. Seats were not reserved, but it was the custom to let the ladies have the center positions. They sat on benches which were drawn up like opposing troops, facing each other and at right angle to the orchestra. The men placed themselves behind the women, and anybody who arrived later than a half hour before the start of the concert stood in danger of being pressed to the wall, with the weight of a corpulent Leipziger leaning against him. Clara Novello, the English soprano, reported:

> . . . the benches are arranged that one sits as if in an omnibus—and no lady and gentleman ever are allowed to sit together here or in their churches. So that the women sit in rows opposite one another staring at each other's dress which is celebrated for being as ugly as the men and women—the men standing round looking at you through an immense eyeglass the whole night.

They were willing to stand, they were willing to be uncomfortable— the heat must have been oppressive—they were willing to arrive long before the beginning of the concert. The music their conductor made stirred them and gave them joy. Mendelssohn was fond of quoting Seneca's words, "Real joy is a serious business." [10] In his honor, these words were later inscribed

[10] *Verum gaudium res severa est.*

on the Gewandhaus building. The building was destroyed in World War II.

The contribution he made to the "serious business" of musical interpretation could not be destroyed. We might draw a line from him to Nikisch, Bruno Walter, Toscanini, Reiner, Beecham, Szell, and Karajan, as we might draw a line from Wagner to Bülow, Richter, Muck, Mahler, Weingartner, Strauss, Furtwängler, and Bernstein. Without continuity there is no course.

Cécile, painted by Edouard Magnus in 1836, a year before her marriage.

Eight

LOVE AND MARRIAGE

I

THE woman whom Mendelssohn loved with the profoundest love of which he was capable, the woman with whom he was united for the longest period of his life, who understood him best and whose way of thinking and feeling came nearest to his own, was his sister Fanny. She not only reciprocated his love but her fondness often o'erflowed the measure. It is not too much to say that, at least until she had a husband and a child of her own, Fanny saw in Felix husband, child, brother, and dearest friend. All the tenderness which this girl possessed, along with her high talents, were put at the service of her brother, four years younger than herself, who roamed the world while her thoughts and letters followed him. Conversely, Felix's love for her never wavered and never lost its luster, not in the midst of turbulence or fame and not after he had found a wife.

When we speak of Fanny's love for Felix or his for her, no sexual relationship is implied. No overt one, at any rate. Who can divine whether an attraction suppressed or unexpressed spun itself between them? A cognate eroticism between these two could not have come to the surface; Felix and Fanny Mendelssohn were not Siegmund and Sieglinde. Nor were they William and Dorothy Wordsworth. Much as they needed each other, they did not live together, and each entered what may be called a successful marriage, satisfying and being satisfied by the partner.

Fanny was not really beautiful, though men found her looks "interesting." Of the two sisters she was the better-looking and the more intellectual one; Rebecka, a considerable personality in her own right, compensated by developing an impish sense of humor. Fanny, the more intense and the more sentimental of the two, did not possess much humor. Her figure was attractive, though her left shoulder was slightly higher than her right one; perhaps that was a throwback to her hunchbacked grandfather. She hid the defect adroitly. She had also inherited her grandfather's eyes, huge and dark and nearsighted. Her teeth were perfect, her hands those of a pianist, her movements quick and decided. Unlike her brother, she was neither a gourmet nor luxury-loving. She cared little about social amenities and like Felix could be very rude to people who bored her. Being rich, both girls were dressed in the latest fashion and made the most of their looks. Fanny rather resented the time which she had to give to the hairdresser. Rebecka enjoyed it. While Fanny read Goethe and Jean Paul and the whole family read Shakespeare, Rebecka did take a breather once in a while by perusing "with pious devotion" (Fanny said) the latest fashion magazine.

Music was the very breath of life to Fanny. She sang, she played the piano superbly, she composed, her theoretical knowledge almost equaling that of her brother. Or so *he* said. Chorley, invited to the Mendelssohn home, heard her play and wrote that her playing had "a touch of that southern vivacity which is rare among the Germans." Her father was proud of her for her extraordinary virtuosity; he was delighted with the songs which she composed and the learned Protestant motets and psalms which came from her pen. But under no circumstances would he allow her to undertake a professional career. Whatever talent she had could not develop by being exposed to public performing, by being wounded through public criticism, by being brought into competition with the musician who had to earn money. Felix held her in such high esteem as a composer that he gave out several of her songs as his own. Love alone prompted him: it was a way to bring her productions into the open and strengthen her confidence in herself. In the other aspects of her life she was the captive cricket on the hearth. Even when Fanny got married, she and Hensel took up their residence in the Leipziger Strasse; fortunately, the estate was large enough to

Fanny, drawn by Wilhelm Hensel. (National Gallery, Berlin)

ensure a certain amount of privacy to the newly married couple. Hensel painted and drew pictures of the family, while Fanny took over the task of organizing those Sunday concerts in the Mendelssohn home which had become a tradition and invitations to which were regarded as marks of distinction by Berlin's society.

While people came to her, she did not go out to people. She did appear publicly—or semipublicly—once at a charity affair. It was a grand affair at which, as she wrote Klingemann (Feb. 27, 1838), the chorus consisted of duchesses, ambassadors' wives, and officers. "Well, I, the elegant lady, was urged to play and did play publicly, for the first time in my life; Felix's G-minor Concerto. I wasn't the least afraid; my acquaintances were kind enough to take care of feeling afraid for me."

Most of her life the "elegant lady" led her existence as the quiet daughter of the house. She accepted her fate as a matter of course. If she resented the waste of her talent, she kept quiet about it. Felix, in a sense, was her compensation. She worried about him. To his newly married wife she wrote:

Oct. 5, 1837

If I could but once hear that Felix has conquered his restlessness! This constant race which he runs year after year takes my breath away, I who live in deepest quiet. . . .

The evidence of their love runs through their lives. Though often expressed lightly and laced with playfulness, the strength and depth of it are unmistakable. Sometimes their letters to each other read like love letters. When he was a boy of fifteen and on a holiday, he wrote to her, "My sweet—I love you terribly." (July 21, 1824) He sends her a song from Munich, composed for her (June 14, 1830) and writes that while he thought of her he felt quite weak. "That I am yours, you know." Three days previously, in the letter in which he tells his "darling little sister" about Delphine von Schauroth, he has her portrait before him as he is writing.

Yesterday a noble countess graciously praised my songs, and remarked, interrogatively, wasn't the one by Grillparzer altogether delightful. Yes,

I said, and she thought I was conceited until I gave her a full explanation by telling her that you were the composer. . . .

Her feelings become apparent the first time that Felix departs on more than a summer journey, the first time he goes out into the great world: his voyage to London in 1829. In her diary she writes: (Entry of April 3) "I stayed with Felix, helped him to get dressed and packed. It was very cold. I followed him with my glance until he disappeared from sight." (April 20) "Today at noon, if God is with him, he arrives in London. It is hard, very hard. This week we received much correspondence and a detailed letter from Felix. Father is much moved by the separation." This is the year in which she is to be married. But there are more entries in the diary about Felix than about Hensel. "Felix our soul is departing"—she is worried about that as early as January. In March, she writes to a friend in England: "I do not know what I shall do without him; all will be mute and desolate." Referring to Hensel, she writes in the same letter, "A bride-groom is no more than a man, after all." She notes in the diary that she is happy that Felix likes Hensel. Five days after Felix departs from Berlin for London, she writes him a letter which is to reach him in Hamburg before he embarks.

April 15, 1829

Although we wrote as late as yesterday, I still have the desire to send you a few lines on this, the last day before you board. Call it what you wish, if you like call it sentimentality, the strongest term of disapprobation you use. Nevertheless, from the point of view of our twinship it gives me pleasure to think about your new life, which will be so much more exciting. Even though you are far away, you will at this moment have time to think of me and my state of mind. All that goes without saying. It is an old story. Every one really writes to himself; I write to myself. . . .

In September there is an entry in her diary: "Sept. 23, 1829. My marriage approaches and everything would be well—if I didn't feel so un-well. I have suffered again with my teeth and had a tooth pulled. Now I have a swollen jaw. Altogether I feel low." Tooth or no tooth, it is hardly the tone one would expect from a bride-to-be in two weeks.

Similarly, she writes in July of the same year to Felix:

> I was afraid that my engagement would tear me from you . . . but the
> contrary is true; having gained a fuller knowledge of myself, I have come
> nearer to you and think even more often of you, if that is possible. . . .
> It is not possible that your love might decrease, for you know full well
> that I cannot spare even a jot of it.

And again on July 29:

> I play your *Hora est,* stop before your portrait and kiss it every five min-
> utes, imagining your presence. . . . I love you, adore you, immensely.

On her wedding day, she writes to the ailing Felix:

> I have your portrait before me, and ever repeating your dear name, and
> thinking of you as if you stood at my side, I weep! . . . every morning
> and every moment of my life I shall love you from the bottom of my
> heart, and I am sure that in so doing I shall not wrong Hensel.

Fanny could be quite possessive about Felix, too much so for him not
to protest:

> Sept. 20, 1827
>
> You must get a rap on the knuckles . . . are you the Inquisition? Do you
> spy on me? Is the string, on which I flutter, long, but unbreakable? You
> were in my room? Prying into my things? . . . Take care, fair flower,
> take care . . . !

Fanny's feelings could not be kept secret in the Mendelssohn house-
hold, except perhaps from Lea and Abraham! Parents often *don't* know.
Rebecka knew all about the Felix-Fanny closeness and mockingly wrote to
Felix that "Last night, in lovely moonlight, during charming conversation,
by the side of the most ardent betrothed, Fanny fell fast asleep. . . .
Why? Because you are not here."

Poor Hensel! After having been kept waiting for more than five
years, he married into a family where he must often have been made to feel
like a speck in the eye. Felix was polite to him and really did like him. But
Hensel could never penetrate the spellbound circle in which brother and
sister moved, in an understanding which surpassed that of consanguinity.

Fanny and Felix used an Esperanto of their own; Hensel told his son Sebastian that he often found their chatter incomprehensible. He could hardly have enjoyed the joke going around Berlin that Fanny nearly married Felix and it was high time that Hensel came to rescue her.

Yet that marriage grew into a loyal attachment. Fanny, while losing none of her love for Felix, was devoted to that gentle man with his modest talent, his academic correctness, his understanding kindness. Hensel admired the whole Mendelssohn family: if he had not, the marriage could hardly have lasted. They had only one child, Sebastian.

Her diary of later years is as full of references to little Sebastian as that of any conventional suburban mother's: how clever the child is, what funny things he says, how much he is learning at school. Yet she did not give up her music. She wants to give morning concerts to interest the distinguished men who frequent her mother's home; she sketches various suggestions for such concerts, in which of course her brother's music plays a leading part. In the summer of 1833, Felix is once again with her. And if she had her health—she was pregnant and then gave birth to a dead child —she would be entirely happy. She is especially glad that Felix now knows better how to get along with father, in spite of "daily little quarrels, mostly about politics, but then about everything."

Felix considered her his musical peer. She was his confidante in all artistic questions and he hardly wrote a note without asking for her comments or criticism. She was honest with him, though she could hardly be objective. He thought he was being objective when he overestimated her as a composer. From Coed-du he writes her: "These songs [Fanny's] are more beautiful than I can say. By God! I speak as an objective critic." He cannot do without her appraisal. From Leipzig he writes:

Jan. 30, 1836

And then, neither in this letter nor in your former one, do you say one word about "St. Paul" or "Melusina," as one colleague should write to another—that is, remarks on fifths, rhythm and motion of the parts, on conception, counterpoint, et cetera animalia. You ought to have done so, however, and should do so still, for you know the value I attach to it, and as "St. Paul" is shortly to be sent to the publisher, a few strictures from you would come in just at the right moment.

Rebecka, drawn by Wilhelm Hensel. (National Gallery, Berlin)

In submitting his compositions to her, he jokingly called her "Talley-rand," Napoleon's brilliant minister. He does not spare himself when he writes to her: "My Third Etude is really a piece of junk (*Saustück*). Please pardon me for having sent it to you." (Dec. 29, 1838) He also calls her "Cantor," referring to the supervisor of the church musical service of Bach's time. These are his birthday greetings (Nov. 13, 1843): "You angel, birthday devil, Cantor-face, Druid, source of inspiration . . . continue to love me. Think of us on a happy birthday. And give thanks that you exist and that you are as you are. That's not very poetically expressed but it is true." He is forever giving her things to do for him, to her delight. He asks her to copy manuscripts in Zelter's library, and if for such service she wishes to charge him an exorbitant fee, he will pay it! When he and his wife plan to come to Berlin, he asks her to get their lodging ready, hang the engravings, place the furniture, etc.

Brother and sister are linked to each other not only in feeling and in their absorption in music but in an interchange of fooling. Felix loved pranks, occasionally quite soggy ones, and Fanny went along. While he is in Vienna on the Grand Tour, she gets a birthday letter in a disguised handwriting—probably Abraham's, but Felix composed the epistle. This is the letter:

Vienna, November 8, 1829

Honored Fräulein:

The fame of your endeavors in my behalf has penetrated to Vienna. A fat gentleman with a moustache and a thin man with a Parisian accent—I can't remember their names—have reported to me that you have succeeded in interesting a cultivated audience in my Concertos in E-flat and G, and my Trio in B-flat. Your audience was supposed to have listened with decent respect and only a few of them were reported to have run away. So much approbation could almost trouble me and make me doubt my own worth; yet the charming way in which you played these works must have been the persuasive factor.

It's no great trick if people enjoy my first trios, my first two symphonies, and some other of my early works. As long as one composes music similar to other composers, as long as one is young, and one's music is appealing and trivial, people understand and buy one's pieces. I am tired of that and I have composed music fitting of a Beethoven. At my age and in the isolation of my empty chamber, I get ideas in my head such as would not be to everybody's taste. When I then find somebody who understands this music and who is sympathetic to my spirit, and who treats my old lonesome self in a friendly way, I consider that a great gain and worthy of gratitude. Such persons are my true friends, and others I don't have.

As a token of my friendship, I take the liberty of sending you for your birthday my Sonata in B-flat Major, Opus 106. [The *"Hammerklavier" Sonata*] . . . I did not write this sonata idly. Some time when you really have leisure, play this sonata. It is not one of the shortest, and it does need time, but then I had so much to say.

If the sonata doesn't put a strain on your friendship and you want to know more about it, by all means ask that specialist, Marx: he will explain it all to you, particularly the *adagio*—there he will have lots of opportunity to pontificate.

. . . I enclose an awful picture of myself. I am as much of a potentate as a good many others who give away their portraits and I consider myself not such a bad fellow. Please remember me kindly.

Your devoted Beethoven.

2

Before Felix could begin his work in Leipzig, the event occurred— foreseen by nobody in the family—which changed his life profoundly. After one night during which Abraham complained that he was not feeling well and that he could no longer distinguish objects, he awoke, fully conscious, though a little thick of speech. Presently he said that he wanted to sleep a little more and turned over in his bed; a half hour later he was dead (Nov. 19, 1835). Felix rushed to Berlin from Leipzig, unweeping, silent, enclosed within himself, and distracted to a point that Fanny feared for his sanity.

Refusing all condolence, he returned after ten days to Leipzig, shut himself up, and emerged only to do his work with the orchestra. To Klingemann he wrote: "What all of us have lost, and particularly I, you must realize because you knew him. He loved you. In what manner my life can go on I have no idea, not as yet." (Nov. 24, 1835) Fanny added a postscript: "You know how he worshipped Father."

To Pastor Bauer he wrote: "I do not know how I can continue my life. . . . He was my one complete friend during the last years." It was not only the death of his father but the consciousness of the failure in what he attempted to do in Düsseldorf which threw him into the shadows. The quarrel with Immermann, the obstacles at the opera house, the inferior quality of the orchestra, the difficulties he experienced in finishing *St. Paul* —all these weighed on him. His heart was too soft, his disposition too kindly, for him to slough off the troubles he saw around him:

> I had to engage the members of the orchestra, make out two contracts for each member, quarrel like a miser over one thaler salary per month. The men went away. Then they returned and did sign the contract. Then they didn't want to sit at the second desk. Then came the aunt of an absolutely horrible musician whom I could not engage, then came the wife, with her two small children, of another poor fellow to put in a good word with the Herr Director. Then I auditioned three lugs and they fiddled beneath all dignity, so that I couldn't engage one of them; then they became meek and went away sadly and I had robbed them of their livelihood. Then the wife came once again and shed tears. Among thirty people there was only one who said simply, "I am satisfied," and signed his contract; all the others bargained and haggled for an hour until I convinced them that with me it was strictly *prix fixe*.

> (Letter to Rebecka, November 23, 1834)

No, this kind of work was not meant for him. He had better go back to conducting, playing the piano, and composing. The composition of *St. Paul* became an obsession with him because it was the work that his father had longed to see finished. *St. Paul* was finally given at the Düsseldorf Festival in May, 1836. Fanny was there. She was singing in the chorus among the contraltos, and when one of the solo singers missed his cue, she whispered it to him and saved the situation.

Back in Leipzig the University conferred an honorary doctor's degree on him. Mendelssohn was not impervious to distinctions, honorary degrees, and medals. Friends came and went to attempt to cheer him or to discuss musical problems with him. He met and exchanged views with Schumann,

Chopin, and again with Moscheles. Yet neither honor nor activity nor friends could dislodge the melancholy which was sitting in Mendelssohn's heart. He felt lonely when he returned to his room at night: he seems deliberately to have set out to look for a wife. At least, he was now receptive.

In the fall of the year, *St. Paul* was to be given at Frankfurt by the Cäcilienverein under the direction of its leader, Johann Nepomuk Schelble. Schelble fell ill and at the urgent request of the Verein, which threatened to suffer a substantial financial loss if some miracle would not save the concert, Mendelssohn went to Frankfurt to take over *St. Paul*. He was not a stranger in Frankfurt. His aunt Dorothea Schlegel was living there, after the death of her second husband, Friedrich Schlegel. She was very old and yet still so brilliant and witty that Felix enjoyed her company. Friend Ferdinand Hiller too was stationed in Frankfurt. Rossini turned up and with his charm quite captured Mendelssohn, though Felix, as usual sensitive, resented Rossini's remark about some of the early Mendelssohn piano works which Felix played for him. Rossini said that they smelled of Scarlatti sonatas. Hiller did not think that comparison odious. Mendelssohn did.

A year had now passed since Abraham's death. Felix wrote to Klingemann: "You knew me in joyful days and so you must have observed in the spring in Düsseldorf how everything seemed finished and done with to me, and I could not get reconciled to life and gladness. And now . . ." (Dec. 4, 1836)

And now? He had met a girl he liked. "Because of Cécile I am once again merry and glad and as carefree as I have not been since I parted from my parental home, since the times of the garden, since the 'Garden Times' . . ."

Who was this girl who had wrought the change?

3

Cécile Jeanrenaud was the daughter of a pastor of the Reformed French Church. The father had died young; her mother, a member of a patrician family, the Souchays, was still pretty, vivacious, sociable, young.

Mother and daughter lived in the grandfather's house, one of Frankfurt's gabled mansions; there Mendelssohn met them both. Cécile was not yet nineteen, Felix was twenty-seven, and Cécile told him that before she knew him she had imagined him as a stiff old man, sitting at the organ with a velvet cap on his head and playing interminable fugues. Felix began to call more and more frequently during his six weeks stay in Frankfurt, and the town gossips were sure that it was the mother the young man was interested in. Naturally, Fanny and Rebecka heard all about it. Hiller remembers that "he treated the girl with such restraint that for several weeks it did not occur to her to refer Mendelssohn's visits to herself."

He seems to have gone about the business of marriage with diffident circumspection. Should he or should he not? He seems to have been more in search of a companion, one who could make a home for the homebody, than a man who longs for a beloved, a man who is physically and mentally enchanted. After Abraham's death, Felix may have remembered Abraham's admonition to find "a center of gravity for his personal life," a thought to which the wish for the continuation of the Mendelssohn line must have been father.

His relation with Cécile did not, as most love stories do, begin with flashing infatuation that cools into a life together. If anything, the relationship grew more ardent after marriage. At first there was too much prudence and not enough enchantment, though I think it is overstating the case to say as H. E. Jacobs does that his "marriage was the very model of passionlessness."

Cécile was certainly a pleasure to look at. She was blonde and blue-eyed, the skin tawny, the figure full and soft, but not heavy. She could have posed as a painter's model for the Victorian girl. Though she was of French extraction, living in Germany, she looked English—which must have attracted Mendelssohn. In a word, she was beautiful, remarkably so. Felix wrote to Cécile's mother: "I no longer want to walk with her in the streets of Berlin: the continuous staring of the passers-by is absolutely ridiculous. Not a soul do we encounter who doesn't open his eyes wide. Cécile herself has often had to laugh about it, though she protests it isn't meant for her . . ." (June 19, 1838) Another testimonial to her beauty comes from Heinrich Brockhaus, the son of the famous lexicographer:

Feb. 9, 1837. At the concert I was quite transported by the performance of a concerto by Mendelssohn. Today a higher spirit seems to have possessed him: his playing was wonderful, full of poetry. It was the same with the *Hommage à Handel* by Moscheles, performed by Sterndale Bennett and him. . . . His bride was there—that explains his being inspired. The girl, who sat quite close to me, really could inspire one: a charming apparition, one to be called beautiful. She looked so happy. Her joy in the triumph of her beloved was mirrored in her eyes. I could gaze at her forever. . . .

Sterndale Bennett described her as "one of the handsomest girls I ever saw."

Yet, except aesthetically, she was not an exciting creature. Gentle and submissive, pink and white in her soul, she was a lackadaisical Lorelei. She was never very strong, never very demanding, never a woman about whom one could feel violent or who felt violently herself. She went through her five pregnancies, some of them difficult and at least one of them dangerous, with matter-of-fact docility. She wanted to be petted, to be treated tenderly, to be made a fuss over, but she accepted Felix's frequent absences and his moods with quiet patience. From the first she was utterly devoted to him, though she could not follow him when he climbed mountains or rode over the fields. She was not an uncultured woman. She loved to read and she shared her husband's worship of Goethe.[1] But she was not at all musical. There is not a single instance recorded of Felix asking her opinion on a musical question. She made the home for him for which he had wished, and Felix's friends, Klingemann or Devrient or Hiller, as well as the celebrities who came to Leipzig—Chopin or Liszt or Berlioz—all liked her and enjoyed being entertained by her. She was a family diplomat, getting along with the sisters and with Lea, as long as she didn't have to stay with them too long. Lea, who was suspicious of her at first, grew fond of her. Rebecka liked her well enough. Fanny could not entirely suppress her jealousy.

And Felix? Before he left Frankfurt he was "more frightfully in love than ever before," he wrote Rebecka, but "I do not know what I

---

[1] Felix gave her a handsome "Souvenir Album" for Christmas, 1836. In it she continued her previously begun collection of drawings, manuscripts, and autographs. She stopped collecting after Felix's death. The album contains autographs of Haydn, Mozart, and Bach, letters by Schiller, Goethe, Lessing, and Zelter (now in the Bodleian Library).

should do." He intends to come back to see the girl again—but "I don't know whether she sees anything in me, and as I say, I also don't know what I should do." (July 24, 1836)

What he did was rather strange. He fled. With his friend the sculptor and painter, Wilhelm Schadow, he went to Scheveningen—far away in Holland—and lay on the beach and reflected. His sisters were in his confidence. Rebecka wrote him:

July 28 [1836]

. . . Write me a real love letter to describe her, how she looks, talks, walks, and whether she is musical. At the same time write me that I am still your dear sister. My claim on your love I will not renounce for any beloved in the whole world. . . . You are sad, depressed. When you returned from the music festival to Berlin you let slip something to the effect that "You will try to get married." Did this intention and your longing to live once again for and through another human being, enlarge your love in your imagination? Or do you really love her? For her sake? And not because you need somebody? Twice you ask, "What should I decide?" Do you really love her? Then decide. Amen. . . .

How well Rebecka knew her brother!
Fanny:

July 30, 1836

Your beautiful girl from Frankfurt interests me not a little. You can't imagine how I long to know your "bride." I think it will be good for you. . . . I got it into my head that this time you mean it seriously. If it's going to be as it was so often when you fell in love—with Doris Zelter at a dance—and once again nothing will come of it, I'll be highly *disappointed* [in English]. It occurs to me that I have never seen you truly in love. All your great amours were . . . superficial. . . .[2]

Finally he made up his mind and rushed back to Frankfurt. He was sure now. Yes, he was in love. On Sept. 9, 1836, he announced his engagement to Cécile. They were married on March 28, 1837, in the

[2] Both of these letters were found in the "Green Books." They are, to the best of my knowledge, unpublished.

Reformed French Church in Frankfurt. The ceremony was performed in French and the couple did *not* exit to the strains of Mendelssohn's Wedding March: it had not as yet been written. But Hiller had composed special music for the event. Neither Lea nor Fanny nor Rebecka was at the ceremony. Why?

Their honeymoon included only a limited territory. They went neither to Switzerland nor to Italy, probably because Felix did not want to expose the frail Cécile to the rigors of travel. Together they kept a diary which, in a way, is an astonishing document. Few are the entries of ecstacy and copious those of people visited, places seen—Cécile as well as Felix drew and painted and the diary is full of sketches—and dishes eaten. Figs cooked in milk and veal garnished with plums play major roles. Still, here and there we read an entry which indicates that the diary was not written by a staid middle-aged couple, but by two young people, as yet uncertain of each other and trying to understand:

From the Diary of their Honeymoon, March 29 to August 29, 1837.

Entries by Cécile:

April 11, Strassburg

My indisposition in the evening decided Felix the next morning to call on Mme. Passavant to ask her for the name of her doctor. We met each other in the street [accidentally]. Felix is all joy and jubilation. We run to the fortifications, where he tells me that the doctor reassured him.

April 23, Freiburg

Our intention to climb the Loretto was not accomplished. After about half of the hill, I couldn't manage it any longer and Felix returned with his useless wife.

April 24, Freiburg

On our way we see a very pretty flower-girl and Felix notices her at once and turns around several times to look at her. That and a few indifferent gestures and words were quite sufficient to render me melancholy and jealous. . . . We begin to climb the mountain behind the inn. Felix com-

(Fig. K.)

A page from the diary of the honeymoon, showing Felix and Cécile in a carriage. Probably drawn by Felix. (Bodleian Library, Oxford)

plains of pains. I behave very badly; after a little while I begin to force back my tears. Felix cannot find out why. He insists. My mood becomes ever blacker and angrier. Felix's begging and his anger result in my becoming quite silent and stupid. I weep copiously, torturing him and myself. In the meantime the carriage is made ready, we return home, and now we once again become as before. I tell Felix all my crazy thoughts and he is sweet again and tender with me. I make a firm resolution never again to be silly without giving a reason to my husband. During the whole evening Felix plays all my favorite compositions for me. That was the end of our marital quarrel. [Underneath this entry Felix wrote, "Don't be angry with me, dear Cécile."]

May 16, Frankfurt

Afternoon excursion to the Frankfurt Forest, where the whole town is to be found these days. Felix enjoys all that going to and fro and riding under the beautiful trees, which are only now beginning to burgeon. . . . Then Felix sits down in his room and scribbles one little musical dot after another, to the end of the day.

May 20, Frankfurt

In the afternoon Felix and Hiller play piano, sing psalms, and make fun of a whole lot of people. Hiller stays on until late at night.

June 11, Frankfurt

Felix is beginning the month by being extremely considerate. He sends me to the milliner to buy grandmother, with whom he was furious yesterday, a new hat. He wants to bury his anger under grass, or rather, under flowers. He is working steadily, as always. What I am doing is so unimportant that I cannot remember. . . . On Monday. I am quite unwell, lie around in bed and on the couch. Tuesday, the same. Felix takes care of me and spoils me, as does my mother. Nevertheless, I am still not up and about on Wednesday.

July 5, Bingen

Unfortunately, the very first day I am unwell. After dinner, I take my medicine with horrible grimaces. Curious what such a little creature can do.

July 6, Bingen

In the morning, because of the medicine and my total laziness, I remain in the garden. In the afternoon . . . we climb a very steep footpath which I could never have managed if Felix had not pushed me from behind. . . . The weather this evening is magnificent and the whole landscape lies before us without a trace of fog. We lie under the young trees which are planted around the church, we sing, dance on the thin grass, count the many islands in the Rhine . . . and love each other very much.

Entry by Felix, who is now in England.

London, Sept. 10

In the afternoon, Cooper [of the Royal College of Arms, an expert on Bach] invited me to play the organ in St. Paul's. In the choir and every-where there was a huge mass of people. I could hardly make my way to the organ, though the service had ended. After I had played a half an hour and the crowd increased rather than decreased, I began the great A minor Prelude and Fugue of Bach. It went fine. . . . But suddenly, at the final passage of the fugue—there was no air in the organ. Cooper runs away like a man possessed . . . finally comes back with the infor-mation that the man who works the bellows simply made himself scarce. The beadle told him to, because not a soul could be chased out of the church. . . . Now I had the opportunity to observe the *public spirit* [in English] of the mass of the English people. There was a tremendous outcry, as if something really important had happened, and from all corners one heard cries of *"Shame! Shame!"* Three or four clergymen came and gave the beadle what-for in front of all the people. . . . Cooper cursed along.

Felix avoided a personal meeting between Cécile and his family. They did not, as I have mentioned, come to the wedding, nor did Felix include Berlin in his honeymoon itinerary. No doubt he knew what he was doing; no doubt he did not want to submit his bride to family scrutiny or Fanny's jealousy. Fanny complained to Cécile:

Oct. 5, 1837

. . . How maddening that it is written in the book of Fate that we can't live together and that for eight months now he has a wife whom I don't know. I have to confess to you that when people come and tell me about your beauty and your beautiful eyes, I growl at them. I've heard enough about that, and beautiful eyes are not meant to be heard.

Fanny finally went to Leipzig to meet Cécile. Once there she was charmed by her and even thought that the girl's placid temperament might successfully counteract Felix's instability.

When after a marriage of fewer than four months he went to England, he worked there with much eagerness, as if the two weeks were to be the last of his career: he not only played the organ at St. Paul's Cathedral but at Christ Church as well, put the finishing touches on a performance of his *St. Paul* at Exeter Hall, played his second piano concerto, and led the Birmingham Festival, the culmination of which was a performance of *St. Paul* conducted by himself. Though he met with the usual acclaim, the yellow grass of England now did not seem quite so green as before, the gray air not quite so blue. He wanted "to let Birmingham be Birmingham," as he was desperately anxious to get back to Cécile. Mendelssohn here again gives the impression of being "always seated askew, as if on the arm of a chair," as Gide once expressed his own restlessness. He left Birmingham at midday directly after a morning concert, arrived in London toward midnight, after a ten-and-a-half-hour journey, was in the mail coach again at half-past midnight, arrived in Dover at nine o'clock in the morning, and, without breakfast, was obliged to "go off directly to the small boat which conveyed us to the steamer." The steamer took him to Boulogne—he was seasick as usual—and without rest or sleep he went through Belgium to Cologne. There he took another steamer down the Rhine. He could sleep on that boat, the first of five nights for such an opportunity. In the middle of the night he awoke: the noise of the engine had stopped. They were fogbound. He gathered his belongings, got two sailors to help him, got off the boat, took a carriage, and arrived at 3 A.M. at Coblenz. He finally reached Frankfurt in the afternoon, where Cécile was waiting for him. He had now been under way for six days and nights. But the journey was not over. Three days more he spent behind the postilion, until he got to Leipzig at two o'clock in the afternoon of the day he was scheduled to conduct the first concert of the season. Did he conduct? He did, indeed, mounting the podium at six o'clock sharp. He confessed, however, that at the end of the concert he was "a little *kaput*."

4

From this fragmented honeymoon and a conflux of less than ecstatic force grew a relationship which became ever more close, secure, and tender. In after years—but one cannot speak of Mendelssohn's life in terms of "after years"—in the ten years, then, which were still given to Felix, he proved himself the most content of husbands and a father who, unlike his own father, had the light touch. Cécile bore him five children; the first was born on Feb. 7, 1838, and was christened Karl Wolfgang Paul. (The middle name, whether given in memory of Mozart or more probably of Goethe, was a heavy burden for a child to carry.) Cécile was seriously ill; the birth was difficult and Felix was in despair. After she recovered, Felix took Cécile to spend some time with the family in Berlin: so at last they met their son's wife. Of the five children, four grew up, one died in childhood.

In the first years of his marriage he composed a number of small works, such as the Preludes and Fugues for Piano, Op. 35, and the Organ Preludes, Op. 37; chamber music such as the three String Quartets, Op. 44; various *Lieder;* as well as the Piano Concerto in D Minor and the beginnings of the Violin Concerto. He thought seriously of an oratorio on the subject of Elijah. It is impossible to fix dates of composition of Mendelssohn's major works: they were not only long in gestation but longer in reworking.

Cécile did not "inspire" him to compose music. Nor did she cause his work to lift itself to a higher plane. She exercised no influence on his genius. Fanny continued to be the confidante and critic of his musical plans. Some observers have claimed that after his marriage his music retrogressed in quality, for a time at least. Was that the price he paid for the peace he found when, after a concert with the Gewandhaus, he came home, all perspiration and tingling nerves, or when the rattle of the cobblestones which was the obstinate obbligato of his journeys receded in the silence of the woman who looked at him with worship?

Whatever her influence, or lack of it, the two could not do without each other, once they had truly become a couple. It is touching to come across stray evidences of their love, those few which have escaped destruction. (They date from the last years.)

Felix to Cécile:

Berlin, Oct. 10, 1843

Dearest Cécile: I can only write to you today and would like so much to speak to you, to kiss you, to spend the whole day with you, to gaze at you, to enjoy the festive occasion [her birthday], to celebrate my happiness and to wish you happiness. Good, dear Cécile! If I were with you I would kiss you ever so often and then kiss you again and you would have to take notice of my presence because the whole day I wouldn't leave you in peace, with my love and my joy over your birthday. . . .

He then explains that he is retained in Potsdam, the rehearsal for *A Midsummer Night's Dream* going wretchedly. But he hopes not to have to postpone the performance . . . "and so I hope to take the first train on Saturday and at half past two to be there where I belong, with my darling, wonderful Cécile, my birthday child! . . . Love me!"

Cécile to Felix:

Leipzig, April 15 [1844]

Time hangs heavy on me till you announce your return. My treasure, why did you not write me a few lines? I think if I had to live a long time without you I would fall bodily ill. I have no appetite; I merely swallow a few bites because one has to eat. I don't enjoy anything. . . . You don't write at all. Is it a revenge for my stupid joke in Naumburg? . . .

Felix to Cécile's mother:

Berlin, Nov. 15, 1844

When I am with her I myself don't understand how indispensable to my life, every moment of it, she is. But every time I am away from her, the absence becomes heavier to bear, more insupportable. Impatiently I count the hours till I see her again, her without whom I no longer know gladness or happiness. . . . Something which comforts me now is the plan (another plan! you will say) that beginning three weeks from now, when with God's help I will be reunited with Cécile and the children, I will not absent myself till the following autumn, neither for long nor for short, neither small nor extensive journeys, no performances, in short, nothing . . .

Cécile to Felix:

Sunday [undated, 1844]

My beloved Felix: I just received your dear letter of the 24th, which makes my intention of answering your last letter in detail unnecessary. These lines are simply to congratulate you. But for what? Well, for your extraordinary talent to lead and influence people so that they fulfill your wishes. It's all like a dream, like Karl's stories of the shepherd boy and the paladin. The King has granted your wish, his regard for you seems to be unselfish. And I will see you again soon. . . .

That you could not depart immediately, that I knew in advance; therefore the end of your letter did not embitter me. I realize you are doing the right thing. I know that you owe this [his presence] to all, including your sisters and brother. I bear the separation patiently, fixing my eyes on a ray of light in a gloomy November. God bless you, my beloved husband, and let Him aid you in the future as he has in the past.

As far as our future plans are concerned, let me say once again today what I have said often and what I feel ever more firmly: the place where I live is a matter of total indifference to me, so long as I am with you and you are content and happy. Such a place is beautiful to me—any place where I am alone is desolate and all the charms of the earth cannot embellish it. That sounds exaggerated, but it is true, and not a momentary mood, but the result of all my thinking. Once this winter has passed, and if God gives us our health, we must choose a place in which our children can be educated and in which we can remain quietly for several winters. I don't care where that is. The pleasant and the unpleasant aspects of the three cities I know balance each other out, more or less. . . .[3]

She subordinated her personality to his, not in conscious sacrifice, but because it befitted the noiseless tenor of her ways. She remained calm, reserved, considerate of Fanny, of whose feelings she must have had an inkling; elegant without being the least flirtatious or ostentatious. She remained pious, stuck to the orthodox Protestant prayers, and called on God. Felix, who did not pray—at least not as a ritual—told her not to bother

[3] All these letters are unpublished.

the good Lord with trivialities. In a word, she was a soothing woman. That is not the kind of woman a man of talent usually chooses: Cosima Wagner, Clara Schumann, Giuseppina Verdi, Constanze Mozart were anything but soothing women. It says much about Mendelssohn that he *did* choose such a wife, though it is idle to speculate whether a sharper personality could have aided his talent. It is perhaps significant, too, that Fanny married a soothing man, thus playing, as she herself said, a double counterpoint in their relationship.

However we may regard the marriage, and acknowledging that the musician loved his sister more, the man did not love Cécile less. Though he never stinted on the house room which in his heart he gave to Fanny, he was yet able to become a gallant, joyful, amiable husband, accommodating to all Cécile's wishes except one, the one for tranquility. As far as the spying biographer can tell, he was never again attracted to another woman. Not seriously. In a hundred ways he tried to please Cécile:

Felix to Chopin:

[In French] Berlin, Nov. 3, 1844

This letter arrives to ask you for a favor. Would you for the sake of our friendship write a few bars of music and sign your name at the bottom to show that you wrote them for my wife (Cécile M. B.) and send them to me? We last met at Frankfurt and I was then engaged. Since that time, whenever I wish to please my wife, I have to play to her, and her favorite compositions are those you have written. There you have another reason (although I have plenty of valid reasons since I have known you) for my wanting always to be informed what you are composing, and for my taking a livelier interest in you and your works than perhaps you yourself do. That is as well the reason why I hope you will grant the favor I ask. Forgive me if I have added thereby to the tiresome requests with which you must be inundated.

Mendelssohn as an autograph collector! Chopin, of course, complied, though somehow it took almost a year.

5

There was no division in Cécile's heart. She lived for him. A month after Felix died she wrote to Conrad Schleinitz, Mendelssohn's friend and president of the Gewandhaus:

Berlin, Dec. 2 [1847]

. . . There are corners in the desolate garden of my mother-in-law where I must martyr myself to be able to grasp that what has happened has happened. Here are the same trees, bower, benches, there is the ruined fountain, and they all still exist. . . . Felix's grave bears a marble cross with his name. Behind it I planted a lilac and a rosebush. I wanted to keep the mound free and green, but it is always heaped with flowers and wreaths. I find that touching but it suffocates me. Quietly I placed my tributes at his feet. . . .

She outlived him by only six years. She, too, died young, at the age of thirty-six.

Portrait of Felix, drawn by F. H. Schramm at the time Felix went to Berlin. Note the weary and melancholy expression. (Bodleian Library, Oxford)

Nine

THE ROYAL DILETTANTE

I

A conscientious chronicle of Mendelssohn's next few years—roughly
from his engagement in 1836 to the end of 1840—would merely weary the
reader: it would link work with more work, string success upon success,
place tribute next to tribute, and enumerate an ever larger register of acquaintances and friends, men important in their times and now but distant
names.

Suffice it to say that as he neared thirty and gained strength and ma-
turity, he proved a sturdy swimmer in the sea of music; he found the water
fine and enjoyed every moment of it. Engaging him as a conductor became
the safe way to turn a festival into a box-office success; from right and left
he received offers. But he liked Leipzig and Leipzig liked him. He spoke
with satisfaction of "establishing a new Gewandhaus tradition" and of firm-
ing this tradition.

What with taking care of other men's music, guest engagements here
and there, social pleasures to be shared with Cécile, and demands for help
and advice leveled at him, there was even time left for composing. He
began much and discarded much. Of the works he finished during those
years, the most valuable are the set of three Quartets (Op. 44), the Preludes and Fugues for Piano (Op. 35), and a group of songs. All three
quartets are interesting, but No. 3 (in E flat) is an altogether fine work,

its slow movement as poignant as a Beethoven slow movement—or almost. The six songs which make up Op. 34 (composed between 1834 and 1837) include the triply famous *"Auf Flügeln des Gesanges"* (Heine) and the mysterious, deeply felt *"Suleika"* (Goethe).[1] Less known but very fine are the six Duets (1836–1844), my favorite being *"Abschiedslied der Zugvögel"* (Fallersleben).

Now that he was firmly established as conductor and regarded as one of Europe's leading composers, now that he felt secure, he was able to exercise effectively the generosity and helpfulness which were so integral a part of his character. Something exciting, one meritorious musical event after another, was always happening in Leipzig; the stellar personalities were arriving in town at frequent intervals, all because Mendelssohn was there, his orchestra and his home ready to welcome. Liszt came and caused a ruckus. Rather, his manager did: he raised the prices for Liszt's concerts and the frugal Leipzigers were incensed. The newspapers made much of the affair. Mendelssohn took Liszt's part, acting unselfishly. As he wrote to Lea:

March 30, 1840

> Liszt was here for fourteen days and caused a mountain of a scandal, in a good and bad sense. Fundamentally I consider him a good, warm human being and a superb artist. . . . Unfortunately his behavior toward our public displeased everybody. . . . The Philistines who worried about the expensive tickets and who wanted to make sure that an excellent artist wasn't going to have too easy a time of it—well, I could have done without them very nicely. And those newspaper scribblers! Explanations and counter-explanations, reviews, accusations—this and that poured down, having nothing to do with music. His stay here caused almost as much irritation as pleasure. . . .
>
> I thought that the inimical atmosphere could best be cleared if the people here really got to know him and heard him. So I decided quickly to give a *soirée* at the Gewandhaus for 350 persons, with orchestra, chorus, bishop cake, *Calm Sea*, psalm, Bach's Triple Concerto (Liszt, Hiller, and I), choruses from *St. Paul*, *Fantaisie sur la Lucia di Lammermoor* [played by Liszt], *"Erlkönig,"* the devil and his grandmother. Everybody had

[1] The duet *"Suleika und Hatem"* (published in Op. 8) is composed by Fanny.

such a good time, we all played and sang with such enthusiasm, that the people swore they had never experienced so diverting an evening. I accomplished easily what I set out to do. . . .

Another pleasant incident occurred on this, Liszt's first visit to Mendelssohn's home. I give the anecdote as it was told by one of the musicians who was there: [2]

There was an evening of music at Mendelssohn's home at which such well known artists as David, Kalliwoda, Hiller, and others were present. Liszt, who was dressed in the Hungarian national costume, looked wild and handsome and announced that he had prepared something special for Mendelssohn. He sat down at the piano and played first a Hungarian folk song and then three or four Variations on it, one more incredible than the other, all the while swinging to and fro on the piano bench. We stood around, totally overcome. After praising the hero of the hour, one of Mendelssohn's friends said to him: "Well, Felix, now we can pack up! Nobody can play like that. All of us had better give up." Mendelssohn smiled and when Liszt approached him, saying that now it was his turn, he burst out laughing and replied that he wasn't going to play, surely not tonight. Liszt wouldn't take no for an answer, and after some back and forth Mendelssohn said, "Well, I will play but you must not get angry with me." So saying, he sat down at the piano and played—what? First the Hungarian folk song and then all the Variations, reproducing them so accurately that only Liszt himself might have discerned a difference. We all were afraid lest Liszt might feel a little peeved, because Mendelssohn, like a real prankster, couldn't prevent himself from imitating Liszt's grandiose movements and extravagant gestures. But Liszt laughed, applauded enthusiastically, and admitted that nobody else, not even he himself, could have managed such a piece of bravura.

By the time Liszt left Leipzig, it was all "pleasure" and no "irritation." His parting gesture was a benefit concert for the Gewandhaus Fund for old and invalid Musicians, at which he played Mendelssohn's Concerto No. 2, Schumann's *Carnaval*—both of these "almost at sight," Schu-

[2] Max Müller. It was printed in the Journal *"Signale für die Musikalische Welt,"* Leipzig, January 2, 1902. Walter Ducloux, of The University of Texas at Austin, kindly called my attention to it.

mann reported—and his own Bellini Variations, the *"Hexameron."* Admission for this concert (March 30, 1840) was 2 thaler, a high price indeed.

On another occasion, after a strenuous concert season, Mendelssohn was asked to help raise money for a Bach monument. He did not have to be asked twice. He prepared an organ recital at St. Thomas Church, practicing the pedal movements so diligently that he could "hardly stand upright any longer and walked down the street in nothing but organ passages." He brought in 300 thalers for the monument. Lea said: "He could announce that he will be standing in his nightcap in the middle of the Leipzig market square; people would come and pay admission."

At the end of the 1839–40 concert season, Schumann wrote:

> One must confess that in this Leipzig which nature treats so shabbily German music blooms to such a degree that, without arrogance, it can compare with the richest and largest orchards and flower gardens of other cities. What an abundance of great works of art were produced for us last winter!

It would seem, then, that Felix's activities were kaleidoscopic enough to have contented him. But no. Contentment? It was still not a state he understood. He had conquered Leipzig, he had conquered London. What next was to be conquered?

2

Frederick William III died in 1840, a bitter old monarch. Failure was stamped on his record. He had never delivered to his people what he had originally promised: a representational Constitution. Worse, in his last years he had tried to suppress new liberal tendencies—"subversive tendencies," the king's friend, Metternich, had called them—by such measures as banishing the seven members of the faculty of the Göttingen University, who included the brothers Grimm and the famous orientalist Heinrich Ewald. Fair-minded Germans resented this "anachronistic tyranny over teaching"; Göttingen Seven Associations sprang up all over Germany.

When the old king died, many heaved a sigh of relief and some made hopeful prophecies. As Crown Prince, the new king had made a favorable impression, expressing publicly his interest in social reforms and the arts. Frederick William IV was no longer quite so young, being forty-five years old when he succeeded his father. All the same, he was welcomed by youth.

The time was propitious and prosperous in a Prussia which was making strides industrially. The Prussian Customs Union, signed in 1834, assumed new significance now that the building of railroads had begun in earnest. The first major German railroad, running from Dresden to Leipzig to Magdeburg, began operating the year that Frederick William IV ascended the throne. Within ten years most of the German cities, at least west of the Oder, were linked by visits of clanking locomotives. Banking and finance kept pace with expanded communication. There was a chance for Germany to become a leading member of a business and political confederation of a united Europe. A remarkable political philosopher came on the scene, Friedrich List. As a young man he had been jailed as a rebel and was pardoned only on condition that he emigrate to America. There he observed the growth of the American economy; he now returned to Germany to publish in 1840 his book, *The National System of Political Economy*. He wanted to see all of the German lands and all of the Habsburg empire brought into a union to be called *Mitteleuropa,* to create something like a United States of Europe bound together by free trade and aided by a vast system of railroads for which he himself designed the plan. One railroad system based on his plan eventually came into being, but List was excluded from its management. Most of his ideas having met with a hostile reception, he killed himself in 1846.

The first actions of the new king seemed promising. Though his father had saddled him with a political creed in which he had warned his son against giving in to the demands for wider representation in Prussian general assemblies, and though this testament was constantly being held up before his eyes by Czar Nicholas I and by Metternich, he nevertheless tried to liberalize the laws. He eased Prussian censorship and did away, at least officially, with the Central Investigation Agency which had done its best to turn Prussia into a police state. The leader of the Göttingen Seven was recalled and made a professor; the Grimm brothers were invited to Berlin as members of the Berlin Academy. It was symbolic that Frederick William IV was the only king after Frederick the Great who took up residence in Sans

Souci. Was Sans Souci once more to become a home for philosophy, an abode for liberal thought, a place for a latter-day Voltaire? No, it turned out to be an empty gesture. The new king was not another Frederick the Great, but Frederick the Vague. He possessed neither his predecessor's firmness of purpose, nor his worldly wisdom, nor his healthy cynicism. Frederick William lost himself in confused and medieval religious dreams. Through religion he wanted to conjure up anew the "glorious past" of German history. Noble knights, now dressed in Biedermeier clothes, were to unite themselves in groups—he founded such associations as the "Order of the Swan" and the "Order of Mary"—and promote Christian universalism. All very troubadour style—and quite impractical. Christian universalism was soon traduced into German Christian nationalism. In 1841 one A. H. Hoffman wrote the song *"Deutschland über Alles"* (the king spelled *Deutschland "Teutschland,"* in the medieval fashion). It was around this time, too, that a poem became popular with the truculent words *"Sie sollen ihn nicht haben, den freien deutschen Rhein"* ("They shall not have it, the free German Rhine"). Mendelssohn was offered a substantial fee for setting this xenophobic verse to music. It is to his credit that he refused.[3]

Golo Mann describes Frederick William IV:

> He was intelligent, full of good intentions, educated, longed for affection and was appreciative of beauty. But he was weak and a prey to temporary influences, a complacent improviser, dependent on advisers whom he liked to dupe, superstitious, arrogant and faithless. In the end he became insane. His ideas were those of the romantic at odds with his age. He wanted to rule with the consent of the people, but this consent must find mediaeval expression, and society must be a hierarchy consisting of happy peasants, honest townsmen, pious clergy, faithful nobles, the prince among his nobles. In 1845 there could be no such society.

The History of Germany Since 1789

In short, he was a dilettante, though his love for art and for music particularly was genuine enough. In dilettante fashion he started one scheme after another, only to drop it and pursue some other idealistic will-o'-the-

---

[3] At least three other composers set the poem to music. Mendelssohn, who continued to find the poem "repellent," must have given in to pressure, because he performed a setting of the song by Konradin Kreutzer.

wisp. Immediately upon accession to the throne he asked that a plan be drawn up to make Berlin the capital of Germany's culture. At that time, Wilhelm von Humboldt and Josias von Bunsen, Prussia's Vatican representative and nicknamed the "Chevalier," were his close advisers. They suggested the establishment of an Academy of the Arts, with four divisions: painting, sculpture, architecture, and music. As early as October 30, 1840, Bunsen handed a memorandum to the king in which he recommended that "Germany's most famous living composer," Felix Mendelssohn, be called to realize three aims:

1. An outstanding educational institution for all music especially on the higher levels.
2. Performance of really appropriate music for the Divine Service, according to Your Majesty's directions.
3. Performance of great old and new oratorios, as a future branch of the theatrical productions—for the present, as royal festivities and celebrations.

Bunsen added:

Is that not enough for one man and master? I rather think it would be too much for anyone but Felix Mendelssohn.

After sounding out Paul Mendelssohn, who was the "practical" member of the family, his Excellency Ernst von Massow, the king's deputy, approached Felix with a comprehensive proposal by which Mendelssohn would be engaged as: 1. Director of the music class of the Royal Academy of Arts; 2. Composer for the Royal Theater; 3. Director of the Royal Orchestra; 4. Conductor and organizer of the Cathedral Choir, in which last position he would supervise all of the evangelical church music and compose such sacred works as might be suggested by the king. In a word, Mendelssohn was to become the head of Berlin's musical activity.

Mendelssohn had had enough experience with officialdom in general and Prussian bureaucracy in particular to be hesitant. All the same, he was flattered.

The Berlin proposal is very much in my mind and I ruminate on it quite a bit. I am still doubtful that it will lead to a result which both of us envisage (I believe). I still doubt that Berlin is the place where an artist like myself can feel himself at home, despite all honors and money. Yet the very fact that it was offered to me gives me an inner push, a certain satisfaction which I value, even if I will never be able to talk to anybody about it. In short, I feel that I have been awarded an honor and I am glad of it. . . .

(Letter to Paul, February 13, 1841)

He did not want to consult Fanny, or for that matter his mother, knowing that they would become excited and do their best to persuade him to come and live again in their midst. But he did consult Klingemann, after binding him to absolute secrecy. In a long letter he begs him for advice:

Leipzig, March 10, 1841

The reasons for it you will at once recognize: mother and sisters and my parental home. But there is a reason against it, a not unimportant one: I am happy here and live contentedly. An official position remains a minor distinction. What people call official honors—and that is what the call to Berlin represents—mean little to me. I am interested in composing a variety of new works. And believe me, I know that a strenuous official position, the bickerings with public, musicians, and officials could hinder me in my chief endeavor, if not destroy it for a considerable time. Here I have experienced none of these disturbances. There I fear them. Therefore is it wise to pick up my wife and child, particularly since a return, possibly even to Leipzig, would then become impossible? You who live so far away, you who know me inside and out, what do you think of this proposal? Advise me soon and with complete honesty. Remember that among all the musicians in Berlin there isn't one really accomplished one whom I could use; I would have to change the personnel completely, etc., etc. And all just to make the Prussian musical life flourish. That wouldn't put down a single note on paper, and that, as I just said, remains my chief concern. Here I could considerably improve my pecuniary and other conditions. My contract is up and they would not willingly let me go. I know what I have here and how much both I and Cécile like it here. What do you say? Does the call to Berlin appeal to you or not? I repeat my request about secrecy. My mother and my sisters, as well as my relatives here, do not know a syllable of the affair. They should be the last to learn anything until I have resolved a matter about which I have vacillated for so long. . . .

Klingemann answered him on July 1 after a long hesitation, apologizing for the delay, he himself being quite uncertain as to what to advise his friend. Ferdinand David had come to London; he was privy to the secret and he and Klingemann had talked it over. Though they weren't sure, perhaps the best move would be to accept a provisional position for one year. Yet if it were his, Klingemann's, decision, he would immediately work for the king because he believed in him. Peace for composing? Nonsense! If Felix really wanted such peace, he could put his nightcap on in whatever place he lived and shut himself up. "*Summa summarum*: Why can't you create that magnificent privacy and quiet of yours in Berlin just as well as some place else? Think about it."

Well, he accepted.

3

What elements in Mendelssohn's nature cozened him into accepting an engagement which was to end in frustration and near tragedy? Why did he leave Leipzig, where he was happy, for a Berlin where his saner self knew from the outset that he was going to be unhappy or, at the least, chafed with irritation? He had no illusions about Berlin and had expressed himself about its low musical standards versus its high arrogance. Yet he went, not like a lamb led to slaughter but like a lion voluntarily entering a cage.

The first and superficial reason one may cite is the desire of an ambitious artist to change the province for the metropolis. Berlin was not only the largest city of the German-speaking people but the center where the yeast of the mind was grown.[4] In the beginning of Frederick William IV's reign, the German states looked to Prussia for leadership; their rulers were knocking at the doors of the Berlin Chancellery. Political hegemony was mirrored in intellectual hegemony. Talent gravitated toward the big town. In the 1840's Berlin's relationship to Leipzig was comparable to New

---

[4] Vienna in the 1830's and early 40's under Metternich decreased in vitality and importance.

York's to Boston: one was the finer city, but an artist could not do without the other.

The tempo of Berlin was a metropolitan pace, such as suited Mendelssohn. An example, possibly extreme, of the Berlin *allegro con fuoco* was furnished by the famous physician Dr. Ernst Ludwig Heim, whose practice comprised 1,400 patients, who said that he paid for as many as 975 prescriptions for the poor every month, who could be consulted at five o'clock in the morning while he was shaving, and who died, still practicing, at the age of eighty-seven.[5] Another example was Johann Gottfried Schadow, the "Court Sculptor" who wielded his chisel for some sixty years, fashioned an incredible number of the muscular statues which dotted Berlin, and was regarded as the supreme instance to decide what was and what was not good art. (It was his son Friedrich Wilhelm Schadow who headed the Düsseldorf Academy.) Still another driving personality was Ida Pfeiffer, born in Vienna. She was an early proponent of women's liberation; in 1842 she made two trips, all alone, around the world and gave birth to a book, *A Woman's Voyage around the World.*

Mendelssohn asserted that the prospect of living close to mother, sisters, and brother was a temptation. The sentimental side of his nature imagined it as idyllic. But his realistic side must have warned him that too much family is a dish to be taken with caution, a soup that's either too hot or too cold. (And so it turned out. It is significant that he moved from the parental home and took a house of his own, opposite the Leipziger Strasse No. 3.)

A stronger reason for his acceptance may have been the promise of large musical forces to be put at his disposal. In Berlin he would be relieved of the stricture of tight budgets and could combine the *Singakademie,* the opera house, and the orchestra in cooperative efforts. He wrote to Ferdinand David of "great concerts" to be planned "with the use of all their best means." He was challenged by the task of lifting the standards of Berlin's music-making organizations and performing the works he loved most, the Handel oratorios, the Bach passions, and the Ninth Symphony.

While he was turning these reasons over in his mind, a deeper impulse pushed him on. It is difficult for us, almost a century and a half later, to

[5] See *The Berliners* by Walter Henry Nelson for a report on him and other Berlin characters.

understand how much veneration the citizen of that period offered to his sovereign, a veneration which in a German was knotted with his general respect for authority in uniform. Mendelssohn was dazzled by what Montaigne defined as "the strange lustre that surrounds a king." It was hard to escape that luster, hard not to heed a king's summons, doubly hard when that king lighted so desirable a goal. Eight years after that summons came the revolution of 1848—but even that revolution was directed more specifically against the Metternichs than against the monarchs.

Finally, the increase in salary, though unimportant to a man who had inherited the major share of Abraham's fortune, must have pleased his self-esteem. He was to receive 3,000 thalers a year, about $27,000 as against $18,000 in Leipzig.

Yet Mendelssohn was astute enough to insist on certain cautions. First, he demanded an official title, that of "Royal Kapellmeister." That was not vanity; he knew the importance of a title to the Prussian mind. He was already "Kapellmeister" to the King of Saxony, but that wouldn't be sufficiently impressive to the Berliners. Second, he prepared a detailed "Pro-Memoria" with his recommendations for the Musical Academy and reform of musical organizations. He asked that this be approved and his duties defined. Third, and most important, he bound himself to the king for one year only, a "trial year," instead of the longer affiliation proposed to him. He did not resign from the Gewandhaus but took what in effect was a sabbatical, appointing Ferdinand David as substitute conductor. (Though Mendelssohn returned to Leipzig frequently as guest conductor and remained concerned with the well-being of the orchestra until his death, it was not until 1845 that he returned as the regular conductor, Hiller succeeding him officially for the season of 1843–44 and Niels Gade for 1844–45.)

Mendelssohn's wishes and recommendations had to be transmitted through "channels," the key man being the Minister of Arts, one Johann Albrecht Friedrich von Eichhorn. His name fitted him—*Eichhörnchen* means squirrel in German—a paper-collecting bureaucrat, dull and timid of decisions. Fanny wrote about him:

. . . Germany is really blossoming, but the interior political conditions are all the more pitiful. That man, that Eichhorn, he seems to have sworn death to every free intellectual endeavor. He is afraid of a mouse. God! What a jerry-built edifice the Prussian state must be if it is really in danger of tottering as soon as three students form a *Verein*, or three professors publish a periodical. . . .

(Letter to Rebecka, September 4, 1844)

Mendelssohn's proposal for the Academy was shelved. Indeed, it soon appeared that the entire plan of an Academy was being quietly filed in a cubbyhole, the usual grave of idealistic ideas which are not nurtured by a nurse who is persistent enough. Mendelssohn's ideas were sound, though perhaps overambitious, but they needed a follow-through which the royal dilettante would not give. Mendelssohn's plan was never refused: it was always "being considered," meaning that it was shuffled from one ministerial office to the next, collecting ever more copious memos in its peregrinations. "Grand plans, tiny accomplishments, huge demands, teeny achievements; sophisticated critics, miserable musicians; liberal ideas and the street full of court employees; the Museum, the Academy—and the sand! I doubt that I'll be able to stand it for more than a year, but of course I'll do everything possible not to waste that year, either for myself or for the others." That is how Mendelssohn wrote to Klingemann in 1841.

He did not waste that year entirely, nor the following. He composed for his own use the piano *Variations sérieuses,* a brilliant work, in my opinion his finest work for the piano. As official composer to the king he executed a commission proposed by Frederick William: to write music for Sophocles' *Antigone.* Mendelssohn needed no urging to do so. He was heart and soul for the task, for the humanity and the nobility of Antigone's character —was she not a sister who defied the law to give proper tribute to a brother? —made a deep appeal to him. He was the one who spurred the production of the play. When "everyone was talking back and forth about it and nobody wanted to begin and they wanted to postpone the thing till late next year, and since the beauty of the play had taken hold of me, I appealed to old Tieck and said: 'Now or never.' He was gracious and said 'Now.' At once I started to compose to my heart's content." (Letter to F. David, October 21, 1841) "Old Tieck" was Ludwig Tieck, a poet of the early romantic movement, who worked with Wilhelm Schlegel on the translation of Shakespeare; he was now sixty-eight years old, one of the directors of the Royal Theater, and official "Reader" to the king.

From the first Mendelssohn had his doubts about the reception of the work in Berlin. In the same letter to David he wrote: "Naturally all of Berlin thinks I am scheming to be the court favorite or court musician or court jester. . . . Up to now everybody admires me; after the performance the pundits are going to come and reveal to me how I should have composed it had I been an honest-to-goodness Berliner!"

The première of *Antigone* was given to invited guests at the New Palace in Potsdam (Nov. 28, 1841). The king was there, of course, as well as dignitaries, scholars, and artists who had come from Germany, England, and Russia. Everybody was wildly enthusiastic and the ecstatic king ordered that a medallion be designed to commemorate the event. It was done: the obverse showed the head of Sophocles, the reverse Antigone—with the profiles of Tieck and of Mendelssohn.

When *Antigone* was exposed to Berlin, it was—after the initial curiosity—coldly received. It bored the audiences. The Berliners must not be blamed for this: Mendelssohn was not the composer whose music could follow the cothurned tread of Greek tragedy. One doubts that this play of ideas, dealing with the problem of law versus love, with the figure of Creon equivalent to that of Antigone, could be expressed in music.

But the king was delighted with it and with his court composer. Early in 1842 he commanded a series of concerts which included a performance of *St. Paul*, but once again the people remained indifferent and Mendelssohn did not achieve a true rapport with the orchestra, whom he called a "bunch of court servants impossible to hold accountable."

4

In the summer of 1842 he and Paul and their wives took a joyous tour through Switzerland. He went for long walks, thought of music—the idea of *Elijah* was now very much in his mind—filled his sketch book, sought out the guides and innkeepers with whom he had made friends on his previous tour, and altogether was in a gay, free-breathing mood. Only one cloud darkened his mind: the prospect of returning to Berlin, with "nothing accomplished." The year was up and there was no Academy, not even the blueprint of one. Once again he appealed to Massow and Eichhorn. What of the future? Had anything definite been decided? Why are you so impatient? they asked him. Why torment yourself? Enjoy the 3,000 thaler and await developments. Why not take advantage of a sinecure?

That was precisely what he did not want. "I wish to do something officially for the money I get officially," he wrote. Enough of delays, excuses, promises! He was tired of it all! He resigned and asked for a "farewell audience" with the king.

After some days Massow informed him that the king was ready for the interview; Mendelssohn might as well know that Frederick William had not looked tolerantly on his behavior: the king was angry and he was going to say good-bye in a few curt words and *basta!*

The evening before the audience, Felix had to tell Lea that he was going to leave Berlin. They walked up and down the garden, and Lea, whose temperament was usually controlled, began to weep. She was old, her husband was dead, and now her famous son was abdicating his place at home. Fanny joined them and helped console Lea. They remained together until late at night.

In the morning Massow called for Mendelssohn. They went to the Palace, everybody bowed, and they were admitted to the king's presence.

Now Frederick William, who could summon more than a pennyweight of charm when he needed it and who could "talk as persuasively as a traveling salesman," according to Karl Marx, turned on all that luster available to a king. It was obvious that he had carefully thought out what he was going to say. Far from being angry, he was all sympathy and understanding. No, he was not the sort of sovereign to issue commands to an artist. Yes, Felix was at perfect liberty to depart should he so choose, even if, without his presence, all the plans, the new as well as the old, which Frederick William dearly desired, would come to naught. What new plans? The king proposed that until the Academy could take shape—and he admitted that this would still take quite some time—he would create for his "favorite composer" a small but expert chorus, let us say about thirty singers, each one most carefully selected. In addition, he would bring into being a small orchestra, perhaps forming it from the elite of the opera orchestra. Both chorus and orchestra he would put at Mendelssohn's disposal, an entirely free disposal. Mendelssohn could conduct the church music for Sundays and holidays, perform oratorios, and compose and perform whatever music he pleased. This was practical, said the king, and could be realized at once. Well, if not at once, very shortly. He knew of course that a musician needed an instrument on which to play, and he saw it as the king's task to create the instrument. But would there be a Mendelssohn ready to use it? Of that he had to be sure. Until this chorus and this orchestra were in working order, Mendelssohn would be free to return to Leipzig or to go to London or to make another Italian journey. "It seems you adore traveling," the king said several times during the interview. Mendelssohn was not to give his decision immediately. He was to go home, think about the matter, and relay his answer through Massow. The king extended his hand; the audience was ended. As the king left them, Massow, his face red as a beet, kept murmuring, "You cannot possibly think of leaving now!"

The king had beguiled Felix. He was half-ready to agree during the interview, and when he got home and told Lea and Fanny and saw their smiles of happiness, he was altogether ready to give in. He confirmed what the king had told him in an official letter (Oct. 28, 1842). He asked that his salary henceforth be reduced by half, since he did not feel that his activities merited the full salary. In turn, the king confirmed his promises on November 22 and in addition awarded Mendelssohn the title of "General Music Director" (*Generalmusikdirektor*), the highest musical title he was able to bestow.

For a while Mendelssohn seemed to have the best of both possible worlds. He returned to Leipzig, after a sojourn in London, for the official founding of his dearest project, the Leipzig Conservatory. It was in operation a few months later, and one of the first pupils enrolled there was a twelve-year-old prodigy, a violinist who came to Leipzig and was befriended by Felix, Joseph Joachim.

The Leipzig Conservatory turned out to be a model of a music school in its day; Mendelsson worked for it as eagerly as if he had nothing else to do but teach.

He was busy executing the king's wishes for new music and he thoroughly revised his *Walpurgisnacht*. He wrote notes "until his head was burning." And he was still waiting for the "new plan" of the king to become reality. Then suddenly he got a memorandum from Massow which, as he wrote his brother Paul (July 21, 1843), infuriated him so that he nearly fell ill. While Massow again confirmed the topics of the meeting, he added six to eight glossary conditions, of which not a syllable had been mentioned at the audience, and which changed the whole tenor of the proposal. For example, the orchestra was to be selected by the management of the Royal Theater and the dates as well as the details of the concerts were to be approved by the Royal Intendant. This meant, of course, that Mendelssohn would be deprived of freedom of artistic action. His first impulse was to break off entirely. He worried about it for four days and decided to make a third try, being now deeply committed to composing music for Berlin: he would ask Massow whether the conditions of his employment were to remain exactly as they were originally outlined or not. If not. . . .

Later Massow agreed to restore the original conditions. Nonetheless, the plan never progressed. Mendelssohn did move to Berlin in the fall of 1843, "with bag and baggage, wife and children," but he made music with the regular Royal Orchestra and the regular Cathedral Choir. It did not satisfy him, though he was now more popular with the Berlin public. The king was content to have it so—and nothing more. Mendelssohn pleaded and asked for a further reduction in salary or outright dismissal. Instead, Frederick William came forth with still another idea: he wanted Mendelssohn to set Aeschylus' *Orestia* to music, or "at least" the *Eumenides*. Mendelssohn had had enough of Greek tragedy or French. He refused. Bunsen, no doubt with the full approval of the king, wrote Mendelssohn an emotional letter on April 28, 1844, in which he spoke of the "extreme sadness" of the king and begged Mendelssohn to remember how misunderstood the king was, how many bitter deceptions he had experienced, how many obstacles trusted members of his government had thrown into his path. Did the king now have to cry about Mendelssohn, *"Et tu, Brute?"* The king's spell did not work second-hand and long distance. Mendelssohn remained adamant. He saw the king in the fall of the year. Two months after this interview he left Berlin. The "long, bitter business" was over.

5

It was during Mendelssohn's second attempt in the king's service and after the satisfaction *Antigone* had afforded to Frederick William that further official commissions were offered him. One was the incidental music to Racine's *Athalie*, a biblical play. The composition has been characterized as "very undistinguished" and "pompous." (Radcliffe) Its famous "War March of the Priests" used to turn up at Pop concerts, but now it has disappeared even there. Another commission was the incidental music for Sophocles' *Oedipus at Colonus*, a play for which Frederick William showed great enthusiasm in his Grecophile phase; Mendelssohn's contribution consists mostly of choruses; these are impressive, at least two of them possessing real dramatic force. But here again Mendelssohn moved in what was for him insalubrious territory.

The third commission—a project suggested by old Tieck—was something else, indeed. Would Mendelssohn expand his famous *Midsummer Night's Dream* Overture to write music for Shakespeare's entire play? He loved the play, that was obvious, and surely the play invited the touch of music. Was he willing to return to it?

It is one of the instances where the talent enters a subject and produces an inspired fusion, as Verdi did with *Falstaff*, as Berlioz did with *Romeo and Juliet*. Fanny understood it well: "From our youth on we were entwined in *A Midsummer Night's Dream*, and Felix particularly made it his own. He identified with all of the characters. He recreated them, so to speak, every one of those whom Shakespeare produced in the immensity of his genius."

He produced twelve additional numbers; five usually live on in concert performances (Overture, Nocturne, Intermezzo, Scherzo, Wedding March), though at least one other, the "Spotted Snakes" song for two sopranos and chorus (IV), is as rewarding as the rest.

Altogether the work is as refreshing as the smile of a child. Mendelssohn succeeded in expressing both worlds of the play, the elfin world and the world of the hempen homespuns. Perhaps a good way to pay tribute to this achievement is to quote what a Shakespearean scholar has said

about the play: his words fit Mendelssohn's music. In his introduction to
the Aldus edition of the play, Henry Hudson writes:

> Great strength of passion or of volition would obviously be out of place in
> such a performance: it has room but for love, and beauty, and delight—
> for whatsoever is most poetical in nature and fancy; and therefore for
> none but such tranquil stirrings of thought and feeling as may flow out in
> musical expression: any tuggings of mind or heart, that should ruffle and
> discompose the smoothnesses of lyrical division, would be quite out of
> keeping with a dream, especially a midsummer-night's dream.

As to the threadbare Wedding March, "Mendelssohn's Greatest Hit"
—I can do no better than quote Donald Francis Tovey from his *Essays in
Musical Analysis:*

> Neither the greatest music nor the greatest poetry in the world was ever
> meant to stand the strain that custom has put upon *The* Wedding March.
> It has stood the strain remarkably well, and would have suffered no strain
> at all if performances of it had been restricted by law to the exact full
> orchestra for which Mendelssohn composed it. It is festive and regal, and,
> to all appearance, quite unromantic. It precisely suits Duke Theseus and
> his Hippolyta, who are neither more romantic nor younger than any favour-
> able specimen of an Elizabethan Lord of the Manor with his Lady. . . .

Can we still enjoy the *Midsummer Night's Dream* music? It depends,
I think, on whether we can still reach the bank where the wild thyme grows
or make our way to a promontory so that we might hear a mermaid, on a
dolphin's back, utter dulcet and harmonious breath. It depends, to an extent anyway, on whether the play can still make us believe in magic, whether
we can still respond to its poetry, which is musical poetry in a special sense
and with a special cadence. *A Midsummer Night's Dream* has never been,
nor is today, everybody's cup of nectar (Samuel Pepys thought it "insipid
and ridiculous"), though in the twentieth century it has been sumptuously
staged and that several times, such as Beerbohm Tree's production in 1911,
in which he introduced live rabbits in the woods, or Max Reinhardt's production, without rabbits, but with Moissi as Oberon. These stagings used
Mendelssohn's music. Peter Brook's recent production, which I thought an
abomination but which won high critical praise, did not.

William Hazlitt said about the play that it was "like wandering in a grove by moonlight." Such, too, is the music, a moonlit stroll. Our pleasure in the music depends on our willingness to stroll and let ourselves experience "tranquil stirrings of thought and feeling."

Whatever our attitude, we can admire the music for what it sets out to do: it is an almost unique example of successful transference of one art to another.[6]

Worth mentioning, too, is the fact that Mendelssohn was able, after seventeen years, to take up his pen and continue the style of the Overture without, so to speak, one false tone. We have a similar instance when Wagner left Siegfried in the forest in 1857, when the composer was forty-four years old, and did not bring him out of the forest until 1868, after an interval of eleven years. Here again no rift in the web is discernible.

The first performance (Oct. 14, 1843, in Potsdam) did not come off entirely to Mendelssohn's satisfaction. Tieck had divided the play into three acts while Mendelssohn had followed the older four-act version in the Schlegel translation. Two of the entr'actes (the *Intermezzo* and the *Nocturne*) had to be played on an open stage on which nothing was happening. In addition, the performance was prolonged by an endless intermission during which, in the royal box, tea was served and the king held his reception. Ferdinand David, who had come with a contingent of Mendelssohn's friends from Leipzig, wrote that during the whole introduction to the third act the clatter of teaspoons and the chatter from the royal box caused such a disturbance that Mendelssohn flushed, grew pale, and had to exercise the utmost self-control to continue to conduct. Young Niels Gade had scraped together enough money to come to Berlin from Leipzig. He didn't much care for the female interpreters of the play—but the music: "Fantastic, light, graceful, fine, yet comic," he wrote to his parents. With young and old *A Midsummer Night's Dream* scored triumphantly. After the Wedding March the audience jumped to its feet. A Prussian nobleman did say to Felix, "What a shame you wasted your beautiful music on so stupid a

---

[6] The *Nocturne* and *Scherzo* played in sequence were one of Toscanini's favorite program pieces. He played the selections thirty-five times between 1928 and 1950 (according to R. C. Marsh). Of his performance of the *Scherzo* Spike Hughes wrote: "Here all Toscanini's magic was displayed—the perfect instrumental balance and 'matching dynamics,' the irresistible rhythm and lightness of touch, the translucent quality of the orchestral texture combined to produce what one can only describe as a magical realization of a magical score. It was a bewitching occasion equaled but never surpassed even by Toscanini himself."

play!" One remembers that something similar happened to him years before in Italy. Then he laughed about it. This time he was coldly sarcastic.

Lea, who had loved the Overture, no longer could hear the incidental music. She had died the previous December, quietly and tranquilly, the morning after an evening when she acted as hostess to a large gathering. Felix mourned her, but not so much as he had mourned the death of his father. He was having too many troubles of his own, too many embroilments, to pause for grief. Nor had he been as close to his mother as to his father.

The great house in the Leipziger Strasse was now his. Without a moment's hesitation he offered it to his sisters.

6

Early in the Berlin days he accused himself of being unreasonable. He himself recognized that he did not approach the task with quite the goodwill which was the salient ingredient he usually carried to his efforts. There was a frown on his high, smooth forehead as he wrote:

> Since I am here [Berlin], I have led a distracted, confused life. I don't have to tell you how glad I am to be once more with my mother and my sisters and brother. But I feel myself all too estranged from this city. . . . I feel like arguing as soon as even an unimportant conversation starts, I disagree so profoundly with their way of thinking. And if I do what is the result? Merely an ill-tempered dispute or an out-and-out quarrel. I can't help it but neither can I change myself. . . . I used to be part of them here, but now I am an outsider. To be on the inside once more, to become comfortably one of them, that I can't imagine. Not now, not ever again. That is what I call being estranged. . . . All that between ourselves, dear friend. . .
>
> (Letter to Schleinitz, August 9, 1841)

Note that this letter was written in August, before Mendelssohn had really begun his work.

Yet he forced himself to carry on the year after he could have called quits, and again a second and a third time. Was this an unconscious self-punishment, a penalty paid for a realization, never consciously formulated, that life had been too easy? Was it a masochistic penance for a feeling that he had obtained what he wanted with almost unbroken success and at too small a cost? More than stubbornness was involved and more than disavowal of failure. Had he succeeded he might have been more unhappy than he was in his frustration, rooted as he then would have become to an uncongenial city.

It is interesting to compare Mendelssohn's four-year-long experience with the mottled monarch to Berlioz's casual contact with the same king. To Berlioz, who had met with indifference from all the official circles of Paris, Prussia seemed a veritable Eden and the king its guardian angel. He wrote in his *Memoirs:*

> Though neither a favourite nor influential, I am none the less profoundly grateful for the good will which the King of Prussia has so often shown to me; and there was no trace of flattery intended when I said to him, that day, during a few moments' serious conversation:
>
> "You are the artists' King."
>
> "How so? What have I especially done for them?"
>
> "To speak only of musicians, a great deal, Sire. You have royally rewarded Spontini and Meyerbeer and loaded them with honours. You have had their works magnificently performed. You have had Gluck's masterpieces restored to the stage in the most imposing fashion; nowhere else but in Berlin can one hear them. You brought the ancient world to life again when you had Sophocles' *Antigone* produced, and you commissioned Mendelssohn to write some choruses for the occasion. You got the same composer to write music for Shakespeare's exquisite fantasy *A Midsummer Night's Dream*. And so one could go on. What is more, the direct interest you take in all these high artistic enterprises is a stimulus to greater activity, a living encouragement to creative artists in their work. And this support that Your Majesty gives them is all the more valuable because it is the sole support of the kind they have in Europe."
>
> "Well—perhaps what you say is true. Only, one shouldn't talk so much about it."

Wagner's experience paralleled Mendelssohn's. In *Mein Leben* he speaks of the vacillating character of Frederick William, with whom he sought in vain to obtain an audience. This was in 1847. Wagner called on A. B. Marx, Mendelssohn's former friend, who told him that he too tried to interest the king in a plan for a new musical Conservatory. The king expressed enthusiasm, but then he, Marx, had been passed on from one official to the other and nothing was accomplished. Wagner found old Tieck even more discouraged. The king would listen, Tieck said, and agree to new ideas, without the slightest hope of their being realized.

Whatever Mendelssohn's feelings for the city and its king were, his sincerity in wanting to help the cause of music in Berlin cannot be questioned. And had he had his way, unencumbered by the sand strewn by dry hands, had he been given a helping hand stronger than the hand of the king, he would no doubt have accomplished improvements to establish Berlin as a place of music rivaling Vienna—or his own little Leipzig. The worst of the failure was not that after all those sheafs of memoranda, heaps of paper, dozens of letters, and calamitous coloquies, Mendelssohn left the state of music in the metropolis exactly where it had been; the worst of it was the toll in energy and frustration the affair exacted from him. Energy he had to spare; with frustration he could find no compromise. The Berlin years sucked his nervous substance. He could not find the inner peace to develop his talent in the years where such development could most naturally be expected; only one major successful work, the *Midsummer Night's Dream,* can be placed to his credit between 1841 and 1844, though he finished his Violin Concerto—begun in 1838!—as soon as he had made up his mind to withdraw from Berlin. It is probable, indeed, that the fruitlessness of the attempt, and not his strenuous travails, nor his tempestuous travels, hastened his death. No doubt it was his fault; no doubt he should have recognized his mistake after one year and climbed out of the muddle.

But he didn't—and one knows that from the beginning there was a conflict in his mind. One part of him did not want any part of Berlin. Yet the stronger the negation the stronger became his wish to stifle it. Were submerged memories of the Berlin failure of his first opera and his rejection by the *Singakademie* coming to the surface and did he feel the need to expunge them? It was the severest psychological conflict he experienced.

When it was over, Fanny wrote: "Felix has once again become loveable."
Yet for some time after he left Berlin his creative faculty showed signs of
fatigue. I think it was fatigue and not a drying-up of invention. The disappointment he had experienced left a blotch on his talent. Time was
needed to heal the bruise. Only with *Elijah* and the last chamber works
did he recover. Perhaps he never fully recovered.

Mendelssohn playing for the young Queen Victoria and Prince Albert. From a contemporary drawing. (Mendelssohn Archive, Berlin)

Ten

QUEEN VICTORIA, JENNY LIND, AND *ELIJAH*

I

"You have to play Mendelssohn if you wish to enjoy a great success," Chopin wrote from London. He was right, of course: Mendelssohn was England's favorite adopted son, all through the years when Queen Victoria was a young girl, when Prince Albert cared about music, and old Lord Melbourne represented the elegance of the empire. To the men and women of the early Victorian age, Mendelssohn's music was like eau de cologne, sweet-smelling but not too heady.

The Victorian age, discussed, admired, sneered at, yawned over, envied —we have arrived at a juster understanding of it than the one we used to hold. Even the least thoughtful no longer imagine it as a period populated largely by starched shirts who prated of morality, or by vice-admirals on their way to "Indjia," or by clerks from the Foreign Office—as thin as their umbrellas—who suspected anybody whose mother tongue did not happen to be English. Nor do we any longer believe that all respectable Victorian women were frigid and watery-eyed.

The compass of the age was wide; at the top of the social periphery stood superbly dressed Count D'Orsay—the "Phoebus Apollo of dandyism," Carlyle called him—gambling his fortune away at Crockford's;

while at the bottom were the ragtag and bobtail to whom a penny earned was a penny that could be spent on gin. Within the circle there grew the mass of working people, now more decently paid and perhaps therefore loyal to their Queen, pushing and perspiring, crowding and expanding the cities and seeking relief from factory noise in every kind of pleasure, including escape from town:

> Our inns are filled to bursting, our private houses broken into by parties desperate for lodgings. . . . A great steam monster ploughs up our lake and disgorges multitudes upon the pier; the excursion trains bring thousands of curious, vulgar people, who mistake us for the authoress next door,[1] and compel us to forge her autograph; the donkeys in our streets increase and multiply a hundredfold, tottering under the weight of enormous females visiting our waterfalls from morn to eve; we are ruthlessly eyed by painters and brought into foregrounds and backgrounds as "warm tints" or "bits of repose"; our hills are darkened by swarms of tourists; our lawns are picnicked upon by twenty at a time, and our trees branded with initial letters. . . .
>
> James Payne, quoted by Stella Margetson in
> *Leisure and Pleasure in the 19th Century*

Thomas Cook, a Baptist missionary, conceived the idea of inexpensive organized tours, and in 1845 ran a conducted excursion from Leicester to Liverpool, charging 14 shillings for first-class and 10 shillings for second-class passengers. The train left at five o'clock in the morning, and Cook furnished a little guidebook listing the places of interest.[2] No doubt some of these tour members liked music entitled "Scottish" Symphony or *Hebrides* Overture.

As wide as the social life of the Victorian age was its art. There was Sir Edwin Landseer, who painted noble stags with soulful eyes (and modeled the lions in Trafalgar Square), but there was as well Joseph Turner with his "Rain, Steam and Speed." There were Bulwer-Lytton with *The Last Days of Pompeii* (1835) and *The Last of the Barons* (1843) and Disraeli with *Conningsby* (1844) and *Sybil* (1845); but this period, which

---

[1] The author was Harriet Martineau, a popular political writer, who on the advice of Wordsworth built herself a retreat in Westmorland.

[2] Bradshaw's first *Railway Guide* was published in December, 1841. *Murray's Switzerland* was another popular guidebook. In the midst of his Berlin troubles, Mendelssohn took time out to ask Klingemann to use his good offices with Mr. Murray to have a certain inn recommended in this book, the proprietor being an old friend.

sometimes "threatened to become humdrum and conventional" (Edmund Gosse), contained as well the genius of Alfred Tennyson, Elizabeth Browning, Thomas Carlyle, Thomas Macaulay, the young Thackeray, and John Ruskin. Charlotte Brontë's *Jane Eyre* and Emily Brontë's *Wuthering Heights* appeared during the last year of Mendelssohn's life. In the years in which Mendelssohn worked in England, Charles Dickens reached the height of his productivity: *The Posthumous Papers of the Pickwick Club* (1836) and *Oliver Twist* (1837), *Nicholas Nickleby* (1838–39), *Old Curiosity Shop* (1840), *A Christmas Carol* (1843), *Martin Chuzzlewit* (1844)—these books made him, who was three years younger than Mendelssohn, the most popular of the English writers. The two met in 1844 and Mendelssohn became Dickens' favorite composer (according to Dickens' daughter).[3]

No generality can be applied to an age as variegated as the Victorian age. Nothing one says of it is wholly true. Yet one characteristic may be suggested: that is its occupation with the overt, its involvement with the practical side of living. Less than the French of Rousseau's time or the Germans of the *Werther* years did the English concern themselves with dark dreams or flights to an imagined world. Macaulay spoke for the age: "An acre in Middlesex is better than a principality in Utopia."

Mendelssohn's music sounded fine in Middlesex. English audiences found in it the right mixture of decorous gaiety and decorous sentimentality. It was not "problematic" music; they took it at its face value. As to the personality of the composer—it suited the notion (as held by Lord Grey, Lord Brougham, Sir Robert Peel, the Duke of Wellington, etc.) of what a gentleman is and does. (See Klingemann's remarks, page 166.)

From the first the press liked him, though he never curried favor with journalists. The two most powerful critics, Chorley and later Davison, were all for him. If only to give an idea how the press reported musical events, I cite two extracts from reviews of leading British periodicals. They appeared after Mendelssohn's first visit in 1829:

The Atheneum, July 22

We omitted to make mention of the excellent concert given by Mdlle. Sontag last week for the benefit of the sufferers from the inundation in Silesia. Our silence was not voluntary, inasmuch as we received from the

---

[3] I owe this point to Professor Edgar Johnson, a biographer of Dickens.

performance a pleasure which had not been equalled in any previous concert of the season, and which we were prepared to express, but the graver matters of the week shut out our notes of admiration. All that can now be permitted are a few words in praise of a most extraordinary man, whose name we have not hitherto presented to our readers, and whose appearance here was one of the grand features of the concert. We allude to M. Mendelsohn [sic], a piano-forte player of almost transcendent talent, which becomes more admirable when something of the *man* is known. He is very young, apparently not more than twenty-two years of age [he was twenty], independent in station, his father being an opulent banker in Leipsic [sic]; and with a thirst and love of music nearly unparalleled, his modesty blinds him to the success with which he has cultivated it. After reading the "Midsummer's Night Dream," he composed that spirited overture of the same title, and in it has represented, not feebly, the emotions and anger which the pencil of the drama left on his mind. He is now gone to the Irish lakes, and it is expected that he will employ them as a subject for some future exercise of his skill in composition. As a performer, his abilities are quite first-rate. In the act of playing he is lost to everything beside the instrument before him; and, indeed, in the most ordinary affairs of life, his musical enthusiasm is always present, and directs his thought and actions into the universal channel. His memory is represented as being the most wonderful of his faculties. After playing one of Beethoven's most intricate symphonies, he can close the book and repeat it accurately by rote.

The Literary Gazette, June 6

A German gentleman—with a long Christian name, too long for any Christian to pronounce with impunity—made his *debut* on this occasion, and performed on the piano a piece termed on the card a "concert-stück." The pianist, however, never once *stuck* in his performance; but on the contrary appeared to get through his work with no less satisfaction to his audience than to himself.

In every subsequent visit he multiplied the affection in which musical England held him. He was offered the Chair of Music at Edinburgh University and the directorship of the Royal Philharmonic Orchestra, both of which he had to refuse. As Klingemann wrote Rebecka: "We, the John Bulls that we are, are more naïve and more sincere than the people of the continent. . . . We possess the *organ of veneration* [in English] and we admire willingly and honestly." (May 18, 1844) That willing admiration extended itself to the queen, who was hardly "naïve."

2

Mendelssohn met Queen Victoria in 1842. The Queen was a young girl, but five years a queen and but two years married to her Prince Albert, "that beautiful man" with whom she was ecstatically in love.

Only one deep fissure jagged the even ground of the marriage: that was the subordinate rank of Albert as a consort. It took time and diplomacy before Victoria managed to obtain for him, an outsider and a German, a position as a co-reigning sovereign, as a respected adviser to and helper of Victoria.

Prince Albert, who had genuine musical gifts, used music as a compensation and comfort in those days when his abilities as a statesman, abilities which he knew to be strong and seminal, lay fallow. The loneliness and homesickness he must sometimes have felt, with all the joys of his marriage, were expressed in his sitting at the organ for hours at a time. One of Victoria's attendants, Lady Lyttleton, observed Albert's face while he played: "She saw something in his face which made her feel that only the instrument really knew what was in his soul." [4] Albert had a pleasant voice, and loved to sing duets after dinner with Victoria, who completely shared with him his distaste for the English custom among the gentlemen of remaining in the dining room for port, with the ladies not present. He got away from what he called "the stayers" as soon as he possibly could and joined Victoria, sometimes to make music, sometimes to listen.

The Queen, too, enjoyed music. In her Journal, which she kept punctiliously, we find such entries as:

Mozart: The Magic Flute: Covent Garden, 1852
The opera itself was performed in a slovenly manner. The three lady attendants (on the Queen of the Night) sang very badly, the scenery was very inferior, and Mario really walked through his part (Tamino). . . .

[4] *Queen Victoria*, by Elizabeth Longford.

Bach: St. Matthew Passion: St. George's Hall, 1859
Though so fine, it is a little fatiguing to listen to, there being so much sameness.

Wagner: Lohengrin: Waterloo Gallery, 1899
It is the most glorious composition, so poetic, so dramatic and one might almost say religious in feeling, and full of sadness, pathos and tenderness.

> (Quoted by R. C. Mackworth-Young,
> Librarian of the Royal Library, Windsor Castle.
> From his article "Music and the Monarch.")

Yet it was chiefly to Albert's initiative that Mendelssohn owed the invitation to Buckingham Palace. King Frederick William IV had given him a letter of introduction to Albert, although that was hardly necessary. He called on Albert once, but it was only on his second visit that Victoria made her appearance. What first impression must Felix, thirty-three years old and filled with vitality, have made on the Queen? Victoria was not insensitive to a handsome man:

> The Queen's susceptibility to beauty was one of her most interesting characteristics. Whether in men, women, children, animals, landscapes, houses or clothes, she hailed it with an enthusiasm unexpected in one who set such store by sterling worth. Just before her marriage she frequently emphasized her admiration for male beauty, often discussing the handsome figure of one or other of her courtiers.[5]

The Queen, who at least in her younger days was far less "Victorian," less conventional, than is ordinarily supposed ·(Prince Albert being stiffer in behavior than she), met Felix on easy terms. He wrote a full account of the meeting to his mother:

> July 19, 1842
>
> Prince Albert invited me for Saturday at half-past two in order for me to try the organ [at Buckingham Palace] before I was to depart [for Frankfurt]. I found him quite alone, and just as we were in the midst of a conversation, in came the queen, also quite alone and dressed in a housedress. She said that she had to leave for Claremont in an hour. "My God, what a mess there is here!" she exclaimed, noticing that the wind had

[5] *Queen Victoria*, by Elizabeth Longford.

scattered single sheets of a large, unbound score which was lying on the organ . . . and blown them into all corners of the room. So saying, she knelt down and began to gather the sheets. Prince Albert helped, and I deigned to do likewise. The prince explained the various registers to me, and she said: never mind, she would straighten up the room all by herself. Then I asked the prince to play something for me so that I could boast about that in Germany. He played a Chorale by heart, pedaling nicely, cleanly, and without mistakes, so well that many a professional organist could have taken it as an example. The queen, who had finished her work, sat down and listened with pleasure. Now it was my turn to play, and I began my chorus *"Wie lieblich sind die Boten"* from *St. Paul*. Even before I had finished the first verse, both of them began to sing along. While I played, Prince Albert manipulated the registers skillfully: first a flute, then at the *forte* at the C-Major passage everything full, then an excellent *diminuendo*, and so on until the end of the piece, and everything by heart. I was enchanted and happy.

The Prince of Gotha came along, and we conversed back and forth. The queen asked if I had composed any new songs. She loved to sing those which had already been published. "You must sing for him," said Prince Albert. At first she let herself be coaxed a little. Then she felt that she could try her luck with the "Spring Song" in B-Major. "That is, if it is still here, because all the music has been packed away for Claremont." Prince Albert went to look for it but returned: "It's packed up." I said, "Well, perhaps we can unpack it again." She answered, "We have to send for Lady NN." (I didn't catch the name.) She rang the bell, the servants ran in and came back quite embarrassed. Whereupon the queen went herself. During her absence, Prince Albert said to me, "She asks you to receive this gift as a memento," and handed me a little case which contained a beautiful ring engraved with "V.R. 1842." The queen appeared again and said, "Lady N.N. has gone off and has taken all my things with her. I find that improper to the highest degree." (You can imagine how that amused me.) Now I said that she ought not to punish me by this little mishap; rather she ought to choose something else to sing. After she had consulted her husband several times, he said, "She will sing you something by Gluck." In the meantime the Princess of Gotha joined us and so all five of us ambled through the corridors and rooms to the salon of the queen, where beside the piano stood an enormous fat hobby horse and two big bird cages. . . . The Duchess of Kent [Victoria's mother] joined the party, and while they all talked I browsed among the music papers and found my first "Song Collection." Of course I asked that she choose one of those songs rather than the Gluck. She acquiesced willingly, and what did she choose? *"Italien."* [This song is not by Mendelssohn but by Fanny.] She sang it most charmingly, strictly in tempo and cleanly in diction; only after the words *"der Prosa Last und Müh,"* when the melody goes to a D and then rises harmonically, she twice sang a D-sharp; then because both times I suggested the D on the piano, she sang D at the third verse where D-sharp is written. But apart from that little error, it was really enchanting, and the last long G I have never heard better, cleaner, and more naturally sung by an amateur. Now I had to confess that Fanny was the composer of the song. (This was hard, but pride goeth before a fall.) I asked her to sing one of the songs that were really mine. "If you would help me, I'd do it gladly," she said, and sang, *"Lass dich nur nichts dauern"* without a single mistake and with truly felt expression. I thought it was not the occasion to indulge in extravagant compliments and therefore I merely thanked her several times. But when she said, "Oh! if I hadn't been so nervous—usually I have a pretty long breath," then I praised her with a good conscience. . . . Then Prince Albert sang, *"Er ist ein Schnitter, der heisst Tod."* Then he said I had to play before I left. He gave me as the two themes for improvising the Chorale which he had played just before and the *"Schnitter"* song. If proceedings had gone as they usually do when I really want to improvise well, I would have played horribly. Yes, that happens to me frequently—and then I remember nothing but my anger. Yet this time, as if the gift I should receive were to be an unclouded memory, I played exceedingly well; I was in the vein, played for a long time, and even I enjoyed it. You can imagine that in addition to the two themes I also used the two songs which the queen had sung. But I wove them in so naturally that I could have continued forever. Both of them followed me with an understanding and an attention which put me into a better humor than usual when I improvise for an audience. . . .

I forgot to say that I asked permission to dedicate the A-Minor Symphony to the queen. This symphony was the real reason for my journey. [He conducted it with the Philharmonic Society on June 13.] . . . Also that just as the queen was about to sing, she said, "Out with the parrot! He screams louder than I can sing." Whereupon Prince Albert rang the bell and the Prince of Gotha said, "I will carry him out myself." And I said, "Please permit me to do it." And I took the big cage and handed it over to the astonished servants.

Victoria's entries in the Journal confirm Mendelssohn's report: [6]

Buckingham Palace

June 16, 1842 . . . After dinner came Mendelssohn Bartholdy, whose acquaintance I was so anxious to make. Albert had already seen him the other morning. He is short, dark, & Jewish looking—delicate—with a fine intellectual forehead. I should say he must be about 35 or 6. He is very pleasing & modest, & is greatly protected by the King of Prussia. He played first of all some of his *"Lieder ohne Worte"* after which, his Serenade & then, he asked us to give him a theme, upon which he could improvise. We gave him 2, "Rule Britannia", & the Austrian National Anthem. He began immediately, & really I have never heard anything so beautiful; the way in which he blended them both together & changed over from one to the other, was quite wonderful as well as the exquisite harmony & feeling he puts into the variations, & the powerful rich chords, & modulations, which reminded one of all his beautiful compositions. At one moment he played the Austrian Anthem with the right hand he played "Rule Britannia", as the bass, with his left! He made some further improvisations on well known themes & songs. We were all filled with the greatest admiration. Poor Mendelssohn was quite exhausted, when he had done playing.

Claremont

July 9. . . . Mendelssohn came to take leave of Albert, previous to his returning to Germany, & he was good enough to play for us, on Albert's organ, which he did beautifully. As he wished to hear me sing, we took him over to our large room, where, with some trepidation, I sang, accompanied by him, 1st:, a song which I thought was his composition, but which he said was his sister's, & then one of his beautiful ones, after which he played to us a little. We thanked him very much, & I gave him a handsome ring as a remembrance. . . .

Windsor Castle

December 24. . . . We played part of Mendelssohn's last Symphony, he has just sent us. . . .

[6] These entries are reproduced by gracious permission of Her Majesty, Queen Elizabeth II.

The "Scottish" Symphony was duly dedicated to Queen Victoria.

On this visit to London, Cécile accompanied Felix. She charmed all the London friends, the Horsleys and the Moscheleses and Klingemann. Frau Moscheles especially became fond of her: she was the "lovable Cécile, as pretty as an angel." Curiously, Cécile was not invited to Buckingham Palace.

Two years later, Mendelssohn was again in London, this time alone; he wrote that this season was as "mad" as any he had experienced. Not once did he get to bed before half-past one in the morning, and in the two months he made more music than in the entire year just passed. He was once more the guest of the Queen, again under quiet, homey circumstances. They played and sang together, chatted, gossiped about court life in Berlin and Dresden; and Mendelssohn invited her to one of the concerts. Victoria accepted, obviously much to the excitement of the directors of the Philharmonic Society. The Queen recorded these entries in her Journal:

> Buckingham Palace
>
> May 30, 1844. . . . We went over to the Drawingroom to see Mendelssohn, & talked to him for some time, then, he played to us beautifully, some of the fine compositions, he has written lately, amongst them music for the "Midsummer Night's Dream", 2 of his *"Lieder ohne Worte"*, & improvised wonderfully on Gluck's beautiful Chorus: "Que de grâces, que de Majesté", bringing in besides a song by his sister, which I often sing. He is such an agreeable clever man & his countenance beams with intelligence & genius. . . .
>
> Buckingham Palace
>
> June 10. . . . We played some of the *Lieder ohne Worte*, which Mendelssohn has kindly arranged for us as Duets, adding an unpublished one. . . .

The Philharmonic Society, which had recorded a deficit of 300 pounds in 1842, could in 1844 add 400 pounds to their reserve fund, so potent was Mendelssohn's popularity. He had become the Pied Piper of London. On May 27 he introduced Joachim, now thirteen years old, to London; they performed the Beethoven Violin Concerto. The Society had a rule forbidding the appearance of child prodigies; the rule was calmly set aside on Mendelssohn's say-so. Davison wrote that "no master could have played it better." Mendelssohn, however, advised the boy's relatives to take him out of the life of the prodigy for at least two years and to let him grow up physically and spiritually. Fortunately, the advice was heeded.

In addition to music-making, Mendelssohn accepted the task of editing a critical edition of Handel's *Israel in Egypt*. The English Handel Society commissioned it, and while he was still in London he closely examined the autograph and the first editions. What he finally turned out was unretouched Handel. Perhaps it was not quite what the Society wanted at a time when conductors, Mendelssohn not excluded, swelled eighteenth-century instrumentation with nineteenth-century brass.

Only one disappointment did he experience. He thought he could bring to his English audiences the Schubert C-Major Symphony, which he had introduced to the Leipzigers. But the orchestra would have none of it, being utterly puzzled, particularly by the last movement. Mendelssohn lost his temper at the rehearsal and set the symphony aside. He was angry enough to refuse to conduct his own Overture to *Ruy Blas* which had been urgently requested. The Overture was not played in England until after his death.

He received an invitation to take charge of a major festival planned in Birmingham for 1846. He was to have an entirely free hand in choosing the programs and the executant artists. He declined the invitation, because even he could foresee that it would entail too heavy a task for his strength. Yet later, when he weighed the English satisfaction against the Prussian chicanery, when he knew that virtually unlimited means were to be at his disposal in Birmingham, he determined that the work which from the first he hoped would represent the apogee of his talent was to be first performed in England. He offered *Elijah* to the Birmingham Festival.

3

The soprano role of *Elijah* was shaped by him for the voice of a singer he met in 1844 and with whom he formed the last of those warm and open friendships of which his nature had so constant a need. The singer was Jenny Lind.

Jenny Lind was one of the most bewildering of the great singing stars of the nineteenth century, a creature passing strange, so strange indeed that even today no agreement exists as to her true character. When Mendelssohn met her she was twenty-four and had made a sensational debut in Berlin. She was a slight, snub-nosed little girl, simply dressed, unassuming, and with nothing of the diva about her. As Chorley wrote, "her apparition was indeed a godsend among the clumsy and exaggerated women who strode the stage, screaming as they strode." That simplicity, say her detractors, was manufactured. In reality she was an egocentric woman who hid ambition behind a factitious self-portrait of the God-fearing girl from the country who hated crowds, shunned adulation, and longed to flee from the grease-paint-scented air of the opera house to the fields and woods. Henry Pleasants, in *The Great Singers*, writes:

> There was always a smugness and primness about Jenny Lind, a readiness to judge and deplore and condemn, a constant dwelling upon her own virtue and high-mindedness. Her whole life was a series of pious, sanctimonious attitudes, relieved, when she chose to turn it on, by compelling charm. More astonishing than any of her vocal miracles is the plain fact that she could put these attitudes over.

She was very much like the David Garrick that Oliver Goldsmith described in *Retaliation*:

> On the stage he was natural, simple, affecting:
> 'Twas only that when he was off, he was acting.

Yet she was not altogether acting off the stage. Jenny Lind's greatest role may indeed have been herself. Her artificial self often became her real self. Again, like Goldsmith's Garrick:

> Our Garrick's a salad; for in him we see
> Oil, vinegar, sugar and saltness agree.

Lind was sugar and salt. Here is a sample of her behavior, as reported by the daughter of the painter Wilhelm von Kaulbach: [7]

[7] Josefa Dürck-Kaulbach: *Erinnerungen an Wilhelm von Kaulbach und sein Haus.* Munich, 1917.

She did not want to stop in a hotel but be entertained by a family . . .
My father, quite taken with her, offered the hospitality of our home. One
day the huge carriage which had been specially built for her arrived at
our garden-portal, packed high with trunks and boxes. At once the carriage destroyed our carefully cultivated flowers and ruined our neat garden paths.

My father flew into a temper: he had made himself a different image
of the Swedish Nightingale. Jenny Lind was a charming woman but as
moody and as capricious as she was charming. She was even more variable
than Kaulbach himself. My mother must have had a difficult time: the
two artists were continuously at opposite poles. . . . The crisis came the
evening she sang Ännchen in *Freischütz*. During the performance she had
the ill-luck to lose a shoe. That ruined her mood, the public noticed it,
the interaction between artist and audience was disturbed, the expected
success did not materialize. There was an enormous company invited to
our house and everybody was dying to meet the famous singer. Who did
not put in an appearance? Jenny Lind. She locked herself in her room and
would not answer knocks or pleas. My father, furious over this lack of
consideration, locked himself in *his* room, and to my mother was left the
task of entertaining the astonished guests. She told them both the next
morning that it was an exceptionally successful and happy party. . . .

A different report from Leipzig. After her Gewandhaus debut, at
which Mendelssohn conducted, a supper was given in her honor by the
Brockhaus family. Fritz Brockhaus:

December 5, 1845. After the concert, Fräulein Lind promised to come to
our house but she stipulated that there were to be no other guests except
the Mendelssohns. It was easier said than done. In point of fact, the evening
became a meeting of all the artists. Mendelssohn's joy over Lind as an
artist and as a noble woman was infectious; he was all enthusiasm.

April 9, 1846. We were at the Mendelssohns for lunch with Lind. One
has to like this girl from the bottom of one's heart. She is such a fine and
beautiful character. Yet she is not happy. I am convinced that she would
exchange all her triumphs for domestic happiness. That sort of happiness
she observes in Mendelssohn's home with his wife and children.

Those who, like Fritz Brockhaus, believed in her did so implicitly. Hans Christian Andersen, who to be sure was in love with her, said that she "showed me art in its sanctity." Others could not praise enough her goodness of heart. All that goodness could not have been false. Mendelssohn, who was no fool in his judgment of people, could not have valued her as greatly as he did, had it been all make-believe. Still, the contradictions, the sugar and salt, remained. No one could be more skillful in creating publicity for herself while slipping out through the back door of the theater to avoid the admirers. No one could be more ruthless in exacting the last pound of a contract or in signing a more favorable contract, regardless of promises given previously, while again and again putting her singing at the service of charitable causes. No one was as competitive as she, while indulging in self-deprecation. She kept the public on tenterhooks by continuous doubts as to whether she would or would not appear. She was almost always late in making her appearances. When she came to America, she was more indebted to the flamboyant Phineas Barnum than she ever acknowledged. As Joan Bulman, one of her biographers, put it, his own reputation for wickedness made her "angel face" appear all the whiter before the public. She earned $130,000 in two years in America, of which she gave nearly $100,000 to Swedish institutions.

Whatever this complicated woman was, as an artist she was simple and affecting, her voice of virginal purity with a quality unlike that of any other singer—a phantom quality. Grillparzer wrote that when he heard her he could not think of body or space, he heard "a soul singing." On the other hand, she did not portray convincingly a part that called for great dramatic force. Her Norma was as ladylike as her Adina.

When she made her London debut on May 4, 1847, in Meyerbeer's *Robert le Diable*, the press at the theater was so great that men were thrown down, women fainted, and dress suits were torn to pieces. Mendelssohn was there and so was the Queen. At the final curtain Victoria threw a wreath at the artist's feet, an unprecedented gesture. The Queen noted in her diary:

> It was all *piano*, and clear and sweet, and like the sighing of zephyr; yet all heard. Who would describe those long notes, drawn out till they quite melt away; that "shake" which becomes softer and softer, and those very

Jenny Lind, an oil painting by L. Asher. On the piano is the score of a song by Mendelssohn that he composed in Leipzig in 1839: Op. 47, No. 6, Bei der Wiege. (Swedish National Museum, Gripsholm)

piano and flute-like notes, and those round fresh tones which are so youthful?

From then on, everything was Jenny Lind: servants' caps, cigars (needless to say, Jenny Lind disapproved of smoking), flies for trout fishing, meerschaum pipes, spectacle cases, and several Staffordshire pottery figures modeled in her image.

To Mendelssohn she showed the finest side of her nature. Bulman believes that she could have fallen in love with him, but as he was married, "she clamped down on her feelings at once." Yet she spoke so openly of her feelings toward Mendelssohn that others were sure she was in love with him. Clara Schumann believed that, as did Hans Christian Andersen. Their companionship was close and exhilarating to both. It is not to be wondered that Cécile looked at Lind with something less than whole-hearted enthusiasm.

Mendelssohn invited her to appear at the Gewandhaus on December 4, 1845. It was an occasion which was spoken of for years after. Ticket prices were raised and free admission for the Leipzig Conservatory was canceled. The students protested and sent a delegation to Mendelssohn. Their spokesman was a young man with flaming red hair who was later to become Jenny Lind's accompanist and husband, Otto Goldschmidt. Mendelssohn conducted Mozart's "Prague" Symphony among other selections, while Jenny sang the "Casta Diva" and the "Non mi dir" from *Don Giovanni*. Toward the end Mendelssohn accompanied her on the piano while she sang various songs by him and other composers.

Mendelssohn helped Jenny Lind whenever she wanted help. She was nervous about appearing in supercritical Vienna, so Mendelssohn wrote two letters to old friends: to Baroness Ertmann and to Aloys Fuchs, one of the directors of the Society of the Friends of Music. In these letters Mendelssohn called her his "cherished friend."

To please him, she took part in the Lower Rhenish Music Festival held in Aachen in 1846, the last festival Mendelssohn was to conduct. She sang in Haydn's *Creation* one day and Handel's *Alexander's Feast* the second day. Mendelssohn and she—chaperoned by a friend—undertook two Rhine journeys together, ebullient excursions for both of them, when Mendelssohn was able to show Jenny the Cathedral of Cologne and Beethoven's birthplace at Bonn. He did not say much about the journey to Fanny, mentioning Jenny Lind only casually, in connection with rice pudding, which the French cooks in Aachen did not prepare to his taste.

He gave her a manuscript album of his songs as well as his portrait painted by Magnus, which in later years Lind gave to Mendelssohn's eldest daughter, Mrs. Victor Benecke. She had as much influence on him as he on her, perhaps more. She reawakened his desire to write an opera, especially for her. In the meantime, there was *Elijah*.

> Mendelssohn wrote it at a time when they were in almost daily contact, when the sound of her voice was ringing in his ears. He had studied her voice minutely, knew the *timbre* of every note. Each had a quality of its own. Of them all he loved best the upper F sharp, and often spoke admiringly of her *"wunderbares Fis."* It is for her that the F sharps ring out in the opening bars of "Hear ye, Israel" . . .
>
> (*Jenny Lind*, Joan Bulman)

Yes, she was going to England:

To Amalia Wichman

October 27, 1846

> Now let me tell you that I am going to London, and that Mendelssohn alone was able to persuade me to do so. For you know what confidence I place in his advice; and besides, things have really so shaped themselves that I can clearly see that God Himself has so ordained it—and against one's destiny one can do nothing. . . .

But by that time *Elijah* had been performed, *without* Jenny Lind. She had decided—or was it God who decided?—that she would rather make her English debut in an operatic role. It gave her a better opportunity to promote her "destiny" under glamorous auspices. Much as she loved Felix she loved Jenny more. She was not to sing *Elijah* until its author was dead. She mourned him as "The only person who brought fulfillment to my spirit, and almost as soon as I found him I lost him again . . ."

4

His last two English voyages were devoted principally to *Elijah*.
Moscheles had been appointed to direct the Birmingham Festival of 1846,
and *Elijah* was to be its chief attraction. Many details of the performance
had to be settled, the text of the Oratorio translated into English by William
Bartholomew (who had previously submitted an opera libretto to Mendelssohn), with the ever-faithful Klingemann[8] watching over it, the manuscript edited, the cast discussed with Moscheles, with whom Felix kept up
a continuous correspondence. One letter is typical of Mendelssohn's character: when Joseph Moore, the Birmingham festival manager, suggested that
certain members of the orchestra who had behaved recalcitrantly on a
previous occasion, be excluded from the performance, Felix wrote to
Moscheles:

Leipzig, June 26, 1846

> The reason for this letter is a remark in a recent letter of Mr. Moore, who
> writes me: "*Nearly the whole of the Philharmonic Band are engaged;
> only a few are left out, who made themselves unpleasant when you were
> there.*" [In English] I don't like that at all and because I believe that
> these matters fall within your jurisdiction I appeal to you, asking you to
> communicate with Mr. Moore.
>
> Nothing is more odious to me than to stir up old, past wrangles.
> Bad enough that they happened! The Philharmonic incident is forgotten
> by me and must under no account influence the hiring for the Birmingham
> Festival. If you wish to dispense with people who are not capable, that's
> not my affair and I have nothing to say. But should anyone be dismissed
> because *he made himself unpleasant when I was there* I call that an injus-
> tice. I ask that it will not happen. . . .

Though, as we have seen, Mendelssohn had intended the soprano role
for Jenny Lind, he himself refused to negotiate with her: as a friend he
did not like to do so, and besides, it was "highly unlikely that I could get
anything like a definite answer from her." The part was therefore assigned

---

[8] The confirmed bachelor had finally married, much to Felix's joy. He married Sophie
Rosen, sister of Friedrich Rosen, professor of oriental languages, who was a good friend of both
Mendelssohn and Klingemann.

to a Madame Maria Caradori-Allan, who seemed to have had little appreciation of the importance of the occasion: she demanded that Mendelssohn transpose her aria, "Hear ye, Israel," a whole tone lower.[9] Mendelssohn replied that he had not the slightest intention of doing so, but he was quite willing to look for another soprano. The lady decided that she could sing the aria after all.

Mendelssohn arrived in London on August 18 and plunged immediately into piano rehearsals, held in Moscheles' home, then two orchestral rehearsals in the Hanover Square Rooms. On the twenty-third the whole cast and the orchestra, as well as a contingent of members of the press,[10] traveled by special train to Birmingham, where further rehearsals were held with the full chorus. Mendelssohn worked far into the night correcting the parts. The orchestra numbered 125, the chorus 271, a huge complex. The role of Elijah was sung by Josef Staudigl (he looked a little like Schubert), a bass-baritone well known in Vienna.

The performance, on August 26, was a triumph, "something quite incredible," as Moscheles wrote his wife. It had not been the custom to applaud oratorio performances, but custom and restraint were swept away by a "volley of plaudits, vociferous and deafening" (London *Times*) by an audience which numbered two thousand. Mendelssohn himself put aside his usual self-critical reserve:

> . . . No work of mine ever went so admirably at its first performance, nor was received with such enthusiasm by both the musicians and the audience, as this oratorio. It was quite evident at the very first rehearsal in London that they liked it, and liked singing and playing it; but I confess, I was far from anticipating that it would possess such vigor and attraction at the first performance. If only you had been there! During the whole three hours and a half that it lasted, the big hall with its two thousand people and the large orchestra were all so concentrated that not the slightest sound could be heard from the audience, and I was able to sway at will the enormous mass of orchestra and choir and organ. . . . No fewer than four choruses and four arias were encored, and in the whole first movement there was not a single mistake. Later there were several in the second half, but

[9] She had sung the soprano part in the first London performance of Beethoven's Ninth in 1825. She was now forty-six years old, her voice no longer fresh.

[10] J. W. Davison had written a long analytical essay about the work before its première.

even these were unimportant. A young English tenor [11] sang the last aria so beautifully that I was obliged to exercise great self-control in order not to be affected, and to beat time steadily. . . .

(Letter to Paul, from Birmingham, August 26, 1846)

All the same, the soprano did not measure up. Mendelssohn wrote to Livia Frege, a cultivated singer and friend of his in Leipzig, for whom he had played parts of the score, that

August 31, 1846

With so much light the shadows were not absent, and the worst was the soprano part. It was all so pretty, so pleasing, so elegant, at the same time so flat, so heartless, so unintelligent, so soulless, that the music acquired a sort of amiable expression about which I could go mad even today when I think of it.

Moscheles was suddenly taken ill, and Mendelssohn helped out at some of the Festival events. Returning home he felt such exhaustion that he had to interrupt his journey from Ostend to Leipzig three times. He was no longer the same Mendelssohn who could travel five nights virtually without sleep.

Once back in Leipzig, he began revising *Elijah*. As always, dissatisfaction crept over him. "What?" wrote Moscheles in astonishment. "Are you trying to make the beautiful work more beautiful?" He was doing just that: he called his habit of constant alteration his "dreadful disease." But there is no doubt that he improved the work.

This revised version was scheduled for performance the following year by the "Sacred Harmonic Society" in London. The Society asked Mendelssohn to conduct the performance—and once again he could not resist. Once again he set out on a journey across the Channel; it was to be his last. The one performance of *Elijah* turned into six, four in London (April 16, 23, 28, and 30, 1847, at the large Exeter Hall), one in Manchester (April 20), and one in Birmingham (April 27). George Eliot, overcome with emotion, wrote that *Elijah* represented "a kind of sacramental purification of Exeter Hall." Queen Victoria and Albert were present at the performance of the twenty-third, and Albert wrote in Mendelssohn's copy of the libretto:

[11] Charles Lockey.

To the Noble Artist who, surrounded by the Baal-worship of debased art, has been able, by his genius and science, to preserve faithfully, like another Elijah, the worship of true art, and once more to accustom our ear, amid the whirl of empty, frivolous sounds, to the pure tones of sympathetic feeling and legitimate harmony: to the Great Master, who makes us conscious of the unity of his conception, through the whole of his creation, from the soft whispering to the mighty raging of the elements.

Inscribed in grateful remembrance by   Albert.

Fulsome though this tribute sounds, it gave Mendelssohn as much pleasure as a good mark in school. Victoria was again present at a concert of the Royal Philharmonic: incredible as it may seem, the day before the Birmingham performance Mendelssohn conducted his "Scottish" Symphony and *A Midsummer Night's Dream* music and appeared as a soloist in Beethoven's G Major Concerto. "I wanted to play especially well," he said, "because two ladies were present whom I wished to please, the Queen and Jenny Lind." Nor was this the full measure of his activity; with an almost neurotic eagerness he took part in several chamber music concerts, made two appearances at Buckingham Palace, and played at two receptions at Baron Bunsen's—now Prussian ambassador to England—for whom he could hardly have harbored the warmest of feelings. At least he met Mr. Gladstone there.

The Queen noted:

Buckingham Palace

April 23, 1847 . . . After a very early dinner, we went at ¼ to 7 with the Dss. of Sutherland & the Ladies & Gentlemen, to Exeter Hall, to hear Mendelssohn's new Oratorio of "Elijah", which is extremely fine. He conducted himself, & the whole went off very well. The Choruses are all very fine, in particular the one "Hear our cry oh Baal",—the concluding Chorus of the 1rst. part, & the concluding one of the 2nd. There is one very fine Motett "Cast thy burden", &c, also a recitative & chorus between Elijah & a youth, which precedes the conclusion of the 1rst. part. Then the Chorus descriptive of the fire coming down, & the Motett & Chorus "Holy, Holy". The recitatives might be shortened, but the whole is a splendid work. We talked to Mendelssohn between the different parts.

Buckingham Palace

April 26 . . . We dined after 7 & then went to a Philharmonic Concert, one of the best I ever remember. Costa conducted admirably Beethoven's very fine Symphony, but nothing came up to Mendelssohn's playing of that beautiful Concerto, also by Beethoven. It was so full of feeling & soul, & his touch was wonderful. He played entirely by heart, which, when doing so with the Orchestra, must be most difficult. He is a wonderful genius & is deservedly an amazing favourite here. The applause was immense. We spoke to him & also to Costa between the parts, & found him, as always, so pleasing & amiable.

Buckingham Palace

May 1 . . . We had the great treat of hearing Mendelssohn play, & he stayed an hour with us, playing some new compositions, with that indescribably beautiful touch of his. I also sang 3 of his songs, which seemed to please him. He is so amiable & clever. For some time he has been engaged in composing an Opera & an Oratorio, but has lost courage about them. The subject for his Opera is a Rhine Legend & that for the Oratorio, a very beautiful one depicting Earth, Hell, & Heaven, & he played one of the Choruses out of this to us, which was very fine. . . .

On May 8 he took leave of Victoria and Albert. Tired so that he could hardly lift his arms, he started on the homeward journey.

5

"There has never been a foreigner more honest in his love for, more discriminating in his appreciation of England," wrote Chorley. Neither English enthusiasm nor English generosity was without precedent: Haydn could have testified to the one, Beethoven to the other. Mendelssohn gave the English what they understood. They gave him what he needed at all times, a full measure of approbation. Indeed, the measure brimmed over.

For two or three decades after his death one "had to play Mendelssohn" in England to score a success. The melodious predilection continued. Mendelssohn's charm wove a posthumous spell, for a time making it difficult for the new music of Berlioz and of Chopin—not to mention Wagner

—to be listened to with open ears. Creatively Mendelssohn's influence on British music was damaging, his musical descendants being weaklings. After *Elijah* there occurred a notable revival in England's interest in the oratorio style: Hubert Parry, Alexander Mackenzie ("The Rose of Sharon"), Charles Villiers Stanford, John Stainer ("The Crucifixion," his most popular work, which survived almost to our own day), all earnest Victorians, all dulcet, all wrote accommodating oratorios. Sterndale Bennett, a contemporary, and Edward German, a follower, were symphonic composers of Mendelssohnian stamp. Only one of these men reached genius: Arthur Sullivan. He was the first to win the Mendelssohn Scholarship at the London Royal Academy of Music; this enabled him to go to the Leipzig Conservatory and study under such men as David, Rietz, and Moscheles. He returned full of symphonic and operatic ambition. He wanted to compose serious works and did. But when he met his brimstone partner, he was seduced into giving out the finest wit to be found in English music.

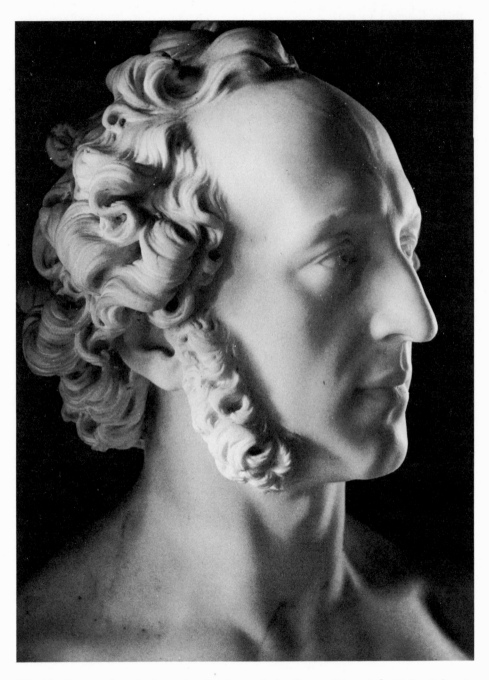

Marble bust sculpted after the death mask by Ernst Rietschel. (Mendelssohn Archive, Berlin)

Eleven

TIME RUNS OUT

I

$\mathcal{A}$NY time now he was going to lay down his baton, step off the podium, refuse public appearances, and put away his travel clothes. What he wanted, or what he thought he wanted, was to withdraw to a spot where he could walk in quiet fields, canter his horse in a friendly forest, invite a guest or two for the midday meal, be with Cécile, play with the children—now five in number—and set down his ideas on music paper. He had been before the public for almost a generation: he was ready to cease being the cynosure of Europe's concert world. Well, perhaps not quite ready. Not today. To-morrow, surely.

He could not quite give up. Just before the Birmingham engagement in 1847 he was to be found, aside from Aachen, at Düsseldorf, at Lièges, and at Cologne. After Birmingham, he and Gade alternated as conductors at the Gewandhaus. There David shone with Mendelssohn's Violin Concerto; he played it on a magnificent tan Guarneri violin (one which came into Heifetz's possession). On November 5, 1846, Mendelssohn gave the première of Schumann's Second Symphony. On that occasion he met with an ugly reminder of the fact that he, the foremost composer of Protestant church music and one who had just composed a setting of the Catholic ritual, *Lauda Sion*, was after all a Jew. He had programmed for the first half of the evening in which the Schumann symphony was to be heard

Rossini's Overture to *William Tell*. This delighted the public to such a response that the Overture had to be repeated. A hostile Leipzig journalist thought this repetition a cheap trick, derogatory to Schumann; he called it a "Mosaic" trick. Who in his right mind would pay attention to such an ink-stained insult? But Mendelssohn, who used to laugh at such snipes, had become sensitive; he withdrew into a hurt silence. When Clara Schumann shortly after wanted to give a concert of her own and begged Mendelssohn to conduct her husband's symphony again, he refused, and it took the combined persuasion of Clara and Cécile to make him change his mind.

As to his compositions, he planned to write another symphony, of which nothing remains, and he began to work on a third oratorio, a *Christus*, of which only fragments are extant. Operatic thoughts occupied him chiefly; what libretto would be suitable for Jenny Lind? Lumley, a London operatic manager, suggested Shakespeare's *The Tempest*. Here was a follow-up to *A Midsummer Night's Dream*, another world of magic, with Miranda as the kind of gentle girl whom Lind could portray. Difficult though it is to believe, Mendelssohn fell in with Lumley's suggestion that Augustin Scribe adapt the play. It would be hard to think of a less likely choice, the author of some four hundred precise and rationalistic plays pouring his glass of water into the sea of Shakespeare's mysteries. Scribe actually completed an adaptation, and the expected happened—Mendelssohn refused it. Then a German lyric poet, Emanuel Geibel, inexperienced as a dramatist but highly regarded as a poet, suggested *Lorelei*. A German legend, a blond siren, the Rhine—of all the subjects which Mendelssohn considered, this lay nearest to the world he understood and loved. Devrient offered to help Geibel, and they submitted a fully worked out libretto with which Mendelssohn was overjoyed. He began to compose, but soon enough discouragement set in and he let the project drop.[1] Three numbers survive.

Tranquility seemed constantly just beyond where Mendelssohn was standing. He could envisage it, he could wish it, but he could not reach it. That is not to say that he was distraught or dispirited all the time. For that his disposition was too sanguine. His thirty-eighth birthday was celebrated with great gaiety on February 3, 1847. Paganini was there to visit him, as well as the Moscheleses and Joachim. But more frequently now he com-

---

[1] Eventually Max Bruch used the libretto for an opera.

plained of headaches. His doctors could find no cause for them and they had no remedy to offer except the oft-repeated plea that he slow down, a plea in which Cécile joined again and again and which Felix disregarded.

2

In the last days of his last visit to London, a change came over him. While he was conducting or playing, he seemed as youthful as ever; at other times he gave the impression of a much older man than one just entering his thirty-eighth year; his skin was gray, his eyes veiled, and his dark hair showed premature streaks of white. The Klingemanns were worried about his health. Sophie Klingemann was about to visit the Continent and decided to travel with him. But at the last moment Klingemann was sufficiently concerned to go along as far as Ostend. From there Mendelssohn proceeded alone. At a little German border town, an officious customs officer mistook him for a Dr. Mendelssohn who was wanted as a political fugitive. Before Felix could establish his identity, almost the entire day was gone. Finally, however, he was permitted to proceed and he went to Frankfurt, where Cécile was waiting for him.

He had been home for only two or three days when the most horrible news reached him. Fanny was dead. A few days before—May 14, 1847— she had been rehearsing for one of her Sunday matinee concerts. She was sitting at the piano when suddenly both her hands fell from the keyboard. She was carried into the next room. She never recovered consciousness and by eleven o'clock that night she was dead.

When Felix got the news, he uttered a piercing cry and collapsed. He remained insensible for some time. When he came to, he could not stop crying.

Fanny's death wrote out his own death warrant.[2] He lived on for a little more than five months, and though he eventually went to work again, though his behavior to his family seemed normal, though he made an effort to recover from that first terrible shock, in the depth of his being he felt himself doomed. He would talk about the future and make plans for further

---

[2] In Marianne Kirlew's *Famous Sisters of Great Men* she writes that Fanny's demise was Felix's "death-blow."

compositions, only to interrupt himself, saying, "What's the use? I will not be here." He wrote about Fanny on May 24:

> What we all have lost, and I above all—that we are not as yet able to measure. With her kindness and love she was part of myself every moment of my life. There was no joy I experienced without thinking of the joy that she would feel with me. The wealth of her sisterly love spoiled me and made me prideful. . . . I make myself believe that the tragic news will suddenly prove to be false; yet I know very well that it is all true. I will never, never be able to get used to it. Perhaps she is lucky, in her marvelously harmonious existence, not to have experienced the pain of old age, of life gradually ebbing—but for us it is hard.

Cécile thought it wise to take him away on a holiday. At first the family went to Baden-Baden, where they had arranged to meet Paul and Hensel. Yet their being all together was not the best thing for Felix, chiefly because Cécile and Paul's wife, Albertine, were unsympathetic to each other and showed it. He decided once again to visit Switzerland, which previously had acted as a tonic for his spirit, and they settled at Interlaken, where he remained until mid-September. Chorley visited him there. He described how old Mendelssohn looked, how he no longer walked upright but a little bent. Yet his smile was as charming as ever, his mind as curious. He had, wrote Chorley, become more tolerant of music which previously he had dismissed: Donizetti, Rossini, among others, and he was much interested in learning about the young Verdi. He vacillated from one moment to the next. He could not bear to touch the piano and yet he thought he might write another concerto. He shrank from the organ and yet he did play one in the little village church of Ringgenberg on the Lake of Brienz. That was the last time he touched the organ keys. He did draw and sketch a good deal.

While he was in Switzerland, he went for extended walks, staying away for hours at a time and worrying Cécile. It was the only way, he said, that he could find some sort of peace. On these walks he sketched in his mind his final completed quartet (Op. 80), which he meant as a memorial for Fanny. It is his most deeply felt composition of chamber music. After that, he composed another quartet, which he never finished, two movements of which appeared posthumously as Op. 81.

Fanny playing the piano, drawn in Rome in 1845. She died two years later. Pencil drawing by A. Kaselowski. (With kind permission of Fanny Hensel Kistner, Erlangen, Germany)

Somewhat restored, at least outwardly, he returned to Leipzig. He was scheduled to conduct the first German performance of *Elijah* in Berlin and then to go to Vienna to conduct *Elijah* there, where Jenny Lind was to sing the part. When he got to Berlin, he was shown the room in which Fanny had held her last rehearsal and the room in which she died. When he entered the room, his grief returned with renewed intensity. Nothing had been changed in the two rooms and the score of his *Walpurgisnacht* was still on the piano. He burst out weeping and canceled the Berlin performance. He could no longer face the public. He resigned as well from the direction of the Gewandhaus, and even Jenny Lind could not tempt him to fulfill the Vienna engagement.

On October 8 he took part in the examination of the Leipzig Conservatory and wrote some examples of *Generalbass* on the blackboard.[3] Next day he went for a walk with Moscheles and Cécile. He walked slowly and answered the questions of how he was feeling with "Gray on gray." He had recently composed a song, a quiet "Night Song" ("*Nachtlied*") to words by Eichendorff. That evening he took this song and some others to the house of Livia Frege to have her sing them for him. When she sang the "*Nachtlied*" he said, "Oh, that sounds sad! But that's how I feel nowadays." Livia Frege left the room in order to fetch more lamps. When she returned she saw him sitting on the couch, his hands rigid and cold. He wanted to walk home to warm himself and she suggested that a carriage be called. He would not hear of it. She gave him a stimulant in a glass of sugar water and he left. At home Cécile found him, again with stiff hands. The following day he suffered with a terrible headache. The doctor was called and the headache was treated with leeches. It was nothing, an upset stomach perhaps or overworked nerves.

He recovered a little, after staying in bed. Paul had written that he was ready to bring "the entire medical faculty of Berlin" to Leipzig by special train; he was reassured by Cécile. Felix himself remained pessimistic: "I feel as if somebody were lying in wait for me who is saying, 'Stop! No more!'" Yet his condition improved. He went out for walks. He laughed occasionally and even toyed with the idea of going to Vienna to

---

[3] The description of Mendelssohn's last days is based on the testimonies of those who were with him: Paul Mendelssohn, Schleinitz, F. David, Moscheles.

conduct *Elijah.* On October 15 he held a long conference with Moscheles about the future of the Leipzig Conservatory. But all the time the fear of dying seemed to possess him, and when he wrote to Paul on October 25, he begged him to come and see him, because such a visit "would do more for me than those bitter medicines."

On October 28 he was with Cécile, took his morning walk with her, ate his lunch with good appetite, when a sudden paroxysm occurred. He lost consciousness, and then in great excitement he began to speak—in English. The doctor came, knowing not what to say or do. Two days later brother Paul arrived from Berlin. Felix spoke pleasantly with him but then became agitated. Toward two o'clock on October 30, Paul having left the room, Cécile called him back. She was trembling because she could not manage to quiet Felix. Paul jokingly scolded him for making such a commotion. He smiled, then suddenly he uttered a horrible cry of pain, his whole face contorted, and he sank back. He screamed the whole night through. The following day, "it seemed as if the pains had lessened, but his face was that of a dying man." Cécile did not leave the room, and when occasionally they forced her to find an hour of repose, she could not find it, because Felix's moaning could be heard through the whole house. Then he sang at the top of his voice. The doctor said to him, "Don't make so much music. You get too excited." He stopped for a while and smiled, but then began again. He now lost consciousness and entered the final struggle with death. He still recognized those around him but spoke no more except to mumble, "Tired, very tired."

On the fourth of November everybody knew that his condition was hopeless. He lay quiet, not asleep, yet not yet dead, though his color "revealed the terror of death." He died at nine-thirty at night. The children were asleep. Cécile said: "Life lasts so long—how shall I live it alone?"

3

No clear medical diagnosis as to the cause of his death exists. Klingemann said that he died of a series of strokes and that "the dissolution of his body had begun years before, of which severe nosebleeds, vertigo, headaches and an irritability which often changed his whole temperament, were symptoms. They wanted to call Dr. Schönlein from Berlin, who could not get away because he was treating a princess; at any rate, he predicted that there would be no hope, 'a repetition of the attacks being fatal.' "

Dr. Dieter Kerner, who made a study of the subject in his book, *Krankheiten Grosser Musiker* (*Illnesses of Great Musicians*), believes that in spite of the evidence of Fanny's and Felix's early death under somewhat similar circumstances, it is not possible to conclude scientifically that there existed hereditary brain weakness in the Mendelssohn family. Felix died of a subarachnoid hemorrhage due to aneurysm: in layman's language this means that a brain artery distended or ruptured, and while this is not invariably fatal, it was severe enough in Felix's case to cause the early death. To say that this condition was caused by hypertension is speculation and, as I have said, it is impossible to make an accurate medical diagnosis of a man who died over a hundred years ago.

The death mask was cast. Hensel came and made a drawing of his face. A mob of people stormed the house; they stood around the coffin and many wept. If Cécile or his friends wanted to view him, the doors had to be forcibly closed. The room, lit by torches, was heaped with flowers and laurel wreaths. Cécile took a bunch of flowers and five little bouquets for the children and placed them on his hands. Cécile was quiet; she smiled, and whispered, "Who could believe it?"

Germany began to mourn him as a national hero. The first of the many commemorative services was held in Leipzig's Paulinerkirche on November 7, the church draped in black, with the pupils of the Conservatory, the dignitaries of the city, and representatives of the Saxon government being present. A chorus of six hundred intoned a Chorale by Bach and one from *St. Paul*. Cécile's strength had given out; she did not attend the service but later she went into the empty church, accompanied by Paul, to take a last look. At eight o'clock that night a thousand people bearing torches carried the coffin to the railroad station. A special train left at ten o'clock; it halted at midnight at Koethen, at half-past one at Dessau, the city of his grandfather, and at Halle. Wherever it stopped it was greeted by groups of men and women singing tributes. At seven in the morning the train arrived in Berlin. Mendelssohn was buried in the churchyard of Trinity Church, next to Fanny.

A Gewandhaus concert scheduled for the evening of November 4 was canceled. The following week's concert began with Mendelssohn's music, with Livia Frege singing the *"Nachtlied"* in a tear-choked voice; the second part consisted of the *Eroica*. In most other German cities memorial concerts were held. The planned Vienna performance of *Elijah* took place, but without Jenny Lind on November 14, 1847; it was done with Viennese theatricality. The music stands were draped in black, the singers dressed in black; on the conductor's desk lay a score and a laurel wreath, but there was nobody standing at the desk, the performance being led from a lower stand by the chorus master.

Musical England's grief was as real as Germany's. The Queen just then was greatly perturbed over the Irish famine and the violence resulting from it. She and Albert set their own worries aside to send a message to Cécile, whom they had never met, in which the sadness and sincerity surpassed the usual formal expression of condolence. From the Queen's Journal:

> Windsor Castle
>
> November 10, 1847 . . . We were horrified, astounded and distressed to read in the papers of the death of Mendelssohn, the greatest musical genius since Mozart, & the most amiable man. He was quite worshipped by those who knew him intimately, & we have so much appreciated & admired his wonderfully beautiful compositions. We liked & esteemed the excellent man & looked up to & revered, the wonderful genius, & the great mind, which I fear were too much for the frail delicate body. With it all, he was so modest & simple. . . . Saw Mrs. Anderson, who was in great sorrow at Mendelssohn's death. She told me he had been very unwell, & had never got over the death of his sister last July, who was also a most talented person, & full of genius. Mrs. Anderson had known Mendelssohn very well. . . .
>
> Windsor Castle
>
> November 13 . . . Mrs. Anderson gave me some most touching, interesting letters to read, from Moscheles & Mme. Moscheles relative to the last moments, of that great, good, & ever to be regretted Mendelssohn. It

was a succession of fits of apoplexy, which killed him. At 1rst. the physicians hoped, as consciousness was returning, that he might do well, provided there were no further attacks. But alas! they returned & from that hour all consciousness vanished. The great soul passed peacefully away, without a struggle, after 9 o'clock. Moscheles & his wife were there the whole time with poor Mme. Mendelssohn & his brother Paul. . . . We read & played that beautiful "Lied ohne Worte", which poor Mendelssohn arranged & wrote out himself for us this year. To feel, when one is playing his beautiful music, that he is no more, seems incomprehensible! . . .

Osborne

December 4 . . . Before dinner Ld. Palmerston brought up Bunsen, who came with a letter from the King of Prussia. . . . Bunsen much regrets Mendelssohn, whom he had known very well. He had settled & arranged with him the text for the new Oratorio of "Earth, Hell & Heaven" & said it had been wonderful to see how beautifully Mendelssohn chose the text from Scripture. . . .

Osborne

December 8 . . . I received a pretty letter from Mendelssohn's poor Widow, who is touching in her great grief. What must it be for her to lose *such* a husband! We got this evening his last songs, the last of all being the very last thing he composed or ever played, being in the act of playing it, when he was taken ill, the 2nd fatal time, & never recovered consciousness. It is a beautiful song but very melancholy, & made me feel so sad. . . .

(The Mrs. Anderson mentioned here was Lucy Anderson, a prominent pianist, who taught Victoria as a girl and later taught the Queen's children. She died in 1878.)

Jenny Lind offered tribute by accomplishing now what she might have done better when Felix was alive. She had been so shocked by her friend's death that she could not bring herself to sing any of his songs for two years, but *Elijah*—that work she would now essay. She gathered a cast of singers familiar with the Oratorio and on the anniversary of Mendelssohn's death organized a performance at Exeter Hall. Julius Benedict, who when Felix was an eleven-year-old boy had first met him, conducted. She sang with all the love and art of which she was capable. Joan Bulman describes the performance in her biography of Lind:

> She had thrown off the ways of an opera singer. It was noted from the start, *The Times* approvingly observed, that Jenny Lind's approach to singing sacred music was the right one; she "would not use her great vocal facility to any other purpose than to give the text in its integrity." Her style was pure, almost to the point of severity. Not a single note was altered, not one ornament added. This was Mendelssohn's music, just as Mendelssohn wrote it and as Mendelssohn would have delighted to hear it.

The concert raised the remarkable sum of a thousand pounds for a "Mendelssohn Foundation." That Foundation, too, was Lind's idea.

With Felix's end the talent which had flowed from grandfather to father to son ebbed. Four of Felix's five children lived on: the last-born, Felix, died when he was nine, Karl at fifty-nine, Marie at fifty-eight, Lili at sixty-five; while Paul, his third child, died at thirty-nine. None of the children was exceptionally gifted. Felix's brother Paul reached sixty-two, Rebecka forty-five. No conclusion of a family disease causing early death can therefore be drawn.

Cécile lived for a time in Berlin. Then, wanting to get away from too intimate a contact with Felix's relatives, she went to Baden and finally back to Frankfurt to her own relatives. For a year before she died she was so ill—probably with tuberculosis—that she had to be carried up and downstairs. In spite of her wasting disease, she remained beautiful. She died on September 25, 1853, silent and sad.

The Mendelssohn family, the various branches of it, became more numerous and ever more wealthy. Uncle Joseph's son Alexander (1798–1871) saw Germany united under Bismarck, and Alexander's son Franz (1829–1889) was ennobled. Franz had two sons, Robert (1851–1917) and Franz (1865–1935), who was president of the German Chamber of Commerce. Ernst von Mendelssohn-Bartholdy (1846–1909), the third son of Paul, added greatly to the wealth of the banking house. When he died he was supposed to have been the richest man in Berlin. In the Berlin Modern Museum hangs one of Manet's finest paintings, "In the Wintergarden," given to the city by Ernst and Robert. A great-nephew of Felix, Arnold Mendelssohn (1855–1933), was a composer of church music and a teacher of Hindemith. Here and there, distinguished descendants are still living. Dr. Karl Mendelssohn is a physicist, a Fellow of the British Royal Society, and has recently advanced an important theory on the building of the Egyptian pyramids. A great-grandson, Felix Gilbert, is at the time of this writing a professor of history at the Institute for Advanced Study in Princeton.

The banking house was forcibly liquidated in 1939. The Mendelssohns still living in Germany dispersed, some to America, some to Switzerland, some into oblivion. Like the twenty china monkeys, the family was broken up.

4

In 1892 a monument to Mendelssohn was erected in Leipzig, the statue standing in front of the Gewandhaus. When Hitler came to power, the press agitated for the removal of the monument. A sample of the propaganda is found in an article in the *Leipziger Tageszeitung*, Sept. 16, 1936, entitled "About Jewish Music and the Monument of a Jew":

> . . . Without wishing to discuss the merits of the composer, it is certainly true that it goes against the healthy instinct of our nation when—prompted by false piety and consideration—we let stand a monument to a Jew, while we consistently endeavor to expunge the damage done to our cultural heritage by Judaism.

The Nazi city government gave orders to remove the "monument standing before the Gewandhaus of the hundred percent Jew (*Vollblutjuden*) Mendelssohn-Bartholdie [sic], because it created public resentment." The mayor of Leipzig, Carl Goerdeler, however, protested. (This was the same man who eventually planned the unsuccessful attempt on Hitler's life on July 20, 1944. He was executed in February, 1945.) Goerdeler felt that this action would "damage Leipzig's reputation as an international music-city." Shortly afterward, Sir Thomas Beecham and the London Philharmonic were scheduled to come to Leipzig as part of a Continental tour by the orchestra. Sir Thomas, who did not know what was going on, inquired of Goerdeler whether he and a deputation from the orchestra would be welcome to place a wreath at the monument. Hadn't Mendelssohn built a bridge between Leipzig and London? Goerdeler replied that this good-will gesture would be most appropriate. Unfortunately, he was out of town the night of the concert. In the morning after the concert, Sir Thomas and the delegation marched to the entrance of the Gewandhaus. *There was no statue.* They looked in the back, on the right, on the left side. No trace of a statue. What had happened? During the night before—November 10, 1936—acting Mayor Haake, a Nazi bigwig, had commandeered a troop of workmen and removed the statue to a cellar, where it was hacked to pieces. The German press kept silent.

The German press did not keep silent in its campaign of derogation:

> The almost hundred-year-old enthusiasm for Mendelssohn is the more incomprehensible since at all times men have spoken up who declared his music to be quite superficial. Not even the most audacious Mendelssohn partisan could deny such a judgment. . . . If Mendelssohn had written music expressive of his race, then perhaps Judaism could boast of a great composer. He was unable to form an indigenous style and had to content himself with imitations of the German character. That character, however, he could not fathom. . . .

> (Otto Schumann, *History of German Music,* Leipzig, 1940)

Here is another Nazi verdict:

> Mendelssohn was an *"Ersatz"* for German masters. . . . That is the decisive point, which ought to regulate our behaviour from now on. We no longer have any need for such substitutes, either in the concert hall, or in the home, or in church. Mendelssohn can perhaps still be used as material for practicing, but never as a full-valued work of art. This holds true of the oratorios *St. Paul* and *Elijah* as well as the rest of his church music; Mendelssohn furnished easy *"Ersatz"* and through his own products hindered the acceptance of Bach, in which he himself was active. There is no excuse for the exaggerated value which the musical world has assigned to Mendelssohn in all branches. Kretzschmar's *Concert Guide* dedicates

eleven pages to Mendelssohn's five symphonies, while Bruckner's seven symphonies, those composed before 1890, occupy little more than one page. Surely a crass example of imbalance between the jewish and the aryan in a German book!

(Karl Grunsky, *Thoughts on Mendelssohn*. Westdeutscher Beobachter, March 3, 1935)

. . . His *Midsummer Night's Dream* music, though it is manufactured with almost unbelievable skill in a musical never-never land, remains without true creative force and the value of its sentiments is false . . . [proving] that a Jew is not, and can never be, creative, at least not like a German genius. . . .[4]

(Richard Litterscheid, *Mendelssohn, Mahler and We*. Die Musik, March, 1936)

A now-forgotten Nazi musician composed an *Ersatz* for the Wedding March.

5

In a woody suburb of Berlin called the Dahlem district, the rebuilt University, the "Museum Dahlem" (housing the unique collection from the former Kaiser Friedrich Museum, including twenty-six Rembrandts), the dramatic new Ethnological Museum, and the Prussian State Library are all located. It is a concentration of artistic wealth, fortunately housed. Adjacent to the Music Division of the Library stands an old-fashioned little building: there is the Mendelssohn Archive, a museum entirely devoted to the Mendelssohns, Moses, Fanny, Felix. The place is chockfull of memorabilia, not only manuscripts, letters, and documents, but such things as Felix's toilet kit which he used on his travels and the silver goblet Felix presented to his parents on their silver anniversary. As new material about Felix comes to light, the Archive eagerly bids on it. His letters, widely scattered, are being examined and collected. Musical texts are being corrected.

Mendelssohn's music is once more considered a national treasure and by no means a museum treasure alone.

A Visitors' Book lies on a table; the inscriptions show that curious

---

[4] These quotations are taken from a compilation of documents published as *Music in the Third Reich*, edited by Joseph Wulf. (Gütersloh, 1963) The book makes unbelievable reading.

music-lovers have come from all over the world. Yet the museum is a quiet place, a place primarily devoted to study.

As one sits in the Mendelssohn Museum and looks at the portrait Goethe—that most un-German of the German poets—gave Felix, one may remember Goethe's lines:

> Man's soul—how like the water,
> Man's fate—how like the wind! [5]

[5] From *Gesang der Geister über den Wassern.*

The monument that stood in front of the Leipzig Gewandhaus. Sculpted by Werner Stein in 1892 and destroyed by the Nazis.

Twelve

WHAT REMAINS?

HE was lifted too high by his contemporaries, the musical world gaping at this gracious figure, every part of him life-enhancing. They appreciated those melodies fluttering nonchalantly in the breeze, but they recognized as well that his music could do more than "do observance to a morn of May"—and many responded to its melancholy strains. However, they heard in it profound meanings which were not there; some thought of him as a second Mozart or, listening to *Elijah*, of a master of equal girth to Handel. It was inevitable that a reaction should set in. So it did, shortly after his death. He was toppled from his high rank to the level of a "harmless" composer. During that patronizing period, he was demoted to a man whose music could be heard by the senior class of St. Timothy's Finishing School without fear of upsetting the emotional equilibrium of the pupils.

As early as 1852, J. W. Davison noted regretfully that in certain circles Mendelssohn had become "the object of pitying disparagement." Not all circles, of course. Wagner excepted, most men of music continued to value him. Brahms was not to be swayed; he would listen silently to condescending discussions about Mendelssohn and then mumble, "Yes, yes, Mendelssohn—he was the last of the great masters." In a long essay (*Mendelssohn in Italia*, 1864) Boito wrote of him as "more than a musician, a thinker, a contemplative, a poet." He must have talked to Verdi about Mendelssohn; can one hear Mendelssohnian reminiscences at the beginning of the last act of *Falstaff*? The young Richard Strauss studied Mendelssohn so assiduously that the influence is clearly perceptible in his early works, such as a piano sonata "for all intents and purposes one of Mendelssohn's *Lieder ohne Worte*." (Norman Del Mar) Echoes of the Mendelssohn influence can still be heard in some of the beautiful passages of *Ariadne auf Naxos*.

To the broad public, however, Mendelssohn's work for some years did not mean much; it was not vital to, it did not excite, listeners inculcated by the fever of *Tristan*. Later, on the other hand, when Till Eulenspiegel was hanged and Electra screamed "Strike once again, Orest!", Mendelssohn served as a relief for those who wanted to hear "music with a tune to it." By and by his output was again recognized as being more than merely melodious, his subtleties of style and grace of design appreciated. Today we live in an age of antiquarian curiosity. For good or bad reasons, forgotten music from Gabrielli to Busoni is pulled out of the archives and Mendelssohn is no exception: his immature compositions are being sought out, chiefly for recordings, but occasionally for the concert hall as well: for instance, the Concerto for Two Pianos and Orchestra in E Major, written when he was fourteen, and one in A flat Major, composed when he was fifteen; as well as a Double Concerto for Violin, Piano and Strings in D Minor, dating from his fourteenth year, and his Symphony No. 1 in C Minor.

While all immortality is relative and all but the few greatest artists —and perhaps even they—undergo fluctuations in strength and meaning, Mendelssohn's appraisal has kept changing more than most musicians. From generation to generation he has experienced ups and downs more extreme than those of other composers, though of course he has never lacked for a public, never lacked for a quantity of fame, never lacked for understanding by perceptive minds. He always did give pleasure to people ready to receive it. He seems especially useful now because we can find no satisfaction in so many of the disorganized, jejune, and cerebral modern productions; yet our capacity for beauty—which Moses Mendelssohn defined —still needs to be nurtured. If a swing back to the romantic does exist, Mendelssohn benefits.

His clear art made a particular appeal to the Anglo-Saxon temperament. At the beginning of 1845 he received an invitation from New York to come and conduct several orchestras, including the New York Philharmonic, then but three seasons old. He was offered $5,000, an enormous sum for those days, plus a benefit concert that would bring him an equal amount. He declined, partly because his boy Felix was severely ill just then. But Mendelssohn societies sprang up in many American cities: New York, Philadelphia, Boston, Chicago. These were mostly choral groups, and to "sing along" with Mendelssohn became a popular pastime. One of the first American chamber music groups took his name, the "Mendelssohn Quintette Club" of Boston. *Elijah* and the symphonies became early successes. One of the remarkable men of the Civil War period was George Templeton Strong, a lawyer who served his country well by organizing the "Sanitary Commission" to care for war-wounded soldiers and prevent the spread of epidemics in New York. Strong kept a diary. As a plain music-lover, not a professional, he gave his impression of the "Scottish" Symphony which he set down in 1864, a few days after Abraham Lincoln was re-elected:

November 19, Saturday

Thence to Philharmonic rehearsal; Mendelssohn's Symphony, *vulgo vocento* the "Scotch Symphony"—why Scotch rather than Welsh I cannot say. Very delightful work. No end of talent, taste, culture, skill, fertility of resources, copiousness of musical language. Every movement beautiful and original and full of splendid points. No fault can be found with it, except that it is without the surpassing, almost supernatural, vigor and beauty that Mozart and Beethoven make an orchestra express. It is first-rate work of the second order, and different *in general* and not merely in degree from work of the first order. But the scherzo is marvellous, and so is the finale.

George Bernard Shaw's opinions on music sound often as if they were written expressly to be iconoclastic. Yet the bristly anti-Victorian loved Mendelssohn, the "Italian" Symphony being one of his favorites. As to the *Midsummer Night's Dream* Overture, he could feel its "novelty now, after sixty-six years." He had this to say about the *Songs without Words*:

At one of his [Paderewski's] recitals he played four of Mendelssohn's Songs without Words, which have dropped out of the stock pianoforte repertory lately, ostensibly because they are too easy for our young lions, but really, I suspect, because they are too difficult. If you want to find out the weak places in a player's technique, just wait until he has dazzled you with a Chopin polonaise, or a Liszt rhapsody, or Schumann's symphonic studies; and then ask him to play you ten bars of Mozart or Mendelssohn.

He was bored by *St. Paul*, though:

I had as lief talk Sunday-school for two hours and a half to a beautiful woman with no brains as listen to *St. Paul* over again.

Germany was more respectful, listening seriously even to the weaker church music, because it was "uplifting." The young Mahler achieved his first prominence by conducting *St. Paul* in Cassel in 1885. Still, there must have been many who felt about Mendelssohn's pontifical compositions, those motets and psalms, as Christopher Sly did about the play: " 'Tis a very excellent piece of work; would 'twere over."

2

What remains?

More and more the art of the past, that part of art which has a gentle constitution, assumes the function of a reminder. When we look at Manet's "In a Boat" at the Metropolitan Museum, we are reminded of a loveliness which no longer exists in the world, or if it does, it exists only in places so far away as to be impossible for most of us to find. The corporeal world has grown harsher and much of it uglier. But the sense of beauty still exists within us and longs to be touched and reminded.

Mendelssohn's music is a reminder of vanished beauty. He conjures up for us the two people in the little boat with the blue sea behind them, or the field of poppies. His mind was not of a tragic bent, and though much of his music is elegiac in tone, tinted darkly, he did not descend to the abyss. Paul Henry Lang in his *Music in Western Civilization* said he did not possess "the mysticism of the unutterable. A certain sober clarity permeates his music." What he did possess was the ability to administer a tonic to tired spirits. To put it plainly, he knew how to make us feel good. If he did not transport us into the seventh heaven nor down into the First Circle, he did offer us a place in a serene Utopia.

He was the Leigh Hunt of music, not the Wordsworth; the Chardin, not the Watteau; the Perugino, not the Signorelli. Yet he was more than merely agreeable or pretty.

Was he a classicist or a romantic? What difference does the label make? Pablo Casals called him "a romantic who felt at ease within the mold of classicism." That is certainly true of his symphonies. Of these, the best loved —deservedly so—is the "Italian," a work he began when he was little more than a boy and had not finished to his satisfaction when he died. More than almost any of his other compositions it brings his excellence to full expression. Exciting in the first movement, stately in the second, elegant in the third, jaunty in the fourth, the "Italian" is a paradigm of Mendelssohn's genius. It, too, is a reminder of vanished glories, of a Rome of the past, a city now half devoured by a locust swarm of vehicles.

The "Reformation" Symphony—originally composed for the 1830 tercentenary of the Augsburg Confession, Protestantism's "Constitution"— is less good: there are noble passages in the score, inspired by Bach, there is power in the first movement and grace in the third; but *in toto* it is a let-down and religiously as unconvincing as some of his other churchly music.[1] The "Scottish" is another story: in a sense it is an early tone poem, the four movements connected and containing a theme which recurs throughout the work; but more importantly it is an enchanting blend of misty and clement moods with an especially beautiful third movement which owes something to Beethoven's "Harp" Quartet. As I have mentioned, we know that the idea of the "Scottish" Symphony was born in Mendelssohn's mind when, as a young man of twenty, he and Klingemann went on the tour of Scotland. At that time (July 30, 1829) he wrote:

In the twilight today we went to the Palace [Hollyrood] where Queen Mary lived and loved; there is a little room to be seen there with a spiral

---

[1] The fact that Mendelssohn after a while said that he "could not stomach" the "Reformation" and wanted to burn it (letter to Julius Rietz, February 11, 1838) means little. We have seen that he was uncertain about the worth of most of his compositions.

staircase at its door; they went up that and found Rizzio in the little room, dragged him out, and three chambers away there is a dark corner where they murdered him. The chapel beside it has now lost its roof, it is overgrown with grass and ivy, and at the broken altar Mary was crowned Queen of Scotland. Everything is ruined, decayed, and open to the sky. I believe I have found there today the beginning of my Scotch Symphony . . .

That is not to say that one can safely read into the symphony echoes of Scottish music. The symphony is Mendelssohn, and not a highland fling. It is significant that so sensitive a listener as Robert Schumann once succumbed to a hoax: while the symphony was being performed, a friend assured him he was listening to Mendelssohn's "Italian" Symphony. Schumann entirely accepted it as visions of the Italian landscape.

We know too the immediate circumstances which led to the composition of the *Fingal's Cave* Overture. On the same visit to Scotland, the two friends had embarked on a sea voyage, their goal being the famous cave. Klingemann wrote:

The more the barometer fell, the higher rose the sea. Its thousand questing tongues licked ever more roughly, and it swirled with increasing violence. . . . The ladies went down like flies, and here and there a gentleman did the same; I wish my companion Felix had not been among them, but he gets on better with the sea as an artist than his stomach does. . . . We were taken off in boats, then clambered along by the hissing sea on the stumps of pillars to the celebrated Fingal's Cave—with its many columns it resembles the interior of an immense organ. It lies there alone, black, echoing, and entirely purposeless—the grey waste of the sea in and around it. . . .

Mendelssohn took the initial idea for the overture, conceived on this visit, and carried it with him to Berlin and then to Rome, and then to Paris, where he completed the first version of the overture. He was, as usual, dissatisfied:

The middle portion in E is too stupid, and the whole working out smells more of counterpoint than of train oil, seagulls, and salt fish, and must be altered. . . .

He completely revised the overture.

All these Overtures, the *Fingal's Cave*, *Calm Sea*, *Melusina*, *Ruy Blas*, and *A Midsummer Night's Dream*—they are all short masterpieces. As Donald Francis Tovey wrote about *Fingal's Cave*: "If those compositions . . . were set apart and regarded as the only authentic works of Mendelssohn, there would be no disputing his claim to rank among the great composers." The Concertos are uneven, though no pianist will want to forsake the Piano Concerto No. 1 in G Minor, the charm of which may have been inspired by young love; and certainly no violinist can do without the E Minor Concerto, one of the few great concertos in the sparse violin repertoire.

Much of his piano music has dated. It is too slight and facile. Mendelssohn never reached the thrust of Liszt or the intensity of Schumann, not to speak of the passion of Chopin. The *Variations Sérieuses* in D Minor (Op. 54), however, is a brilliant work, when a Horowitz plays it.

Shaw was not wrong about the "Songs without Words," of which eight collections were published, six during Mendelssohn's lifetime and two posthumously. It is interesting that Busoni thought highly of them. Some of them—such as the Spring Song (Op. 62, No. 6)—are jam made with too much sugar. Yet if we choose the best of them, they turn out to be more than merely sweet encore pieces: Venetian Boat Song No. 3 (Opus 62, No. 5), Reverie (Opus 85, No. 1), Duet (Opus 38, No. 6), Funeral March (Opus 62, No. 3), etc.

His Songs are most appealing when they are most lyrical. To him the *Lied* was as natural a musical expression as it was to Schubert, Schumann, Brahms, and Richard Strauss. Sometimes he becomes coy and the path is strewn with too many *"Blümelein,"* but the best of the songs are suffused with warm and poetic sensibility. He made an indispensable contribution to an art which is still understood when a Fischer-Diskau or a Janet Baker sings *Scheidend* or *Gruss* (Heine) or the *Venezianisches Gondellied* or *Die Liebende schreibt* or *Der Mond* or the *Nachtlied*. The Duets (Op. 63 and 77) belong to the finest of his songs, such as the *Abendlied* (Heine), *Gruss* (Eichendorff), and the melancholy *Herbstlied* to words by Klingemann.

Beethoven exercised a strong influence on Mendelssohn's chamber music. That was both good and not so good. He was not only steeped in Beethoven's music but we can imagine how often those who had known Beethoven must have talked to Mendelssohn about him. No one who met Beethoven ever forgot him. Whatever the visitor's feeling—admiration, pity, awe, irritation at his rudeness, anger at his intransigence—Beethoven remained indelible. Mendelssohn was surrounded by men and women who had lived in Vienna or gone there before 1827, the year of Beethoven's death, and who must now have discussed him for hours on end. Julius Benedict, Marie Bigot, Bettina Brentano, Johann Baptist Cramer, Dorothea Ertmann, Goethe, Ferdinand Hiller, Johann Nepomuk Hummel, Anna Milder-Hauptmann, Moscheles, Heinrich Rellstab, Ferdinand Ries, Rossini, Sir George Smart, Henriette Sontag, Caroline Unger, and probably Anton Schindler, Beethoven's famulus—that is but a partial count of those whose lives first touched Beethoven's and then Mendelssohn's. Mozart, Handel, and Bach were historic figures to Mendelssohn, however vivid in his imagination. Beethoven had died yesterday.

Beethoven's portrait must have stood on Felix's desk when he composed the String Quartet in A Minor (Op. 13). He was eighteen, and it is extraordinary how much serious intensity he gathered in the work. Beethoven's spirit was still present when Mendelssohn finished the last Quartet (Op. 80). He got off to a good start with the wonderful Octet (Op. 20) and never lost interest, finishing nearly twenty compositions. His corner movements here and there scurry too much—a reflection of his restlessness—but the slow movements are relaxed and tender and often astonishingly somber. As to the scherzos—one would expect them to be brilliant and they are. His chamber music is now coming to the fore,[2] again partly due to recordings.

What can be said of Mendelssohn's fortunes in general can be said of *Elijah:* during much of the nineteenth century it was regarded as *the* oratorio to stand beside the *Messiah.* Its reputation suffered a decline in the twentieth century up to the fifties and is now rising once more.[3] It is a flawed work: Mendelssohn is not at his best when he attempts to be imposingly

[2] The most popular are the Piano Trio in D Minor (Op. 49), the Quartet in A Minor (Op. 13), the Quartet in F Minor (Op. 80), and of course the *Octet.*

[3] It has suffered from amateur and church performances. But recently three full-scale recordings have been published which respect the composer's intention: one is conducted by Frühbeck de Burgos, one by Ormandy, one by Böhm.

dramatic. He thunders weakly. The libretto is smug, particularly in the English translation, with every third phrase being "The Lord." The exciting parts of Elijah's story, such as his ascending in a fiery chariot, are unexciting. But there are marvelously beautiful things in *Elijah:* the unconventional beginning leading into the Overture, the double quartet, "For He shall give His angels," Elijah's aria, "Draw near, all ye people," preceded by the powerful summoning of Baal, the scene of "The fire descends from heaven," Elijah's raging, "Is not His word like a fire," the alto arioso, "Woe unto them"—these are some of the finest features of the first part. In the second part we have Elijah's "It is enough," the gentle expression of a wounded soul, very moving whether it be autobiographical or not. This is soon followed by the sublime chorus "He watching over Israel," by the famous alto solo "O rest in the Lord" and the contemplative chorus "He that shall endure." In short, hearing *Elijah* is still a touching experience, in spite of its prosy passages.

3

The survey here given [4] pretends to be little more than a listing designed to show how much of Mendelssohn is alive. He *is* alive and, as far as one can prophesy, he is in no danger of oblivion.

When Elgar composed his *Enigma* Variations he paid tribute to Mendelssohn by quoting a melody from the *Calm Sea and Prosperous Voyage* Overture (Variation XIII). That was in 1899. The quotation shines out. If in 1999 we will still be able to find a calm sea, if we still will be able to undertake a prosperous voyage to whatever goal as yet unforeseen, we may still be able to love Mendelssohn's music.

To love, lovable—dare we still use such expressions? They come to mind when we think of Mendelssohn.

---

[4] I have not even mentioned several large works which at one time were considered important but are now hardly ever performed. For example, the dramatic cantata, *Die erste Walpurgisnacht*, which in spite of some interesting ideas must be considered a failure; the cantata *Lauda Sion*; the *Lobgesang* (Hymn of Praise), a symphony of three movements with a choral finale, obviously inspired by the Ninth but a long way away from it.

A Mendelssohn Calendar

THE purpose of this Calendar is merely to set Mendelssohn's life within the framework of contemporary events and thoughts. No attempt is made at completeness; I have given preference to such developments as may have impinged on his life and to those books and musical works which he came to know and which influenced him, to some degree at least.

DATE	MENDELSSOHN'S LIFE AND PRINCIPAL WORKS	MUSICAL EVENTS	ARTISTIC AND SCIENTIFIC EVENTS	PRINCIPAL POLITICAL EVENTS
1809	February 3. Born at Hamburg.	Death of Haydn (77). Beethoven: "Emperor" Concerto.	Goethe: *Elective Affinities.* E. Malus discovers polarization of light.	Napoleon wars against Austria; second occupation of Vienna. Metternich becomes Chief Minister. Napoleon divorces Josephine. Peace of Schönbrunn.
1810		Birth of Chopin and Schumann. Beethoven: music to *Egmont.*	Scott: *The Lady of the Lake.* Goya: *Disasters of War* engravings.	Napoleon marries Marie Louise of Austria. Annexes Holland and tightens Continental blockade. In December annexes north German cities, including Hamburg.
1811	Parents flee from Hamburg to Berlin.	Liszt born. Beethoven: *Les Adieux* Sonata.	Jane Austen: *Sense and Sensibility.* Goethe: *Dichtung und Wahrheit.*	Devaluation of Austrian currency. George III insane; Prince of Wales becomes Regent.

1812	U. S. declares war on Britain. Napoleon's Russian campaign. Burning of Moscow. Retreat of Grande Armée. Wellington victorious in Spain.	Byron: *Childe Harold's Pilgrimage.* J. and W. Grimm: *Fairy Tales.*	Beethoven: Seventh Symphony.	
1813	Austria declares war on Napoleon. Napoleon-Metternich interview. "Battle of the Nations," Leipzig.	Jane Austen: *Pride and Prejudice.* Chamisso: *Peter Schlemihls wunderbare Geschichte.*	Births of Verdi and Wagner. Schubert composes First Symphony. Rossini: *Tancredi.* London Philharmonic Society founded.	
1814	Napoleon abdicates. Congress of Vienna begins. War of 1812 ends.	Wordsworth: *The Excursion.* Goya: "May 2" and "May 3" paintings.	Beethoven: *Fidelio* (3rd version), and Eighth Symphony.	
1815	Napoleon enters Paris—"The Hundred Days." Battle of Waterloo. Napoleon banished to St. Helena.	A. Fresnel researches diffraction of light. J. Macadam invents new road construction.	Schubert: *Der Erlkönig.*	Begins piano lessons in earnest.
1816		Coleridge: *Kubla Khan.* Elgin Marbles acquired by British Museum.	Rossini: *Barber of Seville.*	Visit to Paris. Takes lessons from Marie Bigot.

DATE	MENDELSSOHN'S LIFE AND PRINCIPAL WORKS	MUSICAL EVENTS	ARTISTIC AND SCIENTIFIC EVENTS	PRINCIPAL POLITICAL EVENTS
1817	Begins lessons from Zelter (59).	Rossini: *Cenerentola.* Clementi: *Gradus ad Parnassum.*	Byron: *Manfred.* Hegel: *Encyclopaedia of Philosophy.* Grillparzer: *Die Ahnfrau.*	German Students Union formed at Jena.
1818	First public appearance at a chamber concert.	First public piano concert given by Chopin.	Keats: *Endymion.* Grillparzer: *Sappho.* Byron: *Don Juan.* First steamship, *Savannah*, crosses Atlantic in 29 days.	Tariff Reform Law abolishes internal customs in Prussia.
1819	Enters Zelter's Singakademie.	Beethoven: *Hammerklavier Sonata.* Schubert: *Trout Quintet.*	Schopenhauer: *The World as Will and Idea.*	Kotzebue's assassination gives Metternich opportunity to formulate oppressive "Karlsbad Decrees" (censoring the press and universities).
1820	First dated composition, a cantata.		Scott: *Ivanhoe. Venus de Milo* discovered. Ampère formulates laws of electrodynamics.	Death of George III. Revolutionary outbreaks in Spain, Portugal, Naples.

1821	Piano Quartet, Op. 1. Meets Weber. Zelter takes him to visit Goethe (72).	Weber: *Der Freischütz.* Beethoven: Last two piano sonatas.	DeQuincey: *Confessions of an English Opium Eater.* Heine: *Poems.* Constable painting: *Hay Wain.*	Greek war of independence against Turks begun. Death of Napoleon.
1822	Visits Switzerland. Meets Spohr, Hiller.	Schubert: "Unfinished" Symphony. C. Franck born.	Pushkin: *Eugen Onegin.*	
1823	Piano Quartet, Op. 2. Composes much.	Beethoven: *Missa Solemnis.* Schubert: *Rosamunde* music. Weber: *Euryanthe.*	Schleiermacher: *Christian Doctrine.* Ingres painting, *La Source.*	Monroe Doctrine.
1824	Moscheles gives him lessons. Beginning of friendship. Symphony No. 1, C Minor.	Beethoven: Ninth Symphony. Births of Bruckner and Smetana.	Leopardi: Poems. London National Gallery founded.	Death of Louis XVIII and accession of Charles X.
1825	Visit to Paris, examined by Cherubini; meets many musical celebrities. Piano Quartet, Op. 3, dedicated to Goethe. *Die Hochzeit des Camacho,* opera, composed. Octet for strings, Op. 20.	Beethoven: String Quartets, Op. 132 and 130. Johann Strauss, Jr., born. Chopin publishes his Op. 1, a Rondo.	Manzoni: *I Promessi Sposi.* Pushkin: *Boris Godunov.*	Britain passes child labor law, restricting work to 12-hour day.
1826	Overture to *A Midsummer Night's Dream.*	Beethoven: String Quartets, Op. 131 and 135. Weber: *Oberon.* Weber dies.		Russo-Persian War begins.

DATE	MENDELSSOHN'S LIFE AND PRINCIPAL WORKS	MUSICAL EVENTS	ARTISTIC AND SCIENTIFIC EVENTS	PRINCIPAL POLITICAL EVENTS
1827	*Die Hochzeit des Camacho* a failure in Berlin. String Quartet, Op. 13.	Death of Beethoven. Bellini: *Il Pirata*. Schubert: *Die Winterreise*.	Heine: *Buch der Lieder*.	Russia defeats Persia. Turks capture Acropolis. Robert Peel reforms criminal law.
1828	Overture *Calm Sea and Prosperous Voyage*.	Schubert: C Major Symphony. Death of Schubert.	Webster's *Dictionary*. Carlyle: *Essay on Goethe*. F. Wöhler founds organic chemistry.	Wellington forms Tory administration. Greek independence secured.
1829	Revives Bach's *St. Matthew Passion* in Berlin. First visit to England. Conducts London Philharmonic. Friendship with Klingemann, Attwood, Rosen, etc. Visit to Scotland. String Quartet, Op. 12. *Singspiel*, "*Die Heimkehr aus der Fremde*" for parent's 25th anniversary.	Rossini: *William Tell*.	Balzac begins *La Comédie Humaine*. Delacroix painting, *Sardanapalus*.	Robert Peel establishes London Metropolitan Police Force.

1830	"Reformation" Symphony begun. Piano Fantasy, Op. 28. Overture *Hebrides* (*Fingal's Cave*) in its first form. Begins "Grand Tour" to Italy, etc.	Donizetti: *Anna Bolena.* Bellini: *I Capuletti e Montecchi.*	V. Hugo: *Hernani.* Stendhal: *Le Rouge et le Noir.* Tennyson: *Poems Chiefly Lyrical.*	July Revolution in France. Charles X abdicates. Louis Philippe elected King. George IV dies, succeeded by William IV. Wellington resigns. Cholera epidemic in Europe.
1831	In Rome meets Berlioz. "Scottish" and "Italian" Symphonies begun. Milan, Switzerland, then Munich. Piano Concerto, Op. 25. Relationship with Delphine Schauroth. Meets Liszt in Paris.	Bellini: *Norma.* Berlioz: "Fantastic" Symphony.	V. Hugo: *Notre-Dame de Paris.* Charles Darwin's voyage on the *Beagle.* Exhibit in Paris of "Barbizon" painters.	
1832	Meets Chopin in Paris. Second visit to London. *Capriccio brillant,* Op. 22. "Songs Without Words," Book I. Revises *Hebrides.*	Chopin, Mazurkas, Op. 6. Donizetti: *L'elisir d'amore.*	Goethe: *Faust II* published. Goethe dies. Samuel F. B. Morse invents telegraph.	Austrian troops, led by Radetzky, occupy Ancona after new Italian uprisings. Mazzini founds "Young Italy" movement.

DATE	MENDELSSOHN'S LIFE AND PRINCIPAL WORKS	MUSICAL EVENTS	ARTISTIC AND SCIENTIFIC EVENTS	PRINCIPAL POLITICAL EVENTS
1833	Turned down by *Singakademie* after Zelter's death. Finishes "Italian" Symphony for London. Third and Fourth visits to England. Conducts Lower Rhine Festival at Düsseldorf. Overture, *Die schöne Melusine*.	Brahms born. Chopin: 12 Etudes, Op. 10, and Piano Concerto No. 1. Donizetti: *Lucrezia Borgia*.	Carlyle: *Sartor Resartus*. R. Browning: *Pauline*.	Prussia establishes "Customs Union."
1834	Music director Düsseldorf. *Rondo brillant*, Op. 29. *St. Paul*, oratorio, begun.	Bellini: *I Puritani*. Berlioz: *Harold in Italy*. Schumann founds *Neue Zeitschrift*, hails Chopin. Schumann: *Carnaval*, Op. 9.	Balzac: *Le Père Goriot*. C. McCormick invents reaping machine.	Abolition of slavery in British Empire.
1835	Appointed conductor Leipzig Gewandhaus. Meets Schumann. Abraham dies (59).	Donizetti: *Lucia di Lammermoor*. Death of Bellini.	H. Andersen: *Fairy Tales*. T. Gautier: *Mademoiselle de Maupin*. N. Gogol: *Dead Souls*. A. de Tocqueville: *De la Démocratie en Amérique*.	Franz I of Austria dies, succeeded by Ferdinand I. "September Laws" suppress radical tendencies in France.

1836	*St. Paul* performed at Lower Rhine Festival, Düsseldorf. Then at Frankfurt. Meets and becomes engaged to Cécile Jeanrenaud.	Meyerbeer: *Les Huguenots.* Chopin: Piano Concerto No. 2.	Dickens: *Pickwick Papers* (publication begins). Emerson: *Nature.* Arc de Triomphe, Paris, completed.
1837	Marries Cécile, March 28. String Quartet, Op. 44, No. 2. Preludes and Fugues for Piano, Op. 35. Organ Preludes, Op. 37. Piano Concerto, Op. 40. To England and conducts Birmingham Festival. Six Songs, Op. 34 (composed between 1834 and 1837).	Berlioz: *Benvenuto Cellini.* Requiem Mass.	Dickens: *Oliver Twist.* Carlyle: *French Revolution.* Death of William IV. Accession of Queen Victoria. Seven professors at Göttingen University dismissed by King of Hanover.
1838	String Quartets, Op. 44, No. 1 and 3. Cello Sonata, Op. 45. Violin Concerto begun. Schumann sends him Schubert's C Major Symphony; he performs it following season.	Berlioz: *Romeo and Juliet.* Jenny Lind's debut, Stockholm. Birth of Bizet.	V. Hugo: *Ruy Blas.* K. Immermann: *Münchhausen.* Dickens: *Nicholas Nickleby.* Building of Kremlin begun.

DATE	MENDELSSOHN'S LIFE AND PRINCIPAL WORKS	MUSICAL EVENTS	ARTISTIC AND SCIENTIFIC EVENTS	PRINCIPAL POLITICAL EVENTS
1839	Overture *Ruy Blas*. Psalm CXIV. Piano Trio, Op. 49. Very active as conductor in Leipzig.	Verdi's first opera: *Oberto*. Moussorgsky born.	Stendhal: *La Chartreuse de Parme*. Longfellow: *Voices of the Night*. Faraday: *Researches in Electricity* begun. Ranke: *History of the Reformation in Germany* begun.	"Opium War" between China and Britain. Hong Kong taken by British.
1840	*Hymn of Praise* composed for commemoration of invention of printing. Visit to England. Conducts *Hymn of Praise* at Birmingham. Negotiates with Frederick William IV about call to Berlin.	Paganini dies. Tchaikovsky born. Chopin: Preludes, Op. 28. Nocturnes, Op. 37. Polonaises, Op. 40. Schumann: *Dichterliebe*. Wagner: *Faust* Overture.	Dickens: *Old Curiosity Shop*. E. A. Poe: *Tales of the Grotesque*. F. List: *The National System of Political Economy*.	Frederick William III of Prussia dies, succeeded by Frederick William IV.

1841	Appointed director of non-existent Academy of Arts in Berlin. Incidental music to *Antigone*. *Variations sérieuses*, Op. 54. "Songs Without Words," Book IV published.	Schumann: "Spring" Symphony.	Carlyle: *On Heroes and Hero-Worship*. R. W. Bunsen invents carbon battery. D. Livingstone discovers Lake Ngami.	
1842	"Scottish" Symphony finished. Played in Leipzig and London. Meets Queen Victoria. King of Prussia commissions music for Racine's *Athalie*, Sophocles' *Oedipus at Colonus* and *A Midsummer Night's Dream*. Founds Leipzig Conservatory. Meets Wagner.	A. Sullivan born. Schumann: 3 Quartets and Piano Quintet, Op. 44. Wagner's *Rienzi* premièred. New York Philharmonic Society founded. Verdi: *Nabucco*.	Tennyson: *Morte d'Arthur*. C. Long uses ether for anesthetic in operation.	Frontier between Canada and U.S. settled by treaty.
1843	Opening of Leipzig Conservatory. Incidental music to *A Midsummer Night's Dream* performed at Potsdam. Cello Sonata, Op. 58. Berlin plans aborted. Lea dies.	Grieg born. Wagner: *Flying Dutchman* premièred. Donizetti: *Don Pasquale*.	J. Ruskin: *Modern Painters* begun. Dickens: "A Christmas Carol." Wordsworth poet laureate.	

DATE	MENDELSSOHN'S LIFE AND PRINCIPAL WORKS	MUSICAL EVENTS	ARTISTIC AND SCIENTIFIC EVENTS	PRINCIPAL POLITICAL EVENTS
1844	Works on Six Organ Sonatas. Retires from Berlin. Completes Violin Concerto, Op. 64. Conducts five Philharmonic concerts in London.	Rimsky-Korsakov born. J. Joachim debut in London —Beethoven Violin Concerto conducted by Mendelssohn. Verdi: *Ernani*. Berlioz: *Traité de l' Instrumentation*. Debut of Johann Strauss, Jr.	Disraeli: *Coningsby*. A. Dumas: *The Three Musketeers* and *The Count of Monte Cristo*. Heine: *Deutschland, ein Wintermärchen*.	
1845	Returns to Leipzig. Conducts Gewandhaus and teaches piano and composition at Conservatory. String Quintet, Op. 87. Piano Trio, Op. 66. Friendship with Jenny Lind.	Wagner: *Tannhäuser*. Schumann: Piano Concerto. Chopin: Piano Sonata, Op. 58. Liszt: *Les Preludes*.	F. Engels: *The Condition of the Working Classes in England*. The Madeleine, Paris, completed.	
1846	*Lauda Sion* Cantata. Works on *Elijah*; finishes it late July. Departs for England. First performance *Elijah*, Birmingham Festival, Aug. 26. Returns to Leipzig exhausted.	Berlioz: *Damnation of Faust*. Schumann: Symphony II.	F. Dostoievsky: *Poor Folk*. H. Melville: *Typee*. P. J. Proudhon: *Philosophie de la misère*.	U.S.–Mexican War. German professors meet at Frankfurt to discuss German unification ("The Intellectual Diet"). Irish famine.

| 1847 | Works on opera *Lorelei*, also oratorio *Christus*, both unfinished. Fanny dies May 14. Felix ill, taken to Switzerland. Recovers sufficiently to finish String Quartet, Op. 80. Returns to Leipzig September. Dies in Leipzig November 4, 38 years old. | Verdi: *Macbeth*. Flotow: *Martha*. | Charlotte Brontë: *Jane Eyre*. Emily Brontë: *Wuthering Heights*. W. M. Thackeray: *Vanity Fair* (published partly). P. Merimée: *Carmen*. H. Helmholtz: *On the Conservation of Energy*. | Gold discovered (1848) in California. |

Bibliography

ACHTERBERG, ERICH, *Lebensbilder deutscher Bankiers aus fünf Jahrhunderten.* Frankfurt, 1863.

ADLER, H. G., *The Jews in Germany.* Notre Dame, Ind., 1969.

Allgemeine Deutsche Biographie (Encyclopedia, 56 vols.). Leipzig, 1893.

BADT-STRAUSS, B. (ed.), *Moses Mendelssohn, der Mensch und sein Werk.* Berlin, 1929.

BENEDICT, J., *A Sketch of the Life and Works of the late Felix Mendelssohn-Bartholdy.* London, 1850.

BERLIOZ, HECTOR, *Memoirs* (David Cairns, ed.). New York, 1969.

BESTERMAN, T., *Voltaire.* New York, 1969.

BÖHMER, G., *Die Welt des Biedermeier.* Vienna, 1968.

BRAUSTEIN, DR. JOSEF, *Felix Mendelssohn in der Schweiz.* Vienna, 1930.

BULMAN, J., *Jenny Lind.* London, 1956.

BUTTERFIELD, H., *Napoleon.* New York, 1939.

CARSE, ADAM, *The Orchestra.* New York, 1949.

——, *The Orchestra from Beethoven to Berlioz.* Cambridge, 1948.

CHORLEY, H. F., *Thirty Years' Musical Recollections.* London, 1926.

COPLESTON, F., *A History of Philosophy* (7 vols.). Westminster, 1964.

COWAN, F. H., *Mendelssohn.* New York, 1912.

DAHMS, WALTER, *Mendelssohn.* Berlin, 1922.

DAVISON, J. W., *From Mendelssohn to Wagner.* London, 1912.

DEVRIENT, EDUARD, *Meine Erinnerungen an Felix Mendelssohn-Bartholdy.* Leipzig, 1872.

DÖRFFEL, A., *Geschichte der Gewandhaus Konzerte zu Leipzig.* Leipzig, 1884.

DORIAN, FREDERICK, *The History of Music in Performance.* New York, 1942.

DROYSEN, J. G., *Ein tief gegründet Herz, Briefwechsel Felix-Mendelssohn-Bartholdys.* Heidelberg, 1959.

DURANT, WILL and ARIEL, *The Age of Voltaire.* New York, 1965.

———, *Rousseau and Revolution.* New York, 1967.

EDWARDS, F. G., *The History of Mendelssohn's Oratorio* Elijah. London, 1896.

ELBOGEN, I., *Die Geschichte der Juden in Deutschland.* Berlin, 1966.

ENGEL, EDUARD, *Geschichte des deutschen Literatur* (2 vols.). Vienna and Leipzig, 1917.

———, *Goethe.* Berlin, 1910.

FERGUSON, DONALD N., *Masterworks of the Orchestral Repertoire.* Minneapolis, 1954.

FOSTER, M. B., *The History of the Philharmonic Society of London.* London, 1912.

FRIEDEGG, E., *Millionen und Millionäre.* Berlin, 1914.

FRIEDENTHAL, R., *Goethe, His Life and Times.* Cleveland, 1963.

GALTON, F., *Hereditary Genius.* New York, 1870.

GAY, PETER, *The Enlightenment: an Interpretation.* New York, 1966.

———, *Age of Enlightenment.* New York, 1966.

GECK, MARTIN, *Die Wiederentdeckung der Matthäuspassion im 19. Jahrhundert.* Regensburg, 1967.

GEIGER, L., *Berlin, 1688–1840; Geschichte des geistigen Lebens der preussischen Hauptstadt.* Berlin, 1892/3.

GRAETZ, H., *Geschichte der Juden von Beginn der Mendelssohn Zeit (1750) bis in die neueste Zeit (1848).* Vol. XI. Leipzig, 1870.

GROSSMANN-VENDREY, S., *Felix Mendelssohn Bartholdy und die Musik der Vergangenheit.* Regensburg, 1969.

Grove's Dictionary of Music and Musicians, Edition of Philadelphia, 1927. (Article by George Grove)

———, 5th Edition, 1960 (Article by Percy M. Young)

HAMEROW, THEODORE S., *Restoration, Revolution, Reaction.* Princeton, 1958.

HAMPSON, NORMAN, *A Cultural History of The Enlightenment.* New York, 1968.

HEDLEY, ARTHUR (ed.), *Selected Correspondence of Chopin.* New York, 1963.

HENDERSON, W. D., *The Industrialization of Europe, 1780–1914.* New York, 1969.

HENSEL, S., *Die Familie Mendelssohn, 1729–1847* (2 vols.). Berlin, 1891.

HERMANN, G., *Das Biedermeier.* Vienna, 1968.

HERTZBERG, ARTHUR, *The French Enlightenment and the Jews.* New York, 1968.

HERZ, HENRIETTE, *Ihr Leben und ihre Erinnerungen.* Berlin, 1858.

HIBBERT, CHRISTOPHER, *The Grand Tour.* New York, 1969.

HILLER, FERDINAND, *Felix Mendelssohn-Bartholdy, Briefe und Erinnerungen.* Cologne, 1874.

HOLBORN, HAJO, *The History of Modern Germany, 1648–1840.* New York, 1964.

——, *The History of Modern Germany, 1840–1945.* New York, 1969.

HOLLAND, H. S., and W. S. ROCKSTRO, *Jenny Lind, Ihre Laufbahn als Künstlerin.* Leipzig, 1891.

HOLMES, EDWARD, *A Ramble among the Musicians of Germany.* New York, 1969.

HORSLEY, FANNY and SOPHY, *Mendelssohn and his Friends at Kensington.* London, 1934.

JACOB, H. E., *Felix Mendelssohn and His Times.* London, 1963.

JACOBI, DR. M., *Felix Mendelssohn-Bartholdy.* Leipzig, n.d.

KAYSERLING, M. *Moses Mendelssohn, Sein Leben und seine Werke.* Leipzig, 1862.

KELLER, WERNER, *Diaspora.* New York, 1969.

KERNER, DR. D., *Krankheiten Grosser Musiker.* Stuttgart, 1969.

KIRLEW, M., *Famous Sisters of Great Men,* London, n.d.

KÖHLER, KARL-HEINZ, *Felix Mendelssohn-Bartholdy.* Leipzig, n.d.

KOHN, HANS, *The Mind of Germany.* New York, 1960.

LAMPADIUS, W. A., *Felix Mendelssohn-Bartholdy: ein Denkmal für seine Freunde.* Leipzig, 1849.

LANG, PAUL HENRY, *Music in Western Civilization.* New York, 1941.

LAUBE, H., *Erinnerungen, 1810–1840.* Vienna, 1875.

LAZARUS, BENDAVID, *Selbstbiographie.* Berlin, 1806.

LONGFORD, E., *Queen Victoria.* New York, 1964.

MANN, GOLO, *The History of Germany since 1789.* London, 1968.

MARGETSON, STELLA, *Leisure and Pleasure in the 19th Century.* New York, 1969.

MENDELSSOHN, MOSES, *Phaedon oder über die Unsterblichkeit der Seele.* Berlin, 1767.

——, *Jerusalem oder über religiöse Macht und Judentum.* Berlin, 1783.

——, *Lichstrahlen* (selections from his works). Leipzig, 1875.

——, Four unpublished Letters to—— (F. Baumberger, ed.). New York, 1963.

——, *Brautbriefe* (Ismar Elbogen, ed.). Berlin, 1936.

MENDELSSOHN-BARTHOLDY, F., *Ein Brief von F.M.B. an Goethe.* Berlin, 1869.

——, *Briefe an deutsche Verleger* (Dr. R. Elvers, ed.). Berlin, 1968.

——, *Briefe 1833 bis 1847* (Paul Mendelssohn-Bartholdy, ed.). Leipzig, 1864.

——, *Meisterbriefe* (Ernst Wolff, ed.). Berlin, 1907.

——, *Reisebriefe 1830 bis 1832* (Paul Mendelssohn-Bartholdy, ed.). Leipzig, 1862.

——, *Letters* (G. Selden-Goth, ed.). New York, 1945.

——, *Denkmal in Wort und Bild* (Max F. Schneider, ed.). Basel, 1947.

MENDELSSOHN, FELIX, and KARL KLINGEMANN, *Briefwechsel* (Karl Klingemann, ed.). Essen, 1909.

MENDELSSOHN-BARTHOLDY, DR. KARL (ed.), *Goethe and Mendelssohn*. London, 1874.

MITFORD, N., *Frederick the Great*. London, 1970.

MORTON, FREDERIC, *The Rothschilds*. New York, 1961.

MOSCHELES, IGNAZ, *Recent Music and Musicians*. London, 1879.

———, *Aus Moscheles Leben* (2 vols.). Leipzig, 1872.

Musik in Geschichte und Gegenwart, IX (Bärenreiter Encyclopedia) (13 vols.). Cassel, 1961.

NAUMANN, E., *Musikgeschichte* (2 vols.). Berlin, 1886.

NELSON, W. H., *The Berliners*. New York, 1969.

NEWMAN, ERNEST, *The Life of Richard Wagner* (4 vols.). New York, 1933–1946.

———, *The Man Liszt*. New York, 1935.

NÖSSELT, H. J., *Das Gewandhaus Orchester*. Leipzig, 1943.

PETITPIERRE, JACQUES, *The Romance of the Mendelssohns*. New York, 1937.

PLEASANTS, HENRY, *The Musical World of Robert Schumann*. New York, 1965.

———, *The Great Singers*. New York, 1966.

POLKO, E., *Erinnerungen an Felix Mendelssohn Bartholdy*. Leipzig, 1868.

RACHEL, H., and P. WALLICH, *Berliner Grosskaufleute und Kapitalisten* (2 vols.). Berlin, 1938.

RADCLIFFE, PHILIP, *Mendelssohn*. London, 1954.

REISSNER, H. G., and EDUARD GANS, *Ein Leben im Vormärz*. Tübingen, 1965.

ROCKSTRO, WILLIAM SMYTH, *Mendelssohn*. London, 1883.

RUNES, D. D. (ed.), *Treasury of Philosophy*. New York, 1960.

SAMPSON, G., *A Day with Felix Mendelssohn Bartholdy*. London, 1919.

SCHENK, H. G., *The Mind of the European Romantics*. New York, 1966.

SCHINDLER, ANTON FELIX, *Beethoven as I Knew Him* (Donald W. MacArdle, ed.). London, 1966.

SCHNABEL, F., *Deutsche Geschichte im Neunzehnten Jahrhundert*. Freiburg, 1950.

SCHONBERG, HAROLD C., *The Great Conductors*. New York, 1967.

———, *The Great Pianists*. New York, 1963.

SCHULZE, F., *Hundert Jahre Leipziger Stadttheater*. Leipzig, 1917.

SCHUMANN, ROBERT, *On Music and Musicians* (Konrad Wolff, ed.). New York, 1946.

SHAW, B., *Music in London*, Vol. I. London, 1932.

SITWELL, S., *Liszt*. Boston, 1934.

SMART, G., *Leaves from the Journal of Sir George Smart*. London, 1907.

STRATTON, STEPHEN S., *Mendelssohn*. London, 1901.

STRONG, G. T., *Diary 1835–1875*. New York, 1952.

TALMON, J. L., *Romanticism and Revolt, Europe 1815–1848*. London, 1967.

THOMAS, H., *Biographical Encyclopedia of Philosophy*. Garden City, 1965.

THOMPSON, OSCAR (ed.), *The International Cyclopedia of Music and Musicians*. New York, 1939.

TOVEY, DONALD FRANCIS, *Essays in Musical Analysis*. London, 1935–1944 (7 vols.).

TRUMBULL, J., *Autobiography*. New Haven, 1953.

VALENTIN, V., *Illustrierte Weltgeschichte* (2 vols.). Stuttgart, 1968.

WAGNER, RICHARD, *My Life* (2 vols.). New York, 1911.

——, *Zum Vortrag der Neunten Symphonie Beethovens* (from complete edition of prose works, 10 vols.). Leipzig, 1888.

WALTER, H., *Moses Mendelssohn Critic and Philosopher*. New York, 1930.

WEINSTOCK, HERBERT, *Rossini*. New York, 1968.

WERNER, E., *Mendelssohn*. New York, 1963.

WILLIAMS, NEVILLE, *Chronology of the Modern World*. New York, 1966.

WOLFF, E., *Mendelssohn-Bartholdy*. Berlin, 1906.

WOOLDRIDGE, DAVID, *Conductor's World*. London, 1970.

WULF, JOSEPH, *Musik im Dritten Reich*. Gütersloh, 1963.

Zelter-Goethe Briefwechsel (6 vols.). Berlin, 1834.

Index